Robert Christie

A History of the Late Province of Lower Canada - Parliamentary and Political

Vol. V

Robert Christie

A History of the Late Province of Lower Canada - Parliamentary and Political
Vol. V

ISBN/EAN: 9783337076740

Printed in Europe, USA, Canada, Australia, Japan

Cover: Foto ©ninafisch / pixelio.de

More available books at **www.hansebooks.com**

A HISTORY

OF THE

LATE PROVINCE

OF

LOWER CANADA,

PARLIAMENTARY AND POLITICAL,

From the commencement to the close of its existence as a separate Province;

BY ROBERT CHRISTIE.

IN SIX VOLUMES.

VOL. V.

MONTREAL:
RICHARD WORTHINGTON,
PUBLISHER AND BOOKSELLER.
1866.

NOTICE.

This volume terminates an undertaking which, whatever critics and the fastidious in literature may think of it, has cost considerable labour and time, without any expectation, nor indeed desire, of a pecuniary return. It is, and from the commencement was, intended as a votive offering by a native colonist of a neighbouring province to that of his adoption, and will be found a faithful record of the principal political matters in LOWER CANADA, during the FIFTY YEARS of its existence as a separate province and government. The whole, or nearly so, has been gathered from official or authentic documents, and where these were not to be had, from such other sources as seemed fully entitled to credit. The reader, it is hoped, will find the various subjects brought under his notice, detailed in a clear and intelligible order, *sans fard*, and as the writer can conscientiously vouch they have been, *sans fiel*, fear, favor, affection, or resentment towards any political party, partisan, or person whomsoever, living or dead.

Some of the details given in this, as in the preceding volumes, will no doubt be deemed prolix and perhaps unnecessary. We who have witnessed the more recent events of stirring interest in our career, and in which, indeed, many of us have been actors, may indeed well so opine, for surfeited by them, it must be to ourselves more agreeable, nay profitable, to forget than commemorate much of what has taken place; but time, notwithstanding this, will give to all those details, however minute or tedious they now may be deemed, an interest and the future historian in conning them over will, it is hoped, find no fault with the redundancies.

I must not, however, while proclaiming my own disinterestedness in a pecuniary sense, in this publication, forget to acknowledge the obligations under which I am towards my friends and publishers; in the first place, Mr. Thomas Cary, for the impression of the three first volumes, and in the next, to Mr. John Lovell, for this and the preceding volume. It is entirely to the public spirit and liberality of these gentlemen that I owe the impression of the work, which I should not, indeed could not, have undertaken at my own expense, and which at no inconsiderable risk to themselves, they generously assumed, and which I beg them to be assured I am very sensible of and justly appreciate. It is therefore but natural I should entertain a desire that they should be indemnified for, at least,-their outlay, in its impression and publication. On his head, I have also to acknowledge my obligations to the members of the Library Committee of the last and previous Legislative Assemblies, for their sense of the work, as signified by their recommendation for the purchase, (and complied with by the Assembly), of a considerable number of copies, contributing, by so much always, towards reimbursing my esteemed friends in the outlay they have incurred. For myself, I desire nothing beyond the approval of a reading public.

I have previously announced my intention to publish in a separate volume a collection of interesting papers, hitherto unpublished, relating to public matters in Lower Canada. Not knowing how long it may be before those papers will appear, I have thought it advisable to insert a few of them at the end of this voluma. The report of Chief Justice Sewell to the Govenor in Chief, Sir Jamas H. Craig, on "the situation of Canda," and the latter's despatch on the same subject to the Colonial Minister, Lord Liverpool, will be found interesting, as giving the opinions and views of those high functionaries on the state of the country and people, with the administration of whose government and laws they were at the time)1810(intrusted—views certainly any thing but flattering to the governed, had they but khown them. The reader is recommended to begin by the persusal of these documents,—rather an anomalous advice I must admit,—" *to begin at the end,*" but as they precede *in date*, the matters contained in the volume, there is nothing out of the way in it, and he will, if I mistake not, find it to his advan- to take the course suggested. Whatever the reader may think of the views given in those papers, their authenticity, he may be assured, is unquestionable. In the volume hereafter to be published there are several of equal interest, and which it is but right that the public should see.

The appendices referred to in this and the antecedent volumes, under the letters A. B. C., &c., must lie over for the volume just alluded to.

R. C.

Quebec, June, 1854.

A HISTORY

OF THE LATE

PROVINCE OF LOWER CANADA.

CHAPTER XL.

Outbreak under Mr. Mackenzie, at Toronto—Sir John Colborne proceeds in person to St. Eustache, at the head of the Troops—Affair at that place, and submission of the Patriots at St. Benoit—Excesses—Mr. Papineau—Loyal movements in the neighboring Provinces--Reaction in public opinion, particularly in the District of Quebec—Proclamation of Governor Jenison, of Vermont—Memoranda relating to Major Gugy.

The leading Patriots in Lower Canada had been in correspondence with the Agitators in the Upper Province, including Mr. William Lyon Mackenzie, under whose auspices an Insurrection intended to be auxiliary to that in the Lower Province, broke out near Toronto a few days after the affair at St. Denis, which had put that restless and most unscrupulous, I might without sin say accomplished, demagogue and his associates into high spirits. It was suppressed, however, by the loyal Militia of Toronto, aided by a handful of brave Volunteers from Hamilton and Niagara, headed by the gallant Lieut. Colonel Allan (now Sir Allan) MacNab, who, marching upon the insurgents, posted at a place known as Gallows Hill, a short distance north of Toronto, put them to flight —Mackenzie himself narrowly escaping his pursuers. But as these occurrences in the Upper Province do not properly appertain to our subject, which is confined to Lower Canada, we shall not enter upon them.

The gatherings on the Richelieu having been dispersed, and nothing further to be apprehended from insurrection south of the St. Lawrence, in the District of Montreal; Sir John Colborne—strengthened by the reinforcements from the lower Provinces, whom the loyal zeal of the citizens of Quebec* had allowed to join him—now determined upon paying a visit in person to the patriots, who had collected in considerable numbers at St. Eustache, a village eighteen miles north-west of Montreal, under Amury Girod, an adventurer (a Swiss by birth as alleged by some, and by others, a native of Louisiana), who having by his agitation, attracted the attention, and ingratiated himself with Mr. Papineau, was named by him to the command of the Insurgent or Patriotic Army, in the North, and were busy in plundering the British inhabitants there, nearly all of whom, threatened with massacre, had fled

---

* The following from a gentleman, who served as a Volunteer during the winter, is interesting, and to be relied upon as authentic.

"In 1837, when accounts were received in Quebec of the rebellious movements in the District of Montreal, the whole of the British inhabitants volunteered their services to the then Governor General, the Earl of Gosford, to take up arms in defence of Her Majesty's Crown, and the safety of the Province—their offer was accepted; and independent Companies were speedily raised, amounting to a force of 1,600 bayonets of unpaid Volunteers, ready to perform such duty as might be required of them for the defence of the Province in addition to these, a Regiment of 1,000 rank and file was raised, also Volunteers, for general service in Canada This Regiment was under, and subject to, the rules and regulations in force for the government of Her Majesty's Regular Troops; when they were armed and clothed, and returned ready for duty, they then took to Garrison duties, thereby leaving all the troops, which consisted only of the 66th Rement and three Companies of the 15th, ready to be moved up the country. The Regiment thus raised was disbanded in May, 1838, when the Rebellion was supposed to have been subdued; but the Fall of that year saw the Rebels again increased by the arrival of a Brigade of Guards and the 34th, 43rd and 85th Regiments—the Grenadier and Coldstream Guards formed the Garrison of Quebec. On the 5th of November, an Express Steamer arrived with despatches from

for their lives, and taken refuge in Montreal. The Patriots in this quarter were as much as possible kept, it seems, in ignorance of the turn the patriotic cause had taken on the south of the Saint Lawrence, being assured by their Chiefs that it was prospering in that section to the fullest extent of their wishes.

Accordingly, on the 13th of December, Sir John Colborne left Montreal for St. Eustache, at the head

---

Sir John Colborne (Lord Seaton) to Lieut. General Sir James Macdonell, desiring him to send up as many of the Guards as he could spare, and to raise a Volunteer Regiment for the general service. Lieut. Colonel the Hon. James Hope of the Guards, was selected to superintend the organizing this Regiment, and Lieut. Colonel Irvine was appointed the Major. On the 7th, they had a sufficient number of men ready to take the whole of the Garrison duty, thereby enabling Sir James Macdonell and the whole of the Grenader Guards to go up to Montreal; and on the 10th they had their complement of men.

"In 1837 and 1838, three Companies of Volunteer Artillery were also raised in Quebec. It may be remarked that the whole number of Volunteers raised, amounted to about 3,000, and not any Canadian—that is, of *French origin*, was among them—nor did one offer their services on the part of the Government during either of the years that Volunteers were required."

I do not clearly understand whether my friend intends his concluding remark as a reflection upon, or a compliment to, the Canadians of French origin. It certainly may be viewed in both lights; but I am inclined to think that most men will interpret it as rather a good trait in the French Canadian character than otherwise. It is a strong proof (taking it to be fact,) of the feeling and unanimity that prevailed among that class of our fellow-subjects, and that at least they were not untrue to each other. I have reason to believe, however, that offers of service were made, in some instances, by Canadians of French origin to the Government, but which, for obvious reasons, it thought proper to decline. As things have turned out, they would, if employed, have had little or no after credit with the Government for their loyalty and zeal in its service, and very probably be now and in all time to come; branded as traitors to their compatriots as their sole reward. R. C.

of a considerable force, consisting of the 1st Regiment or Royals, under Lieut. Colonel Wetherall: the 32nd Regiment, under the Hon. Lieut. Colonel Maitland: the 83rd, under Lieut. Colonel Dundas: a strong party of Artillery, commanded by Major Jackson : the Queen's Light Dragoons (Provincials), under Captain Walter Jones, the Montreal Volunteer Cavalry and rifle corps; constituting in all, an effective force of about two thousand men in arms, besides a multitude of followers unarmed—the citizens vehemently cheering them as they marched out of the city. A small force had, a few hours previously, proceeded to, and was posted at St. Martin, a place near St. Eustache. The Patriots at this place were now hemmed in; there being at Carillon, on the Ottawa, in their rear, two Companies of Regulars, besides the loyal Volunteers of St. Andrews, and Argenteuil, and they consequently had little chance of escaping, and none of success by fighting. The troops passed the night at St. Martin : and having early next morning, crossed the river on the ice, moved onward to the village of St. Eustache, in the church of which the Patriots had taken post, and were awaiting the attack. Their force at this place is said to have consisted of about one thousand men. The 1st, or Royals, entered the village by the road leading from it to the place known as "Grand Brulé"—a few straggling shots being fired at them just before entering. Two pieces of artillery being placed in position, soon effected a breach in the barricade erected round about the church, which was immediately stormed and carried by a party of the Royals led on by Major Gugy,* Provincial Assistant

---

* MONTREAL BARRACKS, 21st Dec., 1837.

SIR,—In obedience to the orders of the Lieut. General Commanding, I have the honor to report the progress of the Brigade under my command, comprising the 2nd Battalion of the Montreal Volunteer Rifles, (Globensky's Volunteers)

Quarter Master General, and commanded by Major Warde,—many of the Patriots escaping by the windows, others seeking refuge in the steeple. The Presbytére (parsonage house) occupied by the patriots, had, in the mean time, after a stout resistance, been carried by storm, in which several of the defenders were slain, and were set fire to, as were also the Manor House and Church. The flames, the wind

in the operations against St. Eustache and St. Benoit. The Brigade assembled at St. Martin's on the 13th instant. On the following morning the 14th, Globensky's Volunteers were detached on the upper road to St. Eustache, the roads bordering on which were occupied by some pickets, which the Volunteers drove in or dispersed. The other Troops of the Brigade proceeded with the rest of the force by the St. Rose road, crossing the Ottawa on the ice, about three miles below the village of St. Eustache. At about 600 or 700 yards from St. Eustache, the artillery were found in position, battering the church and adjoining houses.

I was here directed to follow the 1st Brigade, which was making a detour of the village, for the purpose of cutting off the retreat of the Rebels by St. Benoit road; but on arriving opposite the centre of the village, I was directed to enter it, which I did, and having advanced up the main street, occupying the most defensible houses, and meeting with no opposition, I reported the circumstance to the Lieut. General who desired me to detach an officer to bring up the artillery. In executing this duty, the officer was driven back by a fire from the church, and the Artillery entered the village by the rear, and opened their fire on the Church door, at the distance of 280 yards, while some Companies of the Royal Regiment and the Rifles occupied the houses nearest to the church. After about an hour's firing, and the church doors remaining unforced, a party of the Royal Regiment assaulted the Presbytery, killed some of its defenders, and set it on fire.

The smoke soon enveloped the Church, and the remainder of the Battalion advanced; a straggling fire opened upon them from the Seignior's house, forming one face of the square in which the church stood, and I directed the Grenadiers to carry it, which they did, killing several, taking many prisoners, and setting it on fire.

At the same time, part of the Battalion led by Major Gugy, Provincial Assistant Quarter Master General, and commanded by Major Warde, entered the church by the rear, and drove

being fresh, extended to an adjoining Convent, and a number of neighbouring buildings, about sixty in all, which were speedily involved in one general conflagration, the Patriots, after a short but ineffectual contest, retreating under it before the victorious Troops and Volunteers. Some who had taken refuge in the steeple of the Church, most miserably perished in the flames, to the distress and horror of the spectators, excited even as they were in the midst of battle and slaughter. Doctor Chenier, a brave young man much esteemed by his compatriots, and who had enthusiastically embraced the miscalled patriotic cause, was among the slain, supposed, although the number has not been pre-

out, and slew its garrison and set the church on fire; 118 prisoners were made in these aassaults. Lieutenant Ormsby's conduct was very conspicuons, Major Gugy was severely wounded, and the Royal Regiment had one man killed and four wounded; and no other casualty occurred in the Brigade. On the morning of the 16th, Globensky's corps was left as St. Eustache in charge of prisoners, and the remainder of the Brigade with the force under His Excellency's orders, marched to St. Benoit, where no opposition was offered. On the 17th the Brigade returned to Montreal, bringing with it the prisoners.

I have the honor, &c.

G. W. WETHERALL,
Com. 2nd Bat. or Royal Regt.

The Dep. Quarter Master General,
Montreal.

Return of killed and wounded of the Troops under the command of His Excellency Lieut. General Sir John Colborne, K. C. B., and G. C. H., in the operations against St. Eustache, on the 14th December, 1837:—

MONTREAL, 20*th December*, 1837.

Royal Artillery—1 Corporal, 2 Privates wounded; 2nd Battalion of 1st or Royal Regiment—1 Private killed, 4 Privates wounded : 32nd Regiment—1 Private wounded. Total —1 Private killed, 1 Corporal and 7 Privates wounded.

N. B.—Major B. C. A. Gugy, Prov. Assistant Quarter Master General, was also severely wounded.

JOHN EDEN,
Dep. Adj. General.

cisely ascertained, to have exceeded two hundred.* The loss of the Queen's Troops and Volunteers was inconsiderable, only one or two killed, and but six or seven wounded, among the latter, Major Gugy, severely.† In the pockets of many of the slain Patriots, marbles (used instead of leaden bullets,) were found, which it was said, in some measure, accounted for the little effect their fire had upon the troops, many more of whom, it is probable, must have fallen, had the Patriots been sufficiently provided with balls, but of which there was a

---

* Among the prisoners at St. Eustache, an eye witness noticed the ex-Magistrate, St. Germain. A wounded prisoner, one Major, from St. Benoit stated, that when the attack was made upon St. Eustache, the Rebel force at that place amounted to about 1,000 men ; but a considerable number of them fled upon the first discharge from the artillery. It is supposed that nearly two hundred of the rebels fell, or were suffocated in the flames of the buildings which had been fired, and from which they defended themselves. Upwards of twenty bodies were found in the church-yard, and in the garden attached to the Nunnery. Forty Rebels were killed in attempting to make their escape towards the woods. In imitation of General Brown, at St. Charles, upon pretence of bringing up reinforcements, the Rebel Commanders, Girod and Pelletier, are said to have made their escape soon after the fire of the troops commenced ; but they have not since been heard of, except calling at Inglis's tavern, about four miles from St. Eustache, where they stated that the troops had been complety defeated. These heroes are now supposed to have taken refuge in the woods ; but it is probable they will soon be traced out.—*Montreal Gazette.*

† This gentleman who was Provincial Assistant Quarter Master General, accompanied the detachment under Lieutenant Colonel Wetherall, to St. Charles, as a Volunteer, and rendered important service both to the expedition and to numbers of the unfortunate captive patriots, who through his influence with the Commanding Officer, Lieut. Colonel Wetherall, obtained their release and permission to return to their homes, from which as alleged, they had been forced by threats and intimidation to join the patriots. He is still approvingly spoken of by many of those misguided people for his generous and humane bearing towards them on that and other occasions,—*See end of the Chapter.*

deficiency. Girod, the General commanding, accompanied by Pelletier, his coadjutor or aide-de-camp, like his confrére General Brown, at St. Charles, a few days previously, decamped on horseback from the scene of action, a few minutes after the fire on the part of the troops commenced, pretending that he was going for a reinforcement, but reporting as he went that Her Majesty's troops and the Volunteers were put to the route, and irretrievably defeated by the Patriots. This adventurer committed suicide at Pointe aux Trembles, a short distance below Montreal, on the 18th December, the fourth day after his flight from St. Eustache, by the discharge of a loaded pistol through his head, when on the point of being seized by the police, who had closely pursued him from Montreal, whither with a view of concealing himself among his friends he had made his way, on deserting his comrades.

The official correspondence inserted below, taken from the papers of the day, is explanatory of the progress of the expedition and the results. The Commander of the Forces issued a proclamation, immediately after taking possession of St. Eustache, calling upon the Insurgents to come in and lay down their arms.* Sir John Colborne moved forward the

---

* ST. EUSTACHE, 14*th December*, 1837.

SIR,—I am directed by the Lieutenant General Commanding to inform you that the forces under his command crossed the river about three miles below St. Eustache and invested the town about mid-day. Many of the Rebels made their escape on the appearance of the troops; but others attempted to defend themselves in the church and the surrounding buildings, from which they were driven in about an hour. Our loss has been trifling. One hundred and twenty have been taken a great many arms. The loss of the rebels in killed and wounded has been great. Dr. Chenier their leader is among the killed.

I have the honor, &c.&c,
(Signed,) JOHN EDEN,
Deputy Adj. General.

Lieut. Colonel Hughes,
   Officer Commanding, Montreal.

day after the affair at St. Eustache, with his force for St. Benoit, where the Patriots were said to be strongly fortified, and which he entered at noon. Previous to his leaving St. Eustache in the morning— a flag of truce from the Patriots at St. Benoit came in to Sir John, tendering submission, but it did not prevent his march upon that place, which had been the very centre and hot bed of the Rebellion. White flags, as he passed along, were displayed from most of the houses on the way, in token of the peaceable disposition of the inhabitants, and they were accordingly respected. Simultaneously with this movement by the Commander of the Forces upon St. Benoit (Grand Brulé), another was made upon St. Scholastique by a division under Colonel Maitland. At St. Benoit, Sir John Colborne found upwards of 250 men drawn up in line, and exhibiting white flags. They declared to Sir John that they surrendered themselves at discretion and implored forgiveness of their error in taking up arms against their Sovereign and Government.*

DEPUTY ADJUTANT GENERAL'S OFFICE,
ST. BENOIT, *Dec.* 15, 1837.

SIR,—I am directed by the Lieutenant General Commanding, to inform you that the forces under his command arrived here to-day, having on the march from St. Eustache been met by a Deputation from this place, which on the part of the few Rebels who remained, communicated their anxiety to lay down their arms, and to surrender unconditionally. Girouard escaped last night, and the greater part of the *habitants* have returned to their homes.

I have the honor to be,
Sir,
Your most obedient servant,
JOHN EDEN,
Deputy Adj. General.
Lieut. Colonel Hughes,
Officer Commanding, Montreal.

* TO THE CLERK OF THE PEACE—DISTRICT OF MONTREAL.

HEAD QUARTERS,
MONTREAL, 17*th Dec.*, 1837.

SIR,—I am directed by the Lieutenant General Command-

The Commander of the Forces dealt with much
humanity towards them, dismissing most of them,
detaining only those who were known to have been
the ringleaders whom he sent prisoners to Montreal.
The total number of those sent from this place and
St. Eustache, was stated in the newspapers at 105.
Papers of importance, it was reported, were found
in Mr. Girouard's house, throwing considerable light
on the revolutionary scheme and its ramifications;
but as they have not been published we are ignorant
of the particulars. Major Townsend, of the 24th
Regiment, with the Troops, previously at Carillon,
in the rear of the Insurgents, and a strong body of the
St. Andrews Volunteers arrived at St. Benoit shortly
after the main body from St. Eustache had marched
in. As usual on occasions when the minds of men
are exasperated by intestine broils, much wanton
mischief, in the destruction of property belonging to

---

ing, to acquaint yeu for the information of the Magistrates
of Montreal, that the Force under his command from St.
Eustache, and that from Carillon, marched on the 15th inst.,
on the Grand Brule, and halted that day at St. Benoit, where
the arms of the Rebels, who had for several weeks been pil-
laging that section of the country, were delivered up. The
farmers who had been compelled to fly from their homes in
consequence of the menaces of the insurgent leaders, Girod,
Girouard, Chenier, Dumouchelle and Chartier, and the outrages committed by them, are returning to their farms.

Colonel Maitland, as you will perceive by the following
extract of a Report from him, marched to St. Scholastique
yesterday, and will return to Montreal by St. Thérèse.

The Royal Artillery, Royal, and 83rd Regiments, and the
Montreal Cavalry and Rifle Corps have returned to Montreal.

I have the honor to be, Sir,
Your most obedient humble servant,
(Signed,) JOHN EDEN,
Deputy Adjt. General.

Extract of a letter from Col. the Hon. John Maitland,
dated St. Scholastique, 16th December, 1837 :—
" On my approach to St. Scholastique, I was met at the

unfortunate Patriots, was perpetrated, particularly by the party under Major Townsend, on their march from Carillon to St. Benoit, who, on returning to his quarters at the former place, with two Companies of the 24th Regiment, writes, on the 18th December:—
"CARILLON, *Dec.* 18, 1837·

SIR,—I have the honour to report for the information of His Excellency the Lieutenant General Commanding, that I commenced my march from the Grand Brulé, at half-past two o'clock P.M., on Saturday last, with the troops under my command, proceeding by the route of Cote Double and Cote St. Pierre, and arrived at my quarters at Carillon, at about 9 o'clock the same night.

Prior to my leaving Grand Brulé, almost every house in the town had been set fire to, as well as the Church, Priest's house, &c. No exertion on my part was spared to save as much as possible, but the irregular troops employed were not to be controlled, and were, in every case, I believe, the instruments of the

---

entrance of the village by about 300 men with white flags, who came to surrender themselves, and deposited in my custody about 50 stand of arms. On my getting into the village I saw several groups of *habitants* assembled from different parts of the parish, amounting to about 5 or 600 persons. They all appeared to be very humble, and received the Troops with frequent cheers for the Queen."

Mr. Girouard, surrendered himself a few days afterwards at Coteau du Lac, to John Simpson, Esq., the Collector at that port, by whom he was hospitably treated, but of necessity forwarded to Montreal, where he was committed to prison. Mr. Girouard, though a warm patriot, and as such implicated in the Insurrection, was highly esteemed by all his British neighbors and acquaintances. He did, as I have heard several of them declare, his utmost, when he saw matters coming to a crisis, to dissuade his compatriots, and prevent it; and during the time the Insurgents were assembled, exerted all his influence with them to prevent them from violence upon the persons or property of their British neighbors. He was detained some time in prison, with a multitude of others, at Montreal, but with them finally released by Lord Durham. R. C.

infliction. Two houses were burnt on the line of march by the same hands, both belonging to individuals who have taken a lead in the rebel ranks—the one belonging to a man of the name of Tique, the other Chenier.

I have the honour to be, Sir,
Your obedient servant,
H. D. TOWNSEND,
Major, 24th Regt.

The Hon. Col. Chas. Gore, &c."

It is however, to be observed, that many of those who served as Volunteers on the occasion, were persons who had been exceedingly ill-treated and plundered by the Patriots, while in the ascendant, during a great part of the preceding summer, and who, therefore, now siezed the opportunity of retaliating, and which it was not in the power of the Commanding Officer to restrain.

Sir John Colborne having effectually suppressed the Rebellion in this quarter, and re-established order throughout the District, returned on the 17th December to the city of Montreal, the Troops and Volunteers following at intervals by divisions. The prison was now filled to overflowing with the captive Patriots, awaiting with anxiety their fate; but to the credit of the Government be it said, though martial law was in force, no examples were made, nor did even a trial take place before a Court Martial. It would indeed have been worse than folly to have brought any of them to trial, when in the excitement of the times, dispassionate jurors could not be found, before the Courts of Criminal jurisdiction, and whose functions, for that reason were now suspended. The Courts of Civil Jurisdiction, nevertheless, continued without interruption, in the usual exercise of their functions. Numbers of the prisoners were discharged during the winter, who went home, thanksgiving to

Providence, and to an indulgent Government for being allowed so cheaply to escape the penalty of their treason. Mr. Papineau, who, as previously stated had made good his retreat a day or two after the affair at St. Charles, very prudently passed the winter incog in the neighbouring Republic, (a portion of the time at Albany, and the remainder at Philadelphia,) not even writing to his lady to acquaint her of the place of his retreat, who, nevertheless, must have been informed by his friends that he had effected his escape and was beyond danger. This, however, was not generally known, and as many believed him to be still in the Province, he, to encourage the belief, preserved silence in his retreat, rightly thinking that so long as the Government entertained a prospect of securing him as the chief offender, it would be the less disposed to be severe upon those in its power, and that time might thus be gained as well for instructions from England, which he believed would be the case, to deal humanely with the unfortunate Patriots, as to let the passions of those in whose immediate power they were, cool down.*

During these occurences in Lower Canada, the neighboring Provinces were not indifferent spectators. In Nova Scotia and New Brunswick, as well as in Upper Canada, Volunteers by thousands were offering their services to march upon the Insurgent Patroits.†

* Montreal, Monday evening.—About 20 of the prisoners in custody for high treason, against whom decided evidence was not forthcoming, were liberated this day. When they were taken from their cells they thought they were going to the place of execution especially as the Rev. M. Mignault of Chambly was present at the time. The Rev. gentleman addressed them in the most pathetic terms; and when they found that they were to be liberated, they one and all fell upon their knees and offered up their prayers for their unexpected deliverance.— *Quebec Mercury, 14th Dec.*, 1837.

† GOVERNMENT HOUSE, 9th December, 1837.
F. B. HEAD.

Militia General Order.

His Excellency the Lieutenant Governor apprehends, from

The brave Highlanders of Glengary were on the point of marching, when by notification from Sir John Colborne that the Rebellion had been suppressed, their services were dispensed with for the present. The following from the Quebec Gazette of the 22nd December—

the recent accounts, that it may be necessary for the Militia of this Province to unite their efforts to those of their brave and loyal fellow subjects of Lower Canada, in order to put down Rebellion, and to maintain the integrity of the glorious Empire of Great Britain.

His Excellency therefore directs, that upon the requisition of the Commander of Her Majesty's Forces in Lower Canada the Colonel or Officer commanding any Regiment of Militia in the Bathurst, Johnstown, Ottawa or Eastern Districts respectively, shall take all measures in his power, agreeably to the Militia Laws of the Province, for furnishing whatever number of men may be required for military Service in aid of the Queen's Forces or the Militia of Lower Canada, in either Province.

His Excellency relies upon the zeal, loyalty and bravery of the Militia of Upper Canada, for rendering effectual service to their Sovereign,and maintaining that character which His Excellency is aware has distinguished them wherever they have been called into the field.

His Excellency is further pleased to authorize the forming of any Independent Volunteer Companies, for the above service."

10*th December*, 1837.

His Excellency the Lieutenant Governor directs, that no Officer, whatever may be his rank, or on whatever service he may be employed, shall take upon himself, to release any Prisoner taken in arms against the Government, or any one apprehended on suspicion of treasonable practices; but all such persons are to await the decision of the Government, upon a careful investigation of the charges against them."

"The Cornwall Observer of the 21st instant mentions that on the day previous, the four regiments of Glengarry Militia, mustering about 2,000 strong, assembled at Lancaster for the purpose of marching down to Montreal, under the command of Cols. D. McDonnell, Fraser, Chisholm, and A. M'Donnell. The field pieces belonging to the different regiments were mounted on strong sleighs, with horses and everything necessary for active service, which, with the flags and martial music of the pipes, formed a most interesting spectacle. It was intended that the troops should march on

ber, 1837, shews the reaction in public opinion that was now in progress.*

---

the 21st, but an express arrived from Sir John Colborne, with a communication ' expressing his warmest thanks to the Colonels of the different regiments for their exertions and activity in this critical period, and requesting them to inform the officers and men of these brave Glengarry Regiments that in consequence of the Rebellion being put down he does not wish them to march from their homes at present.'

We can appreciate the feeling of disappointment, says the Cornwall Observer, with which this communication was received by the hardy Highlanders, anxious as we know they are to distinguish themselves as brave and loyal subjects of their Queen."

* " The following accounts of Public Meetings recently held in different parts of the Province, to express the fidelity of the inhabitants to Her Majesty, and the connexion with the United Kingdom of Great Britain and Ireland, are abridged from the French Gazette of yesterday.—*Quebec Mercury,* 23rd December, 1837.

" *County of Dorchester.*—A meeting was held at St. Henri, on tne 15th instant, Mr. Bouffard, Member of the County, in the chair, the report of which is not yet received.

" *County of Champlain.*—A meeting was held at St. Genevieve, on the 19th instant, David Trudel, Esquire, J. P., in the chair, Frs. Filteau, Secretary. The resolutions are decidedly against the late rebellious movements, and in support of the public authority.

" Another meeting was held on the 17th instant, at Champlain, L. E. Dubord, Esq., J. P., in the chair, and N. J. Martineau, Esq., J: P., Secretary.

" The resolutions are decided, but are in favor of reform by peaceable means.

STATE OF VERMONT.

A PROCLAMATION.

By the Governor.

" It is known to my fellow citizens that disturbances have broken out in the neighboring Province of Lower Canada, which have resulted in bloodshed. The head of the Provincial Government has issued his Proclamation, declaring Martial Law in the District of Montreal.

" This state of things necessarily changes the relations which have heretofore existed between the inhabitants of this State and that Province, and the possibility that any, through the influence of ardent feelings, may be betrayed into acts of unauthorized interference, induces me to call the attention of my fellow citizens to the subject.

" With the Kingdom of Great Britain we are in a state of profound peace. We have treaties with that Government which it is our duty, and I trust our desire, to fulfil to the letter.

" *County of Nicolet.*—A meeting was held at Becancour, on the 18th instant, when Captain Reaux, the senior captain, read the Governor's Proclamation of the 20th November, and two resolutions were passed, expressive of the attachment of the meeting to a religious observance of their duty to Her Majesty, and the maintenance of public peace.

" *County of Terrebonne.*—A meeting was held at St. Vincent de Paul, on the 12th December, Arthur Webster, Esq., in the chair, and Captain Germain and Dr. Joseph Pratte, Secretaries, when nine decidedly loyal resolutions were passed, and an association formed in support of the public authority, and the Address of St Roch Suburb adopted and numerously signed.

" *County of Laprairie.*—A meeting was held at Laprairie, on the 9th December, when an Address to the Governor was adopted, containing decided expressions of fidelity and duty.

" *County of L'Acadie.*—A loyal Address to the Governor was adopted in that County on the 9th December.

" *County of Portneuf.*—A public meeting of the western

"It is obvious that as a nation we have no right to intermeddle with the Constitution of any neighboring power. While as Republicans we prefer that form of Government under which it is our happiness to live, a decent regard for the opinions of others, will prevent all dictation as to the form of that Government.

" Principles which have been admitted for ages, forbid all national interference, unless in the character of allies, and it is scarcely necessary to add, that individuals should not do that which the Government *cannot—must not do.*

" It has been represented to me, that in some few instances arms have been furnished, and hostile forces organized within this State. No one can be ignorant of the consequences of such a state of things if allowed. Such forces may be repelled, and our territory be made the theatre of active warfare. This is not to be tolerated for a moment, and every good citizen will ap-

---

division of the County of Portneuf was held according to public notice, on the 17th instant, at eleven o'clock.

" Frs. X, Larue, Esq., Member for the County, in the chair, and L. A. De St. George, Secretary.

" Mr. Huot, the other Member for the County, also attended and moved an Address to His Excellency the Governor in Chief, partly the same as that adopted at the meeting of the city and county of Quebec, on the 4th instant, expressing the regret of the inhabitants at the Insurrection in the District of Montreal ; their loyalty to Her Majesty, adherence to the connection with the United Kingdom, and determination to maintain the public peace and promote harmony among all Her Majesty's subjects in the Province.

" Another meeting of the Eastern Division of the County was held, at St. Augustin, on the 18th instant, at which Mr. Larue also presided, and Mr. F. Laroche was Secretary.

" The same Address was adopted at this meeting.

" At both places Committees for each Parish were appointed to receive signatures. That of Cap Sante was immediately subscribed by 402 names, and for St. Augustin, by upwards of 200.

" Meetings of a similar character have also been held in several Parishes of the Counties of Dorchester and Lotbiniere.

" A meeting is announced for the County of Saguenay,

preciate the importance of rebukiug all such acts as may tend to produce it.

"That comity which binds nations to each other condemns all interference in their intestine broils, and the laws of Congress are explicit in their denunciation, subjecting those who improperly interfere to heavy penalties and imprisonment.

"Under these circumstances and with those feelings, I have thought it my duty to issue this my Proclamation, cautioning my fellow citizens against all acts that

---

and also for the County of Bellechasse, on the 26th instant.

"The only places in which Agitation Meetings were held in the Districts of Three Rivers and Quebec, were—for St. Maurice, at Machiche; for Quebec, at St. Paul's Market, Glacis School House aud St. Roch's Church door; for Portneuf, at Deschambault; for Saguenay, at Malbaie; and for Bellechasse, at St. Thomas.

"The Right Reverend JOSEPH SIGNAY, Catholic Bishop of Quebec, has issued a *mandement* or pastoral letter, dated 11th instant, addressed to the Clergy and the faithful of the diocese, on the occasion of the events which have occurred in the District of Montreal.

"The object of the letter is to exhort the Clergy and their flocks to be on their guard against the disorganizing doctrines which have been circulated by the misguided persons concerned in the late resistance to the established authority, and to enjoin submission conformably to the principles of the Catholic Church, founded on the example and precepts of the Saviour, as set forth in the Gospel.

"The *mandement* concludes by earnestly recommending peace throughout the country, and establishes certain religious observances on the day on which it shall be received and read in the Churches, and on every Sunday and Holiday, to be continued till notification is given to the contrary.

"How happy would it have been for thousands of persons and their families, had they listened to the exhortations of the Bishop! The Districts of Quebec and Three Rivers have been preserved from the scourge and disgrace of rebellion, and it is to be hoped, if any have been misguided in those Districts, they will profit by the present warning, and a knowledge of the evils which a contrary conduct has brought on the District of Montreal, and indeed on the whole Province."—*Quebec Gazzette.*

may subject them to penalties, or in any way compromit the government.

"Our first duty is to our own Government; and the greatest benefit we can confer on the world is by giving them a perfect example in the action of that government. With other nations our conduct should be regulated by the principles of an enlarged and enlightened philanthropy. In war we may treat them as enemies; but in peace they are to be regarded as friends. In the present posture of affairs our duty is manifest—that of strict neutrality—neither lending such aid to either as would be inconsistent with that character, nor denying the rights of hospitality to either so long as they are within our borders, and maintain the character of quite and peaceable citizens.

"My fellow citizens will appreciate the feelings by which I am actuated. The nation's honor cannot be confided to better hands than our own. Their zeal in the cause of liberty was never doubted. It is only necessary to caution them against such interference with the rights of others as might jeopardize the peace of the country

"Given under my hand, this 13th day of December, 1837, and of the Independence of the United States, the sixty-second.
  S. H. JENISON.
" By the Governor,
  G. B. MAIER, Secretary."

"Mr. Gugy originally served," says a Memoir relating to him in a Montreal paper, (the Transcript, 30th March, 1841,) "in the regular army. He was Gazetted in 1812, and promoted in 1813. He is also a very old Militia Officer, his majority dating back as far as somewhere about 1828. Besides this, he raised at Quebec the first* and best equipped body of Volunteer Cavalry ever seen in Canada, at a heavy personal cost. These things were not done in a corner ; all the orderly duty of that portion of the country was performed by them ; they appeared and acted on field days with the regular troops on the Plains of Abraham, and were presented with a standard by Lord Dalhousie, who entertained the highest opinion of their efficiency.

"During the period that occurred immediately after Mr. Gugy left the regular service he studied the Law. No man in Canada has exhibited talents of a higher order at the Bar. Mr. Gugy was also in Parliament an active member, a zealous advocate for the preservation of British connexion, and an able speaker.

"Now comes a period when Mr. Gugy rendered most essential services to Canada and to the British Government. As a Magistrate,† with a species of roving commission and an immense discretionary power, during the rebellious times (1837 and 1838), he was found indefatigable, supplying intelligence that very few could have obtained, and exercising the powers of his mission with remarkable judgment and lenity : and when the extent and intent of the Rebels were known, Mr. Gugy was attached to the three successive demonstrations at St. Charles, St. Eustache, and Colonel Gore's second visit to St. Denis. The letters subjoined speak for themselves. Sir John Colbourne promoted Major Gugy to the rank of Lieut. Colonel in the Militia, promising to make him Adjutant General in this service, and earnestly recommended him for that post to his successor the Earl of Durham."

Copy of a Letter from Colonel Wetherall, commanding

---

* An error.—The late Hon. Matthew Bell, an eminent merchant of Quebec, preceded him in this respect, having for several years, previously, realized and commanded a Volunteer troops.

†Mr. Gugy was in fact appointed Inspector of Rural Police for the District of Montreal, and in that capacity rendered very important service to the Government, exercising his delegated power in those anxious crises, with a diligence, humanity and judgment that did him infinite honor, as testified by many of the most vehement of the Patriots themselves.

Royal Regiment. to Major Gugy, Depy. Asst. Qr. Master General.

" MONTREAL, 29th December, 1838.

" MY DEAR SIR,—It not only affords the greatest pleasure to record my opinion of your service whilst attached to the force under my command, during the operations against St. Charles in November last, but in so doing I only acquit myself of a duty I owe to your merits.

In my despatch to His Excellency the Lieut. Gen. Commanding, I deemed it necessary to mention how much I was indebted to you for your valuable aid, and I subsequently stated the same personally.

I also wrote to the Attorney General, by whose advice you were attached to the force, stating more fully my sentiments; and so far as I was competent to do, recommended your being further employed.

I have no copy of that letter, but the substance was that from your zeal, unwaried activity, and peculiar tact in eliciting intelligence from the most unwilling, your hardy courage and promptitude in execution, you were the best partisan soldier* I ever met with, and that with a select troop of Mounted Police, you would do more to secure the peace of Lower Canada than any other measure that could be devised, for that no rebel or treasonable agitator could escape your vigilance and decision. Subsequent events have made me better acquainted with your character, and have strengthened the opinion I had before deliberately formed and which I shall be always happy to vouch.

I was sorry to hear from Doctor Farnden, yesterday, that your wound was not in so wholesome a condition as he wished. You must be patient. Confinement is irksome to one of your active habits, but be patient.

Believe me to be always most truly yours,
G. D. WETHERALL,
Lieutenant Colonel,
Commanding the Royal Regiment.

Major Gugy,
D. A. Quar. Master General.

I hoped before this to see your promised rank announced.
G. D. W.

---

* It may not have been so intended, but there is something if I mistake not, fastidious in the terms " partisan soldier," too often observable in Officers of the Army towards Provincials or native Colonists, exceedingly offensive to the latter. Colonel Wetherall, it is true, speaks in all other respects very approvingly of the services rendered him by the partisan soldier, as well indeed he might, it being mainly

Copy of a Letter from Colonel the Hon. Charles Gore, to Major Gugy, dated 9th March, 1840.

"MY DEAR SIR,—(The first paragraph relates to matters of a domestic nature.) From your having served under my orders in the Outbreaks of 1837 and 1838, you certainly have a right to expect that I should speak to your conduct, and I am happy in being able to say that during the period you served with me, your conduct was highly gentlemanly, gallant and most zealous. On your being attached to me on a particular service, finding you were also equal to military duties, I requested Lord Seaton to attach you to my Department as a Provincial Assistant Quarter Master General, which His Excellency very willingly consented to, and you performed the duties to my entire satisfaction, and particularly at the attack on St. Eustache, where you were severely wounded while endeavoring to find out a practicable entry to the Church, which was then stoutly defended.*

After your recovery you were detached to the Counties on the Richelieu, and also to St. Hyacinthe, and employed in disarming the habitans in conjunction with Captain Crompton, of the 66th Regiment and other Military Officers. You were also directed to exert yourself in quieting those sections of the country, and you addressed the habitans at St. Hyacinthe and other places, at the Assembly called by the Priests in their Parishes, with good effect. Altogether I consider your services in 1837 and 1838 as highly meritorious, and shall be happy should any testimonial from me be of any service to you.

I am, my dear Sir,
Yours faithfully,
CHARLES GORE.

---

owing to his local knowledge, foresight, judicious advice and arrangements in proceeding through a hostile population to the scene of action that the Colonel owed his success. So precarious, indeed, was deemed the expedition to St. Charles, after news of Colonel Gore's defeat at St. Denis, that a Messenger was despatched after Colonel Wetherall while on the march thither, with an order to return to Montreal, which luckily he did not receive, the despatch being intercepted by the Patriots. Without in the least intending to detract from the known merit of this excellent officer, there is cause to believe that but for Mr. Gugy's knowledge of the country and advice. in which happily he had confidence, he would have rushed head foremost like Colonel Gore at St. Denis, against the Patriots at St. Charles, and very probably with the like result, and not a man of the detachment have returned alive to Montreal—such was the excitement of the

P. S.--I should have mentioned that, although you reported yourself fit for duty, after your wound, it was still open, and you proceeded on your duty to the Richelieu, still suffering from its effects. O. G.

The above are testimonials selected from the public prints of the times, highly creditable certainly to Major Gugy, as coming from Military men of rank and consideration, intrusted with the Queen's authority in subduing the unhappy outbreaks at the periods in question. But he also was, it is due to him to observe, still more fortunate in obtaining vouchers which are to be seen in prints of the same period, though of later date, far more gratifying to a generous mind than even those, as bearing testimony of the moderation and spirit of conciliation, wherewith he acquitted himself of the delicate mission as Inspector of Rural Police entrusted him, and to which several of the most respectable names in the rural Parishes of the District of Montreal are subjoined, including also some of the Parochial Clergy in the same quarter, all testifying Mr. Gugy's humanity and kindness towards such of the Patriots as fell into the hands of the troops, in country through which they had to pass. But directed by Mr. Gugy, whose thorough knowledge of the sate of things in the neighborhood was of the highest utility, he proceeded with circumspection by slow and easy marches, as well to avoid fatiguing his men as to guard against surprise, and arrived at St. Charles fresh and fit for action. Each man of the Detachment had 60 rounds of ball cartridges, but, strange to say, only one day's rations, on leaving Fort Chambly for St. Charles. Mr. Gugy had consequently to discharge on the emergency the duties both of Commissary and of Quarter Master General, taking upon himself the responsibility of purchasing cattle to provision the party, and of quartering them by night upon the inhabitants, of all which he acquitted himself, as I have heard the military and several of the inhabitants declare, greatly to the advantage of the service and not less to the public satisfaction, the habitants being liberally paid for the supplies they furnished on the occasion.

R. C.

* Major Gugy, I have good authority for saying, received his wound after he had actually entered the Church, and it was matter of surprise that he survived it. The musket ball entered on the left side of his neck, passing through which, near to the carotid artery, it came out a little above the elbow of his right arm.

R. C.

conjunction with whom it was his duty to act, and his respect for, and protection of the persons and property of those whom the fortune or rather misfortune of war had made " prisoners and captives."

Having said this much, certainly in no cold or indifferent manner, I must—not to do the absolute panegyrist in this rather long memoir of him into which I have been drawn—also state that Col. Gugy, who from his first entry upon public life, was a consistent Conservative, or rather a high Tory, has recently (since the Parliamentary Session of 1849, in which he vigorously and most vehemently opposed the famous Rebellion Losses Bill), by abandoning the Conservative ranks, and ranging himself at the following Session in those of the self-styled Liberals, forfeited the confidence and good will of his former partisans and political friends. It is to be observed, however, that some of this party had previously, while in power, most unjustifiably sacrificed him, to suit a time-serving purpose, which nevertheless failed them. The Draper-Daly Administration, during Lord Cathcart's Government, removed him, under the sole flimsy pretence that he was unpopular among the French Canadian population, from the office of Adjutant General for Lower Canada, which he filled with impartiality and ability, to make room for one of their political adversaries, Dr. E. P Tache, and no doubt with the view of propitiating them—a piece of unworthy suppleness, which, with other meannesses, characteristic of that Administration, to carry favor with their opponents, helped finally to swamp them in the estimation of all parties, and drove them deservingly from office. The treatment alluded to could not, however, considering the lapse of time and other circumstances between it and Mr. G's abdication of his party, justify this last but untoward step, leaving on the score of political inconsistency a spot on his escutcheon. But who is spotless ? Mr. Gugy, though as a public speaker, much of a mannerist, approaching indeed to affectation, enjoys nevertheless, the reputation of an acute, cool and able debater in Parliament, as well as of a sound jurist and skilful practitioner in the Courts of Law.

Tius much relating to this gentleman had been composed as a pendant or note to the last chapter (in the 4th volume) in which it was intended that notice of the affair of St. Eustache, where he was severely wounded, should have been included, as may be seen by referring to the contest prefixed to the chapter; but the volume, not admitting of room, it was unavoidably transferred to the present. Not seeing his name mentioned in connexion with the affair at St. Charles Mr. Gugy, with excusable sensibility, deeming his services entitled to some notice at the hands of an impartial annalist, hastily concluded that they were overlooked, and addressed me the following letter, to which—*ex debito justitioe* —I most willingly make room. R. C.

DARNOC, 8*th April*, 1853.

MY DEAR SIR,--You have no doubt occasionally reflected upon the hard fate of those men, who in the great American contest for liberty, took the Royal side. Those who perished in the field, as well as those who withered by slow decay in the Acadian or Canadian wilderness, having in many instances sacrificed enormous wealth and the highest social atanding, are all alike ignored and forgotten,or remembered only through the hereditary devotion of some generous descendant. The feats of their successful adversaries fill volumes, but where shall we look for the historian of their fidelity, their daring and their worth? To compare very small things to great, I venture most respectfully to submit that while you have enlarged upon the acts and deeds of gentlemen whom I had the misfortune to oppose, allowing them even to make their own statesments, you have altogether overlooked me.

With your permission then, I would say that on the memorable 22nd November 1837. I was requested by Lord Seaton, then Sir John Colborne, to repair to Chambly. I accordingly proceeded in that direction during a storm, which making it unsafe for the steamer to approach the wharf, compelled me to swim my horse for a considerable distance on the South side of the St. Lawrenc. On arrival at about eight P.M., I myself delivered to Colonel Wetherall the order to march that very night, with all the possible secrecy and speed. The Colonel was not to halt; he was to reach St. Charles by a certain hour next morning, and instantly to aftack the place. In many respects the Commander of the Forces reckoned, as I shall show, without his host. In the first place, not one of the Force knew anything of the roads or people, nor do I believe that more than one spoke French, of the body. The storm raged so fearfully, the rain poured in such torrents, and the frost set in afterwards so intensely, that as we approached St. Mathias, men and horses were all equally fatigued. Indeed, though Col. Wetherall, in obedience to his orders, insisted on continuing the march; they were all so exhausted as to be unable to cope, on broken or woody ground, successfully with any resolute enemy. Col. Wetherall, as I have said, was determined to obey his orders literally (as it is now known that General Gore did, in marching upon St. Denis). From this determintaion, I must say, since no other will,that I had the good or bad fortune to dissuade him, I induced him to halt—I billeted his men and horses in the neighboring houses until daylight. It was only at that period, however, that I learned that we had marched without a dollar, without a loaf of bread, without a Commissary and without a spare catridge—a pretty predicament in an enemy's country, surrounded by thousands of armed men.

Reaching Rouville about noon, I purchased bullocks and flour—secured the services of butchers and bakers, procured spirits. and served all out to the troops. Obtaining information which led me to fear that some disaster had befallen Colonel Gore, I recommended Colonel Wetherall to send for Major Warde and an additional Company of the Regiment then at Chambly;* and I pointed out the mode by which it could be effected. He was to enter the scow, then used for ferrying over the Richelieu at night, and having reached the middle of the stream, he was to compel the ferrymen to drop down to St. Hilaire. As you justly say, by adopting this course, the men arrived fresh and ready for service. I thus have at least the merit of having been a little more than merely an extempore Commissary.

It was I too, who, to spare the effusion of blood, sent in the respectable old Canadian, mentioned by Mr. Brown, with a request that the people dispérse. Lastly, I positively state it was not the Queen's Force who fired first. but the gentlemen on the other side.

There. are no doubt, many living witnesses of the foregoing fact. On the 14th of December, being an Assistant Quarter Master General, in order to prove that the ice on the Ottawa was safe, I was the first to cross it. I did so at hand gallop in the presence of the troops, at a spot which suited us, but which had been open two days before. I also pointed out the mode by which the guns could be safely crossed, and guided the horses with my own hand.

Without adverting to facts which are well known, I dare assert that impatient and dissatisfied at finding the Royal Troops so long successfully resisted as they were on that morning; I sought and found a vulnerable spot, and immediately after led the column by which it was assaulted and taken.

You know how my zeal has been rewarded.

Yours, &c.

R. Christie, Esquire.   A. GUGY.

---

* This despatch was carried during the night at very imminent personal risk from Rouville to Fort Chambly by Sidney Bellingham, Esq , accompauied by one of the Montreal Cavalry, and delivered to Major Warde at four o'clock in the morning.   R. C.

(*From Colonel Gugy to the author.*)

Will you listen to an anecdote of another Governor? Lord Metcalfe sent for me one day, and informing me that the Oregon question was likely to end in war desired me as Adjutant General without disclosing that information, to organize the Militia. At that time there were some Officers of the several Volunteer Corps who held higher, some lower rank therein, than they had held in the Militia. There were Officers of Militia who had refused to assist in suppressing the Rebellion; there were many who were implicated in it; more who had been merely passive. All these persons had conflicting pretensions, which were not without great difficulty reconciled during Lord Metcalfe's administration. But when Lord Cathcart assumed the reins of Government, he insisted on managing these matters himself, and his panacea for every compliant was a long parenthetical general order. I have shewn you some of the verbose General Orders which he penned, and you have seen the criticisms which they provoked. They were certainly edited in very questionable English; and as he insisted on my fathering them, I was mercilessly assailed by the Press. In spite of my remonstrances, among other things, in order to elevate to a Lieutenant Coloneley, one of his countrymen, who held no rank whatever, he chose to organize the Fire Companies of Montreal into a Battalion—the text of the Statues and the evident intention of the Law exempting Firemen, to the contrary notwithstanding! Hostilities being then impending, he did me the honor one day among other matters, to express his opinion, that I had talents for war; and he assured me that, in the event of its being declared, he *would give me the command of a Brigade!* But there was no war; and his turn being served, he allowed his Ministers to introduce into Parliament a Bill for *legislating me out of my office.* This was done accordingly, and he thereby summarily removed a public officer, of whom, in his letter of the 3rd February, 1846, he spoke as follows:—

" Admitting fully every consideration, that is due to your
" personal character, and with the highest esteem which a
" knowledge of the zealous services you have so conspicuous-
" ly rendered to your country on many occasions has created
" as well as paying a just tribute to the devoted loyalty to
" your Sovereign which you have always evinced, the Ad-
" ministrator of the government is however satisfied from
" what has come before him during the short period in which
" you have acted under his immediate orders, that your su-
" perior talents and acquirements might be more suitably and

"advantageously employed in some other branch of the pub-"lic service."

The compliment might certainly have been more gracefully expressed, but it could scarcely have been more emphatic. Such were the terms in which he signified the result of an opinion, which he had had previously expressed, " that no Colonist should hold the appointment of Adjutant General.' Such was his style, and I complain only of the inference that what " came before him," was the result of my acts, when in fact I was but the passive instrument of a man who comprehending nothing, meddled with every thing, and not only imagined he could write, but actually borrowed his light from James Smith! He thus punished me for his own mismanagement; for he was himself the Adjutant General. It may be added, that having deprived me of my income in one branch of the public service, he forgot his more than implied promise to employ me in any other.

Such was the reward of " *devoted loyalty*"--such the meed of zealous services conspicuously rendered." It conveys a valuable lesson.

A G.

This most disingenuous " dodge" here alluded to, of legislating Colonel Gugy out of his office, was at the time attributed to private pique on the part of Mr Attorney General Smith—then a leading but most inefficient member of the Government—against that gentleman, who, it was said, and I believe truly, had refused to suggest in his official capacity, to the Governor, certain appointments in the Militia of the County (Missisquoi), represented by Mr. Smith, which this gentleman was desirous of making, to distinguish by his especial favor, some of those by means of whose influence he had seated himself in the Assembly, but which Col. Gugy did not deem consistent with justice, inasmuch as the removal of persons of at least equal merit to that of those whom it was proposed to appoint, and without any just or other cause than Mr. Attorney General's displeasure, was comtemplated, in order to make room for them. If men in power would only bear in mind that they are but guardians and trustees of the rights of others, and in exercise of their trust, have just magnanimity enough to forego the indulgence of their own petty preposseesions and resentments, what an amount of individual heart-burning, public trouble and expense might there not be spared?

Mr. Gugy Adjutant General, it is to be observed, had been honored by Sir Charles Metcalfe, with the rank of Colonel of Militia. This step facilitated in some sort the "dodge" in question which was as follows:—It being necessary--in 1848, owing to the existing discussions between the American and British Governments, relating to the Oregon Territory, to recast the old Militia Laws of the two Canadas, now united, into a single and uniform code; it was among other matters enacted, that an Adjutant General and two Deputy Adjutant Generals one for each section, (Upper and Lower Canada) of the Province, might be appointed by the Governor; the first to be a Colonel in the Militia—the latter, Lieutenant Colonels. Lieut. Col. Plomer Young of the line, was--in conformity with Lord Cathcart's notions that, no Colonist should hold the office of Adjutant General of Militia--appointed to that post, with the round salary of £1,000 a-year, but which being reduced the following Session, he resigned. As Colonel Gugy held the rank of Col. he could not, it was pretended, hold the office of Deputy Adjutant General, which was conferred upon Doctor Tache, one of the opposite class of politicians to that of Colonel Gugy, but it was, nevertheless, a popular appointment, Mr. Tache's character for impartiality and integrity being universally admitted. It was, besides this, more than insinuated, that Colonel Gugy's unpopularity among the great body of Lower Canadians, rendered his removal expedient—an argument which, if he really were unpopular, considering whence it had arisen, namely his activity and acknowledged services during the Rebellion, never could have been used by an upright and honorable Government, and could have proceeded only from a time-serving Administration. It is satisfactory to state, that they obtained no credit for the " dodge" in sacrificing Colonel Gugy, to whom, however, they allowed, on giving him his conge, a year's salary,(£500,) the very party, whom to propitiate, they had sacrificed him, despising them more than ever for it, and under the pressure of whose contempt they soon afterwards were extinguished, to the satisfaction even of most of their old friends, who had seen with disgust their miserable shifts and obsequiousness to their opponents.

There is, and has always been, a tendency, in metropolitan officials originating in selfishness, to undervalue if not trample upon native colonists, as if the latter really were morally, intellectually and physically their inferiors, a delusion by which, among a multitude of others, Lord Cathcart, during his accidental and short administration seems to have been led astray, and which the memorable and glorious struggle for, and achievement of independence by our anglo-saxon kinsfolk the people of the United States of North America, late British Colonisists, ought to have dispelled.

It is but natural that men of spirit among the native colonists should resist the feeling, I have no doubt, induced Mr. Gugy in the prospect of an approaching war, to look for the rank of Colonel conferred upon him by Lord Metcalf. Being restricted in the Militia service to the rank of Lieut. Colonel, no colonist could ever expect to command either in quarters or in the field. In the last war with the United States to make security doubly sure, every Major in the regulars was, by general order, elevated to the local rank of Lieut. Colonel. It was, I am inclined to believe, an unlawful order, but it was obeyed by the Canadian embodied Militia though not without disgust by its best superior officers who felt themselves disparaged, indeed degraded by it, while patriotically serving the Empire in co-operation with regulars, and in defence, moreover, of their own hearths and altars, inasmuch as a regular major was always sure to turn up on the least prospect of active service, to the exclusion of the Militia Lieut. Colonel who was thus excluded from all hope of command. And thus if there were a chance of distinction it was reserved for the regulars. If there were an unpleasant service the Militia were ordered to perform it

Why indeed, it may be asked, should not we as well as our neighbours in the United States, have Generals of Militia. Why should the Provincials be always subordinate to men who buy their commissions, as groccers do their figs, to sell again?"

To talk of exclusion on the ground of a presumed incapacity is idle – for assuredly some might be competent for command, as Lord Cathcart justly deemed Colonel Gugy, and here as elsewhere the right of selection might and would, doubtless, be constitutionally exercised. It is not every General in the army who is entrusted with a command, nor would one in a hundred of the Generals of Militia aspire so high—but the time has come for all right-minded Colonists to assert and maintain their perfect equality with Metropolitans.

R. C.

August, 1853.

CHAPTER XLI.

Lord Gosford proposes retiring from the Government—Correspondence on the subject with the Ministers—*Mandement* of the R. C. Bishop of Montreal—Addresses to the Governor—General Order to disarm the *habitants* in certain Counties of Montreal—Doings on the Frontiers by the fugitive Patriots—Instructions and approval by the Minister of Sir John Colborne's conduct—Act suspending the Constitution proclaimed—Special Council meet—Services of Volunteer Militia dispensed with—Martial Law ceases—Document transmitted to " Working Men's Association of London"—Constitutional Associations of Quebec and Montreal—Mr. Andrew Stuart of Quebec delegated to England by the former, and Messrs. Moffatt and Badgley by the latter—Fixed determination of the British population in Lower Canada, for a reunion of the Provinces -Opinions upon the subject in Upper Canada

THE Earl of Gosford—sensible at length that his Administration had proved a failure, and that all further attempts to conciliate were idle—wrote on the 2nd September to the Colonial Minister:—" It is evident that the Papineau faction are not to be satisfied with any concession that does not place them in a more favourable position to carry into effect their ulterior objects, namely, the separation of this country from England, and the establishment of a Republican form of Government. Mr. Papineau has gone such lengths, that he must now persevere in the course he has taken, or submit to a defeat which would annihilate all his power and influence. The plan he pursues clearly shows that he is determined to do all in his power to obtain his ends."—" Mr. Papineau has enemies in various directions; and though I do not conceive there is any ground for alarm, still great caution and vigilance are required to guard against the evils that might follow from the attempts making to excite discontents among the people, by the most abominable misrepresentations. The Executive requires more power, and under my present impression I am disposed to think that you may be under the necessity of suspending the Constitution. It is with feelings of deep regret I state this, but duty compels me to communicate it to you."*

His Lordship again writes to the Colonial Minister on the 14th November, a few days before the outbreak of St. Denis, as follows :—"Finding from the system pursued by the disaffected in this Province, that the decisive measures I have recently submitted for your consideration become every day more necessary, it naturally occurs to me that, if it should be determined to take a strong course of proceeding, you might feel desirous to intrust the execution of your plans to hands not pledged, as mine are, to a mild and conciliatory line of policy. As I stated in a former letter, I would not shrink from difficulties, nor wish to take any step that would in the least

---

* The following letter marked "Private" from Sir John Colborne to Lord Gosford, affords a glimpse of the agitation which, at this time, was going on at St. Denis, St. Charles, and their neighborhood :

SOREL, Oct. 6. 1837.

Private.

" MY DEAR LORD,—I beg to thank your Lordship for your letter of the 5th ultimo. It appears absurd to attach an importance and influence to tactics of the factious party in this Province heyond their actual progress, and the results of their unchecked movements and language, while the great mass of the Canadian peasantry cannot be excited or indeed to take an active part with the persons who are now sounding the alarm ; but no doubt should be entertained that the system of agitation carrying on by the faction,although chiefly intended to intimidate the Home Government, under present circumstances, and to demonstrate that the country is bordering on a state of revolt, must tend to promote effectually the avowed object of Mr. Papineau.

" In my correspondence with Col. Eden, I have had occasion to refer to the facts and reports that establish the decided character which the agitators have lately assumed. The people have elected the dismissed officers of the militia to command them. At St. Ours a pole has been erected in

degree embarrass Her Majesty's Ministers: but I owe it to you, to myself, and to my sense of public duty, fairly and honestly to declare my conviction that any alteration that may take place in the policy to be observed towards this Province would be more likely to produce the desired result if confided to a successor, who would enter on the task free to take a new line of action, without being exposed to the accusation of inconsistency, which, just or not, always proves injurious to the beneficial working of any Administration. My continuance here, to this time, has been, as you are aware, solely on public grounds; had I been influenced by private considerations, I should long ere this have solicited my recall; but the

---

favor of a dismissed Captain, with this inscription on it— 'Elu par le peuple.'

At St. Hyacinthe, the tri-clored flag was displayed for several days. Two families have quitted that town in consequence of the annoyance they experienced from the patriots. Wolfred Nelson warned the patriots at a public meeting to be ready to arm. The tri-colored flag is to be seen at two taverns between St. Denis and St. Charles. Many of the tavernkeepers have discontinued their signs, and substituted for them an eagle. The bank notes or promissory notes issued at Yamaska, have also the same emblem marked on them. Mr. Papineau was escorted from Yamaska to St.Denis by a numerous retinue; and it is said that 200 or 300 carriages accompanied him on his route. He has attended five public meetings lately; and at one of them, La Valtrie, a priest was insulted in his presence. The occurrence at St. Denis was certainly a political affair, a family at St.Antoine opposed to the proceedings of W. Nelson, having been annoyed by the same mob that destroyed the house of Madame St. Jacques a few hours before the shot was fired from her window."

" The game which Mr. Papineau is playing cannot be mistaken; and we must be prepared to expect that if 400 or 500 persons are allowed to parade the streets of Montreal at night, singing revolutionary songs, the excited parties will come in collision.

" I remain, &c.
" J. COLBORNE.
" His Excellency the Right Hon. the Earl of Gosford, &c."

principles by which I was actuated, would not admit of an abrupt application of this nature; I therefore confined my communication on this head to acquainting you that my private wish was to return home, but leaving it entirely to you to take the course you might think best calculated to promote the public service. I can, however, now assign reasons of a public nature for wishing to be relieved, which I could not well have done sooner; and should you admit their validity, I trust that, after what I have said, you will feel no hesitation, as regards myself, in making such arrangements as you think desirable.

" I have, &c.,
" GOSFORD."

This letter was acknowledged by Baron Glenelg, who, in consequence of it, addressed, on the 23rd of December, the following to the Earl of Gosford:—
" My Lord,—I have the honour to acknowledge the receipt of your Lordship's despatch of the 14th November, stating the grounds on which you consider it advantageous to the public service that you should be at once relieved from the office of Governor General of Canada.

" From my private letter of the 22nd, and my despatch No. 281, of the 27th November, which will probably by this time have reached you, your Lordship will perceive that the Ministers of the Crown, fully appreciating the disinterested views which you have expressed in several of your private communications, had already advised Her Majesty to accept your resignation. It only remains for me, therefore, to repeat the high sense entertained by Her Majesty's Government of the generous motives by which you have been guided in this respect.

I have, &c.
" GLENELG."

The Minister had, in contemplation of Lord Gosford's retirement, addressed, on the 6th December, the following letter to Sir John Colborne :—" Sir,— My despatch of the 27th ult. will have apprised you of the approaching retirement of the Earl of Gosford from the government of Lower Canada—an event which, by the terms of His Lordship's commission, will devolve upon you the temporary administration of the affairs of the Province.

"It is at once my duty and my anxious desire to relieve you, as far as possible, from the arduous responsibility attendant upon the discharge of that duty at the present moment. I do not, however, propose to enter upon any statement of the course to be pursued respecting those questions of permanent policy which have been agitated between the Executive Government and the House of General Assembly. All such discussions, however important, are for the present, superseded by the urgent necessity which has arisen for maintaining the public peace and restoring the authority of the law. To that one great object your undivided attention will be given, and to that alone will my present communication be confined.

" I enumerate in the margin the series of Lord Gosford's despatches, which describe the gradual but rapid advance of the enemies of peace and order, from the complaints urged at least under the forms of the Constitution to the very verge of rebellion. The conclusion from the whole of this intelligence is inevitable, that the leaders of the movement party are restrained only by some remaining considerations of prudence from raising the standard of open insurrection. It is therefore necessary to consider how this crisis is to be encountered.

" You appear already to have concentrated upon the points most exposed to danger, every part of Her Majesty's forces in British America, which it has been possible to withdraw from the adjacent Provinces.

Arrangements have been made for increasing, if necessary, the number of troops under your command with the return of the spring. In the meantime I trust that your present force will be sufficient to awe the seditious, and to suppress any actual rising which the civil power may be unable to control. If, however, your strength should be inadequate to these objects, you will, of course, avail yourself of the voluntary zeal of such of Her Majesty's loyal subjects as may be willing to serve under your authority, and submit themselves entirely to your order.

" The first and highest prerogative and duty of the Crown is the protection of those who maintain their allegiance against the enemies of order and peace. To repress by arms any insurrection or rebellion to which the civil power cannot be successfully opposed is therefore a legitimate exercise of the Royal authority; and, in the attainment of this object, the proclamation of martial law may become indispensable.

" It is superfluous to state with what caution and reserve this ultimate resource should be resorted to, and that it ought to be confined within the narrowest limits which the necessity of the case will admit. But if unhappily the case shall arise in any part of Lower Canada in which the protection of the loyal and peaceable subjects of the Crown may require the adoption of this extreme measure, it must not be declined. Reposing the utmost confidence in your prudence, that such a measure will not be needlessly taken, and relying upon your firmness, that, if taken, it will be followed up with the requisite energy, Her Majesty's Government are fully prepared to assume to themselves the responsibility of instructing you to employ it, should you be deliberately convinced that the occasion imperatively demands it. They will, with confidence look to Parliament for your indemnity and their own.

" It might embarrass, but could hardly assist you, if I should attempt to address to you any more detailed instructions for your guidance in the present emergency. Her Majesty's Government commit to your hands the safety of the important part of the Crown over which your authority will extend. In the discharge of that trust you will have the highest claim to every degree of support which it may be in our power to give.

" I have, &c.,

" GLENELG."

Accordingly, the first news of Lord Gosford's recall reached Quebec on the 13th of January. The Roman Catholic Bishop of Montreal issued, on the 8th of this month, a *mandement* to the Clergy and Laity of his Diocese, referring to his recommendation to them in July, and his *mandement* of the 24th October last, announcing also the restoration of tranquility in the District. The Prelate deplored, in becoming terms, the evils brought upon the country by those concerned in the late Rebellion—declaring that none of them could be admitted to a participation in the Sacraments of the Church, or to Christian Burial, till they had made reparation and shewn meet fruits of repentance. He ordered divine service to be celebrated in this intention, and required the Clergy to urge charitable collections for the relief of those who are suffering.

Various addresses from the inhabitants of French origin in the City and County of Quebec, and from the neighbouring Parishes, expressive of their concern and regret at the recent disturbances, were shortly, before his departure, presented to the Governor. His answer to that from the City and County of Quebec is given below.*

---

* "GENTLEMEN,—I beg to assure you that the sentiments of attachment to Her Majesty's Government contained in the Address which you now present, afford me much satisfaction, and will, I feel persuaded, be graciously received by

The following notice of Lord Gosford's departure from Quebec for England, is from the Quebec Mercury of the 1st March, 1838:—

"On Tuesday His Excellency the Earl of Gosford ceased to administer the Government of this Province, over which he had presided for two years and a half; having arrived at Quebec in August, 1835, as the chief of a commission of inquiry and pacification, whose labors it was hoped, by Ministers, would have led to the adjustment of all political differences, and the establishment of the Provincial Government upon a firm and liberal footing, the grand principles of the British Constitution being always kept in view. That the Mission failed in its object is a matter of notoriety, and that the terms which have been accepted with thankfulness by the other British American Colonies, have been factiously rejected by Lower Canada, is also too well known to render it necessary that we should further dwell upon it at this time. That Lord Gosford, as Governor in Chief executed the instructions of concession and conciliation which had been imparted to him to their full extent, is equally well known. Indeed, he pushed them to the utmost bound, and still held out the olive branch when the enemies of the Constitution and British connexion were sharpening their swords in the hope of overthrowing the Government, and of severing that tie by which the

---

our beloved Sovereign, to the foot of whose Throne I shall, as you request, caus them to be conveyed.

"This declaration of loyalty proceeding under existing circumstances from so large number of respectable inhabitants of the City and County of Quebec cannot fail, I should hope, to remove the false impressions which by wilful and continued misrepresentation have unhappily been too successfully instilled in the minds of our confiding and less enlightened fellow-subjects, have been the means of seducing a portion of them into commission of those acts subversive of lawful order and public tranquillity, that have so justly excited the grief of the memoralists, and of all who desire the welfare, happinesss and prosperity of the Province."

Province has been raised to its present rank in the British Colonial Possessions, whilst its religion, its institutions, its language, and its laws have been preserved inviolate. At length the undisguised language of the declaration, at the meeting of the Six Counties, held at St. Charles, on the 23rd of October last, too plainly proved that the endeavour at governing Lower Canada under the existing Constitution was a hopeless task, and Lord Gosford then apprized Her Majesty's Ministers of his thorough conviction of the necessity of changing the conciliatory policy which had been hitherto pursued for measures of a sterner charater, and at the same time that he declared his inability to conduct the government under the instructions by which he had to that time been guided, added, that if he stood in the way from his adherence to those instructions, of the full execution of the measures which had obviously become necessary, he was willing to resign the trust that had been confided to him, and begged to be relieved from his charge. Her Majesty's Ministers whilst they fully concurred in all that His Lordship had done, in the government of the Colony, and expressed their approbation of the manner in which his important duties had been discharged, consented to his return to Britain, and sent instructions for His Excellency Lieutenant General Sir John Colborne, to assume the reins of government upon His Lordship's departure. This transfer of authority has now taken place. Whatever have been the errors Lord Gosford may have committed during the short but eventful period of his administration, no man can question his motives, we believe none will be found so rancorous in their censure of his conduct as to question the purity of his intentions and the benevolence of his views. But having been instructed to endeavour to form a government, by uniting the most moderate of the two political parties, His Lordship pursued this object with an earnestness that caused him to lend too ready an ear to the representations of designing men, who affected to secede from the majority of the Assembly only to forward their own views of personal advancement, and unhappily, were too successful in palming their pseudo loyalty upon the Noble Lord, and producing a far more favourable impression than their previous conduct, considered with their present professions, ought to have obtained for them. That Lord Gosford has not succeeded in administering the government of Lower Canada and calming the dissensions by which it has been torn, cannot be imputed to him as a disgrace. His predecessors for years past, have not been more fortunate; and if open rebellion, pretended to have been provoked by the necessary interference of the Imperial Parliament in the concerns of the Colony, has broken out under the conciliatory policy enjoined by his instructions, it is fully obvious that such an outbreaking would not have been averted had coercion been resorted to at an earlier period. An appeal to force might have produced for the insurgents a strong sympathy among the people of the United Kingdom and even in the Imperial Parliament, under the idea that they had been driven to desparation by the arbitrary and oppressive conduct pursued towards them; whereas they now stand prominent as reckless and ungrateful rebels, who have refused concessions which have been thankfully received by every other Province in British America, and have been seduced by their own vanity, and the vaunts of their unprincipled chiefs, to wage an unprovoked war against the Mother Country, without even the most distant prospect of success to cloak the crime of treason in the mantle of revolution."

The 26th of February was observed in Lower Canada as a day of General Thanksgiving to the Almighty for the termination of the Rebellion and the restoration of Peace. The Earl of Gosford left Quebec on the following day for England, crossing from this city to Point Levi, and thence taking the Kennebec road for Boston—visiting Philadelphia and Washington previous to his embarking for England. Sir John Colborne, upon the departure of Lord Gosford, assumed the Government as senior Military Officer for the time being, in command of the Forces within the Provinces of Upper and Lower Canada—issuing at the same time his Proclamation to that effect. He issued on the same day, another Proclamation, continuing Martial Law in the District of Montreal, as proclaimed by Lord Gosford, on the 5th December last. A General Order was issued at Montreal on the 22nd February, directing that the *habitans* of the Counties of Laprarie, Chambly and L'Acadie should be disarmed. It enjoined all persons residing in those Counties, within one month after date of the order, to carry and deliver all arms in their possession to the nearest Justice of the Peace, or Officer of the Militia, who was to be held responsible that they should be conveyed and surrendered to the Officer commanding the nearest Military post, either St. Johns, Chambly, L'Acadie, Napierville, St. Philippe, La Tortue, or Isle aux Noix, as the case might be.

The following communication from the Civil Secretary, by order of the Commander of the Forces, to the Clerks of the Peace at Montreal, for the public information, will explain the movements of the fugitive Insurgents who had left the Province after the affairs at St. Denis and St. Charles, and taken refuge in the neighbouring States, where they were preparing the means of annoying their loyal fellow-subjects in Canada, by marauding inroads from time to time along the frontiers.

GOVERNMENT HOUSE,
MONTREAL, *March* 5, 1838.

GENTLEMEN,—I am directed by His Excellency Sir John Colborne, to transmit to you, for the information of the District of Montreal, the accompanying statement of the different attacks made lately by bands of rebels and brigands on several points of the frontier of Upper and Lower Canada.

I have the honour, &c.,

WM. ROWAN, Civil Secretary.

The Clerks of the Peace, Montreal.

" Six or seven hundred of the Rebels who quitted the Province in December, and had for some weeks been cantoned at Champlain, Chazy, and Plattsburg, were observed on the 25th and 26th ultimo, to be actively employed in concentrating and equipping for a movement towards the frontier, having been supplied with arms by their partisans in the States of New York and Vermont, taken, it is said, from the Arsenal in Elizabethtown. They crossed from the Lake Champlain, accompanied by a numerous train of sleighs, with fifteen hundred stand of arms, ammunition, and three field-pieces, proceeded to Alburg, in Vermont, and entered the Province on the 28th, halting at Week's House, about a mile from the frontier line.

" The rebels were chiefly *habitans* from L'Acadie and Laprarie, commanded by Drs. Robert Nelson and Cote, of Napierville. As soon as it was known where they had crossed the frontier, the Missisquoi Volunteers assembled in their flank, but were directed by Colonel Ward, Inspecting Field Officer, to delay their attack till the arrival of the Queen's troops, under the command of Colonel Booth, from Henryville. The rebels and brigands re-passed the frontier, early on the first instant, and surrendered their arms, ammunition and equipage to General Wool, of the United States Army, who had pursued them from Plattsburg.

"Nelson and Cote were arrested and delivered over to the civil authorities of the United States. This incursion of the rebels appears to have been made in combination with similar attempts to disturb the tranquility of these Provinces, by the brigands from Watertown, Ogdensburg, Morristown, and Buffalo, in the State of New York, and from Detroit, in Michigan.

"On the 22st and 23nd ultimo, Gananoque and Kingston were menaced with attacks from the brigands assembled in French Creek; four hundred of them took possession of Hickory Island.

"On the 26th, two hundred and fifty brigands moved from the vicinity of Buffalo, with three field-pieces, across the ice, in the direction of Point Abino, and about thirteen miles from Fort Erie, on the Canadian Shore, and not far from the Western Locks of the Welland Canal. They were pursued by Col. Worth, of the United States Army, and dispersed.

"On the 26th ultimo, three or four hundred brigands from Detroit, passed from the State of Michigan to Fighting Island, (British territory,) with three field pieces, arms, ammunition, and provisions. Col. Maitland, commanding the Western Frontier, ordered them to be dislodged on the following day, by two companies of the 32nd and 83rd Regiments, and a detachment of Artillery, under Captain Glasgow, and two hundred and fifty of the East Kent Militia under Colonel Elliot. This force was commanded by Colonel Townsend. The brigands were soon driven off the island, leaving part of their arms and provisions, and retired to the American shore, where they opened a fire upon the troops.

"The different towns and villages on the frontier of Upper and Lower Canada, are thus constantly exposed to the piratical incnrsions ol the lawless population of the neighboring States.

"The Volunteers and Militia are prepared to receive the Marauders in every quarter, and have had frequent opportunities of shewing their zeal and vigilance, and attachment to the institutions of the country."

The following Declaration of Independence was issued by Doctor Robert Nelson, one of the fugitives, but does not bear date. It, however, first appeared in the Canada papers at the commencement of March 1838, and was probably issued by the *soi disant* President of the imaginary new Republic of the State of Lower Canada some time in the preceding month of February.

"DECLARATION.

"Whereas, the solemn covenant made with the people of Lower Canada, and recorded in the Statute Book of the United Kingdom of Great Britain and Ireland as the 31st Chapter of the Act passed in the 31st year of the reign of King George III., hath been continually violated by the British Government, and our rights usurped. And, whereas, our humble petitions, addresses, protests, and remonstrances against this injurious and unconstitutional interference have been made in vain. That the British Government hath disposed of our revenue without the constitutional consent of the Local Legislature—pillaged our Treasury—arrested great numbers of our citizens, and committed them to prison—distributed through the country a mercenary army, whose presence is accompanied by consternation and alarm—whose track is red with the blood of our people—who have laid our villages in ashes—profaned our temples—and spread terror and waste through the land. And, whereas, we can no longer suffer the repeated violations of our dearest rights, and patiently support the multiplied outrages and cruelties of the Government of Lower Canada. We, in the name of the people of Lower Canada, acknowledging the decrees of a Divine providence, which permit us to put down a Government which hath abused the object and intention for which it was created, and to make choice of that form of Government which shall re-establish the empire of justice—assure domestic tranquility—provide for common defence —promote general good, and secure to us and our posterity the advantages of civil and religious liberty.

"SOLEMNLY DECLARE:—

"1. That from this day forward, the People of Lower Canada are absolved from all allegiance to Great Britain, and that the political connexion between that power and Lower Canada is now dissolved,

"2. The Republican form of Government is best suited to Lower Canada, which is this day declared to be a Republic.

"3. That under the Free Government of Lower Canada, all persons shall enjoy the same right; the Indians shall no longer be under any disqualification, but shall enjoy the same right as all other citizens in Lower Canada.

"4. That all union between Church and State is hereby declared to be DISSOLVED, and every person shall be at liberty freely to exercise such religion or belief as shall be dictated to him by his conscience.

"5. That the Feudal or Seigniorial Tenure of Land is hereby abolished, as completely as if such Tenure had never existed in Canada.

"6. That each and every person who shall bear arms or furnish assistance to the people of Canada in this contest for emancipation, shall be and is discharged from all dues and obligations, real or supposed, for arrearages in virtue of Seigniorial rights heretofore existing.

" 7. That the *douaire coutumier* is for the future abolished and prohibited.

" 8. That imprisonment for debt shall no longer exist, except in such case of fraud as shall be specified in an Act to be past hereafter by the Legislature of Lower Canada for this purpose.

" 9. That sentence of death shall no longer be passed nor executed, except in cases of murder.

" 10. That all mortgages on landed estates shall be special, and to be valid, shall be enregistered in offices to be erected for this purpose, by an Act of the Legislature of Lower Canada.

" 11. That the liberty and freedom of the press shall exist in all public matters and affairs.

" 12. That TRIAL BY JURY is guaranteed to the people of Lower Canada in its most extended and liberal sense in all criminal suits and in civil suits, above a sum to be fixed by the Legislature of the State of Lower Canada.

" 13. That as general and public education is necessary and due by the Government of the people, an Act to provide for the same shall be passed as soon as the circumstances of the country will permit.

" 14. That to secure the elective franchise, all elections shall be had by BALLOT.

" 15. That with the least possible delay, the people shall choose delegates, according to the present division of the country into counties, towns and boroughs, who shall constitute a Convention or Legislative body, to establish a Constitution according to the wants of the country, and in conformity with the disposition of this declaration, subject to be modified according to the will of the people.

" 16. That every male person of the age of twenty-one years and upwards, shall have the right of voting, as herein provided, and for the election of the aforesaid delegates.

" 17. That all Crown Lands, also such as are called

Clergy Reserves, and such as are nominally in possession of a certain Company of Land-holders in England, called the 'British North American Land Company,' are of right the property of the State of Lower Canada, except such portions of the aforesaid lands as may be in possession of persons who hold the same in good faith, and to whom titles shall be secured and granted by virtue of a law, which shall be enacted to legalize the possession of, and afford a title for such untitled lots of land in the Townships as are under cultivation or improvement.

" 18. That the French and English languages shall be used in all public affairs: and for the fulfilment of this Declaration, and for the support of the Patriotic cause in which we are now engaged, with a firm reliance on the protection of the Almighty, and the justice of our conduct, WE, by these presents, solemnly pledge to each other our lives and ·fortunes, and our most sacred honor.

By order of the Provisional Government,

ROBERT NELSON, *President.*

" PROCLAMATION.—No. 2.

" PEOPLE OF CANADA,

" We have been oppressed by the hand of a Transatlantic power, and unjustly and cruelly castigated with the rod of unrelenting misrule for a long series of years— so long, that the measure of Tyranny has filled to overflowing. We unceasingly, but in vain, have attempted to bridle a bad Government, rescind bad laws, enact such as would cause our institutions to merge from the mire of ancient vassalage and rise to the level of those which characterize the recent Government of the nineteenth century. We are now compelled by the force of tyranny, and contrary to our sentiment, to appeal to the force of arms, in order that we may acquire and secure to us such rights as are due to a deserving and free people: nor shall we lay those arms down, until we shal have secured to our Country the blessings of a Patriotic and sympathizing Government.

" To all such persoas as shall aid us, in these our patriotic exertions, WE extend the hand of fraternity and of fellowship, and to such as shall persist in the blind, headlong, plundering, sanguinary and incendiary course that has to our sorrow and of the suffering of our aged people, our women and our children, so disgracefully stamped the heedless career of Sir John Colborne, the Commander of the British-Forces, and his adherents, we shall, in self-defence and in common justice to our people and our cause, inflict the retaliation which their own terrific example has set before us, but as their are now many persons who now repent of their conduct and of the Vandalism of their associates, a course which has driven us to war, and as our sense of humanity, of justice and of honor, is cast in a different mould from that of our oppressors, we cannot reconcile to our principles, or to the morals that elsewhere than in the English Government of Canada, distinguish the age we live in, to exercise their savage example towards them.

"We therefore solemnly promise to afford security and protection both in person and property, to all such as shall lay down their arms and otherwise cease to oppress us,—a promise which our character and the known moral and peaceable habits of our native people sufficiently guarantee. Nor shall we lay down our arms until we shall have effected and secured the object of our first Proclamation.

" By order of the Provisional Government of the State of Lower Canada.

ROBERT NELSON,
Commander in Chief of the Patriot Army.

News reached Canada early in March, of the suspension of the Constitution, and of the appointment of the Earl of Durham as Governor General and her Majesty's High Commissioner, " for the adjustment of certain important affairs affecting the Provinces of Lower and Upper Canada," which produced universal satisfaction among all classes in the Canadas.*

---

* The following, it appeared by the papers laid before Parliament, were part of the Instructions to Lord Durham :—
" In order to lay the ground for the permanent settlement of the questions which agitate Lower Canada, also of those which create divisions between Upper and Lower Canada, it will probably be found necessary to resort to some Legislative measures of a comprehensive nature. But before such measures can be framed and submitted to Parliament, it would be highly disirable to ascertain the wishes and opinions of the people of both Provinces regarding them.

" This object could be best attained by a personal communication on your part with such persons selected from each Province as may be presumed, from their station, character and influence, to represent the feelings of their fellow countrymen in general. It seems advisable, therefore, to authorize Your Lordship, if you should so think fit, to call around you a certain number of such persons with whom you might take council on the most important affairs of the two Provinces; the time of such a committee of advice being left entirely to your discretion. You are therefore empowered to select three Members from the Legislative Council of Upper Canada, to attend such meeting; and to invite the House of Assembly of Upper Canada to nominate ten of its Members for the same purpose. Under ordinary circumstances the same course would be pursued with respect to the Legislature of Lower Canada. But if the Bill now before Parliament should be passed into a law, recourse must be had, during the suspension of that Legislature, to another mode of supplying the deficiency.

" You will accordingly, during such suspension, select three Members of the body at present composing the Legislative Qouncil, and will take measures for calling on the electors in each of the five Districts into which Lower Canada is now divided, to elect two persons to sit in the Committee. Your Lordship can obviate any difficulty which may stand in the way of holding such elections, by an Ordinance for this purpose, to be passed by the authority of the Governor in Council.

It appeared also by papers recently laid before Parliament, relating to Canadian affairs, that Sir John Colborne had received the most gratifying assurances of the approval of his past conduct by the Home Government, and of its reliance on his wisdom. Lord Glenelg, by his Despatch of the 27th November, 1837, informs him that "Lord Gosford

"The Committee will thus consist of twenty-six Members, over whose deliberations you will of course preside.

"The Committee being thus formed, you will bring before them the subjects on which you desire to receive their opinion and advice. Among the most important of these are the questions in debate between the two Canadian Provinces.

"In the last session both Houses of Parliament passed a resolution, ' That great inconvenience has been sustained by His Majesty's subjects inhabiting the Provinces of Lower Canada and Upper Canada, from the want of some adequate means for regulating and adjusting questions respecting the trade and commerce of the said Province, and divers other questions wherein the said Provinces have a common interest; and it is expedient that the Legislatures of the said Provinces respectively be authorized to make provision for the joint regulation and adjustment of such their common interests.'

"It is clear that some plan must be devised to meet the just demands of Upper Canada. It will be for Your Lordship, in conjunction with the Committee, to consider if this should not be done by constituting some joint Legislative authority, which should preside over all questions of common interest to the two Provinces, and which might be appealed to in extraordinary cases to arbitrate between contending parties in either; preserving, however, to each Province its distinct Legislature, with authority in all matters of an exclusively domestic concern. If this should be your opinion, you will have further time to consider what should be the nature and limits of such authority, and all the particulars which ought to be comprehended in any scheme for its establishment.

"The Constitutional Act of 1791 will supply another subject of deliberation, with a view to determine what measures may safely be taken to correct the defects which have hitherto interfered, at least in the Lower Province, with its successful working. The constitution of the Legislative Council has formed the chief topic of complaint with the

retires without the slightest diminution, on either side, of the confidence which has invariably subsisted between himself and the Ministers of the Crown;" and that the circumstances which led to his Lordship's retirement, "greatly enhanced his previous claims on their respect and gratitude." The Minister expressed his consciousness that the duties which

---

House of Assembly of Lower Canada, and they have insisted that the only remedy is to be found in making the Council elective. On this subject the following resolution was last year passed by both Houses of Parliament :—'That in the existing state of Lower Canada it is unadvisable to make the Legislative Council of that Province an elective body, but it is expedient that measures be adopted for securing to that branch of the Legislature a greater degree of public confidence."

HOUSE OF LORDS.

THE EARL OF DURHAM.—" My Lords, I think it necessary to address a few words to Your Lordships in explanation of the principles which will hereafter influence my conduct, and which in point of fact have induced me to accept the office which I now hold. My Lords, it is impossible for language to express the reluctance with which I have consented to undertake this duty, and nothing but the most ardent attachment and most determined devotion to Her most Gracious Majesty's house and interests, and to the service of my country, could have induced me to place myself and my character in a situation where I fear that I cannot answer the expectations of my noble friends who have requested me to undertake this office, or even my own—(hear, hear) The noble and illustrious Duke, who has spoken with so much candour to night, has stated that he regrets to hear that the object of these measures which your Lordships are now called on to consider, is merely the support of a particular part in Canada. I can assure your Lordships that it is with no such view, that I have undertaken my present duty—(hear, hear.) My duty, as I conceive it, is to assert in the first instance, the supremacy of Her Majesty's Government, and to vindicate in the next, the honor and dignity of the law, taking care that it is not set at naught in the remotest cabin, in the remotest settlement of Canada—[hear, hear]—and I shall feel that I have not performed that duty whilst the dignity and supremacy of the Crown and the Law

devolved upon Sir John Colborne would be of grave responsibility, but that he would not shrink from encountering them with calmness and courage. " He was," he observed, " happy to learn, through Lord Hill, that his (Sir John Colborne's military opertions had been conducted with foresight and decision." That without proposing to fetter His Excellency in the Administration of the Government, further instructions would be sent out. "In the mean time," concludes Lord Glenelg, "I will only assure you that your measures will receive the most favorable construction, and that you will be seconded by the most full and cordial support which it is in the power of Her Majesty's Government to afford you.

The Act suspending the Constitution, and "to make temporary provision for the Government of Lower Conada," sanctioned by Her Majesty on the 10th Eebuary, 1838, was proclaimed in the *Quebec*

---

continue to be assailed. [Hear, hear.] Having settled these primary and preliminary objects, I wish, casting aside all considerations of a French, a British, or Canadian party, but will look on them alike as Her Majesty's subjects---[hear, hear.] I wish I repeat, to extend to them all equal justice and equal protection, [hear, hear.] I will protect on the one hand the local rights and privileges of those who may be considered as the proprietors of the soil, and on the other those commercial rights and privileges which are considered more peculiarly to affect the British settlers. The noble and learned Lord at the close of the speech, which he delivered from the bench below me said that I have undertaken but a thankless task in carrying out with me to Canada the suspension of its Constitution. My Lords, on this as on many other points, I cannot agree with that noble and learned personage (Brougham). These acts ought not to be considered in the light in which the noble and learned Lord has been pleased to view them. The Constitution of Canada is suspended, not by any Act of the British Parliament, but by the rebellious acts af individuals in that Province. (Hear, hear.) I do not consider—If I did I would not undertake the task—I do not consider that I go to Canada to suspend its Constitution ; I go there to provide a remedy for an ex-

Gazette by authority, on the 29th of March following. The same Gazette of the 5th of April, contained also Sir John Colborne's Proclamation, summoning the new legislative body—THE SPECIAL COUNCIL, named by His Excellency pursuant to this Act—to meet in session, at Montreal, on the 18th of the month. They accordingly assembled at the appointed time, and proceeded to the despatch of business. The body was constituted of gentlemen of the first respectability, selected from different quarters of the Province,* and of both origins, in equal numbers. The first Ordinances passed, were two, on the 23rd of

---

traordinary state of things, produced by rebels, who have rendered the working of that Constitution impracticable [Hear.] And to execute this honorable, and difficult and dangerous mission—difficult and dangerous I mean as affects my reputation—I implore of your Lordships to give me such powers as will enable me to make such a final settlement of these unfortunate differences as will produce final contentment and satisfaction among all parties, and as will not merely assist the dignity of the Crown and the supremacy of the law, but will also promote the general happiness and prosperity of one of the most important Colonial possessions of Great Britain. If I could accomplish this great object, my Lords, I should consider no personal sacrifice, not even that of my life, too much [hear,] and I can hope to accomplish it by the cordial support of my noble friends below me Her Majesty's Ministers, which I feel sure that 1 shall meet by the active co-operation of Parliament which I expect to obtain, and by that generous forbearance on the part of the noble Lords opposite, to whom I have been opposed politically all my life, which I am induced to believe they will display towards me from the candor which the noble and illustrious Duke has exhibited on this occasion, as on all other occasions where the public interests have been concerned. [The noble Earl then sat down amidst loud cheering from both sides of the House.]

* Constituted as follows :—

District of Quebec.

The Hon. C. E. C. De Lery, of Quebec.
" James Stuart, do.
John Neilson, Esq. do.
William Walker, do. do.

April: one declaring that the Ordinances or Enactments of the Special Council were to take effect from the date of their being passed; the other, suspend-

Amable Dionne, do. Kamouraska.
Charles Casgrain, do. Riviere Ouelle.
The Hon. M. P. De Sales LaTerriere, Ebculemens.

District of Montreal.

The Hon. T. Pothier, of Montreal.
" P. McGill, do.
" P. De Rocheblave, do. .
Samuel Gerrard, Esq. do.
Jules Quesnel do do
Wm. P. Christie, do. do.
Turton Penn, do. do.
John Molson, do. do.
The Hon. J. Cuthbert, of Berthier.
" B. Joliette, of St. Paul, Lavaltrie.
Joseph E. Faribault, Esq., of L'Assomption.
Paul H. Knowlton, Esq., of Brome.
Ichabod Smith do. Stanstead.

District of Three Rivers.

Joseph Dionne, Esq., of St. Pierre les Becquets.
Etienne Mayrand, of Riviere du Loup.

MONTREAL, (*Gazette*,) April, 19.

The Special Council met yesterday, at two o'clock, when sixteen Members appeared and were sworn in. The absentees are marked with an asterisk in the following list. His Excellency the Administrator, after nominating the Hon. J. Cuthbert to preside at the Council Board, and laying before it the drafts of several Bills, retired, and the Council continued in session till five, when it adjourned till one to-day.

James Cuthbert; Toussaint Pothier; * Charles E. C. De Lery; James Stuart; Peter M'Gill; * Mare P. De Sales La Terriere; Barthelemi Joliette; Pierre De Rocheblave; J. Neilson; *Amable Dionne; Samuel Gerrard; Jules Quesnel; William P. Christie; *Charles E. Casgrain; William Walker; Joseph E. Faribault; John Molson; Etienne Mayrand; Paul Holland Knowlton; Turton Penn; *Joseph Dionne; *Ichabod Smith.

The following letter was addressed to each of those gentlemen previous to their appointment:—

ing the *Habeas Corpus Act* until the 24th of August next, so as to give time (it was said), to Lord Durham to adopt such measures in relation to those concerned in the late Rebellion, as he should think fit, conformably to his instructions.

Matters assuming by this time a more peaceful aspect, Sir John Colborne thought it advisable to dispense with the further services of the Volunteer Militia, which had been embodied for the recent emergency—His Excellency accordingly issued the following General Order:

GOVERNMENT HOUSE,
MONTREAL, 31st *March*, 1838.

"SIR,--I am directed to acquaint you that, in exercise of the powers vested in the Queen by the 2nd section of the Act of Parliament, intituled, "An Act to make temporary provision for the Government of Lower Canada," Her Majesty has been pleased to empower the Administrator of the Government to constitute a Provisional Special Council for the affairs in Lower Canada, and that it is His Excellency's intention to assemble the Councillors that may be selected at this important crisis, about the 14th of April, with a view of passing such Laws as the circumstances of the Province may render necessary before the arrival of the Governor General. His Excellency requests, therefore, to be informed whether you will consent to be appointed to the Provisional Special Council which it has devolved on him to form in the first instance, in pursuance of Her Majesty's instructions; and to attend at the opening of the Session.

"I am, however, to state that the Earl of Durham will enter on the discharge of the duties with which he is entrusted, wholly unfettered as to the choice of Councillors, and that your appointment to the Special Council will be entirely provisional, and that the Royal Instructions which have been forwarded to His Excellency on this occasion will, be revoked and superseded by the Commission and the Instructions of which Lord Durham will be the bearer."

"I have the honor to be,
Sir,
&c., &c., &c.
(Signed) W. ROWAN.
Civil Secretary.

HEAD QUARTERS,
MONTREAL, 12th April, 1838.

"Several applications having been made by different paid corps of Loyal Volunteers for permission to return to their former occupations, and the term of engagement of the said Corps being about to expire:—The Commander of the Forces directs that the following Corps be disembodied, and paid up to the 30th instant inclusive, and then their pay is to be discontinued.

"His Excellency cannot allow this opportunity to pass without sincerely thanking the Officers, Non-Commissioned Officers, and Privates, of these Corps, for their zealous and valuable services during the time that they have been embodied:—

Rawdon Loyal Volunteers.
New Glasgow do.
St. Andrews do. (two Companies.)
Two Mountains do. Cavalry.
Henryville do. (two Companies.)
Clarenceville Rangers.
St. John's Loyal Volunteers.
Royal Quebec do. (eight Companies.)
Royal Quebec Artillery.
Eastern Townships Loyal Volunteers, six Companies, excepting 1 Captain, 1 Subaltern, 2 Serjeants, 2 Corporals, and 50 Privates, under Captain Kilburne, until further orders.
Cornwall Loyal Volunteers.
Queen's Own Rifles.

    (Signed,)   W. DICKSON.

A Regiment of the loyal men of Gengarry, in Upper Canada, who had come down during the late insurrection, and had been quartered at St. Phillipps, in the County of Laprarie, had, a few days previous to the date of the General Order, passed through Montreal on their way home—their services being deemed no longer necessary.* Another Regiment (the Lancaster,) from the same County, which had been quartered at Napierville, passed in like manner, on the 1st of May, through Montreal, on their way home.† A Proclamation dated 27th April, appeared in the Quebec Gazette by Authority, of the 3rd May, declaring Martial Law, as proclaimed on the 5th December last, in the District of Montreal, to have ceased with the publication of the present- The Province was consequently now considered in a state of tranquility. But although the Insurrections had been put down, and an apparent calm

---

* There were in Quebec two Companies (unpaid) of the Queen's Own Light Infantry, commanded by Major Temple, late Captain 15th Regiment; 300 Volunteer Artillery, paid, commanded by Major W. B. Lindsay; Queen's Volunteers, paid, under Captain Hale; 4 Companies Light Infantry Rifles, unpaid, under Major John Sewell, late Captain 49th Regiment.

Their passage is thus noticed in a Montreal paper:—

"MONTREAL, [*Herald*], *March* 20.

"One Regiment of Glengarry Highlanders, under the command of Lieut. Colonel Fraser, arrived in town yesterday from St. Phillipps, and created quite a sensation as they marched through our streets to the martial music of the spirit-stirring bag-pipe. They mustered about five hundred strong, and were generally considered as fine and effective a body of Volunteers as could be produced in the Province, such men as would " do or die" for their Queen and Country. They are *en route* for their homes, after having displayed their willingness to defend with their lives the glorious Institutions of their fatherland, from the encroachments of internal traitors or foreign enemies."

" This day [1st May], the Lancaster Regiment of Glengarry Highlanders, under the command of their Colonel, Mr. Sheriff Macdonell, marched into town, en route to Upper Canada, from Napierville, where they were quartered since their arrival in this Province, during the winter.— They are a fine body of men, and presented a very military appearance."

existed, it was, nevertheless, very evident—from the general uneasiness throughout the following summer, among the *habitans*, particularly in the southern parts of the District of Montreal, and the sympathising spirit prevailing among the American population along the Frontier, in their neighbourhood, where the fugitive Insurgents had sought refuge, and were making preparations for an incursion—that another outbreak might be expected. Ths Gaol at Montreal was crowded with prisoners, some only suspected; others known to have been actively concerned in the Insurrections, and taken in the fact, with arms in their hands; and although many of minor note, had, in the course of the winter been discharged, it still remained full to excess. Several, there is cause to believe, suffered, on mere suspicion, imprisonment most unjustly—one of the many great evils usually incidental to civil commotions in all countries. But no trial, either by Civil Courts or by Courts Martial, took place in Lower Canada, in consequence of the disturbances. The forbearance to make examples on the occasion was, it has been said, in consequence of instructions to that effect from the Home Government,* although the Insurgents and their

---

* "In the House of Commons on the 17th January, after the motion of Lord John Russell, for leave to bring in a Bill to make temporary provision for the Government of Lower Canada, had been carried:—Mr. Hawes put a question, 'whether any steps had been taken to prevent the infliction of sanguinary punishments in Lower Canada, previous to the arrival of Lord Durham?'—To this Lord John Russell replied, that though there was no reason to suppose that Sir John Colborne would do anything beyond what might become his painful duty, yet the Government had not neglected to let that officer know its opinion of the inexpediency of inflicting capital punishments on occasions of this nature. He had not the least doubt the feeling of Sir John Colborne was the same as that which had been expressed by the Government, and without enforcing upon him, because from a knowledge of the character of that officer they did not consider it necessary to do so, any positive instructions-they

political associates attributed it to the weakness of the Provincial Government, and its inability, from the general insurrectionary spirit prevalent among the population of French origin—to carry the law against Treason and Rebellion into effect, and it certainly bore that appearance.

The document following after being forwarded to a political and revolutionary Club, recently formed in England, styled "The Working Men's Association of London," some time in 1837, previons to the Insurrections, appeared, but without date, in the Canada papers in January, 1838. It is only interesting as expressing the views of those whose names are attached to it.

"THE PERMANENT AND CENTRAL COMMITTEE OF THE COUNTY OF MONTREAL, TO THE WORKING-MEN'S ASSOCIATION OF LONDON.

"BROTHERS, We have received the Address of the

---

had no doubt that he would fully concur in the suggestions that had been submitted to him.

"Mr. Hawes said nothing was farther from his intention than to imply a charge against Sir John Colborne, and the answer was perfectly satisfactory.

"Sir R. Inglis, Mr. C. Buller, and Mr. Bothwick offered each some observations.—Lord John Russell, in reply to a remark of Sir. R. Inglis, said the Government had not interposed and would not interpose, with respect to the cases of any individuals upon whom judgment might be passed in Canada; all they had done was to give an opinion on the expediency of clemency.

"Sir R. Peel said, if any thing could tend to dim or diminish the high prerogative of mercy, it was the House of Commons, discussing the subject, in the absence of all knowledge of the crimes that might have been committed, and to say that in no case should blood be shed—(hear, hear.) Did the honorable member for Liskeard (Mr. Buller) seriously mean to contend that murder was not to be punished with death? Were the murderers of Lieut. Weir to be pardoned? The honorable member had made no exception.— (Cheers.)

London Workingmen's Association to the people of Canada. It had been read amidst enthusiastic cheers, at a meeting of our Permanent and Central Committee, and published in our newspapers: It has gone abroad over the American Continent, as evidence of that bold democratic spirit which shook off the grasp of sordid Barons, and fixed limits to the prerogatives of arbitrary Sovereigns, still animates a portion of your citizens.

"The glory of your nation has ever been the existence of its recognized democracy, which enabled you throughout long and bitter struggles, to maintain a degree of liberty and political power superior to that possessed by your European neighbors. We axcept, therefore, with grateful thanks, the sympathy of a democracy endowed with such exalted and correct sentiments on the nature of Government.

"Aristocracy is a stranger to us. With it we hold not, have not, any principles in common. Thanks to the facility with which our ancestors have been able to obtain fertile land in a territory of unlimited extent and to our laws which prevent the accumulation of hereditary wealth, nearly our whole population is dependent for a subsistence on manual or mental labour. We respect men for their good works; we despise them for their misdeeds, whatever may have been the deserts of their fathers. We honor him who causes two blades of corn to sprout where only one grew before: who goes forth and makes the forest disappear before his footsteps; we despise the idler who vegetates on the earth a mere consumer of what better men produce. The distinctive names of your various mechanical occupations appear to our eyes more honorable than the pompous titles, oppressive privileges, and unnatural hereditary legislation, which have been usurped and granted by Sovereigns, and registered in herald's offices, in the vain attempt to create two orders of intelligence where nature has made but one.

" We live in a hemisphere chosen for the unentrammelled action and free growth of democracy, unstinted by any proximity to an exhausting, deep-rooted aristocracy. The few exotics of that tribe transplanted from another world, wither and disappear from a soil which affords no nourishment to their order, and upon which Equal Rights were stamped in everlasting characters when it first emerged from chaos,

"The aboriginal masters of the American wilderness knew neither Lords nor King, but freely chose the best deserving as head in Council and Chief in war. When the pilgrims from England, imbued with a dignified taste for freedom, first landed on the bleak shores of New England, they brought good seed to a land already prepared for its reception, and from which it was to spread and fructify; and though Europe endeavoured to quarter her nations in various parts of this sanctuary, the corruptions which followed them dissapeared before the flood of light proceeding from principles recognized, proclaimed and acted upon, by a body of virtuous and enlightened democrats, who braved and overcame the difficulties of their new settlement, not through any motives of wealth or thirst of plunder, but to establish on sounder principles the science and economy of government.

" Long connected with you as fellow subjects, with you we have shared the withering influence of an aristocracy which, pampered in the Eastern hemisphere, has, in our unfortunate case, been permitted to annoy the West. However confident we feel that such an unnatural and baneful principle cannot long keep enthralled this Democratic Continent, yet we fear with you that the hereditary reverence for particular families, the dangerous accumulation of enormous masses of wealth in the hands of a few, and the corrupting practices of a Government depraved in the distribution of the patronage, have so marred the benefits which should arise to you from the glorious charter of your rights, that years must elapse before you can resume and completely enjoy the liberty which you should enherit from your forefathers. The accession of a young Queen afforded a favourable opportunity of reaewing the conditions of the social compact and of your contract of allegiance. Co-heirs with her to the institutions of your country, that country you have often defended with your blood. With the persevering industry of your constant daily toil have you raised it to a pinnacle of redundant wealth, and now in the midst of that dazzling splendor, which has bean created by your indomitable energies, you are robbed by unequal and unjust laws; borne down by grinding taxation which deprives you of the necessaries, in order to minister to the profusions of an overbearing caste occupied in entangling you in its meshes, honestly and devotedly working to create and maintain its enormous wealth, which is at once its portion and the instrument of your political subjection. Whilst in some instances you were successfully acting in the dignity of conscious might, with sorrow have we too often seen some of your worthiest friends neglected at your recent elections, and a portion of the democracy indifferent spectators, willing auxiliaries, or the servile mercenairies of one or the other aristocratic factions, which are contending for the privilege of loading you with their oppressive yoke, totally indifferent to your interests. except, in so far as the reformation of an abuse tends to the security of their own power.

"In the free exercise of our acknowledged principles—in defence of rights guaranteed and dear to us, we have met publicly in our various Counties as a preliminary proceeding, to protest solemnly against the infamous invasion of powers inherently appertaining to us. Conscious of our strength and right, we treated with contempt a silly proclamation of an ignorant Government against these meetings. We hope this lesson will not be lost. We must trust that it will prevent for the future a presumptuous interference with the people's immunities both here and elsewhere. We are gratified that our conduct in promptly repelling the attack of the British Parliament upon our property hrs merited your approbation. Have you reflected on the mighty responsibility to the whole British Empire which has devolved upon the people of this Province?—The British Ministry could never have introduced a monstrous measure which aims at the destruction of the powers of a democracy, acting through their own branch of the Legislature, entirely for the purpose of hastening the payment of a few paltry official salaries, when that object could have been attained by a simple and honest process, were it not that your aristocracy are preparing an unholy scheme for the destruction of your own liberties. Lower Canada is made the theatre of the experiment, because it is imagined that the majority of the population, being of French extraction, though borne down by continued abuse or arbitrary exactions, would excite no sympathy among the English race by which they are surrounded.

" The conviction of the mighty responsibility resting upon us, far from discouraging, invigorates us, conscious that all energetic and free minds throughout the Empire must watch with intense interest our courageous struggle—that their wishes are for us, and that they pray that we may successfully defend the rights of all. For ourselves, rest assured, we are determined never to submit to the intended ministerial usurpation—never to live with the world's finger of derision pointed to us as a people who, more ignorant than slaves that are bought and sold, permitted their birth-right to be wrested from them, thereby establishing a precedent for a similar aggression on the liberties of their brother, Colonists and follow them throughout the Empire..

" Think not that because few in number, we dread

the result of this our determination. Nature has given strong fastnesses to our country; to our people strong hearts. Our arms are now the arguments of justice and reason. They can be easily changed for more decided weapons, if the eyes of the invaders of our rights continue too dull to see, and their ears too obtuse to hear. We deem not that armed bands from Europe would now wage exterminating war upon the democracy of America. They are themselves the offspring of a democracy which, in the nineteenth century, is alike in feeling throughout the civilized world They know they are not blind instruments to do the bidding of a brutal master, but moral agents responsible for their deeds to God and humanity. When the day of trial arrives, they will rather throw away the ensigns of their cruel occupations to be received into the kindred bosem of an American fraternity, than aid in murderous designs against the heart's blood of a generous people acting for the defence of the common Rights of Man.

"We do not assume a tone of defiance to your Government unless forced to it. Our grievances are not of new characters or of recent date. They have been publicly and distinctly stated, and the mode and measures of redress have been plainly defined. Our citizens have at public meetings reiterated them for past years. They have founded upon them humble petitions to your Parliament, which turning a deaf ear, now adds aggression to contempt. Under such circumstances we may safely appeal to the judgmeat of the whole world for our justification in determining to be deluded no longer with vain hopes of redress from beyond the seas, but to depend alone upon our own energies, and that sympathy from our brethren upon this Continent, which a cause so just must inevitably command.

"We have not alluded to a separate independence from the British Crown, but we are not forgetful that the destiny of Continental Colonies severs them from the Metropolitan State whenever the unconstitutional action of a legislative power residing in a distant country is no longer supportable. There is nothing in this prospect to seperate the identity of interest which should exist between the democracy of the old world and that of the new. If Colonies are to be made an instrument of corrupt patronage for providing refuge and maintenance for the poorer portion of your aristocracy; an excuse for maintaining standard armies: for robbing the people of their subsistence to pile up stone and mortar into fortifications, or a pretence for restricting the free operations of your trade, the casting of such as can support themselves can only give stability to to your own liberties and advance your national prosperity. You have the example of the United States, which in one year, as an independent offspring, does more for the honor and benefit of the Parent State than she could have accomplished in ages of weak, puling dependent existence.

" We again thank you for the sympathy which you express for the people of Canada. It is pleasant to receive such sympathy from Englishmen. You have done a noble act, for since a people is responsible for the deeds of its rulers, yours is a manly and virtuous determination, to inform mankind that you hold yourselves guiltless of the enormity attempted to be committed by those over whose actions you, unfortunately for yourselves and for us, have no control. Whatever may be the result of this your noble patriotism and generous self-devotion, we are assured that you will leave your children better fortified against your domineering Oligarchs than you were yourselves at your entrance into life.

" We desire, through your Association, to proclaim, that whatever course we shall be compelled to adopt we have no contest with the people of England. We

D

war only against the aggressions of their and our tyrannical oppressors.

"Signed by order, and on behalf, of the Permanent and Central Committee.

R. PLESSIS, President, · ROBERT NELSON,
L. J. PAPINEAU, J. BOULANGET,
C. H. COTE, LOUIS PERRAULT,
JOSEPH LE TOURNEUX, W. GALT,
PIERRE CADIEX, E. R. FABRE,
CHAMILLY DE LORIMIER, T. S. BROWN,
ANDRE OUIMET, E. N. DUCHESNOIS,
J. PHELAN, JOSHUA BELL,
C. OVIDE PERRAULT, C. DE LORIMIER, } See.
E. B. O'CALLAGHAN, G. E. CARTIER,

We shall now retrace our steps to observe the proceedings of the Constitutional Associations of Montreal and Quebec, on the recent occurences. The Constitutional Association of the City of Montreal met on the 30th December, 1837, when the following Report by the Executive Committee, was made and concurred in by the body.

CONSTITUTIONAL ASSOCIATION OF THE CITY OF MONTREAL.

"The Constitutional Association of this city met on Saturday last, at the St. Ann's Market House, for the purpose of receiving the Annual Report of the Executive Committee, and for the election of a General Committee for the ensuing year.

The Honorable Mr. M'Gill, as Chairman of the Association, stated in few words the object of the meeting,—that the circumstances of the times had prevented an earlier general meeting of the Association —that the period had arrived when some determinate course of action should be adopted for securing the rights of the British inhabitants of Lower Canada —that this Province should be made a British Province in fact as well as in name—and that the chief means of effecting that object were to be found in a re-union of the Canadas. The Honorable Chairman elequently urged the necessity and the advantage of that important measure—that no confidence could be placed in the loyal professions of the French Canadians, who had only come forward after the victory had been won —and, in conclusion, that petitions had been transmitted to the Legislatures of the sister Colonies, appealing to their assistance in our favour, and especially to Upper Canada, for their adoption of the Provincial re-union, which would prevent a suspension of the Constitution in this Province and secure the prosperity of both Canadas.

" The Report was then read by the secretary, and unanimously adopted upon a motion of John Torrance, Esq., seconded by Benjamin Hart, Esq.

" The General Committee was afterwards moved by John Molson, Esq., seconded by John Redpath Esq.

" The thanks of the Meeting to the Honorable Chairman were moved by James Fraser, Esq., seconded by Stanley Bagg, Esq,, and carried by acclamation.

"*Report of the Executive Committee of the Constitutional Association of this City.*

" Your Committee have taken advantage of the earliest opportunity, after a return of tranquility in this District, to assemble together the Members of the Constitutional Association of this city, for the purpose of submitting to you, in conformity with the rules of the Association, a Report of the proceedings of your Committee for the past year.

" Though the commencement of the year was not marked by any appearance of that sedition and rebellion, wfth which it has been so unjustifiably terminated, indications of disorder and disturbance were sufficiently manifest to give to your Committee strong grounds for apprehension, to impel them carefully to watch over the just rights of the British Provincial inhabitants, and to use their best endeavors to promote such measures as would secure the maintenance of British Interests, British rights, and British supremacy in Lower Canada.

"Since the last Annual General Meeting of this Association, the Reports of the Royal Commissioners specially appointed for the investigation of grievances, affecting Her Majestey's subjects in Lower Canada, in what relates to the administration of the Government thereof have been published: and whilst your Committee, in. common with the generality of the British inhabitants of this Province, deplore the loss of time and waste of money lavished upon those unprofitable labors, they have likewise to express their deep regret, not only at the confused and partial views taken by the Commissioners of the real cause of discontent in the Province, ' of the extent to which it has reasonable foundation,' and of the inadequate and inefficient remedies proposed by them for its removal, but also at their disregard of the substantial grounds of repugnance existing among the different races of the Provincial inhabitants, their neglect of the acknowledged grievances of those inhabitants of British origin, and the captious avoidance of their claims for a just participation in the enjoyment of rights deservedly dear to Englishmen, and their utter indifference to the important measure of the legislative union of the Canadas.

"An attentive consideration of these circumstances, and a firm conviction of the extreme importance of that Provincial union, stimulated your Committee to employ every means at their disposal to bring that measure prominently into notice, to urge its immediate as well as prospective advantages, and to direct public attention in both Provinces, to its ultimate and paramount necessity. With this view your Committee prepared and extensively circulated "a Representation upon the Legislative Union of the Provinces,' containing some of the principal reasons in its support, tables of the population and of its increase in both Provinces, particularly the separate increase of the British and French races in Lower Canada, and various statistical details, together with a map exhibiting a new division of Counties in this Province, by which a more equal share in the provincial representation would be given to the British inhabitants; and advantage was taken of the last session of the Imperial Parliament, to transmit copies to the leading Members of both branches of the Legislature, as well as to influential persons resident in Great Britain, who are connected with the Canadas, or interested in their prosperity.

"Your Committee likewise prepared an Address to Her Most Gracious Majesty the Queen, conveying to Her Majesty the most hearty congratulations of Her Majesty's loyal British subjects in this Province, upon her succession to the Throne of her ancestors, and the sincere expression of their condolence upon the death of their late lamented and beloved Sovereign, King William the Fourth, at the same time most respectfully submitting their grievances to Her Majesty's personal consideration, and suggesting the remedies required for their effectual redress; but late events have so materially altered the aspect of Provincial affairs as to induce your Committee to withdraw it altogether.

" The great and increasing necessity of the Legislative Union of the Canadas, impels your Committee to submit to you the propriety of pressing that great object to the desired conclusion, as the experience of nearly 50 years of separation between them, and the late seditious and rebellious movements in the most populous and prosperous portions of this Province plainly shew, that the advantages anticipated from the division of the Province of Quebec into two separate Legislatures have been entirely unfounded, that 'the probability of reconciling by this means, the jarring interests and opposite views of the provincial inhabitants' has been altogether falsified, and that the chief results of that most unwise and impolitic measure are apparent in the growth of a population in ower Canada, who with a few exceptions, have retained and cherished the distinctive characteristics of a separate people, without sympathies, attachments or interests, in common with their British fellow subjects, who have manifested a ready disposition to oppose British institutions and British connections, and who have now extended that opposition to open and unjustifiable rebellion. And your Committee declare their settled conviction, that without a re union of the Provinces, these evils must every year be increasing, as the population of British origin increases, and that true wisdom will be shewn in meeting those evils with boldness, and at once effecting their entire removal. '

"Your Committee have likewise the satisfaction of reporting to you, that they have taken advantage of every favourable opportunity of urging upon their Provincial fellow subjects of British origin, respect for the laws, and obedience to the constituted authorities, while at the same time they have been zealous in their endeavours to animate their loyalty to their Sovereign, and to rouse their determination to resist every attempt at Provincial disturbance. Your Committtee having foreseen that the efforts of the missionaries of Insurrection who paraded through the Province during the past year, and who attended at public meetings of French Canadians, held in various parts of the Province, at which the most unfounded and inflammatory speeches were delivered, would end in rebellion, having for its object the final severance of the Province from the British Empire, and a total destruction of British rights, interests and property, directed the attention of the loyal British population of this city to a system of local organization in their several wards, with the intention of thereby recommending the adoption of a similar system to the British Inhabitants throughout the Province, for the support of Government, the maintenance of order and public peace, and the protection of persons and property. And your Committee most sincerely congratulate their fellow subjects upon the unanimity, spirit, and effect with which that organization has been conducted and completed.

"The mendacious boldness with which the Provincial discontents have been characterized within and without the limits of this Province, by the partisans and supporters of the late unjustifiable disorders and the extraordinary degree of ignorance existing among a number of our fellow subjects in the adjoining Colonies, as well as among the citizens of the neighboring Government, of the true cause of those disorders, induced your Committee to prepare special Addresses to the Legislatures, and a general Address to the inhabitants of the sister Colonies, exposing the real views and designs of the Provincial malcontents, and appealing to their fellow Colonists for their sympathy and assistance in preserving to the inhabitants of Lower Canada, of British origin, the integrity of their birthright as British subjects, and the maintenance of the Provincial connection with the Parent state.

"Your Committee having thus reported to you their proceedings for the past year, are desirous, previous to returning into your hands the trust which your confidence had reposed in them, of most earnestly entreating their loyal British fellow subjects throughout the Province dispassionately to consider, at this period of returning tranquility, the real causes of the late insurrectionary and seditious manifestations, to abandon all minor and secondary points of difference among themselves and zealously to continue their loyal and spirited exertions in support of the Government and the suppression of disorder. But your Committee are also impelled by a sense of imperative duty to direct the most serious attention of the British Provincial inhabitants, to those measures in which they are most especially interested, and to the immediate adoption of the necessary means for carrying them into full and entire effect.

"While the full exercise of their religious worship, the complete enjoyment of their French civil law, the undisturbed use of their native language, and perfect immunity from taxation, the entire control over the Provincial legislation and the redress of every pretended or theoretical grievance, conjoined to render the French inhabitants of Lower Canada the most favoured portion of Her Majesty's subjects, the real and substantial wrongs of the British inhabitants of this Province remain neglected and unredressed: they have been compelled to submit to a system of French jurisprudence, foreign to their habits and injurious to their interests, to the French feudal law, which, to the disgrace of Lower Canada, finds a home in this Province alone; to a denial of those legislative improvements which would have introduced British capital and enterprise, and an increased British population into the Province; and to the privation of their dearest rights as British subjects, by their virtual exclusion from a just participation in the Provincial representation. On the one hand, the possession of every political and civil advantage, and conciliation and concession, to the utmost verge consistent with the dependence of the Colony upon the Mother Country, have been met by disaffection, insurrection and rebellion, attended by atrocious murder, robbery and rapine; while on the other, the privation of their most sacred rights, as British freemen, and neglect and contempt of their grievance, have been followed by obedience to the laws, support to the Government, and loyalty to their Sovereign.

" Impatience under oppression was not, therefore, the movtive of the late disorders; the motive is to be found in the distinctiveness of national origin alone; a continuance of the same evil must of necessity be followed by the same prejudices, while a perseverance in the policy which has so long fostered that national distinctiveness, will inevitably end in the utter ruin and extermination of the British Provincial inhabitants, and a desolation beyond the power of arms or wisdom to prevent or cure: to suppose the contrary is to trust in extravagant contingency, to be fooled with our eyes open, and being fooled, to be undone.

" It is with no intention of keeping alive feelings of animosity or ill will, that your Committee express these sentiments; on the contrary, they rejoice to see the French Canadians returning to a proper sense of their duty; but it is from a most serious apprehension that their numerous professions of devoted loyalty, and the tone and spirit of the answer to those professions, will 'justify the British Government in continuing the paternal policy which has hitherto secured their institutions, their language, and their laws;' in a word, in continuing those very causes of national prejudices and distinctiveness which have produced the late disastrous occurrences, and from a well-founded dread that no change of that policy, commensurate with the just expectations or rights of the British inhabitants in the Province, will be made or can be anticipated, under existing circumstaoces.

" The British Provincial inhabitants must, therefore, not only remember that their applications for relief have been neglected and their grievances have remained unredressed, but they must likewise not allow the present period to pass away, without boldly declaring to the British Government and Parliament, that they insist upon an entire abandonment of the present impolitic system of partiality, concession and conciliation to the French Canadians, upon a speedy and complete redress of the British Provincial inhabitants, which are not the theoretical speculations of designing and revolutionary demagogues, but real and substantial grounds of complaint, affecting alike the integrity of their birthright as British subjects, and the general improvement of the Province, upon the immediate adoption of the means necessary for crushing the blighting influence of French Provincial ascendancy, and for rendering the Colony a British Province in fact as well as in name, and upon a re-union of this Province with Upper Canada, as the only means of promoting the prosperity of both Provinces, of securing their dependence upon the British Government, and of preventing a dismemberment of the Empire.

"The Executive Committee, in conclusion, entreat the loyal British subjects throughout the Province, to urge the above measures with the vigor and perseverance due to their importance, to represent to the British people, that though the ignorance of the French Canadians and their abuse of the advantages of a Representative Government may have caused them to abandon the constitution of the Province, that the intelligence of 200,000 British Provincial inhabitants and their just appreciation of those advantages, should be deliberately considered, previous to recording the virtual annihilation of a Representative form of Government, dear to them as British freemen, to declare that no amalgamation can take place between the British and French Provincial inhabitants, while the policy of the Imperial

Government continues the prejudices and distinct nationality of the French Canadians; and to shew that the preservation of the Province as an integral part of the British Empire, is due to the native spirit and inherent loyalty of its British inhabitants, and that the manifestation of any indifference on their part as to the issue of the contest between the rebellious population of French origin and Her Majesty's troops, would have been followed by the most disastrous results.

"Your Committee cannot permit this occasion to escape without expressing the warmest thanks of the British inhabitants of this city to His Excellency Sir John Colborne, for his prompt and energetic conduct under the late most trying circumstances, and to Her Majesty's troops under his command, for their exertions in putting down the late insurrectionary movements, and to assure His Excellency, that the British inhabitants of this city will be at all times ready to render their best assistance to His Excellency and his brave companions in arms, in maintaining the authority of Her Majesty's Government, and in suppressing sedition and revolution."

P. M'GILL, Chairman.
W. BADGLEY, Secretary.

Montreal, 30th December, 1838.

At a General Meeting of the Constitutional Association of Quebec, on the 7th of February, the following Resolutions were adopted:—

"1. That Her Majesty's subjects in this Province are not less bound by the most sacred duty than impelled by motives of affection and gratitude, and by a due regard to the just interests of themselves and of their posterity, to maintain inviolate the connection of this Province with the United Kingdom of Great Britain and Ireland.

"2. That the Assembly of Lower Canada, as established and composed under the existing laws, is altogether incompetent to the performance of the important duties assigned to it by the Constitution, and that in the exercise of the powers confided to that body, it has disregarded and set at nought those duties, and after encouraging and fomenting sedition and anarchy, has wilfully abdicated its high office, and has thus rendered it of paramount and immediate necessity to provide a remedy for the evil.

"3. That the establishment of an efficient Legislature, capable of providing such laws and of adopting such measures as may from iime to time be called for by the wants of the country, and as may serve to develope its agricultural and commercial resources, to extend the benefits of education therein, and to improve its moral and social condition, will afford the only sure means of perpetuating the ties which happily unite the North American Colonies to Great Britain.

"4. That this object can be only fully and effectually accomplished by a Legislative Re-union of the Provinces of Upper and Lower Canada.

"5. That the Geographical position of the Provinces of Lower and Upper Canada, and the community of the use of the waters of the St. Lawrence as a common highway to the ocean, establish between them as to trade, and navigation and external relations a community of interest which can only be protected and advanced by such Legislative Union,

"6. That in the opinion of this Meeting, it is expedient that some person possessing the confidence of the British and Irish inhabitants of the Province, do proceed to London, to represent their wants and wishes to the Home Government.

"7. That a Petition be prepared, founded on the foregoing Resolutions, and that the Executive Committee be .requested to draw such Petition and to carry the said Resoltuion into effect.

"8. That the prominent part which Andrew Stuart, Esq., has for many years taken in public affairs—his thorough knowledge of the events which have occurred in this Province, and of the causes which have retarded the progress of public improvement, and the high estimation which his talents and integrity have gained for him, are calculated to give weight to his representations to the Home Government and eminently qualify him for the office of Agent to represent the British and Irish inhabitants of this Province— that he therefore be respectfully requested to undertake the mission to England on behalf of this Association, and of the several Branch Associations who shall concur in the said nomination.

"9. That a subscription be now opened to defray the expenses attending the mission of an agent to London."

Mr. Stuart accordingly left Quebec, on the 24th of February, for England. He was well received at the Colonial Office, and had a hearing from the Minister; but the Government having already determined upon its course, the mission was not productive of any particular result.

Messieurs Moffatt and Badgley were named by the Montreal Constitutional Association as their agents; and these gentlemen, as well as Mr. Stuart, were heard by the Mintster on the subject of their mission, and by Lord Durham, previous to his departure from England for Canada.*

---

* The following appeared in an English paper of the 10th April, relating to the Petitions which these gentlemen had taken to England :—

An Union of the Canadas as may be gathered from the above, was now desired by the population of British origin in Lower Canada. The opinion prevalent on this subject in the other Province, may be understood by the following extract from the "Report of a Select Committee of the House of Assembly of Upper Canada, on the political state of the Provinces of Upper and Lower Canada," dated February 8th, 1838, signed by Mr. Henry Sherwood, as Chairman.

"3rd. Your Committee next proceed to the question of a Unirn of the Provinces of Upper and Lower Canada. Were it not that the Inhabitants of Lower Canada of British origin regard this project with much favor, and appear to consider it as the best measure for relieving them from the oppression under which they have long suffered from the conduct of the dominant faction in their House of Assembly, your Committee would at once declare their unqualified dissent; but we feel bound not to overlook or treat lightly any suggestion that offers a reasonable hope of relieving our loyal fellow subjects from their political embarrassments, which now, more than ever claim our sympathy and consideration. Indeed, we feel that unless a change takes

---

"House of Lords, April 10.

"Canada.—Lord Glenelg presented a Petition from the British and Irish population of Lower Canada, expressive of their deep regret at the late disturbances in the Provinces. The Petitioners expressed their sense of the grievances to which the population were exposed, in consequence of the Act of 1791. Amongst other matters on which the Petitioners gave an opinion, was the union of the two Provinces. He (Lord G.) had on a former occasion alluded to this subject; but he felt that it would be premature for him to express an opinion on it at present. This much; however; he might say, that he thought if such a measure were proposed it could only be done with the approbation of the two Provinces themselves. The noble Lord presented a petition to the same effect from Quebec.

place in the Constitution and system of Government in Lower Canada, it is next to impossible that either that Province or this can advance one step in improvement, and that those who desire to continue to live under the British Crown, will be driven to seek some other place of residence.

"If, however the union should be that measure which the Imperial Parliament may ultimately determine upon, care must be taken that the British ascendancy is securely established in both branches of the Legislature: upon no other terms can the measure be sanctioned by this Province; and this should be most clearly and positively stated to Her Majesty.

"In what manner this ascendancy can be secured, your Committee abstain from offering any positive opinion. A variety of modes, however, may be suggested, founded on a division of territory, and the tenure by which lands are held in the two Provinces, and by restraining freeholders in Lower Canada, holding lands by conveyance, from voting until their titles are registered, as in the Upper Province. The introduction of the laws of England, and the use of the English language in all Legislative and Judicial proceedings should also be insisted upon; and lastly it should be stipulated as a *sine qua non* on the part of this Province, that the place selected for the Seat of Government should be within its limits."

The views here expressed with respect to the pro jected union of the two Provinces, it would seem, were adopted by the Assembly, according to the following statement of its proceedings, extracted probably from its Journals of the 24th February, published in the various newspapers of the day.

"Resolved, That a great saving would be effected in the Goverments of the two countries by uniting their Legislatures, and additional facilities afforded in accomplishing any measure by a direct communication with the Home Government, in place of waiting years to obtain the sanction of the two Legislative bodies actuated by different views, feelings, and separate interests.

"Resolved, That the Currency of the two Provinces, the management of the Post Offices, together with every internal regulation, can never be placed on a permanent beneficial footing so long as their separate interests prevail."

"Resolved, That although this House entertain the sentiments expressed in the foregoing resolutions, and feel that they will gather strength from year to year, so strong is their apprehensions that a union of those Provinces would prove injurious to their best interests, unless a decided majority in the Legislature is allotted to this Province, as recommended in the report of the Select Committee of this House during the present Session on the political state of the Provinces—they desire a united Legislature only on the following terms and conditions :—

"1st. That the principles of our Constitution be maintained inviolate—each branch of the Legislature to be constituted on the principles originally intended by the Act of the Imperial Parliament, that all future appointments in the Legislative Council be made in such manner from the different Districts, as best to secure the agricultural, commercial, and other interests of the Province.

"2nd. That the Casual, Territorial, and every branch of the Revenue be placed under the control of the Legislature, upon the same principle as Her Majesty's Government has been pleased to concede them to the Province of New Brunswick and Nova Scotia, which concession has given the greatest satisfaction to Her Majesty's subjects within this Province, as it holds out an evidence of what we may anticipate from the same liberal policy.

3rd. That the Seat of Government be established within the boundary of Upper Canada.

"4th. That in order to give full scope to British enterprise the English language should be established in the Legislature, in Courts of Justice, and in all legal proceedings, which in a few years would produce the beneficial result of converting a Canadian Province into one truly British, and thus draw still closer the ties which bind that section of the Canadas to the British Crown.

" 5th. That for the encouragement of enterprise, the introduction of British and Foreign capital, and the security of property, the abolition of the Feudal Tenure, and the establishment of Registry Offices are indispensable.

" Resolved, That an humble address be presented with the report adopted by the House on the political state of the Provinces of Upper and Lower Canada having reference to the same subject, and earnestly praying Her Majesty graciously to be pleased to take such steps as shall in Her Majesty's wisdom be deemed necessary to carry out the views of Her Majesty's faithful subjects, and thereby permanently place these Provinces and the other North American Colonies as dependencies of the British Caown."

Copy of a Despatch from Lord Glenelg to Lieutenant General Sir John Colborne, K. C. B., dated Downing Street, December 30, 1837:

" SIR,—I have received Lord Gosford's despatch of the 22nd November, describing the occurrences which, up to that date, had taken place in Lower Canada, and the General Commanding in Chief has laid before Her Majesty's Government, your Despatch to Lord F. Somerset of the 29th November, reporting measures which you had adopted in consequence of the demand of the Law Officers of the Crown and the Magistrates of Montreal, for the repression of attempts made by bodies of armed persons to disturb the peace of the country, and to resist the power of the law.

"I have had the honor to lay these communications before the Queen, and I have to convey to you Her Majesty's approbation of the vigor and decision with which you have acted. Her Majesty has also observed with much satisfaction the steadiness and gallantry displayed by the troops on this arduous service; and I am commanded, especially to express Her Majesty's sense of the zeal and judgment evinced by Lieutenant Colonel Wethcrall on the several occasions on which he has been employed. I cordially concur with you in the hope that what has recently occurred may be the means of quickly restoring tranquility to the country. In my despatches of the 27th ultimo and 6th instant, Her Majesty's Government acting on the recent information of the state of Lower Canada, commnnicated to them by Lord Gosford, conveyed to you full authority for using all the resources at your command for the maintenance of order and tranquility, and for the protection of the loyal inhabitants of the Province.

"Her Majesty's Government have since learned, with the most serious regret, the extent of the insurrectionary spirit in the Districts lying near the Richelieu. This information reached them though not officially, on the 23rd instant. Her Majesty's Government felt it their duty, in consequence, to propose that the period for which it was before intended that Parliament should adjourn, should be considerably abridged in order that no time might be lost in submitting to Parliament those measures which they feel the present state of affairs in Lower Canada to demand.

"The proposal having been agreed to, Parliament will meet on 16th of January, on which day this subject will be brought under the consideration of the House of Commons in pursuance of a notice which has been given to that effect by Lord John Russell.

"I shall take the earliest opportunity to communicate to you the result of the proceedings in Parliament on this important question. My separate despatch of this date will inform you of the military arrangements which have been made, in order to give you the utmost support in the adoption of effectual measures to check the progress of revolt and restore the authority of the law.

"Her Majesty's Government place full reliance on the judgment and energy with which you will conduct the affairs of the Province in its present circumstances and I earnestly hope that the unhappy contest which has unfortunately arisen will be terminated at a very early period and with as little injury to the interests and welfare of the Province, as under such circumstances may be possible.

"Her Majesty cannot contemplate the bloodshed and misery in which a portion of her subjects have involved themselves, without the deepest feeling of regret for he necessity which has oceasioned the active services of Ler troops in one of the Provinces of the British Empire.

"The Queen, however, entertains the fullest confidence, that, so far as depends on yourself, these evils will be restricted within the narrowest possible limits, and that on the part of her loyal and faithful subjects in the Province, no vindictive feeling will mingle itself with their zealous and strenuous endeavors. under your guidance, to put down insurrection and revolt, and to vindicate the authority of the law; but that their conduct will be equally marked with moderation and firmness.

"I have to request that you will furnish me with early and frequent intelligence of the course of events, and you may relyon a prompt attention being given to Her Majesty's Government to any suggestion which you may offer, calculated, to strengthen your hands, and give greater efficiency to the local Government.

"I have, &c.,

GLENELG"

Copy of a Despatch from Lord Glenelg to Lieutenant General Sir John Colborne, K. C. B., dated Downing Street, January 6, 1838:

"SIR,—Since I last addressed you on the 30th ultimo, I have received the Earl of Gosford's Despatches of the 30th November, No. 123, and the 6th December, No. 130, which together with your Despatches to Lord Fitzory Somerset of the 3rd and 7th of December, contain a report of the recent progress of affairs in Lower Canada, of the second Expedition, under Colonel Gore, to the banks of the Richelieu, and the Proclamation of Martial Law in the District of Montreil.

"Having had the honor to laythese Despatches before the Queen, I am commanded to convey to you Her Majesty's e i- tire approbation of the course which has been pursued by yourself and by the Earl of Gosford, with reference to the transactions which they detail. I am not in possession of the information on which the warrants for the arrest of certain individuals have been issued, but 1 have no doubt that they were such to justify the proceeding, under the actual circumstances of the country.

"It is highly satisfactory to Her Majesty to find that the measures which you adopted had produced so decided an effect in suppressing the insurrection in the neighborhood of the Richelieu, and that on the occasion of the last expedition-under Colonel Gore, no resistance was offered to Her Majes y's troops, but that, on the contrary the *habitants* gave every assistance which was required for the purpose of t-ansport. The disposition thus evinced by the *habitants*, the abahdonment of St. Denis, and of the other villages in the neighborhood by the armed insurgents, and their apparent dispersion, may, I trust, warrant the expectation that, under a firm but temperate administration of the power at present vested in the local Government, the time is not far distant when the authority of the law will have been fully vindicated and tranquillity restored to the Province. Her Majesty's Government can, however, entertain no doubt that, after the events which have recently occurred, and under the circumstances still actually exieting in a part of the District of Montreal, the Proclamation of Martial Law could not properly have been longer delayed, but had become indispensable to the maintenance of the Queen's authority and the protection of the loyal inhabitants of that District. In the adoption of the extreme measure, Lord Gosford only anticipated the instructions which I addressed to you in my Despatch of the 6th December, for your guidance in the event, which has since unhappily taken place, of this exercise of the prerogative becoming necessary for the suppression of actual revolt. Deeply regreting, while they fully admit this necessity, Her Majesty's Government have observed with much satisfaction, the recommendation addressed to you by Lord Gosford, in his letter of the 5th December, and the determination which you have expressed to the General Commanding in Chief, to restrict the operation of Martial Law within the narrowest limits which shall be consistent with the public safety, and not to withdraw from the ordinary tribunals any cases which can properly be left to their decision. Her Majesty's Government are also assured that Lord Gosford exercised a sound discretion in not having recourse to this measure without the most conclusive evidence of the inadequacy of any milder remedy to meet the existing evil. His Proclamation of the 29th November was directed by a spirit of enlightened humanity, and will. I trust, be effectual in recalling some, at least, of the misguided peasantry to their allegiance to their Sovereign.

" The Queen cheerfully accepts the tender of service which

has been made to Lord Gosford by a considerable number of the inhabitants of Quebec, and is pleased to sanction the conditions proposed by his Lordship, for the corps of Volunteers to be raised in that city. 1 am further commanded to express to you the high sense which Her Majesty entertains of the zeal and loyalty of that large body of Her subjects in Lower Canada, who have enrolled themselves on the present occasion for the defence of the Province and the suppression of revolt.

"I trust that you will have been enabled, as soon as the season may have allowed military movements, to effect the dispersion of the insurgents in those parts of the District of Montreal, in which, from the last accounts, they appeared still to be assembled in considerable numbers. Her Majesty's Government, however, entertain the fullest confidence in the judgment and discretion which will have governed whatever measures you may have adopted with a view to this object, or in reference to the general state of the Province.

" I have, &c.,

GLENELG,"

CHAPTER XLII.

Proclamation of Governor Marcy, State of New York Views of the people of Nova Scotia, of the rebellion in Canada--also of the inhabitants of New Brunswick---Speech of the Lieut. Governor of Upper Canada, Sir F. B. Head, to the Legislature---Mr. Mackenzies letter from Navy Island to the "Watertown Jeffersonian"---Despatches from Sir F. B. Head to the British Minister at Washington and Message to the Legislature with copies thereof addressed to Sir F. B. Head, &c.

The leading patriots in Lower Canada had all along counted upon the sympathy and support, not only of our American neighbors, but of the neighboring Provinces of Nova Scotia and New Brunswick. They now found, however, nothing of the kind among the masses, in either of those Provinces, distinguished as they have ever been, whatever local differences may have existed among themselves, for their loyalty and attachment to the British Constitution and Government. We shall devote this chapter to the demonstrations they respectively presented with respect to the insurrections which took place in the Canadas in 1837. We have previously observed the Proclamation issued by the Governor of the State of Vermont, (Mr Jenison,) warning the people of that State against all interference with the troubles in Canada, and now subjoin one of a similar description by Governor Marcy, of the State of New York.

PROCLAMATION.

BY WILLIAM L. MARCY, GOVERNOR OF THE STATE NEW YORK.

" Whereas information has been received that an armed body of men is assembled at or near the city of Buffalo, with the avowed intention of taking part in the disturbances which prevail in the neighboring Province of Upper Canada, and that similar movements are to be apprehended in other parts of the State, adjoining the Province of Lower Canada: and whereas any attempt to set on foot such military expeditions or enterprises, is in direct violation of the laws of the land, and of the relations of amity subsisting between the Kingdom of Great Britain and the United States:—

"I do hereby call upon the persons who may be assembled, or who may design to assemble, as aforesaid, to desist from their unlawful proceedings, and upon the citizens of this State to co-operate with the officers and Magistrates of the United States in their efforts to suppress all such violations of law, and to bring the offenders to punishment. I do also enjoin upon the good people of this State to abstain from all illegal interference with the domestic concerns of the said Provinces, and they are hereby cautioned not to allow their feelings of sympathy for those who, for political causes, have fled from other countries and taken refuge in our own, to mislead them into any infraction of the laws, or of those principles of neutrality which it is the duty of the Government to maintain, in relation to the dissensions, whether external or domestic, of Foreign States.

"Given under my hand, and the Great Seal of the
[L. S.] State, at Albany, this nineteenth day of December, one thousand eight hundred and thirty-seven.

W. L. MARCY."

By the Governor,

JOHN A. DIX, *Secretary of the State.*

General Winfield Scott, was at the same time earnestly engaged, by order of the General Government of the United States, in counteracting and suppressing the movements along the nothern frontier of that State, and thence westward to Detroit, by the band of sympathisers who, together, with the fugitive refugees from Upper Canada, had assembled at various points, and were threatening a descent upon the Upper Province, with a view rather to plunder, than to achieve the independence of the people thereof,

Shortly after the outbreaks at St. Denis and St. Charles were known at Halifax, N. S., a public meeting of the inhabitants of that town was held, at which the following resolutions were unanimously adopted:

" Resolved, That the recent events which have taken place in Lower Canada, where a number of misguided men have been deluded into rebellion against their Soverign, render it a duty in all Her Majesty's subjects inhabiting the British Provinces of North America, publicly to declare their firm and unshaken loyalty to Her Majesty, their thankfulness to Divine Providence for the many blessings secured to them by the British Constitution, and their firm determination to resist by every means in their power, any dismemberment of the British Empire, of which this meeting is proud to consider this Province an integral part.

" Resolved, That this meeting deeply regrets the necessity which these unfortunate events have created, for the departure of Her Majesty's forces from this garrison, where the conduct of both officers and men has secured to them the respect and attachment of all classes of society.

" Resolved, That this meeting is aware that the noble spirit which animates British Soldiers, will induce them resolutely to encounter the hardships they must endure in marching through a long and dreary wilderness, at this inclement season of the year—but while the soldier at the call of duty spurns both danger and fatigue, the husband and the father cannot but feel deeply for those whom they are compelled to leave without their natural protectors. To alleviate those feelings as much as possible—to lessen the pang which the brave soldier must experience in parting with his wife and children, we agree to contribute towards their comfort, to raise a fund for the relief of the wives and

E

children of tl e soldiers of this garrison, whose husbands and fathers have left, or shall be under the necessity of leaving them behind, when they march to uphold and support the authority of our beloved Sovereign, and to preserve the integrity of the British Empire.

"Resolved, That the Committee be appointed to collect subscriptions of this meeting, and of all who may feel disposed to the benevolent object contemplated in the foregoing resolution.

"Resolved, That S. Binney, E. Kenny, E. Cunard, Hugh Bell, Joseph Howe, Michael Tobin, W. M. Allan, E. Wallace, W. J. Starr, J. C, Allison, and W. A. Black, Esquires, be appointed a Committee for the above purpose; that W. A. Black, Esq., be appointed Treasurer, to receive the sums collected by the Committee.

"Resolved, That a Committee be appointed to regulate the mode of distributing the relief intended to be offered to the wives and children who shall be left by the soldiers who depart from this garrison for Canada.

"Resolved, That the Hon. the Speaker of the House of Assembly and the Solicitor General, with the several gentlemen composing the last named Committee, be the members of this Committee.

"Resolved, That a committee be appointed to prepare an Address to His Excellency the Lieut. Governor, embodying the substance of the foregoing Resolutions, and requesting him to make known to Her Majesty's the sentiments of Her Majesty's loyal subjects in Nova Scotia, as expressed by this meeting.

"Resolved, That the Speaker and Members of the House of Assembly, resident in Halifax, with the Chairman of this meeting, and the Solicitor General, the Hon. T. N. Jeffery, S. W. Deblois, Esq., J. L. Starr, Esq., and the Honourable H. H.. Cogswell, be a committee to carry into effect the last resolution.

The first Resolution was moved by the Hon. Speaker,

and seconded by Thoma Forrester, Esq. The Sheriff was about putting it, when Joseph Howe, Esq. addressed the meeting.

" Mr Howe spoke as follows:—Mr Chairman, I am very happy to see this meeting: I am pleased and proud to meet my fellow townsmen on such on occasion. All are assembled on common ground, ready to express a universal sentiment. When I first heard of this meeting, I was afraid that it would have a tendency to divide the community : but I am highly pleased to find that it will be quite the reverse, and that it is calculated to unite all. I am not anxious to take up time, or to intrude anything that would jar harshly on any man's ear; but now that we are all assembled, if and differences exist, it is right that we should understand each other,—if any misunderstandings have gone abroad, let this day clear them up.

" From my profession and habits, my name has been much mixed up with the public concerns of the country, and during the last few weeks, many expressions have been calculated, coupling me, and those who associate with me, with insurrection and rebellion. I come here, not only to express loyalty to Her Majesty —and heaven knows the Queen has not more loyal subjects, in the same number, in any part of her dominions, than she has in Nova Scotia—I come here not only to express my loyalty, but also to vindicate my public conduct, and that of those with whom I have acted,—to prove that never for a single moment did we harbour a thought which might not be spoken in the presence of our Queen. (Applause.) I have been called the Papineau of Nova Scotia, I have heard it from many quarters, and a connection is attempted to be shown between the Reformers of this Province and the agitators of Canada,—I come forward to disprove this—to throw back upon the slanderers the falsehood they have circulated—to show you what we have said and done—how far, and no further, we sanction opposition to the measures of Government. It has been said that we have been holding treasonable correspondence with traitors in Canada; and so many tales have been invented, that some old woman I really believe apprehend, that when the last company of soldiers marches out of town, the standard of insurrection is to be raised: while others have even gone so far as to refuse to eat Chizetcook eggs, believing that the very hens in that quarter were disaffected. (Much laughter, Mr. H., resided at Chizetcook.)

"I now declare that the only correspondence which ever existed between the Canadian party and myself or those with whom I have been associated, so far as I know, is included in two letters received from an agent in England; these letters are now in my pocket, and any gentleman in the room are welcome to their perusal.

"(The Chairman here interposed.)

"Chair. I am afraid, Mr. Howe, that you are straying from the resolutions.

"Mr. Forrester. Read the letter, it will satisfy the meeting respecting your views.

"Hon. T. N. Jeffery. Mr. Howe has declared his opinions, his word is enough.

"Stephen Deblois, Esq. I believe that no accusation has been made against Mr. Howe.

"Alex. Stewart. Esq. Will not every one be heard in a meeting which is wished to be unanimous? I hope it will not be said, that in a meeting of Nova Scotians, a gentleman of Mr. Howe's character, who wishes to vindicate himself, will be denied a hearing.

"(Loud cries for Mr. Howe to proceed.)

"Mr. Howe resumed: I will not occupy much of the time of the meeting. The letters I allude to were received in the year 1835, and were from Mr. Chapman, who formerly edited a daily paper in Montreal and went home as agent, associated with Mr. Roebuck. The object of these letters, was to further co-operation among tl e Provinces, in reference to Colonial reform, and Mr. Chapman called on me for information respecting Nova Scotia. These letters and their answers are ready for the inspection of any gentleman who wishes to see them. Every one in the community knows my opinions on Canadian affairs; when I received those letters—fearing from some indications in Canada, that extreme results might be expected—I felt it to be my duty, as a Nova Scotian reformer, to put on record the sentiments prevalent in this country, that there might be no mistake on the subject. Contrary to my usual practice, I fortunately kept a copy of that answer. I will now refer to passage or two of it, and would willingly read it all, only for the time it would occupy. After this meeting, I may now perhaps put the letter in print, as a declaration of my own views, and the views of others, on this subject

" (Mr. Howe here read a passage of the answer to Mr. Chapman's letters. The passage remarked on the desirableness of using sincerity and frankness on the subject, and stated that seven-eights of the population of the Lower Province would be opposed to separation from the Crown: that the people were sincerely attached to the Mother Country—that the object of our reformers was the purification of their institutions—and that they never assumed that justice would not be obtained by peaceful and constitutional means.)

" This is the way, said Mr. Howe, in which I have spread disloyalty! This is the way we have encouraged parties to throw off their allegiance. There is not a sentiment in the letter, which any man, woman or child, in the community, need be ashamed to avow. (Applause.)

" Referring to the natural growth of these countries, and to ultimate changes which may be forced on us centuries hence, I stated that our population had no disposition to hasten that period which would witness their separation from the Mother Country, and that the desire was, when it did occur, that it should be an act of peace and mutual good will. The letter may not be understood without the whole being read,—but I cautioned those people, as far as was in my power, that not only need they expect no assistance from these Provinces, in any extreme design—for I anticipated something of the kind, although no hint of that description was contained in Mr. Chapman's letter—that not only need they expect no assistance, but that, from the weakness evident in their own party, they had no chance of success. That is the sort of language reformers of Nova Scotia have used towards the people of Canada. I feel bound to make these declarations—I owe it to those who have been associated with me, both in and out of the Legislature—to those now in their homes in various parts of the country, to declare that not one of them ever harbored a thought of disloyalty to their Sovereign; and I feel that as a public man I am bound thus to publicly state our sentiments and dare those who have defamed us to the proof.

"Although I was not consulted, Mr. Chairman, respecting the proceedings of this meeting, I expressed a hope to some of the gentlemen interested, that the resolutions would be drawn so that they might pass the meeting unanimously. In order to show the spirit in which I came to this meeting, here are four resolutions which I brought with me, similar in substance to those which the meeting are called on to pass. In these I stated our loyalty to the Government, and our abhorrence of the introduction of foreigners into any of the Colonies to settle domestic disputes.

"In these matters my feeling has ever been that which actuates the great Reformer of Ireland; the language I have constantly held has been—keep the peace, never break it, use the means within the law and the Constitution—and these, after patient perseverance, will procure every needful reformation which we require. These are the sentiments by which I have been actuated; and I never in public or private, expressed the contrary. I now stand prepared to maintain and justify every sentiment expressed by me with reference to Canadian affairs.

" I give my sanction to these resolutions unqualifiedly. It is well to shew to Her Majesty the sentiments which we hold—to declare our loyalty and our attachment to the country from which we have descended—whose language we inherit—whose blood is running in our veins. Respecting the soldier, whatever differences of opinion may prevail concerning the causes and result of the present contest, every one here must feel that we are under obligations to the troops, and that they, of all others, are not to blame. They have often assisted us in seasons of danger, they have lived with us on most friendly terms—and it behoves us, as men, as christians, on the present occasion, to relieve their anxiety concerning their families. I am prepared, as one, to give my mite in their behalf.*

---

* Mr. Joseph Howe was at that time Editor of the Nova Scotian published at Halifax, and had hitherto invariably, it is believed, spoken in his paper approvingly, and more than once, with enthusiasm of Mr. Papineau's agitation and career in the work of reform. The Canadian " patriots ' built considerably on Mr. Howe's sympathy and on that of his party in Nova Scotia, whose seeming approbation certainly cheered them on. ' He may, indeed, have imagined that they sought only " Colonial Reform," but the pass to which matters in Canada had at last come undeceived him, and he therefore judiciously availed himself of the present opportunity of "backing out" and setting himself right in the estimation of his fellow countrymen, the Nova Scotians, who though themselves, seeking for reform, by no means contemplated rebellion to accomplish it. Many in Canada judging of Mr. Howe, by his editorials, deemed him in fact a more progressive patriot than Mr. Papineau himself, but the minds he had to work upon were neither so pliable nor confiding as those with whom Mr. P., acted, or, as many in Canada, do him the justice, or injustice, to believe he possibly might have attempted the whole figure.

Afer some conversation the resolutions were put together and passed unanimously. Three times three most hearty cheers followed.

In New Brunswick various Militia Regiments volunteered their services towards putting down the rebellion in Canada. We shall give only an instance or two, as exhibiting the feeling and spirit of all. At a meeting of the officers of the St. John County Regiment of Militia, held at Portland on the 6th of December, present Lieut. Colonel, the Hon. Charles Simond, &c., it was:

Resolved unanimously, That the officers of this regiment deeply lament the progress which rebellion is making in the adjoining Province of Lower Canada, and that they view with abhorrence the proceedings of the faction there, who, under pretence of seeking redress of grievances, have seduced a portion of Her Majesty's subjects from their allegiance, for the wicked purpose of revolution.

" That actuated by those principles of loyalty which happily pervade the entire population of this Province, the officers of this regiment feel it a duty to offer their services to His Excellency the Commander in Chief, to perform garrison on any other military duty, which the absence of the regular troops may render necessary for effectually supporting Her Majesty's Government, and they are assured that the non-commisioned officers and men of this regiment feel a like sense of duty to their Queen and country.

Resolved, That Lieut. Col. Simmonds do communicate the foregoing resolution and tender of services to His Excellency the Commander in Chief.

GOVERNMENT HOUSE, FREDERICTON,
December 6, 1937.

SIR.—I have received with the highest satisfaction the resolutions adopted by the officers of the Saint

John County Militia, at a meeting held in Portland yesterday.

I am so entirely convinced of the ardent loyalty and devoted attachment to British connexion by which the universal population of this Province is animated, that I am not only enabled to detach the whole of the Queen's troops in this Province to the support and assistance of those in Lower Canada, but also to entertain a well founded confidence of being empowered to afford to Her Majesty's loyal subjects in that Province, the assistance and co-operation of the Provincial troops from this, in the event of circumstances rendering it necessary.

To yourself individually I tender my thanks for your spirited offer, and can only assure you that in such an emergency as I have alluded to I should be happy to have you and St. John County Militia at my side.

I have the honour to be, Sir,
Your faithful friend,
J. HARVEY,
Lieut. Governor.

To the Hon. Charles Simmonds,
Lieut. Col. St. John Chunty Militia.

To an address from the officers of the 1st Battalion of Queen's County Militia, expressive of attachment to the Throne and Constitution of England—their abhorrence and concern of the measures pursued by the disaffected portion of the inhabitants of Lower Canada, with an offer of their united services to aid in putting down treason and rebellion in Lower, Canada, Sir John Harvey answered:

"It is unspeakably gratifying to me to receive such declarations of attachment to the Throne and Constitution of England. and of determination to support the royal authority, and put down treason and rebellion in the neighbouring Province, as are contained *is* well in Colonel Peter's address to, as in the resolutions adopted by the officers of the 1st Battalion of Queen's oCunty Militia. That they are concurred in by the 2nd Battalion, I do not for a moment entertain a doubt, believing as I do that they express the sentiments of the universal population of this thoroughly British Province. I am deeply sensible of the expression of confidence and favorable opinion as respects myself individually.

I have called the Legislature together for the purpose of suggesting the propriety of evincing towards our loyal fellow subjects in Lower Canada, the sympathy which the inhabitants of this Province feel for their situation, and of placing at the disposal of the authorities in that Province, the services of such portion of the militia of this, led by myself, as may be required for the support of the royal authority in Lower Canada, and the suppression of the revolt into which many of its naturally contented and well disposed peasantry have been led by wicked and unprincipled, traitorous and reckless men.

Militia of Queen's County, in the name of your youthful and most Gracious Queen, I thank you for the sentiments you have expressed.

(Signed,)   J. HARVEY,
            Lt. Governor.

The Magistrates and other principal inhabitants of St. John presented on the 12th December, 1837, a loyal address to Sir John Harvey, in answer to which we find the following recorded:

GENTLEMEN,—I acknowledge with feelings of pride and pleasure, your truly loyal and patriotic address. Proceeding from such a community, and bearing the signatures of all that is most respectable in that loyal city, I feel that I may justly consider this address as an index, nothing equivocal, of the general feeling of the population of the Province.

Taking it in connection with many others which have lately reached me, I deem myself warranted, not only unhesitatingly to commit the protection of the Province, and of the lives and property of Her Majesty's subjects within it, to its loyal militia; but also (in confident anticipation of the Legislative sanction) to tender, through His Excellency the Governor in Chief, to Her Majesty's loyal subjects in Lower Canada, not only *sympathies* only, but the actual co-operation of a large body of the Militia of New Brunswick, in the suppression of the insurrection in that Province; and should their services be required or accepted, I trust that it is unnecessary for me to say, that I should glory in placing myself at the head of a volunteer force, acting under feelings and upon principles of so high and noble a character.

J. HARVEY,
Lieut. Governor.
Government House, Dec. 12, 1837.

Sir John Harvey addressed, about this time, a despatch to Sir John Colborne, from which the following is an extract:

"I am instructed by Sir Colin Campbell to hold the 34th in readiness to follow the 43rd and 85th, upon your Excellency's requisition, and as I have summoned the Legislature of the Province to meet on the 28th instant, for the purpose of offering to their loyal subjects in Canada, and to the royal authority, something beyond the mere expression of their sympathies with the one, and their attachment to the other, I do not entertain a doubt of being empowered by the representatives of this truly loyal people, to embody and lend to the neighboring Provinces, such numbers of the militia of New Brunswick, as your Excellency and the civil authority of Lower Canada may require, whether for the purpose of assisting in forming the garrison of Quebec, and thereby rendering the whole of the Queen's forces disposable, or of being elsewhere employed in maintaining Her Majesty's authority, by checking and controlling any seditious or rebellious movements in the parts of Lower Canada adjoining *this* Province—in a word, in any way in which their services and my own may be rendered useful in the royal cause. I can depend upon the loyalty of the people of this Province to a man.

I have the honour to be, your Excellency's most obedient and faithful servant,

J. HARVEY, M. General,
Lieut. Governor.

To His Excellency, Lieutenant General Sir JOHN COLBORNE, &c., &c., &c.

In meeting the Legislature of New Brunswick on the 28th December, His Excellency stated that his object in calling them together at this early period was "to invite their attention to the lamentable state to which the treasonable and rebellious proceedings of a certain portion of the deluded inhabitants, have reduced the neighboring Province of Lower Canada. The disaffected having availed themselves of a season of the year when succours from the mother country are believed to be excluded by the rigour of the climate it appears to be in a more special manner incumbent on Her Majesty's loyal subjects in the surrounding Colonies to stand forward, not with the mere expression of their sympathies, but, if required, in active support of the Royal authority, and in aid of their loyal fellow subjects in Lower Canada, now contending against the desperate efforts of a Revolutionary faction, for the preservation, to themselves and their descendants of the inestimable blessings of British connexion. The mode and extent of this aid your own loyalty and wisdom will best devise; for myself I will only add, that my individual services, in the furtherance of such an object, shall be afforded with all the energy of which I am capable, and in any manner in which it may be considered that they can best promote it. I cannot upon this occasion refrain from expressing my high admiration of the unchanged loyalty and gallantry of the militia in our sister colony of Upper Canada, evinced in the prompt suppression of them, unaided by any portion of Her Majesty's Troops, of the Revolutionary outbreak which was attempted by some misguided persons in that Province."

To this the Assembly most cordially responded.

"We the representatives of Her Majesty's Loyal subjects, the people of New Brunswick, beg leave to express our thanks for your Excellency's Speech at the opening of the present Session.

"We can assure your Excellency that the people of this Province have not failed to derive both consolation and satisfaction from the unequivocal manifestation of deep rooted attachment to its ancient Monarchical Institutions, which stimultaneously burst forth in expressions of the most ardent loyalty from every part of the Mother Country after the lamented death of our late beloved Sovereign William the Fourth, of revered and glorious memory, and upon the occasion of the accession of Her Majesty Queen Victoria to the Throne of Her illustrious ancestors.

"The lamented state to which a portion of its deluded and rebellious inhabitants have reduced the neighboring Province of Lower Canada, excites within us that fraternal sympathy for our loyal fellow subjects in that Province, with the mere expression of which we shall not rest satisfied, but shall evince it by our active support of the Royal authority, and in aid of those who are now contending against the desperate efforts of a revolutionary faction for the preservation to themselves and their descendants, in common with us all, of the inestimable blessings of British connexion; and although succours from the Mother Country may be in some degree, cut off at this season of the year by the severity of the climate, yet we hope that the prompt and effective manner in which the surrounding Colonies shall render assistance to the Government, at this important crisis, will be a sufficient assurance, that succours are always at hand, *which no rigor of climate can exclude, while a man remains in these loyal Provinces able to take the field.*

" We shall apply ourselves with diligence in order to devise the mode and extent of the aid which we can best render to our loyal brethern of Lower Canada, and your Excellency's past conduct in your Country's service affords us a most satisfactory guarantee that all the energy by which your Excellency has been heretofore characterized will be readily directed, if required, in that manner which will be best calculated to promote the interests of the Crown, and the security of the Country.

" We were prepared to learn that the loyalty and gallantry for which the Militia of Upper Canada have been so memorably distinguished remain unchanged; and we sincerely hope that the prompt suppression, by them, unaided by any portion of Her Majesty's troops, of the revolutionary outbreak, which was attempted by some seditious and deluded persons in the Province, will have a most beneficial influence in preventing the repetition of such violent outrages on the peace and good order of society."

NEW BRUNSWICK,

HOUSE OF ASSEMBLY,

FRIDAY, 9th, *January*, 1838.

" Resolved unanimously, That the thanks of this Province are due, and should be presented to Sir Francis Bond Head, and the gallant Militia of Upper Canada, for their able, prompt and energetic suppression of the insurrection which lately took place in the neighborhood of Toronto.

" Resolved unanimously, That the conduct of our fellow subjects of Upper Canada, on this memorable occasion, so fully in accordance with their former high spirit and character, affords a glorious example to the Sister Colonies, and cannot fail to quicken the zeal and animate the exertions of every loyal heart in these Colonies, in support and defence of the liberties they enjoy under British Laws and Institutions.

" Resolved unanimously, That our fellow subjects in Upper Canada may rest assured of the lively sympathy of the inhabitants of this Province in their loyalty and patriotic ardor, and of our most zealous co-operation in maintaining the Royal authority, and the inestimable advantages of our connexion with the Mother Country.

" Resolved unanimously, That an humble address be presented to His Excellency the Lieut Governor, praying that His Excellency will be pleased to transmit these Resolutions to His Excellency Sir Francis Bond Head, Lieutenant Governor of Upper Canada.

" Resolved, That the Legislative Council be requested to join in these Resolutions."

CHARLES P. WETMORE,
Clerk.

The House of Assembly voted, the day before the close of the Session, an address to the Lieut. Governor, stating that a sum not exceeding £10,000 should be at the disposition of His Excellency, " to meet any emergency which the interests of the Province or the welfare of the British Colonies may appear to require," and that the Assembly would make provision for the same, the Legislative Council concurring in the address, on this subject. Sir John Harvey, in his speech on proroguing the Legislature, observes :

" In concluding the Address, I advert with feelings

of proud emotion to your joint Resolutions, which have just been presented to me, placing at my disposal the sum of £10,000 for the purpose of enabling me to meet any emergency which may arise out of the state of affairs now existing betwixt the British and American Governments, in consequence of the lawless and hostile proceedings of the armed banditti by which the Frontiers of Upper and Lower Canada are threatened from the United States, and for the object of preserving that connexion with the Mother Country, which is so warmly cherished by the inhabitants of this Province."

The Lieut. Governor of Nova Scotia, Sir Colin Campbell in opening the Legislature of that Province on the 25th, of January, after noticing the recent death of His late Majesty King William the Fourth, observes:

"The Throne of the British Empire is now filled by his august niece Queen Victoria, the daughter of his late Royal Highness the Duke of Kent, who for many years resided amongst you, when Commander-in-Chief in British America. Her Majesty's accession has been hailed, in every part of Her extensive dominions, with the most enthusiastic loyalty: Her youth and sex claim from Her subjects their dutiful affection and support.

"It is with deep regret I have to notice the late unfortunate events in the Canadas; but I have the satisfaction of informing you that the insurrection has been put down in Lower Canada and that the traitorous attempt made to separate the Upper Province from British rule, has been signally defeated by the gallant conduct of the Militia alone: it is true that a small and desperate band still retain possession of Navy Island: but there is every reason to believe, as measures have been adoptad at the recommendation of the President of the United States for the enforcement of neutrality on the frontier, that these deluded men, deprived of all foreign assistance, will be speedily dispersed.

"These rebellious proceedings have called forth in this Province the strongest impressions of indignation and abhorrence, and the addresses from various quarters which have been presented to me, declare the unshaken attachment of the inhabitants of Nova Scotia to Her Majesty's Person and Government.

In answer to this the Assembly observed:

"The regret we feel for the recent insurrection in the Canadas, is mitigated by a knowledge that it has been suppressed in the Lower Province. And we feel proud that the constitutional force of the Upper Province has defended the traitorous attempt to call off British allegiance, are gratified to learn that the Government of the United States is determined to adhere to the pacific treaties subsisting between the two nations, and to preserve that neutrality which may leave the desperate band of conspirators encamped at Navy Island, no alternative but submission to a just and indignant government.

" The attachment of Nova Scotians to Her Majesty's person and government has ever been unshaken, and recent events have only caused it to be more openly and fervently expressed.

Both in St. John and Fredericton, N. B., as well as in Halifax, provision for involuntary subscriptions among the inhabitants were generously made for the women and children left behind belonging to those regiments, (the 34th, 43rd and 85th), who, in course of the winter, marched over land into Canada.

The speech of the Lieut. Governor of Upper Canada, Sir F. B. Head, in opening the Legislature of that Province on the 28th December, 1837, affords the best view, perhaps, of affairs in that quarter that could be given.

" I have deemed it necessary to convene the Legislature of Upper Canada a few days earlier than has been customary, for the purpose of communicating with you on the present state of the Province; but before I draw your attention to this important subject, I cannot refrain from condoling with you on the loss which, since our last meeting, we have sustained in the demise of his late Gracious Majesty King William the Fourth, of blessed memory, whose parental attachment to the Canadas will, I feel confident, long be remembered by its inhabitants with filial gratitude and respect.

" The Throne of the British Empire is now adorned by Her Majesty Queen Victoria, whose youth, education, virtue and sex, endearing Her to Her subjects, claim their loyal protection and support.

" Notwithstanding the prosperity and happiness of this Province, it is with pain I inform you, that I have suddenly been called upon to suppress a rebellion, which must have appeared to the Province at large of so extraordinary a character, that it is proper I should advert to its origin and progress.

" With every disinclination to revive political difference of opinion, which must exist in every free country, and which no liberal man would ever be desirous to suppress, I will merely remind you, that shortly after I arrived in this Province with instructions from His late Majesty to correct whatever grievances might exist, it unavoidably became necessary that I should constitutionally appeal to the sense of the people—I did so, and they unequivocally supported me.

" A few individuals, disappointed at the result, did not scruple to declare, that the people of Upper Canada had been mistaken in their verdict, which it was asserted had been obtained by improper means.

" This second subject of discussion I deemed it advisable to bring plainly before the public—it was accordingly submitted to the consideration of His late Majesty and the Imperial Government, the House of Commons, and the House of Assembly of Upper Canada, and by all these tribunals the question was decided against those, who with groundless slander had assailed their Government, and who being rapidly deserted by their original supporters, were now reduced to a very few individuals.

" Finding that against cool argument they could advance nothing, they desperately determined to try an appeal to physical strength, the avowed object of which was to force Her Majesty's subjects from their allegiance, and to subvert the British Constitution, under the pretext of reform. .

" As soon as this conspiracy became known to me, I determined that for the public good I would allow it to work its own cure : but as I felt convinced that cure would never be admitted to be perfect if Her Majesty's troops were required to take any part in the contest, I cheerfully approved of their leaving the Province in order that the people of 'Upper Canada' in a state of uncontrolled independence, might be allowed another opportunity of unequivocally demonstrating whether they would support me or desert me in the determination I had evinced, " to maintain for them the British Constitution inviolate,"

" Besides parting with the troops, I further resolved to place in the hands of the Civil portion of the community all the muskets, (about 4000)which the Government had in store, and I accordingly delivered them over to the custody of the Mayor, Aldermen and Commonality of the City of Toronto.

" Without either soldiers or weapons to enforce my cause, I allowed the leader of the intended insurrection a full opportunity to make his intended experiment —I freely allowed him to write what he choose—say what he chose, and *do* what he chose—I allowed him to assemble his deluded adherents for the purpose of drill—I even allowed them unopposed to assemble with loaded fire arms, and in spite of the remonstrances which, from almost every District in the Province, I received from the peaceable portion of the community, I allowed him to make deliberate preparation for revolt, for I freely confess that I did underrate the degree of audacity and cruelty which these armed insulters of the law were prepared, as events have proved, to exhibit. It did not seem to me creditable, that in the bosom of this peaceful country, where every one was enjoying the protection of equal laws, and reaping the fruit of his labours almost undiminished by taxes, any number of persons could be found willing to assail the lives, plunder their unoffending fellow subjects, and to attempt the destruction of a Government from which they had received nothing but good.

"The ultimate object of the conspiracy was veiled under a mysterious secrecy which I had no desire to penetrate; and relying implicitly on the people, so little did I enquire into it, or impede it, that I was actually in bed and asleep, when I was awakened by a messenger who abruptly informed me that a numerous body of armed rebels had been congregated by their leader—that the murder of a veteran officer of distinction, a settler in the Province, had already been committed—and that the assailants were within an hour's march of Toronto.

"The long looked for crisis had now evidently arrived: and accordingly, defenceless and unarmed, I called upon the Militia of Upper Canada to defend their Government, and then confidently awaited the result.

"With an enthusiasm which it is impossible for me to describe, they instantly obeyed the summons. "Upwards of 10,000 men immediately marched towards the Capital—and in the depth of a Canadian winter, with no clothes but those they stood in—without food, and generally speaking without arms—Reformers as well as Constitutionalists—nobly rushed forward to defend the revered Constitution of their ancestors, although the rebel who had dared to attack it was offering to his adherents 300 acres of our land, and the plunder of our banks.

" As soon as the people had organized themselves, I saw it would be necessary to make an attack, however feeling the greatest possible reluctance at the prospect of a sanguinary conflict with the deluded subjects of Her Majesty who were opposed to me I despatched to them two of their own party, to tell them that before any collision should take place, I parentally called upon them, as their Governor, to avoid the effusion of human blood.

" The answer I received from the rebel leader was, that he would only consent that his demands should be settled by a National Convention, and that he would wait till two o'clock for my answer.

" Having now, to the best of my ability, performed the religious as well as moral duty which I owed to the Province, I issued a Proclamation calling upon those who had been seduced to join the unnatural rebellion, to return to their duty, in which case I informed them that they would find the Government of their Queen as indulgent as it was just: and having given them this last opportunity to disperse, I allowed the brave Militia of Upper Canada to advance, and the result of this trial by battle was the public verdict which I had always anticipated.

" The rebels dispersed in all directions, surrendered everywhere at discretion; those of their leaders who were not taken prisoners absconded to the United States ; and before sunset the whole conspiracy exploded.

" In the London District, a similar proof of public opinion was particularly evinced. To the Militia, nobly commanded by Colonel MacNab, Speaker of the House of Assembly, upwards of three hundred misguided men laid down their arms—craving pardon for their guilt—asking permission to assist the loyal Militia in capturing the fugitive leaders, who they declared had not only deceived, but deserted them—and the affair being thus concluded, there remained not a rebel throughout the whole Province in arms!—indeed so complete was their defeat, that General Orders were immediately issued by me, announcing that there was " no further occasion for the resort of militia to Toronto"—and that the Militia of the Bathurst, Johnstown, Ottawa and Eastern Distrits, might march to Lower Canada in aid of the Queen's Forces.

"In all the civil contests which History has been compelled to record, I conceive that there has never been a question more fairly submitted to the judgment of the free people, than that which in Upper Canada has just ended in the total defeat, moral as well as physical, of the opponents of the British Constitution.

" The triumph has been that of reason over force —of good laws over anarchy—of bravery, fidelity and generosity on the part of the Militia, over murder, arson and robbery by the rebels.

" Tranquility had returned to the land—angry passions had subsided—the political atmosphere of the Province has become already healthy after the storm which had passed over it, when, I regret to inform you, that the peace of the Province was suddenly invaded from a quarter from which Her Majesty's subjects in this Province had certainly never calculated upon receiving an attack.

" I need not on this Continent declare that Americans are a people with whom the British Empire for many years has assiduously cultivated the most friendly connexion. Our Government has looked upon them as its allies—our people have intimately connected themselves with their commerce—our capital has irrigated their land—unlimited credit has been fraternally extended to them, with that unsuspecting confidence which in the civilized world is reposed in men of character and truth—we have rejoiced in their success, and we have done all that a generous nation could do, to save them from the expense and misery of war. It is true, we were once opponents, but the hatchet of war has long been buried, and I must own I had hoped that the spirits of our mutual ancestors were sacredly guarding its tomb!

"Such are the feelings of the British people towards the Americans, and yet I regret to inform you, that in a moment of profound peace and personal friendship, a considerable number of Americans, regardless of the crimes committed, as well as of the degraded character of the man, have sympathised with the principal rebel, who has lately absconded as a criminal from our land. I regret to inform you the American citizens of influence and great wealth have come forward to coerce the brave and independent people of Upper Canada, to change laws and institutions which they have lately, by open and almost universal suffrage, publicly declared that they prefer.

"The American press has, to my astonishment, in many instances advocated this flagrant act of injustice and such has been the popular excitement, that not only has the body of Americans, headed by American leaders, within a few days, taken possession of Navy Island, (which belongs to the British Empire,) but a Proclamation has just been issued from this spot, declaring that the standard of liberty is planted in Canada—that the Provisional Government is established there—that a reward of five hundred pounds is offered for my apprehension—that three hundred acres of Her Majesty's lands will be freely bestowed by this Provisional Government upon any volunteer who shall personally assist in invading our freedom; and it is added that " ten millions of these lands, fair and fertile, will speedily be at their disposal, with the other vast resources of a country more extensive and rich than the United Kingdom or old France."

"I am informed that Americans from various quarters are hastening from the interior to join this standard of avowed plunder and revolt—that cannon and arms are publicly proceeding there,—and, under these circumstances, it becomes my painful duty to inform you, that without having offered to the United States the smallest provocation—without having entertained the slightest previous doubt of the sincerity of American alliance, the inhabitants of this Province may, in a few days, be called upon by me to defend their lives, their properties and their liberties from an attack by American citizens which, with no desire to offend, I must pronounce to be unparalleled in the history of the world.

"Upon the courage and resolution of the Canadian people, I place the firmest reliance; and if this unwarrantable invasion should proceed, I know I shall not in vain require every British subject coolly to perform that duty to his country which his own pride, spirit and feelings, will spontaneously suggest.

"The interference of foreigners, in the domestic policy of a free country, is an aggression which no Nation of character can ever submit to endure, (especially where a band of people, violating their own laws, our laws, as well as the sacred obligations of national amity, intrude themselves upon peaceable inhabitants, lawlessly, to advocate by force of arms the practical blessing and advantages of Republican Institutions, which, by their own showing, have at least ended with them in anarchy and plunder) and as every country is a natural fortress to its inhabitants—as every village is a strong military position—and as every bridge and ravine can be advantageously defended—I must own that deeply as I should lament a conflict of this nature, I entertain no feeling of anxiety for the result. The peaceful inhabitants of Upper Canada will not be left to defend their country alone, for they belong to an Empire which does not suffer its subjects to be injured with impunity; and if a national war, which it rests with the American Government to avert, should be the unhappy consequence of an intolerant invasion of our freedom, the civilized world, while it sympathises with our just cause, will view with feelings of astonishment and abhorrence this attempt of a body of American citizens treacherously to attack and plunder, in a moment of profound peace, their oldest—their most intimate—and their most natural ally.

"A few days will, I trust, demonstrate that the American Government wants neither the will nor the power to control its people. If otherwise, the defensive course which the inhabitants of Upper Canada must be called upon to adopt, is plain and clear.

'· In the meanwhile, however, it is but justice to the American Nation to allow them, notwithstanding our territory has already been invaded by their citizens, the opportunity of nobly vindicating, as I firmly believe they will, the integrity of their Government and institutions; and I have to inform you that with this peaceful object in view, I have communicated with the Governor of the State of New York with whom I have hitherto been on the most friendly terms, as also Her Majesty's Minister at Washington; and awaiting their replies, I have reinforced the gallant Militia of the frontier, by a strong corps of observation, and have made arrangements for a general call upon the Militia, in case their services should unfortunately be required."

The following from Mr. Mackenzie, addressed by him, while in occupation of Navy Island, to the Editor of an American newspaper, "the Watertown Jeffersonian" may throw further light on the subject of the insurrection near Toronto, and will be found interesting:

NAVY ISLAND, U. C.,
14th January, 1838.

"DEAR SIR,—I received yesterday three or four of your latest papers, with a couple of the *U. C. Heralds* of last month, and letter from Messrs. McLeod and Fletcher, dated at Watertown, the 2nd instant. In one of these Heralds, I find a very incorrect narrative of the insurrection at Toronto; and as your journal probably circulates in the same section of country, and there is no likelihood that the Kingston Editor would permit me to correct his errors, I request that you will publish this statement, at your leisure, in the Jeffersonian. I also send for your perusal the Rochester Democrat of last Thursday, with a long article over my signature, entitled, "*Reasons for a Revolution in Canada*," the perusal of which might perhaps be acceptable to the old friends and neighbours of your cruelly persecuted fellow citizen, John G. Parker.

NARRATIVE, &c.

"On the 31st of July last, the Reformers of Toronto responded to the request of their fellow sufferers in Lower Canada, by appointment of ward committees of vigilance, the passage of resolutions of sympathy and co-operation, and the adoption of a declaration of rights and grievances, which only differed from your great declaration of 1776, in that it did not at once proclaim the Province independent, nor enumerate, in all cases, the same complaints.

" The Reformers had taken great pains to inform the British Government of the true state of affairs in Upper Canada, and many believed that Sir Francis Bond Head would do what he could to remove the chief causes of discontent, until the proceedings of the executive previous to and at the last general election of the House of Assembly, convinced them that nothing but a revolution would relieve the country. This opinion

I was confirmed in, by observing that when the Assembly of Lower Canada deferred granting supplies until their wrongs be redressed, the House of Commons of England, by a vote of about 10 to 1, and the Lords unanimously, (Lord Brougham alone dissenting,) resolved that the proceeds of the Revenue raised in that Colony, both by Provincial and British Statutes, should be expended without the consent of the representatives of the people, or the form of law in keeping up a costly foreign government in which the governed had no share.

" In the Declaration of Grievances of the 31st of July the British Government were distinctly given to understand that revolt might be the consequence of i's duplicity. And that declaration was read, considered and approved at 200 public meetings in the country; 150 branch associations, agreeing to its principles, were speedily organized, and Sir F. B. Head was informed through the press, that the officers of these societies *might* be used as captains and lieutenants of companies, for resistance by force, in case a change of his measures did not soon take place.

" The many scenes of violence and outrage which occurred at our public meetings between July and December I need not recount. Let it suffice to say, that we kept up a good understauding with the reformers of Lower Canada; and concluding that arbitrary imprisonments and a declaration of military execution would follow the anticipated outbreaks at Montreal, we resolved to second the Lower Canada movements by others, equally prompt and decisive.

" Some of the members of our branch societies were kept in ignorance of the intended revolt. Others were fully aware of it. Some whose names were attached to no association were leaders in the revolution —other very active republicans took no part. The presses under my control sent for nearly 3000 copies of a periodical filled with reasons for revolt, and about the third week in November it was determined that on Thursday the 7th of December, our forces should secretly assemble at Montgomery's Hotel, 3 miles back of Toronto, between 6 and 10 at night, and proceeding from thence to the city, join our friends there, seize 4000 stand of arms, which had been placed by Sir Francis in the City Hall, take him into custody with his chief advisers, place the garrison in the hands of the liberals, declare the Province free, call a convention together, to frame a suitable constitution, and meantime appoint our friend Dr. ROLPH, provincial administrator of the government. We expected to do all this without shedding blood, well knowing that the vice-regal government was too unpopular to have many real adherents.

"Only in one instance did we forward a notice of the intended movement beyond the limits of the county of York, and to Whitby and some other towns in it no circulars were sent. We never doubted the feeling of the Province. Sir F. admits in "his speech from the throne," that we would have cheerfully submitted the whole matter to a convention of the people.

"Twelve leading reformers in the city and country agreed, one day in November that on Thursday the 7th of December last, between the hours of six and ten in the evening, the friends of freedom in the several townships, led by their captains, would meet at Montgomery's, march to Toronto, seize the arms we so much wanted, dismiss Sir Francis, *and proclaim a Republic.* The details were left entirely to my management; and *an executive in the city* was named to correspond with Mr. Papineau and our other friends below, afford intelligence, aid our efforts, and finally, to join the army at Montgomery's. It was also stipulated that no attempt should be made by that executive to alter the time on which we were to revolt, without consulting with me in the first instance.

"The country was rife for a change, and I employed a fortnight previous to Sunday the 3rd December, in attending secret meetings, assisting in organizing towns and places, and otherwise preparing for the revolution. On that day, I rode from Southville (where I had two private meetings on the Saturday) to Yonge street; and arrived at Mr. Gibson's in the evening. To my astonishment and dismay, I was informed by him, that although I had given the captains of Townships sealed orders for Thursday following, the executive, through him, by a mere verbal message, had ordered out the men beyond the ridges, to attend at Montgomery's with their arms next day, Monday, and that it was probable they were already on the march.

"I instantly sent one of Mr. Gibson's servants to the north countermanding the Monday movement, and begged of Col. Lount not to come down nor in any way to disturb the previous regular arrangement, because neither of the other towns, nor the citizens of Toronto, were in any way prepared for an alteration which if persisted in would surely ruin us. The servant returned on Monday, with a message from Mr. Lount, that it was now too late to stop, that the men were warned, and moving with their guns and pikes, on the march down to Yonge Street, (a distance of 30 to 40 miles on the worst roads in the world,) and that the object of their rising could therefore be no longer concealed.

"I was grieved and so was Mr. Gibson, but we had to make the best of it; accordingly I mounted my horse in the afternoon, rode in towards the city, took five trusty men with me, arrested several gentlemen on suspicion that they were going to Sir Francis with information, placed a guard on Yonge Street, the main northern avenue to Toronto, at Montgomery's, and another guard on a parallel road, and told them to allow none to pass to the city. I then waited some time expecting the executive to arrive, but waited in vain — no one came, not even a message—I was therefore left in entire ignorance of the condition of the capital; and instead of entering Toronto on Thursday, with 4000 or 5000 men, was apparently expected to take it on Monday with 200, wearied after a march of 30 or 40 miles through mud, and in the worst possible humour at finding they had been called from the very extremity of the county, and no one else warned at all.

"About 8 or 9 o'clock I accompanied Captain Anderson of Lloydtown, Mr. Shephard, and two others, on horseback down Yonge street, intending if no one came with tidings from the city, to go there and ascertain how far an attack and seizure of muskets and bayonets we much needed, was practicable. There were warrants out for my apprehension, but I did not mind them much.

"We had not proceeded far when we met Alderman John Powell (now the Mayor,) and Mr. Archibald McDonald, late of Kingston, on horseback, acting as a sort of patrol. I rode up to them, presented a double barrelled pistol, informed them that the democrats had risen in arms, that we wished to prevent information of that fact from reaching the city, and that they would have to go back to Montgomery's as prisoners, where they would be well treated, fed and lodged, and in no way injured in person or in purse—but they must surrender to me their arms. They both assured me they had none, and when I seemed to doubt, repeated the assurance; on which I said, " Well gentlemen, as you are my townsmen and men of honor, I would be ashamed to show that I question your words by ordering you to be searched," and turning to Messrs. Shephard and Anderson, I bade them place the gentlemen in the guard room, and see that they were comfortable, after which I proceeded again towards the city.

"Not many minutes afterwards I was overtaken by

Alderman Powell, riding in great haste. I asked what it meant, and told him he must not proceed except at his peril.. He kept on, I followed and fired over my horse's head, but missed him. He slackened his pace till his horse was beside mine, and while I was expostulating with him, *he suddenly clapt a pistol quite close to my breast*, but the priming flashed in the pan, and thus I was saved from instant death. At this moment McDonald rode back seemingly in great affright, and Powell escaped from me by the side bar, and by a circuitous route reached Toronto. McDonald appeared unable to explain, I therefore sent him back the second time, and being now alone judged it most prudent to return to Montgomery's, on my way to which I encountered the murdered remains of the brave and generous Captain Anthony Anderson, the victim of Powell's baseness. His body was stretched in the road, but life was extinct. The manner of his death was as follows: Shephard and Anderson was accompanying Powell and McDonald on their way to their guard room at Montgomery's, when Powell was observed to slacken his horse's pace a little—by this means he got behind Anderson, and taking a pistol from his pocket, shot him through the back of the neck, so that he fell and died instantly. . Shephard's horse stumbled at the moment, Powell rode off and McDonald followed. Whether Powell is or is not a murderer let the candid reader say. I give the facts. On arriving at Montgomery's, I was told by the guard that Colonel Moodie of the army had attempted to pass the barrier, that they had told him what guard they were, that he had persisted in firing a pistol at them, on which one of the men levelled his rifle and shot him. He died in an hour or two after. I find it stated in many papers that I killed Col. Moodie, although at the time of his death I was several miles distant, as those then present well known. But I fully approved of the conduct of those who shot him.

"Sir Francis Head admits that he was entirely ignorant of our intended movement until awaked out of his bed that night. His informant, I believed to have been Captain Bridgeford. He had the bells set a ringing, took up his abode in the City Hall, delivered out a few rusty guns, made speeches, and was in great trouble. Of all which particulars our executive neither brought nor sent us any account whatever.

"About midnight our numbers increased, and towards morning I proposed to many persons to march to Toronto, join such of the reformers there as were ready, and endeavour to make ourselves master of the garrison and muskets.

"To this it was objected, that I was uninformed of the strength of the fortress, that the other townships had not yet joined the men from the upper country, that we were ignorant of the state of the city, and that gentlemen who had advised and urged on the movements, and even the executive who had ordered this premature Monday rising, stood aloof, and had neither joined us nor communicated with us.

"Next day (Tuesday) we increased in number to 800, of whom very many had no arms, others had rifles, old fowling pieces, Indian guns, pickes, &c. Vast numbers came and went off again, when they found we had neither muskets or bayonets. Had they possessed my feeling in favor of freedom, they would have stood by us even if armed but with pitchforks and broom handles.

"About noon we obtained correct intelligence that with all his exertions, and including the College boys, Sir Francis could hardly rise 150 supporters in town and country; and by one P. M. a flag of truce reached our camp near the city, the messengers being the Honorables Messrs. Rolph and Baldwin, deputed by Sir Francis to ask what would satisfy us. I replied, "Independence;" but sent a verbal message that as we had no confidence in Sir F's word, he would have to send his message in writing, and within one hour. I then turned round to Colonel Lount, and advised him to march the men under his command at once into the city, and take a position near the Lawyer's Hall, and rode westward to Colonel Baldwin's where the bulk of the rebels were, and advised an instant march to Toronto. We had advanced as far as the College Avenue, when another flag of truce arrived, by the same messengers, with a messenger from Sir F. declining to comply with our previous request. We were proceeding to town, when orders from the executive arrived, that we should not then go to Toronto but wait till six o'clock in the evening and then take the city.

"True to the principle on which the compact was made for our rising, the order was obeyed, and at a quarter to six the whole of our forces were near the toll bar, on Yonge street, on our way to the city. I told them that I was certain there could be no difficulty in taking Toronto; that both in town and country the people had stood aloof from Sir Francis: that not 150 men and boys could be got to defend him; that he was alarmed and had sent his family on board a steamer; that 600 reformers were ready to join us in the city, and that all we had to do was to be firm, and with the city would at once go down every vestige of foreign government in Upper Canada.

"It was dark and there might have been an ambush of some sort, I therefore told six riflemen to go ahead of us a quarter of a mile on the one side of the street, inside the fences, and as many more on the other side, and to fire in the direction in which they might see any of our opponents stationed.—When within half a mile of the town, we took prisoners the captain of their artillery, a lawyer, and the Sheriff's horse. Our riflemen ahead saw some 20 or 30 of the enemy in the road, and fired at them, the 20 or 30, or some of them, fired at us, and instantly took to their heels and ran towards the town. Our riflemen were in front, after them the pikemen, then those who had old guns of various kinds, and lastly those who carried only clubs and walking sticks. Colonel Lount was at the the head of the riflemen and he and those in the front rank fired, and instead of stepping to one side to make room for those behind to fire, fell flat on their faces, the next rank fired and did the same thing. I was rather in front when the firing began, and stood in more danger from the rifles of my friends than the muskets of my enemies. I stept to the side of the road and bade them stop firing, and it appeared to me that one of our people who was killed was shot in this way by our own men. Certainly it was not by the enemy.

"Some persons from town, friendly to us, but not very brave, had joined us during the march, and they, unknown to me, told awful stories about the preparations the tories had made in several streets, to fire out of windows at us, protected by feather beds mattrasses, &c. These representations terrified many of the country people, and when they saw the riflemen in front falling down, and heard the firing, they imagined that those who fell were the killed and wounded by the enemy's fire; and took to their heels with a speed and steadiness of purpose that would have baffled pursuit on foot. In a short time not twenty persons were to be found below the toll bar!

"This was almost to much for human patience. The city would have been ours in an hour, probably without firing a shot; hundreds of our friends waited to join us at its entrance; the officials were terror struck; Governor Head had few to rely on; the colony would have followed the city; a convention and a democratic constitution been adopted, and a bloodless change from a contemptible tyranny to freedom accomplished. But 800 ran where no one pursued, and unfortunately ran the wrong way.

"I rode hastily back until I got in the rear of the main body, stopt a number of them, and implored them to return. I explained matters to them, told them to fear nothing, offered with half a dozen more to go between them and all danger, and reminded them that the opportunity of that night would be their last, that the moment it was known in the country that the reformers were timid and fearful without cause, Sir Francis would instantly gain numbers.— But it was of no use. To successive groups I spoke in vain. Neither threats nor coaxing could induce them to go to the city. I tried to find even fifty or forty to go to town. but the reply was, "we will go in the light but not in the dark." Of these many went home that evening, and although about 200 joined us during the night, we were 200 less numerous on Wednesday morning.

"With the steamers in the hands of the Government, the city, 4,000 muskets and bayonets, perhaps 60 experienced military officers, the well-paid officials and their sons and dependants, abundance of ammunition, a park of artillery well served, the garrison, and the aid of all who are prejudiced in favour of Colonial Government, it had become a difficult task for a collection of undisciplined and half armed countrymen, without cannon, scarce of gunpower, not possessed of a single bayonet, not even of guns or pikes for half their numbers, to contend successfully against the enemy for the city; we therefore stood on the defence on Wednesday. Gentlemen of influence who were pledged to join us, and even the executive who commanded us to make the premature and unfortunate movement, neither corresponded with us nor joined us. To explain their conduct was beyond my power. It discouraged many and thinned our ranks.

"On Wednesday forenoon, I took a party with me to Dundas Street, intercepted the great western mail stage and took a number of prisoners, with the stage, mails and driver, up to our camp. The Editors state that money was taken from the mail, which was not the case. But the letters of Mr. Sullivan, President of the Executive Council, Mr. Buchanan, and others, conveyed useful information. We found they expected soon to have strength enough to attack us in the country, and I wrote to the executive in the city to give us timely notice of any such attack. Some of the leading reformers in the city had left it, *but not to join us* — others semed to have lost their energies; neither messenger nor letters reached our camp; the executive was not there. One man on horseback told us we might be attacked on Thursday.

"My chief hope lay in this, that if we were not attacked till Thursday night, vast reinforcements would join us from the outer townships, and that reformers at a distance would march to our aid, the moment they heard that we had struck for self-Government. With this view, I sought to confine the attention of the enemy to the defence of the city, and on Thursday morning selected 40 Riflemen and 20 others to go down and burn the Don Bridge, the eastern approach to Toronto, and the house at its end, to take the Montreal mail stage and mails, and to draw out the forces in that quarter if possible. I also proposed that the rest of our men who had arms, should take the direction to the right or left, or to retreat to a strong position as prudence might dictate. At this moment Col. Van Egmond, a native of Holland, owning 13,000 acres of land in the Huron Tract, a tried patriot, and of great military experience under Napoleon joined us, and one of the Captains desired a council to be held, which was done. Col. V. approved of my plan, a party went off, set fire to the bridge, burnt the house, took the mails, and went through a part of the city unmolested. But the councilling and discussing of my project occasioned a delay of two hours, which proved our ruin, for the enemy having obtained large reinforcements by the steamers from Cobourg, Niagara and Hamilton, resolved to attack us in three divisions, one of them to march up Yonge street, and the others by way about a mile to the right and left of the road. Had our forces started in the morning, the party at the bridge would have interfered with and broken up the enemy's plan of attack, and we would have been in motion near Toronto, ready to retreat to some of the commanding positions in its rear, or to join the riflemen below and there enter the city.

"We were still at the hotel, discussing what was best to be done, when one of the guards told us that the enemy was marching up with music and artillery and within a mile of us. Our people immediately prepared for battle, I rode down towards the enemy, doubting the intelligence, until when within a short distance I saw them with my own eyes. I rode quickly back, asked our men if they were ready to fight a greatly superior force, well armed, and with artillery well served. They were ready and I bade them to go to the woods and do their best. They did so, and never did men fight more courageously. In the face of a heavy fire of grape and cannister, with broadsides of musketry in steady and rapid succession, they stood their ground firmly and killed and wounded a large number of the enemy, but were at length compelled to retreat. In a more favorable position, I have no doubt but they would have beaten the assailants with immense loss. As it was, they had only three killed and three or four wounded. I felt anxious to go to Montgomery's for my portfolio and papers, which were important but it was out of the question, so they fell into the hands of Sir Francis. All my papers previous to the event of that week I had destroyed, except a number of business letters, and these it took my family upwards of an hour and a quarter to burn. But with all my caution, some letters fell into their hands to the injury of others.

"The manly courage with which two hundred farmers, miserably armed, withstood the formidable attack of an enemy 1200 strong, and who had plenty of ammunition, with new muskets and bayonets, artillery, first rate European officers, and the choice of a position of attack, convinces me that discipline, order, obedience and subordination, under competent leaders would enable them speedily to attain a confidence sufficient to foil even the regulars from Europe. About 200 of our friends stood at the tavern during the battle, being unarmed.

"Mr. Fletcher, Col. Van Egmond, myself and others, held a consultation near Hogg's Hollow, and concluded that it would be useless to re-assemble our scattered forces, for that without arms success would be doubtful and I determined to pass over to the United States, and accomplished my purpose in three days, travelled 125 miles, was seen by 2000 persons at least, and with a reward of 4000 dollars as advertised for my head, speedily reached Buffalo.

"It is said we were cruel to our prisoners, 54 in number, but nothing could be further from the truth. They had the largest and best rooms in the hotel, twelve bed chambers were appropriated to their especial use, and bedding, while our volunteers lay in their wearing clothes on the floor of the bar and other apartments— they fared as we fared; and for their amusement I sent them up European, American and Canadian papers, often without reading them myself. Mr. McDonald wrote to his family that he was kindly treated, and it is unjust for any British officers to allow such slanders as have appeared in the newspapers to go uncontradicted.

"As to Sir Francis Head's story of 10,000 men instantly making for the capital to support him, it is a sheer fabrication. If that were true why has law become necessary since to suspend the trial by jury. Why were his family confined for two days on board a steamboat ? Why did he send us a flag of truce on Thursday, when all the force he couid muster was 150 men and boys, out of a population of 20,000 in and near Toronto ? The truth is, that thousands were on their way to join us on Thursday evening, that being the regular time for which the towns had been summoned ; and they, on learning that we were dispersed, made a virtue of necessity, and professed that they had come to aid the tories ! I Sir Francis, in his speech, says they were, " generally speaking, without arms;" and in fact most of them had none to bring. That was the grand difficulty ; and would have been remedied had our movements been delayed till Thursday, as agreed on. Very few militia men in Upper Canada had been entrusted with arms, and of these few the Government had endeavoured; through Captain Magrath and others, to deprive them previous to the outbreak.

" The burning of Mr. Gibson's house, stables and out houses, by order and in the presence of Governor Head, was highly disgraceful to him, and is a stain upon his reputation. Dr. Horne's premises was head quarters to the spies and traitors who infested our camp, and used for the purpose of the enemy, but this was not the case with those of Mr. Gibson. Yet Government destroyed them, and carried off his cattle, horses, grain and property, and used or sold it, and kept the money. The moveables of hundreds of others were taken in the same way. Sir Francis' advisers may live to see this example followed more extensively than they desire. When the Reformers destroyed the house of Dr. Horne, they did not carry off the value of one farthing of his effects. As to Sheriff Jarvis's premises, they would have been burnt but for two reasons —1st, we had no proof that the Sheriff's house was used as a rendezvous for our enemies ; and 2nd, there were sick people in it, whom we did not wish to make war upon.

"About 3,500 persons joined us during the three days on which we were behind Toronto.

" My large and extensive book store, the newest and most valuable printing establishment in Upper Canada, and my bindery, were entered by Alderman Powell and others on Tuesday, the types upset, the work destroyed, and everything on the premises either rendered useless or carried off.

" The American people well understand the state of society in the Canadas, when informed, that Martial Law obtains at Montreal, and that the Habeas Corpus Act is suspended at Toronto, that the opposition Presses are all destroyed or silenced and their Editors expatriated—and that liberty of speech and of the Press is enjoyed in an equal degree in conquered Poland and in conquered Canada.

" There may be errors in the preceding narrative, and if so, I shall be thankful for their correction. My motives having been impeached by some, I cheerfully refer to those of all parties who have had the best means of observing my public and private conduct for many years past. Whether I am deserving of blame as one who recommended a movement which has been unsuccessful, or for lack of discretion or energy so far as concerned in its execution, are questions which, if worth while, the public have the facts before them to determine. Being of opinion that a vast majority of the people of Upper Canada earnestly desire independence, and firmly persuaded that with perseverance they wi'l attain it, I intend to continue to devote my very humble efforts towards hastening the happy time when colonial vassalage will be exchanged for freedom and peace.

"The Canadian people owe to their American brethern a large debt of gratitude, and will, I trust, ever remember the kindness and sympathy extended towards them. The freemen of this frontier have lost sight of the political and party divisions of the hour, and enthusiastically cheered our aspirations for liberty, indulging a lively hope that heaven would speedily bless their efforts, and hasten the day in which they will be enabled to burst the bonds of ages of tyranny, attain liberal political institutions, and become prosperous and free.

I am, dear Sir,
Your faithful servant,
W. L. MACKENZIE.

The foregoing, with the following message from Sir. F. B. Head to the Legislature of Upper Canada, and accompanying Despatches to the British Minister at Washington, will give the reader a general view of matters in that Province.

Lieutenant Governor Head to Mr. Fox.

GOVERNMENT HOUSE,
TORONTO, Upper Canada, Dec, 23, 1837.

"SIR,—It is my duty to lose no time in apprizing your Excellency that the peace and security of this Province are at this moment threatened, and that its territory is actually invaded by a large band of American citizens from Buffalo, who have taken up arms and established themselves in a hostile manner on Navy Island, in the Niagara river, and within the territory of Upper Canada.

" Your Excellency has, no doubt, learned from the public papers that, in consequence of the insurrection unhappily commenced in Lower Canada, but which, I have reason to believe, is now effectually suppresed, an attempt, as rash and hopeless as it was wicked, was lately made by three or four hundred persons in this vicinity, to involve this Province in the miseries of civil war. In concert with this movement, an endeavour was also made to excite the people in another district, to take up arms against this Government. Both these attempts were promptly and effectually suppressed by the local militia of this Province, unaided by any military force. Most of the deluded persons who were engaged in this rash and criminal enterprise have surrendered themselves or been taken: but the principal leader, William Lyon Mackenzie, and some of the most active of his followers, succeeded with great difficulty, in making their escape to the adjoining state of New York.

"It was soon reported to me that at Buffalo, to which place these traitors fled, strong symptoms were shown by numbers of American citizens to aid them with men and arms, and to supply them with other necessaries, in order to make a hostile invasion of this Province.

"That the public authorities in Buffalo and the most respectable portion of the inhabitants would discountenance such proceedings I had no doubt, and their conduct since has justified that expectation: but as it was doubtful how far they might be able promptly to control this ebullition of hostile feeling towards a nation with which the United States holds the strictest relations of amity and peace, I immediately addressed a letter to His Excellency Governor Marcy, at Albany, of which a copy is herewith sent.

"No reply to this has yet reached me, nor do I know what steps, if any, have been taken on the part of the American Government at Buffalo to repress this hostile rising of their people.

"Since the letter was written, Mackenzie has been joined by some hundreds of American citizens from Buffalo and the adjoining villages, and they have established themselves on Navy Island, as I have before mentioned, with artillery and arms procured in the United States.

"The paper printed at Buffalo, which I send you, will show you the spirit in which this movement is urged forward.

"I am, of course, taking all possible means to repel invasion and insult, and I believe that in a few days a considerable military force will be at hand to sustain our gallant militia in this extraordinary and unlooked for conflict.

"I need not remark to Your Excellency how unfair and unjust it is that a rebellion, which, within this Province, was so insignificant that it was instantly crushed by the civil inhabitants of the country, should be renewed and rendered formidable by the direct and active encouragement of the American people; and that during the existence, not merely of peace, but of the most friendly relations between Great Britain and the Government of the United States, the peaceful population of this Province should be threatened with devastation and plunder, and all the miseries of civil war, by the unjustifiable interference of American citizens.

"Though inhabiting a remote portion of the British dominions, the people of Upper Canada feel that they may rest assured of being ultimately protected by the whole force of the Empire, if it be necessary.

"They are conscious, also, that they deserve kinder offices at the hands of the American people, and I appeal to you in their name, and as the Representative of their Sovereign, to urge upon the Government of the United States the immediate exertion of military force to suppress a movement of their people so insulting and injurious to a neighboring nation, and which, whatever temporary calamity it may inflict, must inevitably, unless promptly checked, lead to a national war, in which any wrongs committed against the people of this colony will, under the protection of a just Providence, be amply redressed,

"I beg Your Excellency will not fail to assure the American Government of my sincere conviction that the facts of which I complain will certainly meet with their most unqualified reprobation.

"I have the honor to be, Sir, Your Excellency's most obedient humble servent,

F. B. HEAD,
Lieutenant Governor.

TORONTO, 12th January, 1838.
F. B. HEAD.

"The Lieutenant Governor transmits to the Legislative Council, the reports and other information which he is possessed of respecting the capture and destruction of a piratical Steamboat, called the Caroline, while engaged in the service of a lawless band avowedly associated for the purpose of plunder; together with a copy of a communication which has been recently made upon the subject to His Excellency, the Minister of Her Britannic Majesty at Washington; and also copies of the correspondence respecting the occupation of Navy Island; and respecting artillery and arms belonging to the Government of the State of New York, and in possession of a piratical force assembled on Navy Island.

"The Lieutenant Governor also transmits to the Legislative Council a copy of another communication made by him to Her Britannic Majesty's Minister at Washington, immediately upon the occupation of Navy Island to which he has not yet received an answer, and he has satisfaction in adding, that no reason has been given him to doubt, that the intentions and inclinations of the Government of the United States towards the United Kingdom of Great Britain and Ireland are perfectly pacific; and it is of course out of the question that any Government can countenance in its subjects such conduct as has been recently pursued by some of the citizens of the United States towards the people of this Province.

Copy of a Despatch from His Excellency Sir Franci B. Head, Bart., Lieut. Governor of Upper Canada, to His Excellency Henry S. Fox, Her Majesty's Minister at Washington.

TORONTO, *Upper Canada*,
8th, January, 1838.

"SIR,—I have the honor to enclose to you the copy of a special message, sent by His Excellency Governor Marcy, to the Legislature of the State of New York, in relation to a matter on which Your Excellency will desire the earliest and most authentic information. The message only reached this place yesterday, and I lose no time in communicating with Your Excellency on the subject.

"The Governor of the State of New York complains of the cutting out and burning of the Steamboat Caroline, by order of Col. McNab, commanding Her Majesty's Forces at Chippewa, in the Province of Upper Canada, and of the destruction of the lives of some American citizens, who were on board the boat at the time she was attacked. The act complained of was done under the following circumstances:—

"In Upper Canada, which contains a population of 450,000 souls, the most perfect tranquility prevailed up to the 4th day of December last, although in the adjoining Province of Lower Canada, many of the French Canadian inhabitants had been in open rebellion against the Government for about a month preceding.

"At no time since the treaty of peace with the United States, in 1815, had Upper Canada been more undisturbed. The real cause of the insurrection in Lower Canada, namely: the national antipathy of the French inhabitants, did not in any degree apply in the Upper Province, whose population like the British and American inhabitants of Lower Canada, were wholly opposed to the revolt, and anxious to render every service in their power in support of the Queen's authority. It had been reported to the Government, some time before the 4th of December, that in a remote portion of the Home Districts, a number of persons occasionally met and drilled, with arms, under leaders known to be disaffected, but it was not believed by the Government that any thing more could be intended than to make a show of threatened revolt, in order to create a diversion in favor of the rebels in Lower Canada. The feeling of loyalty throughout this Province was known to be so prevalent and decided, that it was not thought unsafe to forbear, for the time at least, to take any notice of the proceedings of this party.

" On the night of the 4th December, the inhabitants of the City of Toronto were alarmed by the intelligence that about five hundred persons armed with rifles, were approaching the City—that they had murdered a gentleman of great respectability in the highway, and had made several persons prisoners. The inhabitants rushed immediately to arms—there were no soldiers in the Province, and no militia had been called out. The Home District, from which this party of armed men came, contains 60,000 inhabitants —the City of Toronto 10,000. In a few hours a respectable force, although undisciplined, was collected and armed in self-defence, and awaited the threatened attack. It seems now to admit of no doubt, that if they had at once advanced against the insurgents, they would have met with no formidable resistance, but it was thought more prudent to wait until a sufficient force could be collected, to put the success of an attack beyond question. In the meantime, people poured in from all quarters to oppose the insurgents, who obtained no increase of numbers, but on the contrary, were deserted by many of their body in consequence of the acts of devastation and plunder into which their leader had forced them.

" On the 7th of December, an overwelming force of militia went against them, and dispersed them without losing a man—taking many prisoners, who were instantly released by my order, and suffered to depart to their homes—the rest, with their leaders, fled—some have since rendered themselves to justice—many have been taken, and some have escaped from the Province.

" It was reported about this time, that the District of London, a similar disposition to rise had been observed, and in consequence, a militia force of about 400 men was sent into that District, where it was speedily joined by three times as many of the inhabitants of the District, who assembled voluntarily and came to their aid with the greatest alacrity. It was discovered that about three hundred persons under Doctor Duncombe, an American by birth, were assembled with arms: but before the militia could reach them they dispersed themselves and fled—of these, by far the greater number came in immediately and submitted themselves to the Government, declaring that they had been misled and deceived, and prayed for forgiveness.

" In about a week, perfect tranquility was restored and from that moment not a man has been seen in arms against the Government in any part of the Province, with the exception of the hostile aggression upon Navy Island, which I shall presently notice—nor has there been the slightest resistance offered to the execution of legal process, in a single instance.

" After the dispersion of the armed insurgents, near Toronto, Mr. Mackenzie, their leader, escaped in disguise to the Niagara River, and crossed over to Buffalo. Reports had been spread there, and elsewhere along the American frontier, that Toronto had been burnt, and that the rebels were completely successful; but the falsehood of these absurd rumours was well known before Mackenzie arrived on the American side. It was known also that the ridiculous attempt of four hundred men to revolutionise a country containing nearly half a million of inhabitants had been put down by the people instantly and decidedly, without the loss of a man.

"Nevertheless, a number of American citizens in Buffalo and other towns on the frontier of the State of New York, enlisted as Soldiers, with the avowed object of invading Canada, and establishing a Provisional Government. Public Meetings were held to forward this design of invading a country with which the United States were at peace. Volunteers were called for, and arms, ammunition and provisions, were supplied by contributions openly made. All this was in direct and flagrant violation of the express laws of the United States, as well as of the law of Nations.

"The civil authority of Buffalo offered some slight show of resistance to the movement, being urged to interpose by many of the most respectable citizens, but no real impediment was offered; and on the 13th of December, some hundreds of the citizens of the State of New York, as an armed body, under the command of Mr. Van Rensselaer, an American citizen, openly invaded and took possession of Navy Island, a part of Upper Canada, situate in the River Niagara. Not believing that such an outrage would really be committed, no force whatever was assembled at the time to counteract this hostile movement.

"In a very short time this lawless band obtained from the Arsenals of the State of New York, clandestinely, as it is said, several pieces of artillery, and other arms, which, in broad day light were openly transported to Navy Island, without resistance from the American authorities. The people of Buffalo and of the adjacent country continued to supply them with stores of various kinds, and additional men enlisted in their ranks. In a few days their force was variously stated from five to fifteen hundred of whom a small portion were rebels, who had fled from Upper Canada. They began to entrench themselves, and threatened that they would, in a short time, make a landing on the Canadian side of the Niagara River.

"To prevent this and keep them in check, a body of militia was hastily collected and stationed on the frontier, under the command of Colonel Cameron, Assistant Adjt. General of Militia, who was succeeded in this command by Col. McNab, the Speaker of the House of Assembly, an officer whose humanity and discretion, as well as his activity, have been proved by his conduct, in putting down the insurrection in the London District; and have been acknowledged in warm terms of gratidute by the misguided persons who had surrendered themselves into his hands. He received orders to act on the defensive only, and to be careful not to do any act which the American Government could justly complain of as a breach of neutrality.

"An official statement of the unfriendly proceedings at Buffalo was without delay, (on the 13th December,) made by me to His Excellency the Governor of the State of New York, and after this open invasion of our territory, and when it became evident that nothing was effected at Buffalo for preventing the violation of neutrality, a special Messenger was sent to Your Excellency at Washington, to urge your interpósition in the matter. Sufficient time has not yet elapsed to admit of his return. Soon after his departure, this band of outlaws on Navy Island—acting in defiance of the laws and Government of both countries—opened a fire from several pieces of ordinance upon this shore, which in this part is thickly settled: the distance from the island being about six hundred yards, and in sight of the populous village of Chippewa. They put several balls (six pound shot) through a house, in which a party of Militia-men were quartered, and which is the dwelling-house of Capt, Usher, a respectable inhabitant. They killed a horse on which a man at the time was riding, but happily did no further mischief, though they fired also repeatedly with cannon and musquetry

G

upon our boats. They continued daily to render their position more formidable—receiving constant supplies of men and stores from the State of New York, which were chiefly embarked at a landing place on the American main shore, called Fort Schlosser, nearly opposite to Navy Island. This place was once, I believe, a military position before the conquest of Canada from the French; but there is now neither Fort nor Village there, but merely a single house, occupied as a tavern, and a wharf in front of it, to which boats and vessels are moored. The tavern had been, during these lawless proceedings, a rendezvous for the band, who cannot be called by any name more appropriate than pirates: and was in fact, openly and notoriously resorted to as their head quarters, on the main land, and is so to this time. On the 28th December, positive information was given to Col. McNab, by persons from Buffalo, that a small steamboat called the Caroline, of about fifty tons burthen, had been hired by the pirates, who called themselves "Patriots," and was to be employed in carrying down cannon and other stores, and in transporting men and any thing else that might be required, between Fort Schlosser and Navy Island.

"He resolved if she came down, and engaged in this service, to take or destroy her. She did come down, agreeably to the information he received. She transported a piece of artillery and other stores to the Island, and made repeated passages during the day between the Island and the main shore. In the night he sent a party of militia, in boats, with orders to take or destroy her. They proceeded to execute their order. They found the Caroline moored to the wharf, opposite the Inn, at Fort Schlosser. In the Inn there was a guard of armed men to protect her, part of the pirate force, or acting in their support. On her deck there was an armed party, and a sentinel who demanded the countersign. Thus identified as she was with the force, which, in defiance of the law of nations, and every principle of natural justice, had invaded Upper Canada, and made war upon its unoffending inhabitants, she was boarded—and after a resistance, in which some desperate wounds were inflicted upon the assailants, she was carried.

"If any peaceable citizens of the United States perished in the conflict, it was and is unknown to the captors: and it was and is equally unknown to them whether any such were there. Before this vessel was thus taken, not a gun had been fired by the force under the orders of Colonel McNab, even upon this gang of pirates—much less upon any peaceable citizen of the United States. It must, therefore, have been a consciousness of the guilty service she was engaged in that led those who were employing her to think an armed guard necessary for her defence. Peaceable citizens of the United States were not likely to be found in a vessel so employed at such a place, and in such a juncture: and if there were there, their presence, especially unknown as it was to the captors, could not prevent, in law or reason, this necessary act of self-defence. Fifteen days had elapsed since the invasion of Upper Canada by a force enlisted, armed and equipped, openly in the State of New York. The country where this outrage upon the law of nations was committed, is populous. Buffalo alone contains 15,000 inhabitants.

The public authorities, it is true, gave no countenance to these flagrant acts, but they did not prevent them, or in the slightest degree obstruct them, further than by issuing Proclamations, which were disregarded. Perhaps they could not, but in this case, the insult and injury to the inhabitants of Canada were the same, and their right to defend themselves equally unquestionable.

"No wanton injury was committed by the party who gallantly effected this service. They loosed the vessel from the wharf, and finding they could not tow her against the rapid current of the Niagara, they abandoned the effort to secure her, set her on fire, and let her drift down the stream.

"The prisoners taken were a man who, it will be seen by the documents accompanying this despatch, avowed himself to be a subject of Her Majesty, inhabiting Upper Canada, who had lately been traitorously in arms in that Province, and having fled to the United States was on board for the purpose of going to the camp at Navy Island, and a boy, who being born in Lower Canada, was probably residing in the United States, and who, being afraid to land from the boat in consequence of the firing kept up by the guard on shore, was placed in one of the boats under Captain Drew, and taken over to our side, from whence he was sent home the next day, by the Falls Ferry, with money given him to bear his expenses.

"I send with this letter—1st. A copy of my first communication to His Excellency Governor Marcy, to which no reply has reached me.

"2nd. The official reports, correspondence and Militia General Order, respecting the destruction of the Caroline, with other documents.

"3rd. The correspondence between Commissary General Arcularius, of the State of New York, respecting the Artillery belonging to the Government of the State of New York, which has been and still is used in making war upon this Province.

"4th. Other correspondence arising out of the state of things on the Niagara frontier.

5th. The special message of Governor Marcy.

"It will be seen from these documents that a high officer of the Government of the State of New York, has been sent by His Excellency the Governor, for the express purpose of regaining possession of the artillery of that State, which is now employed in hostile aggression upon this portion of Her Majesty's dominions, and that being aided and favored as he acknowledges by the most friendly co-operations which the Commanding Officer of Her Majesty's forces could give him, he has been successfully defied by this Army of American citizens, and has abandoned the object of his mission in despair.

"It can hardly fail to be also observed by Your Excellency, that in the course of this negociation between Mr. Van Renssellaer and the Commissary General of the State of New York, this individual, Mr. Van Renssellaer, has not hesitated to place himself within the immediate jurisdiction of the Government whose laws he had violated, and in direct personal communication with the officer of that Government, and has nevertheless, been allowed to return unmolested, to continue in command of American citizens engaged in open hostilities against Great Britain.

" The exact position then of affairs on the frontier may be thus described:—

" An army of American citizens joined to a very few traitors from Upper Canada, and under the command of a subject of the United States, has been raised and equipped in the State of New York, against the laws of the United States and the treaties now subsisting, and are using artillery plundered from the arsensals of the State of New York, in carrying on this piratical warfare against a friendly country.

" The officers and government of the United States, and of the State of New York, have attempted to arrest these proceedings, and to control their citizens but they have failed. Although the piratical assemblage are thus defying the civil authorities of both countries, Upper Canada alone is the object of their hostilities. The Government of the United States has failed to enforce its authority by any means, civil or military, and the single question, if it be a question, is whether Upper Canada was bound to refrain from necessary acts of self-defence against a people whom their own Government either could not, or would not control.

loss of life, their conduct would not have been the less justifiable. It is almost too obvious an observation to make, that if any army of American citizens had taken up a position on their side of the Niagara River, at a point where no Island intervened, and had begun battering the houses and people on our shore, and if this shameful aggression, with guns taken from the United States arsenals, had continued for weeks, without any effectual interposition on the part of the American Government, Her Majesty's subjects would have had an unquestionable right to attack the batteries, and disperse the lawless band which carried on this disgraceful warfare—and of course a right to attack any boat or vessel employed in their service, and carrying their guns and men. To call so necessary an act of self-defence a violation of neutrality, would of course be absurd—whatever insult or injury it would occasion to American territory must be ascribed to that portion of their own citizens who were in arms against their authority, and committing outrage on their unoffending neighbours. This being so, it can surely make no difference favorable to the United States, that the army of American citizens did, in this instance, first commit the gross wrong of taking forcible possession of British ground, that they might fire more effectually from thence—It was merely taking two steps in committing the injury instead of one.

"Your Excellency, I dare say, has not failed to observe that at a Criminal Court in the State of New York, an indictment has been found for murder against Captain Drew, and others who are supposed (but some of them erroneously) to have been present at the capture of the Caroline. I cannot but believe that the American Government will feel it to be due no less to their own character than to their relations with Great Britain, to interest themselves in arresting any such proceeding. The act was done by public authority, in the prosecution of a warfare to which this Province was driven by the outrageous aggressions of American citizens. The British Nation is to answer for it, and not individuals zealously acting in her service.

"Your Excellency will have learnt from various channels, the occurrences which have taken place on our western frontier, opposite the State of Michigan. There a large force, stated in the newspapers of Detriot not to be less than 1,000 or 1,200 in number, with arms and artillery taken from one or more Public Arsenals, attempted to invade this Province—and did, indeed, actually possess themselves of the Island of Bois Blanc, in the River Detriot. With an armed schooner they commenced battering the town of Amherstburgh, and intended on the next day to have made a descent on the main land, but their further progress was arrested by the gallant conduct of some militia volunteers, who attacked and boarded the schooner, and took several prisoners, together with the guns, arms and military stores on board of her. A considerable military force is now stationed on our wastern frontier.

"I send you the Proclamations issued by Mr. Sutherland, an American citizen, who styled himself General of the 2nd Division of the Patriot Army, Van Rensellaer band of ruffians, I suppose forming the first. These will shew you the nature and object of the expeditions to whose attacks the people of Upper Canada have been exposed.

"Among the prisoners taken on this last occasion were now several American citizens.

"I need scarcely state to you, that the necessity of being armed at all points along our extensive frontier, has occasioned an enormous expenditure to the British Government. The American, I perceive, has called on Congress to provide $600,000 for the pay and outfit of a force necessary to keep down the excitements on the Niagara frontier alone. You will readily understand, therefore, how much greater must be the expense which the Government is put to by the preparations necessary to meet attacks at various points. The hostile spirit manifested in Michigan, appeared likely to be attended with more serious consequences than the movements along the Niagara frontier.

"I send Your Excellency a copy of some correspondence which has taken place since Major General Scott arrived at Buffalo. Fortunately the pirates have dispersed without any thing farther occurring that can give rise to controversy, and I have no doubt their removal was hastened by the active measures at length taken by the American Government for preventing their receiving supplies of arms and provisions. It would give me pleasure if I could add, that in the conduct of the American militia stationed on Grand Island, or in the construction which the officers of the American Government seemed disposed to put upon the relative rights of the two Countries, under the extraordinary circumstances in which they were placed, I have discovered satisfactory proof of a spirit calculated to contribute to the restoration of permanent tranquillity.

"When a people has been insulted and aggrieved as the people of Upper Canada have been, it is not to be supposed that they can feel it necessary to perplex themselves with researches into books upon the Laws of Nations—they will follow a more unerring guide in obeying the irresistible natural instinct of self-preservation. By the cannonading from Navy Island three inhabitants of this Province have been killed—there is no extenuating circumstance which can make the offence less than murder; and if it can be claimsd as a right on this, or upon other occasions, that the perpetrators shall be allowed to escape with impunity into the country from whence they came in an armed body, to commit these flagitious outrages—if it be maintained that to cross the line of division through the waters of the Niagara to destroy them, or to cut off their resources, is a violation of American neutrality, then it can only follow, that when the American people are suffered to commit such gross outrages upon the Province of Upper Canada, they must bring upon themselves the consequences of a public war, for unquestionably the right of self-defence will be experienced—it is not in the nature of things that it should be forborne.

"I am upon the point of being succeeded in the Government of Upper Canada by Col. Sir George Arthur; and I cannot depart from the Province without offering to Your Excellency on the part of its inhabitants, my most grateful thanks for your prompt and able interposition to protect them from foreign aggression, I have been extremely gratified by the earnest solicitude shown by Your Excellency to discharge your delicate and important duties satisfactorily and with effect. I can assure Your Excellency, that the people of Upper Canada feel deeply how much they are indebted to you, as the Minister of their Sovereign, for your conduct on this anxious and important occasion.

"I have the honor to be, with the highest consideration, Your Excellency's most obedient humble servant.

     Signed "F. B. HEAD.
" His Excellency Henry S. Fox,
   "&c., &c., Washington"

During these occurrences in Upper Canada a multitude of loyal addresses from various parts of the Province were presented to Sir Francis B. Head, tendering aid to the Government, if needed, to put down the troubles. Among them was one from the loyal and true hearted Highlanders of Lochiel in

excitements on the Niagara frontier alone. You will readily understand, therefore, how much greater must be the expense which the Government is put to by the preparations necessary to meet attacks at various points. The hostile spirit manifested in Michigan, appeared likely to be attended with more serious consequences than the movements along the Niagara frontier.

"I send Your Excellency a copy of some correspondence which has taken place since Major General Scott arrived at Buffalo. Fortunately the pirates have dispersed without any thing farther occurring that can give rise to controversy, and I have no doubt their removal was hastened by the active measures at length taken by the American Government for preventing their receiving supplies of arms and provisions. It would give me pleasure if I could add, that in the conduct of the American militia stationed on Grand Island, or in the construction which the officers of the American Government seemed disposed to put upon the relative rights of the two Countries, under the extraordinary circumstances in which they were placed, I have discovered satisfactory proof of a spirit calculated to contribute to the restoration of permanent tranquillity.

"When a people has been insulted and aggrieved as the people of Upper Canada have been, it is not to be supposed that they can feel it necessary to perplex themselves with researches into books upon the Laws of Nations—they will follow a more unerring guide in obeying the irresistible natural instinct of self-preservation. By the cannonading from Navy Island three inhabitants of this Province have been killed—there is no extenuating circumstance which can make the offence less than murder; and if it can be claimed as a right on this, or upon other occasions, that the perpetrators shall be allowed to escape with impunity into the country from whence they came in an armed body, to commit these flagitious outrages—if it be maintained that to cross the line of division through the waters of the Niagara to destroy them, or to cut off their resources, is a violation of American neutrality, then it can only follow, that when the American people are suffered to commit such gross outrages upon the Province of Upper Canada, they must bring upon themselves the consequences of a public war, for unquestionably the right of self-defence will be experienced—it is not in the nature of things that it should be forborne.

"I am upon the point of being succeeded in the Government of Upper Canada by Col. Sir George Arthur; and I cannot depart from the Province without offering to Your Excellency on the part of its inhabitants, my most grateful thanks for your prompt and able interposition to protect them from foreign aggression, I have been extremely gratified by the earnest solicitude shown by Your Excellency to discharge your delicate and important duties satisfactorily and with effect. I can assure Your Excellency, that the people of Upper Canada feel deeply how much they are indebted to you, as the Minister of their Sovereign, for your conduct on this anxious and important occasion.

"I have the honor to be, with the highest consideration, Your Excellency's most obedient humble servant.

Signed "F. B. HEAD.
" His Excellency Henry S. Fox,
"&c., &c., Washington"

During these occurrences in Upper Canada a multitude of loyal addresses from various parts of the Province were presented to Sir Francis B. Head, tendering aid to the Government, if needed, to put down the troubles. Among them was one from the loyal and true hearted Highlanders of Lochiel in

Glengary, expressing their abhorrence of the late foul and unnatural rebellion; and declaring "by the memory of the past—by the hope of the future—by all that is worthy of ourselves, and of being transmitted down to posterity," that they were all ready to a man, and at a moment's warning, to march against the rebels of their adopted Country. The following is the characteristic reply of His Excellency to this spirit stirring address:

Brave and loyal Highlanders of Lochiel.

"The few remaining rebels, who dared to insult the authorities of this noble portion of the British Empire, have absconded from its dominions, and the only enemies we have now to encounter are a band of pirates, who, under American leaders, have invaded our territory, for the avowed object of plundering our lands, and subverting our revered institutions.

"I feel confident, if this unprincipled aggression should continue, that, in one body, you will advance to exterminate the perfidious invaders of our liberties or, like Highlanders, perish.

> "With your backs to the field,
> And your feet to the foe,
> And leaving in battle
> No blot on your name,
> Look proudly to Heaven
> From the death-bed of fame!"

"Government House, January 13th. 1838."

CHAPTER XLIII.

Arrival of the Earl of Durham—Addresses to him—His first measures—Treatment of the political detenus—Negociation with Wolfred Nelson and seven others—His Excellency's ordinance for their transportation to Bermuda and conveyance thither—Opinions in the House of Lords of the ordinance—Visits Upper Canada—Congress of Governors at Quebec—Proceedings in the Imperial Parliament in consequence of the ordinance—Trial at Montreal of Nicholas and others for the murder of Chartrand—The Earl of Durham issues a proclamation notifying his intention and the cause of his retiring from the Government—Addresses to him before his departure—Promotes Mr. (subsequently Sir) James Stuart to the bench—Liberal appropriation of his salary Letter from the political exiles at Bermuda.

The arrival of the Earl of Durham, at Quebec, on the 27th May, in H. M. S. Hastings, from England, whence he had sailed on the 24th of April, relieved Sir John Colborne of the Government. His Lordship did not disembark, however, until the 29th: when landing at the Queen's wharf, he was received by Sir John Colborne, accompanied by the whole of the Military Staff and heads of Departments, and a vast concourse of the inhabitants, who repeatedly cheered His Lordship as he proceeded thence to the Castle. Here the Executive Council and principal Officers of the Civil Government were in attendance, and he immediately took the oath of office, issuing instantly after it the following Proclamation :—

" The Queen having been graciously pleased to entrust to me the Government of British North America, I have this day assumed the Administration of affairs.*

---

* " VICTORIA, by the GRACE OF GOD, of the United Kingdom of Great Britain and Ireland, Queen, Defender of the Faith; To our Right Trusty and Right well beloved Cousin and Councillor JOHN GEORGE EARL of DURHAM, Knight

" In the execution of this important duty, I rely with confidence on the cordial support of all Her Majesty's subjects as the best means of enabling me to bring every question affecting their welfare to a successful issue, especially such as may come under my cognizance as Her Majesty's High Commissioner.

Grand Cross of the Most Noble Order of the Bath, GREETING :—WHEREAS by five several Commissions under the Great Seal of our United Kingdom of Great Britain and Ireland, We have constituted and appointed You, the said JOHN GEORGE EARL OF DURHAM, to be Our Captain General and Governor in Chief in and over each of our Provinces of Lower Canada, Upper Canada, Nova Scotia, New Brunswick and in and over Our island of Prince Edward, in North America. And we have by the said several Commissions made provision for the Administration of the Government of Our said Provinces, and of the said Island respectively, in the event of your absence, by authorizing the respective Lieutenant Governors or Administrators of the Governments of the said Provinces and of the said Island respectively, in that contingency, to exercise the Powers of the said Commissions respectively granted to You; and Whereas, We have by a Commission under the Great Seal of Our said United Kingdom of Great Britain and Ireland, constituted and appointed Our Trusty and well beloved HENRY PRESCOTT Esquire, Captain in Our Royal Navy, to be Our Governor and Commander in Chief in and over Our Is land of Newfoundland and its dependencies; And Whereas, there are at present certain weighty affairs to be adjusted in the said Provinces of Upper and Lower Canada ; now know you that We, reposing especial trust and confidence in the prudence, courage and loyalty of You, the said JOHN GEORGE EARL OF DURHAM, have of Our especial Grace, certain knowledge and more motion, thought fit to constitute and appoint and do hereby constitute and appoint You, the said JOHN GEORGE EARL DURHAM, to be our High Commissioner, for the adjustment of certain important Questions, defending in the said Provinces of Lower and Upper Canada, respecting the form and future Government of the said Provinces; And we do hereby give and grant unto You, the said JOHN GEORGE EARL OF DURHAM, as such High Commissioner as aforesaid, full power and authority in our name and on our behalf, by all lawful ways and means, to enquire into and as far as may be possible to adjust all questions depending in the said Provinces of Lower or Upper Canada, or either of

"The honest and conscientious advocate of Reform and of the amelioration of defective Institutions will, receive from me, without distinction of party, races, or politics, that assistance and encouragement which their patrotism has a right to command, from all who desire to strengthen and consolidate the connexion between the Parent State and these important Colonies; but the disturbers of the public peace, the violation of the law, the enemies of the Crown and of the British Empire will find in me an uncompromising opponent, determined to put in force against them all the powers, civil and military, with which I have been invested.

"In one Province the most deplorable events have rendered the suspension of its representative constitution, unhappily, a matter of necessity; and the supreme power has devolved on me.

"The great responsibility which is hereby imposed on me, and the arduous nature of the functions which

---

them, respecting the form and Administration of the Civil Government thereof respectively. And whereas, with a view to the adjustment of such Questions, we have deemed it expedient to invest You with the further powers hereinafter mentioned. Now know You, that we do in like manner constitute and appoint You, the said JOHN G. EARL OF DURHAM, to be our Governor General of all the said Provinces on the Continent of North America and of the said Islands of Prince Edward and Newfoundland; And we do hereby require and command all our Officers, Civil and Military, and all other inhabitants of our said Provinces and of our said Islands respectively, to be obedient, aiding and assisting, unto You the said JOHN GEORGE EARL OF DURHAM, in the execution of this our Commission and the several powers and authorities herein contained; Provided nevertheless, and we do hereby declare our pleasure to be, that in the execution of the powers hereby vested in You the said JOHN GEORGE EARL OF DURHAM, You do in all things conform to such instructions as may, from time to time, be addressed to You for guidance by us, under our Sign Manual, and Signet, or by our Order in our Privy Council, or through one of our Principal Secretaries of State. Provided also, and we do

I have to discharge, will naturally make me most anxious to hasten the arrival of that period when the Executive power shall again be surrounded by all the constitutional checks of free, liberal and British institutions.

"In you—the people of British America—on your conduct and on the extent of your co-operation with me, will mainly depend whether that event shall be delayed or immediate. I therefore invite from you the most free, unreserved communications. I beg you to consider me as a friend and arbitrator—ready at all times to listen to your wishes, complaints, and grievances, and fully determined to act with the strictest impartiality.

"If you, on your side, will abjure all party, and sectarian animosities, and unite with me in the blessed work of peace and harmony, I feel assured that I can lay the foundations of such a system of Government; as will protect the rights and interests of all classes—allay all dissensions—and permanently establish, under Divine Providence, the wealth, great-

---

hereby declare our pleasure to be, that nothing herein contained shall extend or be constructed to extend to revoke or to abrogate the said Commission under the Great Seal of our said United Kingdom of Great Britain and Ireland, appointing the said HENRY PRESCOTT, Governor and Commander in Chief of our said Island of Newfoundland, and its dependencies as aforesaid. And we do hereby declare, ordain and appoint, that You, the said JOHN GEORGE EARL OF DURHAM, shall and may hold, execute and enjoy the said offices of High Commissioner and Governor General of our said Provinces, on the Continent of North America, and of the said Islands of Prince Edward and Newfoundland as aforesaid, together with all and singular the powers and authorities hereby granted unto You for and during our will and pleasure. In WITNESS WHEREOF, we have caused these our letters to be made Patent. WITNESS ourself, at Westminster, the thirty-first day of March, in the first year of our Reign.

"BY WRIT OF PRIVY SEAL."

ness and prosperity, of which such inexhaustible elements are to be found in these fertile countries.

"Given under my Hand and Seal at Arms at the Castle of St. Lewis, in the city of Quebec, in the said Province of Lower Canada, the twenty-ninth day of May, in the year of our Lord one thousand eight hundred and thirty eight, and in the first year of Her Majesty's Reign.

"By command,
"CHARLES BULLER,
Chief Secretary."

Considerable reinforcements to the army had reached Canada from England previous to his Lordship's arrival. Her Majesty's ships Edinburgh, (74,) Inconstant Frigate, and Troop Ships Apollo and Athol, had arrived in Quebec on the 9th May, bringing the 2nd battalion Grenadier Guards, and 2nd battalion Coldstream Guards, the whole under the command of Major General Sir James McDonnell. Shortly after the arrival of the Hastings, came the Malabar 74, the Pique 46, the Andromache 28, and finally the Hercules 74, and the Dee and Medea, war steamers, all bringing detachments more or less to the several regiments in Canada, and rendering the port of Quebec more lively and interesting than usual by the presence of so many ships of war, and the stir and improvement in business they occasioned.

The appointments mentioned below were immediately after His Lordship's arrival publicly notified.*

---

* " His Excellency the GOVERNOR GENERAL has been pleased to make the following appointments :—

" To be Secretary to the General Commission.

"¶CHARLES BULLER, Esquire, Member of the Imperial Parliament of Great Britain and Ireland :—and

THOMAS EDWARD MICHAEL TURTON, Esquire, Barrister at Law.

To be Military Secretary and Principal Aide-de-Camp, Colonel GEORGE COUPER, K. H.

"One of the first steps"—observes the Quebec Gazette—" of His Excellency after having taken the oaths of office was to enquire for the Attorney General. That functionary was unavoidably absent from the Council Chamber by reason of indisposition, and the noble Earl, before proceeding to other business, desired, that return of the number and names of persons at present under confinement, in the jails should be laid before him without delay, together with the depositions upon which they had been committed, and a statement of the length of time they had been incarcerated. His Lordship also directed that returns should be forthwith made out for his

"To be Attaches to the High Commission.
" GERVAIS PARKER BUSHE, Esquire.
" ARTHUR BULLER, Esquire—and,
"The Hon. EDWARD PLEYDELL BOUVERIE.
 " To be Aides-de-Camp to the Governor General.
" Lieutenant the Honorable FREDERICK VILLIERS, Coldstream Guards ;
" Captain STEPHEN CONROY, Coldstream Guards ;
" Ensign W. H. FREDERICK CAVENDISH, H. M. 52nd Regiment Light Infantry :
" Cornet the Honorable C. A. DILLON, H. M. 7th Dragon Guards
" To be Extra Aide-de-Camp,
" Captain Ponsonby, Royal Fusilier Regiment.
' To be Private Secretary to the Governor General,
" EDWARD ELLICE, junr., Esquire, Member of the Imperial Parliament of Great Britain and Ireland."
The Quebec Mercury observes:—" The following, we believe, is a correct list of the passengers in the *Hastings* :—
Earl and Countess of DURHAM,—and family,
Mr. and Mrs. Ellice, Miss Balfour,
Mr. Charles Buller, Chief Secretary,
Mr. Turton, Legal Adviser,
The Hon. E. P. Bouverie, Mr. A. Buller, Mr. Bushe, Attaches,
Hon. Frederick Villiers, Capt. Ponsonby, C. A. Dillon, Esquire, Frederick Cavendish. Esq., A D. C.
Sir John Doratt, Physician to the Earl of Durham."

information by the acting magistrates throughout the Province, of the number of warrants remaining in force, but unexecuted against persons who had fled from Justice, with a succinct detail of the circumstances or grounds of suspicion, or accusation upon which they had been issued. In calling for this information, His Lordship has, no doubt, satisfied one of the primary executive duties of his high office, and one of the most imperative injunctions of the British laws, viz: the duty of watching with jealousy over the personal liberty of the subject. This is a duty which cannot without impropriety be delegated to other hands, and the EARL OF DURHAM has, with peculiar grace, made the first of his rule, one which ought to inspire all with increased confidence in the administration of the laws."

A circular, cautious in terms, was addressed to the several members of the Executive Council, acquainting them for the present that their services would not be required.* The Special Council was, by Letters Patent of the first of June, also dissolved.

---

* " CASTLE OF ST. LEWIS,
"QUEBEC, 31st May, 1838.

" SIR,—I am directed by His Excellency the Governor General to acquaint you that it is not His intention to continue the Executive Council, according to its present composition, and that your services therefore will not be required for the present.

" His Excellency has come to this determination, not from any feeling of dissatisfaction with the conduct of that Council, or any of its members. On the contrary, His Excellency particularly directs me to express his high sense of your services and his esteem and respect for yourself personally.— But His Excellency deems it essential for the objects of his mission, that during the temporary suspension of the Constitution, the Administrator of Affairs should be completely independent of, and unconnected with all parties and persons in the Province.

" Dissentions and animosities have naturally, during the course of the late unfortunate events, been carried to such an extent, that the necessary abstraction from all party feeling cannot be expected from any, who have been participators in the struggle on one side or the other.

The following gentlemen were called by His Excellency to the Executive Council, by whom accordingly it was now constituted, viz: Charles Buller, Esq., Chief Secretary,—T. E. M. Turton, Esquire, Secretary,—Colonel George Couper, K. H., Military Secretary,—The Provincial Secretary, Mr. Daly and Commissary General- Mr. Routh.

Sir John Doratt, was appointed Inspector General of Hospitals, and of all medical, charitable and literary Institutions in the Province,—and Lieut. Colonel the Hon. Charles Grey of the 71st Regiment was appointed an *Attache* to the High Commission.

The citizens of Quebec waited upon His Excellency on the 4th of June, with a congratulatory address.

" We feel," they observed, " that it would be premature to call for any immediate expression of opinion on the part of Your Excellency on the various grievances which have so peculiarly pressed on us, and which are detailed in our addresses to the Throne and the two Houses of the Imperial Parliament! we beg respectfully to represent that we shall be prepared at a fitting time through the medium of the Executive

---

" His Excellency believes that it is as much the interest of you all, as for the advantage of his own mission, that his administrative conduct should be free from all suspicions of political influence, or party feeling; that it should rest on his own individual responsibility, and that when he quits the Province, he should leave none of its permanent residents in any way committed by the acts which his Government may have found it necessary to perform, during the temporary suspension of the Constitution. When happily the time shall have come for the re-establishment of Constitutional Government, the different powers composing it will return to their natural state, and be confided to those whose station in the Province and personal character, entitle them to the confidence of their Sovereign and this country.

" I have the honor to be, Sir,
" Your most obedient servant.
(Signed,)   CHAS. BULLER, Jr.
   Chief Secretary."

Committee of the Quebec Constitutional Association to expose to Your Excellency the nature resulted from our being virtually unrepresented in the popular branch of the Legislature, as it existed, until the late suspension of the Constitution.

"Your Excellency finds the country impoverished, public improvements retarded, enterprise scarcely existing, and immigration impeded and discouraged. With what feelings of hope may we not look forward to a happy change under your administration, and we hail the future with most pleasing anticipations, looking to Your Excellency's appointment as an earnest of better times, particularly gratifying to us after so many years of suffering under the feudal and obsolete laws of times long gone by."

To this he answered.—" I thank you gentlemen most sincerely for this kind and friendly address.

"Following, as it does, the cordial reception which I experienced on my first landing on your shores, it gives me true satisfaction, for it convinces me that I may rely on your support and co-operation, in the accomplishment of the arduous task which, in obedience to the commands of our Sovereign, I have ventured to undertake.

" I earnestly intreat you, at this crisis, so important to the fate of your country, to lay aside all party feeling and political animosity, let your wisdom and good sense be manifested by restraining the violent, by encouraging the moderate, and by setting the praiseworthy example of charitable forbearance.

"You will thus enable me to proceed without hindrance in accomplishing the great objects of my mission, and placing in a permanent state of security those interests in which you are so deeply concerned.

" I shall thankfully receive from you, and from all Her Majesy's subjects in these Provinces, any information which you can, by personal and individual communication afford me, convinced, as I am, that an intercourse thus freely and unreservedly, but at the same time cautiously and peaceably conducted, can only tend to our mutual advantage to the promotion of your interests, and to the success of my administration."

On the tenth of June, a deputation from the District of Montreal, consisting chiefly of French Canadian gentlemen, waited upon His Excellency with an address, to which, although he graciously received it, he gave an answer rather dry, as many deemed it, savouring also, it was thought, somewhat of severity.* Various addresses from other quarters

---

* " We, citizens, inhabitants, proprietors and others, subjects of Her Majesty, residing in the District of Montreal, have the honor respectfully to approach and congratulate Your Excellency, on your safe arrival in this Province.

" However serious may be the circumstances in which the country is now placed, we trust that under Your Excellency's administration, the rights of Her Majesty's subjects, will be maintained, protected and respected.

" The previous course of Your Excellency's public life, confirms us in our just anticipation that we shall see the laws administered in such a manner as to ensure to all classes of society, without distinction, the protection to which they are entitled.

" These sentiments we consider it our duty to convey to Your Excellency, convinced that they are of a nature to meet with Your Excellency's approbation.

" The following are the names of the gentlemen forming the deputation:—

" James Leslie, Dr. Beaubien, Dr. Lusignan, Jos. Vallee, père, Dr. Vallee, Jos. Bourret, Henry DesRivieres, Jos. A. Labadie, Augustus Tullock, Olivier Frechette, Jos. Grenier, John Dillon—of Montreal ; Pierre De Boucherville, Dr. C. Weilbrennor, Jean Bte. Jeaudoin, Guillaume Roy--of Boucherville ; Paul Lussier, A. Massue, Z. Brodeur, J. Petit dit Lalumiere, Edouard Beaudry—Varennes ; Henry Monjeau, J. B. Desautels, N. Masson—of Longueuil.

" His Excellency was pleased to return the following answer :

" GENTLEMEN,—I thank you for this mark of your respect and good feeling towards me.

" You have truly stated that the Province is now placed in

were also presented to him. To one from the " British Wesleyan Ministers in Lower Canada," concluded in very loyal terms, and highly complimentary to himself, he answered.

" GENTLEMEN,—Your congratulations are most agreeable to me, and demand my grateful acknowledgements.

" I have implicit reliance on your assurances of attachment to the principles of the British Constitution, in which you and all Her Majesty's subjects in these Provinces will ever find protection and encouragement.

" I shall not fail, in obedience to the dictates of that Holy Christian Religion óf which you are Ministers, and in accordance with the prayer of your address, to exercise the high functions entrusted to me with "justice and mercy"—Justice towards the guilty—Mercy towards the misguided.

" Your fervent expressions of loyalty to our beloved Queen, are such as I expected to receive from you and from all who are sensible of the advantages of living under a Constitutional Monarchy."

In the *Gazette*, by authority, of the 21st June, ap-

---

serious circumstances,—but however great may be the difficulties which attend the solution of this important question, they shall be encountered by me with firmness and energy, and, by the blessing of God, effectually removed.

" The only distinctions in any class of society which I can recognize, are those which arise from the just of improper use of those rights to which you refer. When their exercise is marked by loyalty to the Crown—obedience to the laws—and a due regard to the best interests of the country, it will ever be held sacred :—but when it deviates from its legitimate course, for the attainment of seditious and unconstitutional objects, it must and shall be restrained.

" I earnestly hope that by the good conduct of all classes and parties, this lamentable necessity will never recur, and I rely with confidence on your exertions and co-operation, for the purpose of enabling me to accomplish the final settlement of your affairs on a permanent and satisfactory basis.

peared a Commission from the Governor General, appointing Charles Buller, Esq., Chief Commissloner, to inquire into the present mode of disposing of Crown Lands in Lower Canada, and to collect information respecting the operation thereof, as regarded the promotion of emigration from the mother country. Richard Davies Hanson, Esq., and the Hon. Henry Pétre, both *Attaches* from England, were named assistant Commissioners, and Mr. Buller was moreover authorized by the Commission to appoint, if he should see fit, other assistants. He accordingly, shortly after, named Edward Gibbon Wakefield, Esq., of whose subsequent speculation in the construction of the Beauharnois Canal, mention has already been made, and who had followed the Earl of Durham to Canada in expectation of being employed, as did also several others on speculation, some of whom have proved successful in obtaining, by dint of intrigue, some of the most profitable of the Colonial offices and employment. To this Commission, Charles Franklin Head, Esq., a Major in the army, was also subsequently added. The inquiries and report of the Commision are interesting, but too voluminous for further notice here, than observing that by exhibiting the abuses which have prevailed through improvident grants of the waste lands of the Crown of both Canadas, the system was exposed in all its odium. The inquiry was beneficial in other respects. The Report was favourable in particular to those who had sat down upon the wild lands of the Crown, and by their labour and industry improved them, giving to such the right of pre-emption of the lands they had so improved, it being rightly considered, that squatters though they were, they had squatted on the public lands which were awaiting the hands of industry, and by their exertions in reclaiming the forest from a wilderness to productive fields, consequently deserved well of the common wealth. Many so situated had been xceedingly ill treated by speculators and land jobbers, who, without the knowledge of the occupants of the lands so improved, had purchased or otherwise obtained titles from the Government to them, and had been subjected to lose their labour, unless they consented to re-purchase them of the speculators, whom they were thus cruelly compelled to pay for their own improvements.

The following Proclamation issued by His Excellency the Lieutenant Governor of Upper Canada on the pillage and destruction of the Steamboat *Sir Robert Peel*, is worthy of notice.

" By His Excellency Sir GEORGE ARTHUR, Knight Commander of the Royal Hanoverian Guelphic Order, Lieutenant Governor of the Province of Upper Canada, Major General Commanding Her Majesty's Forces therein, &c., &c., &c.

" Whereas information has this day been received that on the thirtieth day of May instant, the British steamboat, Sir Robert Peel, while lying peaceably at an American Island, was treacherously attacked by a body of armed ruffians from the American shore, set fire to, and burned: the passengers, amongst whom were defenceless females, wantonly and brutally insulted and a large amount of money and other property on board the said boat was either plundered or destroyed: and whereas the said robbery and outrage cannot fail to excite feelings of the utmost indignation in the minds of Her Majesty's subjects, who may be induced thereby to resort to acts of retaliation for the redress of injury, without properly considering that it belongs to the Government of Her Majesty to claim that redress, and to the Government of the United States to see that it be promptly rendered.

" The steamboat Sir Robert Peel, with persons and property on board, lay at a wharf on the shore of a friendly power, in the confidence of that security which every civilized nation extends over the sub-

H

jects and property of foreigners within its territory in times of peace, and free commercial intercourse.

"The Government of the United States, it may be confidently expected, will vindicate the national honor, and feel deeply the insult which this act of savage and cowardly violence, committed in the dead of night, has inflicted upon their nation. They will not, and cannot, with regard to national character, delay to bring the criminals to punishment, or to render to the injured subjects of Her Majesty, redress —though it be late, in this instance, to offer them protection.

"The demeanour and conduct of the population of this Province, has been that of people resting securely upon the sanctity of law, and the regular exercise of the power of the Great Empire of which they form part; and accordingly, even during rebellion, and foreign invasion, this country has not been disgraced, by any scenes of individual violence or revenge, on the part of its loyal inhabitants. The character which has thus been gained in this Province has commanded the admiration of the British people —demonstrated the proud superiority of British institutions—and is too valuable to be sacrificed in its smallest part, for the sudden gratification of indignant feelings, however justly they may have been aroused.

"I therefore express to Her Majesty's faithful and loyal subjects, my entire confidence in their dignified forbearance, and that the British flag, which has been so nobly defended by them, will not now be stained, by having outrage or insult offered to the persons or property of foreigners within its territory, and under its protection.

"It need not be said to men who understand the character and institutions of England—that injury offered to one British subject is felt by all, and that the mutual ties of duty and affection, which bind a free and loyal people and their Sovereign together give the strength of the whole Empire to an injured individual. This consideration is all that is necessary to restrain a loyal community within becoming bounds, and to insure their leaving to their Government that claim for redress which this unprovoked outrage imperatively demands.

"Until the American Government shall have taken such measures as will ensure the lives and property of British subjects within the territory of the United States from spoliation and violence, the utmost guard and caution is required, on the part of masters of steamboats and other vessels, in entering American harbours, as it is but too plain, that at present the subjects of Her Majesty may be sometimes placed in the power of a lawless banditti, when they imagine themselves within the protection and authority of a friendly Government.

"Given under my Hand and Seal at Arms, at Toronto, this thirty-first day of May, in the year of our Lord one thousand eight hundred and thirty-eight, and of Her Majesty's Reign the first.

"G. ARTHUR.

"By command of His Excellency,
"C. A. HAGERMAN, *Attorney General.*
"D. CAMERON, *Secretary.*"

Large numbers were still in gaol at Montreal, under charges of high treason, and these remained to be disposed of. No examples, as previously mentioned, had been made, and as the Earl of Durham's mission was one of peace, and, if possible, to restore order without severity, and to heal the wounds that still were bleeding, it was determined that a lenient and humane policy should be pursued, and that the *detenus*, with the exception of a few, known as the most active of the leaders in the late troubles, should be released, taking precautions, however, that those deemed the most culpable, and who by their flight had evaded justice and escaped to the neighboring States, should not return with impunity, until permission at least were obtained to that effect from the proper authority. But how was the Government to proceed in order legally to establish the greater guilt of those who had been most prominent in the disturbances? In the state of public feeling it would have been impossible to find an impartial jury for their trial, and a verdict of acquittal rather than of guilt would, in all probability, be the result. An expedient was adopted, discreditable to the Government of Lord Durham, with a view of extricating him from the dilemma, by enabling him to dispose of the leading insurgents, by an Ordinance of the Special Council, without the preliminary of a legal trial for the offences whereof they stood accused. A general amnesty of all political offences without exception of persons was expected by many, and indeed it would, both as respected the country, and the noble Earl's character, have been infinitely preferable to the course he was advised to take.

Accordingly, a person of consideration taken into the confidence of the Governor General, probably for the purpose, and who through some years residence in the province, being known to the prisoners, was commissioned to wait upon certain of them with proffers of His Excellency's clemency, on condition of their addressing him a petition or letter in accordance with a draft of one he communicated to them. This petition of which we are not aware that a copy has ever been published, and therefore cannot specify the contents of it, seems not to have been acceptable. They, however, addressed a letter to His Excellency, giving it in charge to the gentleman entrusted with the mission who returned with it to Quebec, assuring those who had signed it of his sincere desire to serve them, and of his good offices for the purpose near

His Excellency. This not proving satisfactory the gentleman acting as mediator on the occasion immediately returned to Montreal, for another conference with the *detenus*, pursuant to which a second and more explicit letter than the former was addressed to the Governor General, placing themselves at His Lordship's discretion, and praying that *the peace of the country might not be endangered* by a trial.*

This movement, and the measure we shall presently produce, built upon it, were utterly unworthy of the reputation and fame as a statesman which Lord Dur-

---

* For the previous letter, see end of this chapter. The present was as follows:—

"My Lord.—We have some reason to apprehend that the expressions used by us in a letter addressed to Your Lordship on the 18th instant, may appear vague and ambiguous.

" Our intention, my Lord, was distinctly to avow that in pursuit of objects dear to the great mass of our population, we took a part that has eventuated in a charge of high treason.

" We professed our willingness to plead guilty, whereby to avoid the necessity of a trial, and that to give as far as in our power, tranquillity to the country, but whilst we were thus disposed to contribute to the happiness of others, we could not condescend to shield ourselves under the provisions of an *Ordinance passed by the late Special Council of the Province*.

" Permit us then, my Lord, to perform this great duty, to mark our entire confidence in Your Lordship, to place ourselves at your disposal, without availing ourselves of provisions, which would degrade us in our own eyes, by marking an unworthy distrust on both sides.

" With this short explanation of our feelings. we again place ourselves at Your Lordship's discretion; and pray that the peace of the country may not be endangered by a trial.

. " We have the honor to be, my Lord, with unfeigned respect, Your Lordship's most obedient humble servants.

R. S. M. BOUCHETTE,   H. A. GAUVIN,
WOLFRED NELSON,   S. MARCHESSAULT,
R. DES RIVIERES,   J. H. GODDU,
L. H. MASSON,   B. VIGER,

" The Right Hon. The Earl of Durham,
&c., &c., &c.,

ham had acquired, and injured, not only his character as such, but with it also, it is believed from the annoyance he experienced resulting from it, his comfort and peace of mind to a degree affecting his health, and which brought this high minded and sensitive nobleman prematurely to his grave. His Lordship now provided with the consent of the chief *detenus*, to deal with them as he pleased, and having sufficient authority, as he thought, to transport them beyond seas named on the 28th June, his Special Council* the previous body, having as already noticed been discharged upon his arrival, and on the same day issued the following, intituled ". an Ordinance to provide for the security of Lower Canada."

" WHEREAS divers persons, subjects of Her Majesty in this Province, have been charged with high treason and other offences of a treasonable nature, some of which said persons are at present in custody, and others have withdrawn themselves from the pursuits of justice beyond the limits of this Province; and whereas of the persons so charged and in custody those whose names follow, that is to say : Wolfred Nelson, Robert Shore Milnes Bouchessault, Bonaventure Viger, Simeon Marchessault. Henri Alphonse Gauvin, Toussaint Goddu, Rodolphe Des Rivières, and Luc Hya-

---

*(From the *Quebec Official Gazette*)
" QUEBEC, 28th *June*, 1838.

" His Excellency has been pleased to appoint Vice Admiral, the Honorable Sir Charles Paget, G. C. H,; Major General Sir James MacDonnell, K. C. B. and K. C. H.; Lieutenant Colonel, the Honorable C. Grey ; the Honorable Colonel George Couper, and the Honorable Charles Buller, to be members of the Special Council.

Not one of those gentlemen were personally connected with the Province, nor otherwise concerned in its welfare than officially by the appointments they held in it for the moment. Vice Admiral Sir C· Paget commanded on the Halifax Station, and was on a visit to Quebec. To these, Major General Clitherow was in the month of August following also added.

cinthe Masson, all respectively now in the Gaol of Montreal in custody of the Sheriff of Montreal, have severally acknowledged their participation in such high treason, and have submitted themselves to the will and pleasure of Her Majesty: and whereas Louis Joseph Papineau, a Member of the late Assembly of Lower Canada and Speaker thereof, Cyrile Hector Octave Cote, also a Member of the said late Assembly, Edmund Burke O'Callaghan, also a Member of the said late Assembly, Edouard Etienne Rodier, also a Member of the said late Assembly, Thomas Storrow Brown, Budger Duvernay, Etienne Chartier, a priest, George Et. Cartier, John Ryan, the elder, and John Ryan, the younger, Louis Perrault, Pierre Paul Demaray, Joseph Francois Davignon, and Louis Gautier, all respectively subjects of Her said Majesty, and against whom respectively warrants for high treason have been issued, have severally absconded from this Province and with drawn themselves from the limits thereof, and from the pursuit of justice:—and whereas it is Her said Majesty's most gracious will and pleasure, that no further proceedings shall be had or taken against any persons whomsoever on account of such high treason or other offences of a treasonable nature, save and except as hereinafter provided; but it is nevertheless expedient to provide for the security of this Province by effectually preventing the several persons whose names are hereinbefore set forth from being at large therein: Be it therefore ordained and enacted, by His Excellency the Governor of the Province of Lower Canada, by and with the consent and advice of the Special Council, for the affairs of the said Province of Lower Canada, constituted and assembled by virtue of an Act of the Parliament of the United Kingdom of Great Britain and Ireland; passed in the first year of the Reign of Her present Majesty, intituled, "An Act to make temporary provision for the Government of Lower Canada;"—And it is hereby ordained and enacted by the authority aforesaid, that it shall and may be lawful for Her Majesty to transport to Her Majesty's Islands of Bermuda, during Her pleasure, the said Wolfred Nelson, Robert Shore Milnes Bouchette, Bonaventure Viger, Simeon Marchessault, Henry Alphonse Gauvin, Toussaint H. Goddu, Rodolphe Les Rivières, and Luc Hyacinthe Masson respectively, and to subject them or any of them to such restraints in the said Islands, as may be needful to prevent their return to this Province: and it is further ordained and enacted and with the authority aforesaid, that if the said Wolfred Nelson, Robert Shore Milnes Bouchette, Bonaventure Viger, Simeon Marchessault, Henri Alphonse Gauvin, Toussaint H. Goddu, Rodolphe Des Rivières, and Luc Hyacinthe Masson respectively or any of them, or if the said Louis Joseph Papineau, Cyrile Hector Octave Cote, Julien Gagnon, Robert Nelson, Edmund Burke O'Callaghan, Edouard Etienne Rodier, Thomas Storrow Brown, Ludger Duvernay, Etienne Chartier, George Et. Cartier, John Ryan the elder, and John Ryan the younger, Louis Perrault, Pierre Paul Demaray, Joseph François Davignon, and Louis Gautier, against whom respectively such warrants for high treason have been issued, and also have so withdrawn themselves from the pursuits of justice as aforesaid, or any of them shall at any time hereafter, except by permission of the Governor General of Her Majesty's Provinces on the continent of North America, and High Commissioner for the adjustment of certain important questions depending in the Provinces of Upper and Lower Canada, or if there shall be no such Governor General and High Commissioner, by the permission of the Governor in Chief, or Governor, or other person administering the government of this Province as hereinafter provided, be found at large, or come within the said Province, they or he shall in such case be deemed and taken to be guilty of high treason, and shall on conviction of being so found at large or coming within the said Province without such permission as aforesaid, suffer death accordingly. Provided always that it shall and may be lawful for such Governor General and High Commissioner, or if there shall be no such Governor General and High Commissioner, then for the Governor in Chief, Governor, or other persons administering the Government of this Province, acting for and in behalf of Her said Majesty, so soon as it shall to Him appear consistent with the peace and tranquillity of this Province, by any act or instrument under his hand and seal at arms, to grant permission for the said Wolfred Nelson, Bobert Shore Milnes Bouchette, Bonaventure Viger, Simeon Marchessault, Henri Alphonse Gauvin, Toussaint G. Goddu, Rodolphe Des Rivieres, Luc Hyacinthe Masson, Louis Joseph Papineau, Cyrile Hector Octave Cote, Julien Gagnon, Robert Nelson, Edmund Burke O'Callaghan, Edouard Etienne Rodier, Thomas Storrow Brown, Ludger Duvernay, Etienne Chartier, George Et. Cartier, John Ryan the elder, and John Ryan the younger, Louis Perrault, Pierre Paul Demaray, Joseph Francois Davignon, and Louis Gautier, or any of them, upon giving such security for their future good behaviour and loyal conduct as the said Governor General and High Commissioner, as the Governor in Chief, Governor, or other person administering the Government of this Province shall think fit, to return to this Province and reside therein, and the said Wolfred Nelson, Robert Shore Milnes Bouchette, Bonaventure Viger, Simeon Marchessault, Henri Alphonse Gauvin, Toussaint Goddu, Rodolphe Des Rivieres, Luc Hyacinthe Masson, Louis Joseph Papineau, Cyrile Hector Octave Cote, Julien Gagnon, Robert Nelson, Edmund Burke O'Callaghan, Edouard Entienne Rodier, Thomas Storrow Brown, Ludger Duvernay, Etienne Chartier, George Et. Cartier,

John Ryan the elder, and John Ryan the younger, Louis Perrault, Pierre Paul Demaray, Joseph François Davignon, and Louis Gautier, or such of them as shall receive such permission as aforesaid shall not thenceforth be subject to any penalty or prosecution whatever for any treason or treasonable or seditious practices by them or him at any time heretofore committed. Provided also, that in any indictment for being so found or coming within the Province without such permission as aforesaid, the burthen of proof of having obtained such permission of the said Governor General and High Commissioner, Governor in Chief, Governor, or other person administering the Government of this Province, shall lie upon the party accused or indicted thereof.

"2. And it is hereby further ordained and enacted by and with the authority aforesaid, that nothing in any Proclamation of Her Majesty contained, shall extend or be held, or construed to extend to the cases of François Jalbert, Jean Baptiste Lussier, Louis Lussier, François Mignault, François Talbot, Amable Daunais, François Nicolas, Etienne Langlois, Gedeon Pinsonault, Joseph Pinsonault, or any of them, or to the case of any other person or persons charged with the murder of the late George Weir, a Lieutenant in Her Majesty's 32nd Regiment of Foot, or with the murder of the late Joseph Chartrand, nor shall François Jalbert, Jean Baptiste Lussier, Louis Lussier, François Mignault, François Talbot, Amable Daunais, François Nichlas, Etienne Langlois, Gedeon Pinsonault, Joseph Pinsonault, or any of them, nor shall any other persons suspected of being concerned in the said murders or either of them, nor any person concerned in the escape from the custody of the Sheriff of Montreal of Louis Lussier, charged with the murder of the said George Weir, or who may have harbored the said Louis Lussier after, or aided him in such escape, derive any benefit or advantage whatsoever from any Proclamation of Her Most Gracious Majesty, nor shall any amnesty thereby intended to be granted be taken in any way to apply to such person or persons, or any of them.

"Ordained and enacted by the authority aforesaid, and passed in Special Council, at the City of Quebec, the twenty-eighth day of June, in the second year of the Reign of Our Sovereign Lady Victoria, by the Grace of God, of the United Kingdom of Great Britain and Ireland, Queen, Defender of the Faith, and so forth, in the year of Our Lord, one thousand eight hundred and thirty-eight.

"By His Excellency's Command.
"W. B. LINDSAY,
"Clerk Special Council."

This edict, sentencing eight British subjects in custody to transportation, without trial or form of trial in Her Majesty's Courts of Law, besides subjecting others, who were not in custody (having fled,) to the penalty of death, in case of their return to the Province without leave first obtained, was an exercise of arbitrary power unprecedented in the darkest time we hear of in the Annals of England, more becoming the autocrat of Russia than the representative of the constitutional Sovereign of the British Empire, and created surprise as well it might in the minds of all who entertained a due sense of and respect for British laws, and the safeguards of British justice and liberty.

The following remarks, taken from an English paper of the time, took place on the subject in the House of Lords.

"Lord Brougham had, he said, a question to ask of the noble lord who was at the head of the Colonies which he considered of the very highest importance. He perceived by accounts received in the American papers that two ordinances were said to have been issued by the Governor in Canada, with ordinances, if the noble lord who was at the head of the Government of Canada presumed—he repeated it, presumed—to carry into effect, he would be guilty of murder. So gross and so outrageous was the violation of British law to be found in these ordinances that he did not believe that any man who ever had a gown upon the shoulders as a lawyer could have given his advice for their promulgation. The accounts that he referred to stated, with respect to those ordinances, that a Special Council had been appointed, consisting not of Canadians but of persons not belonging to the Province, and three of them personally dependent upon Lord Durham. Three of that same council were the Military Secretary, the Aid-de-Camp, and the public Secretary of Lord Durham, namely, Mr. Buller. The accounts then proceeded to state that the council had issued the two following proclamations. One of these proclamations declared that certain persons had come in and confessed that they were guilty of the crime of rebellion, and, therefore, without bringing them to trial, Lord Durham's sentence was that they should all, untried, be transported to a certain place, Bermuda, and with the addition that they should be put to death if they left that place [laughter]. Even if these persons had committed the crime of rebellion, they ought to have been tried; they could not be put to death without trial, and without sentence of death in course of law. Even if the Queen—if the Crown had in a certain case commuted the sentence of death to that of banishment, the man returning from banishment could not be put to death. It was only after trial that a man could be ordered to be put to death. The returning from transportation was made a capital felony by Act of Parliament in certain cases; but here death was ordered without a trial, and without the regular sentence of a law to sanction it. This, however, was going upon the vulgar error that a man who returned before the period of his banishment had expired could be put to death by any one. There was, then, the case of Mr. Papineau and one or two others, who had not confessed themselves guilty of any crime."

" Lord Lyndhurst:— And if they had, it would be only evidence."

" Lord Brougham: But who had not confessed; and there had been cases where men had been acquitted notwithstanding their confession. But then there was Mr. Papineau not confessing anything, and not tried, and yet he was also to be put to death! He could not conceive anything more monstrous than this. He thought it was bad enough when they offered a reward of £1000 to those who would give evidence in an American court of justice: but here was the Government proclaiming and promising to commit a capital felony. The Act authorised Lord Durham to make a general law, but it did not at all authorise him to hang men without the form of law."

" Lord Ellenborough admitted that he had been anticipated by the noble and learned lord on this subject: for he was about to move not only for the production of the ordinances, but also for the production of papers connected with them. He was most anxious, especially, for the minutes of the council upon that particular day on which the ordinances had been issued, because he was inclined to think that, beyond what had been stated by the noble and learned lord, three other grave illegalities had been committed in the issuing of the ordinances A rule had been laid down that between the proclamation for the convening of the council and its proceeding to legislate, twenty-one days should elapse. This council had been appointed on the 26th of June, and it had proceeded to legislate on the 28th of June. Another thing that was done which was contrary to rule. was, that the ordinances were read a first, second, and third time on the same day. This was contrary to the standing orders of the council. Five persons only had been appointed as the council; if five were not present, then an illegality in the proceedings had occurred. The council was said to have taken place on the 28th of June, and he found by the papers that one of the persons named on the council had not arrived until the evening of the 29th. Five were stated to have been present—four of these were members of the council, with Lord Durham, who was not a member of the council. There could not be a matter which required more anxious deliberation than that which the council had to determine. They had to draw a line of distinction between persons who were supposed to be criminal. They had upon certain persons to pass sentence of transportation, and also to be hung if they came back. Then there were 16 who were to be banished, and there were another set who, although they had absconded, were yet absolutely pardoned. They were all cases which required to be looked to most particularly; and yet so rapidly did the council proceed that, of the twenty-four cases which were to be punished, and all of the other cases which were to be considered deserving of mercy, they had all been disposed of at once. He certainly should require to see all documents, as he thought it was a matter for grave consideration with the house whether it would not interfere in a matter likely to be so mischievous and to bring so much disgrace upon the Government, as that which had occurred in Canada."

"Lord Brougham observed that the Ordinance referred to Upper Canada as well as to Quebec, and that Lord Durham had no right to make such orders."

"Lord Glenelg was, he said, quite ready to produce all the papers. He had the Ordinance, and would produce some parts of the letters of the Governor. Other parts of them he could not produce. He had not the minutes of the council to produce, as they had not yet arrived. He had only to observe that the noble lords who had spoken had been somewhat premature in coming to a conclusion that Lord Durham had acted improperly. The fact was that the conduct of Lord Durham had gained the confidence of both parties; not the mere confidence and approbation of those who might have been opposed to him, but the general confidence of all parties, who had expressed themselves well pleased with the conduct of Lord Durham."

" Lord Brougham had expressed no disapprobation of the conduct of Lord Durham, What he had done was to condemn the proclamations of Lord Durham, if indeed, he had issued any such proclamations. He appealed to any lawyer in the house whether, without committing murder, the proclamations could be carried into effect; for it was murder to hang a man without his being regularly tried, convicted, and sentenced according to law."

—" Viscount Melbourne said that, considering the manner in which this matter had been introduced—considering the state of affairs in Canada—considering the great interests that were at stake—considering the state of the Empire, and how deeply the empire might be effected by the affairs that were then taking place in that country, it was, he must say, in his opinion, premature—it was in the highest degree imprudent—it was in the highest degree unpatriotic—it was in the highest degree unjustifiable—thus to sacrifice the interests of their country to the interests of party. It was in the highest degree unfair, in their desire to attack individuals, to permit such a proceeding as they then witnessed. It was wrong thus at once to condemn those acts of a noble lord, or what they deemed to be his acts, when they had not the best means of forming a judgment upon measures which the exigency of the circumstances and the state of the country might have convinced him were required He had no objection to the production of the papers, but he must say that he could not refrain from expressing his opinion and his feelings as to the course which had been pursued by noble lords."

"Lord Brougham absolutely and peremptorily dissented from the doctrine of the noble viscount. He told the noble viscount that it was not unpatriotic, that it was not premature, and that it was not unjustifiable, but that it was absolutely necessary, that it was absolutely a matter of duty for that house to keep a watchful superintendence over the exercise of such dictatorial powers as had been entrusted to the Governor of Canada. What had they been told during the passing of this bill? That Parliament would always be at hand—that it would always superintend the exercise of the powers given by the bill—that the House would be always open to control any abuse of the powers given by the bill. Large and ample as the powers were, he was told that they would be controlled by Parliament. And now, when Parliament was called on to interfere, the powers of the bill were not merely to exercise, but they were exceeded. When he had argued against the bill which gave such enormous powers, he had been met with the reply that Parliament would be always ready to interfere, and that the control of Parliament would always be at hand. The noble viscount had talked as if Lord Durham had powers under the Act for what he had done, and as if he (Lord Brougham) was premature in discussing these acts. Lord Durham had not the power to do that which had been done in the Ordinance he referred to. No such powers, he contended, were given by this Act. What, then, was to be said if, instead of exercising the powers given by that Act, he had not only run contrary to it, but to the laws and customs of England, when he condemned men to be executed who had never been tried? And he also said that, under such circumstances, sending a man to Bermuda, and ordering him to be hung if he returned, Lord Durham had as little right to do as he (Lord Brougham) would have to order one of their lordships to be banished to Botany Bay, or to massacre a man he might meet in the streets. As to Lord Durham's judging of the exigency of the circumstances, and the necessity of the case, he asked was it a matter of necessity to commit felony for the good of the country? Was it necessary to hang a man, who had never been tried, for the good of the public? Talking of the good of the empire and the state of Canada never could justify for an instant the issuing of such an Ordinance. Let it not be said that he sought for an occasion of attacking Lord Durham; he had not sought the occasion for attacking Lord Durham; even when he had been given up by the noble viscount himself, upon that very occasion he had defended Lord Durham, and for doing so he had drawn down upon himself a right reverend prelate, whom he should always speak of with respect—he had drawn the rebuke of that right reverend prelate upon himself, because, in his absence, he had been the defender of Lord Durham. He had defended Lord Durham when that noble earl had been denounced by the noble viscount for the appointment of Mr. Turton. He could only say that, in that general attack upon Lord Durham and Mr. Turton, there might have lurked any charge however odious, and yet the noble viscount had said that 'deeply regretted, and was greatly surprised at the nomination of Mr. Turton.' Never should he more desire to be put down, if he were a person appointed to a public and confidential situation, and in consequence of any arrangement he had made, than when those under whom he held a confidential situation had publicly said that they deeply regretted and were greatly surprised at it. He did not mean, however, that the noble viscount had intended to express more than his regret and surprise that an appointment had taken place, which, he assured the houses, had not concurred. As to its being thought that he was influenced by factious motives, he regarded the charge as little as the noble viscount himself on former occasions did when he brought forward charges against the then Governments, and the Government then did, as all Governments did when their opponents, accuse him of being influenced by factious motives."

"In answer to a question from Lord Ellenborough, Lord Glenelg said he was ready to produce all the papers.

"Lord Lyndhurst observed that letters had been received from the noble earl, and he wished now to know if he had any explanation to give concerning these transactions."

"Lord Glenelg observed that he gave the papers themselves; if he declined giving them, then an explanation might be required from him.

"Lord Wyndford thought some explanation ought to be given respecting these matters."

"The motion was agreed to."

Extract from Lord Glenelg's Letter to Lord Durham.

"Your lordship will observe that the Attorney and Solictor Generals are clear'y of opinion that so much of the ordinance as relates to the restrictions to be placed in Bermuda on the eight persons sent by you to that place is void, inasmuch as the legislative jurisdiction of the Governor and Special Council of Lower Canada does not extend beyond the limits ot the Province. In all other respects they are of opinion that the provisions of the ordinance were within the competency of the Governor and Special Council.

"I regret, however, to state that a different view of

the case was taken by several individuals of high legal
attainments, whose station and professional experience
could not fail to secure great weight to their opinions
in the House of Lords, where this question was first
agitated. There were, indeed, some who went so far
as to contend that the whole ordinance was illegal, as
exceeding the legislative authority vested by Parliament in the Special Council; but as this view of the
case has not received the sanction of either House of
Parliament, Her Majesty's Government, in accordance
with the opinion of the law officers of the Crown,
are fully satisfied that the powers confided by Parliament to the Governor and Special Council are sufficiently ample to authorise them to legislate to the full
extent of the ordinance in question, so far as relates
exclusively to acts to be done within the Province of
Lower Canada."

It is not probable that the prisoners, in placing
themselves at the discretion of His Excellency, as
they did distinctly by their second letter, contemplated that it was to serve as the basis of so unusual
and extraordinary a proceeding as that of an Ordinance certainly more like a Russian Ukase exiling
to Siberia some unfortunates, who had incurred
their master's displeasure, than the act of a British
Colonial Legislature. The utmost they expected,
if not Her Majesty's gracious pardon though a general amnesty, of which they no doubt had hopes,
was, it is believed, a voluntary expatriation, until the
return of more happy times should render a return to
their country, no longer objectionable. The Ordinance
was accompanied by a proclamation of the same date,
as follows:

PROCLAMATION.

" Whereas our Province of Lower Canada hath
been long disturbed by political dissensions, and
was recently afflicted with rebellion and civil war,

whereby it hath become necessary to suspend the Constitution of the said Province, and to provide for the temporary Government thereof, by means of extraordinary powers, conferred upon us by the Imperial Legislature; and whereas we are firmly resolved to punish with the utmost severity any future act of insubordination in our said Province, and more especially to prevent in future, as far as is in our power, the occurrence of dissensions similar to those by which our said Province has been long disturbed as aforesaid, by effectually removing all causes of dissension, so that our said Province many be established in peace as a loyal and truly British colony; and whereas in the exercise and in pursuance of the extraordinary powers as aforesaid, it hath been ordained and enacted by an Ordinance this day made and passed, according to law, entituled "An Ordinance to provide for the security of the Province of Lower Canada," that it shall be lawful for us to transport certain persons named in the said Ordinance, to our Island of Bermuda. during our pleasure, and that, if the said persons, or certain other persons, also named in the said Ordinance, who have withdrawn themselves from the pursuit of justice, beyond the limits of our said Province, shall at any time hereafter, except by permission of our Governor General of our Provinces on the continent of North America, and High Commissioner for the adjustment of certain important questions depending in the Provinces of Lower and Upper Canada, or if there shall be no such Governor General, or High Commissioner, by the permission of the Governor in Chief, or Governor, or other person administering our Government of Lower Canada, as provided in the said Ordinance, be found at large or come within our said Province; they shall in that case be taken and deemed to be guilty of high treason, and shall suffer death accordingly;

and whereas, under the peculiar circumstances of our said Province, as aforesaid, it is not less expedient in our judgement, than grateful to our heart, to mark, by an act of royal grace, our recollection of the ancient, and well proven loyalty of all our Canadian subjects, rather than by any severity of punishment, our sense of the recent disaffection of some of them:—KNOW YE THEREFORE, that we have ordained, directed, and declared, and by these presents, do ordain, direct, and declare, that no further proceedings shall be had, or taken, against any persons whatsoever on account of any high treason, or offences of a treasonable nature, with which they now stand charged, or wherewith they may be chargeable at this time, but that all such proceedings, without exception or distinction, save as hereinafter mentioned, shall henceforth cease and determine. And it is our further will and pleasure that with the exception of such persons as are in that behalf named in the said Ordinance, and whose cases are thereby provided for, all persons at present in custody and charged with high treason or other offences of a treasonable nature, and also with such exception as aforesaid, all persons who have withdrawn themselves from the pursuit of justice beyond the limits of our said Province, shall immediately upon giving such security for their future good and loyal behaviour as our said Governor General and High Commissioner, or if there should be no such Governor General or High Commissioner, then the Governor in Chief, Governor, or the person administering the Government of this Province shall direct, be at liberty to return to their homes, and may and shall there remain wholly unmolested by reason of any high treason or other offences of a treasonable nature, in which he or they may have been concerned.

"In testimony whereof we have caused these our

letters to be made patent and the great zeal of our said Province of Lower Canada to be affixed thereto.

"Witness our right trusty and right well beloved John George Earl of Durham, Viscount Lambton, etc., etc., Knight Grand Cross of the most honorable Military Order of the Bath, one of our most Honorable Privy Council, and Governor General, Vice Admiral and Captain General of all our Provinces within and adjacent to the Continent of North America, &c., &c., &c.

"At our Castle of St. Lewis, in our city of Quebec, in our said Province of Lower Canada, the twenty-eight day of June, in the year of our Lord one thousand eight hundred and thirty-eight, and in the second year of our reign.

(Signed,) D. DALY,
Secretary."

In consequence of these, all, with the exceptions mentioned, who were in prison charged with political offences, were released, giving sureties for their good behaviour.*

---

* Strange and unconstitutional as those proceedings are now and ever will be considered, it is to be observed, however, that time, but rather as acts of clemency, on the part of Lord Durham, who, it must be acknowledge, had a most delicate and difficult mission, and as such they were rather approved than the reverse by the generally of people in the Province. The following extracts from the *Quebec Gazette*, (Mr. Neilson's) and *Le Canadien*, papers of opposite politics shew the views generally entertained by both parties on the subject.

"THE LATE REBELLION.—Those who are entrusted with "the peace, welfare, and good Government of the Province,' under the authority of the Crown and an Act of the Imperial Parliament having pronounced on the character of the late rebellion, and the fate of those who were charged with being concerned in it, we should be glad that it were no longer spoken of, and even effected from the History of the Province.

"During the temporary suspension of the Constitutional Act, having no share or voice in the choice of our rulers, it

Simultaneously with the above Ordinance and proclamation, appeared another "Ordinance for establishing an efficient system of police in the cities of Quebec and Montreal." A measure of which both cities had long been much in need.

---

is the duty of good and faithful subjects of the British Crown to submit to the established authority, and throw no obstac'e in the way of the discharge of its duties, for which it is responsibile to those by whom it is constituted.

"We have had enough of dissentions; their effects are visible in the diminished prosperity of the Province; in the loss of liberty and life; in the affliction of families, and in the ruins of once happy dwellings and thriving villages.

"The British Government, far removed from the scene of the passions and predices which have been excited in this Province, has listened to the inspiration of mercy and the spirit of the age in the most enlightened countries of the world.—For death and confiscation of property, which the law had fixed as the penalty of treason and rebellion, it has substituted the temporary exile and detention of eight out of hundreds of prisoners, many of them taken with arms in their hands and declared that sixteen out of a great number who fled from justice, shall not return to the Province without leave. To all others, except eleven, accused of deliberate murder of persons in their power, there is an entire oblivion. merely on their giving security for future good behavoir.—Hitherto, not a single individual in this Prov nce has been put to death for having been concerned in the late treasons and rebellions, excepting those who were killed in action; and it is an act of justice to the rebels to state our belief that, with the exception of Lieuteeant Weir and Chartrand, no person was kille l by them in cold bloo l. In Upper Canada, the only exceptions which have taken place, were those of two leaders of the insurrection who were concerned in the death of Major Moodie, and the burning of Dr. Horne's house, at the first outbreak of a most unprovoked revolt. We wish that the conduct of the British Gov' ernment, on the present occasion, may be duly appreciated it is, we believe, sufficiently powerful to be generous; at all events—

"............pacemque imponere morem,
"Parcere subjectis, et debellare superbos,
are ancient and spproved rules of Empire." *Quebec Gazette.*

Pursuant to this, the first ordinance by the new Special Council of Lord Durham's appointment, the eight *detenues* imprisonment at Montreal, and now destined for Bermuda, were at five o'clock, in the evening of the 7th July, put under a strong military guard on board the steamer "Canada," placed for their reception at the foot of the Current St. Mary, opposite the gaol. The steamer immediately departing for Quebec, embarked them the following

"*Extract from the editorial article in the 'Canadien.'*"

"It must be borne in mind that Lord Durham enjoys one of the finest reputations in Europe, which will be ruined or crowned by his execution of the important task he has undertaken, and that trsk he cannot accomplish with credit unless he meets the views of liberal men in Great Britain: The present Governor General offers then in his past and present conduct, and in his future prospect, the strongest guarantee which Canada can desire, and those must be unreasonable indeed who do not repose their trust in him. We must be fully convinced that he who has been chosen by the reform party in the mother country as their chief, will conduct is administration with as much liberality as circumstances will admit of, and if it, at times, appears that some of his measures are not conceived upon as enlarged a view as we may have desired, it must be remembered thatt the immense responsibility which rests upon his head as despository of the general interests of the empire obliges him to observe the greatest circumspection: he must risk nothing, leave nothing to chance, and may sometimes find himself obliged to draw the rein on the desires of his own heart. When, in an important crisis, a people has the happiness to see its destinies confided to a man of proved talents and of liberal principals, too much confidence and support cannot be given to him. The ancient Romans, in times of eminent danger, chose a dictator, always a man remarkab'e for his virtues and great talents, to whom all the powers of the State were confided, and by such appointment Rome was saved more than once. It is truly a dictatorship we have at this time in Lower Canada, and under the man who exercises it we also may expect public safety, and the reestablishment of order and security upon the ruins caused by anarchy and political dissensions. We have greater benefits to expect—the establishment of a Constitutional Government upon a permanent foundation, and

morning in that port, on board of Her Majesty's Steamer "Vestal," then under sailing orders for Bermuda, and for which she immediately set sail.*

His Excellency with the Countess of Durham, family and suite, left Quebec early in July on a visit to Upper Canada, accompanied by Sir Charles Paget and Sir John Colborne. A very flattering address was presented to him, at Montreal, and indeed from

it is chiefly on this account that all good Canadians ought to exert themselves to give confidence to the author of our new Constitution in the good disposition of the mass of their countrymen; to convince him that there is no danger in his putting in practice as respects the Canadians, those highly liberal principles he has through life professed, and which will be to him a mark of glory, and, we are certain, one of the happiest acts of his public life. Whoever, without the most imperious reasons, such, we hope, as will never arise, shall endeavour to prevent his countrymen from rallying round the present administration, after the generosity shown towards the political prisoners, an act which proves how completely all former disastrous influence is repudiated ought to be branded as the declared enemy of his country, of the cause of reform, and of the return in all their plenitude of those liberties and political advantages which belong to us as British subjects."

" The indulgence of the Government is certainly beyond what could have been expected; it is to be hoped that it will not have exercised its generosity in vain."

*" Wolfred Nelson, Robert Shore Milnes Bouchette, Bonaventure Viger, Simeon Marchessault, Henri Alphonse Gauvin Toussaint Goddu, Rodolphe Des Rivieres, and Luc Hyacinthe Masson, arrived from Montreal at five o'clock this morning in the steamer 'Canada,' and were, without landing, placed in safe custody, on board Her Majesty's steamship 'Vestal,' under sailing orders for Bermuda. These convicts were guarded on the passage down by a detachment of the 71st regiment; they were the only passengers in the steamer. The 'Canada' left Montreal yesterday evening, and took the prisoners on board at the foot of the current, whither they had been conveyed unknown to the great majority of the inhabitants of Montreal. Great excitement, we hear, prevailed in that city from the moment of the receipt of the important documents published here on Friday last."
—*Quebec Mercury.*

thence to Niagara, and on his way in returning, he was, at every place where he touched on his route, received with the utmost enthusiasm.† He put up for several days at the Clifton House, near the Falls, during which he was visited by all the notabilities in the neighborhood, including many from the United States, military reviews, levees, entertainments, and splendid balls, being the order of the day during His Excellency's residence at that place which he reached

---

† The following letter, on His Excellency's arrival at Montreal, was addressed by Mr. Buller to the Attorney General, Mr. Ogden :—

"MONTREAL, *July* 8, 1838."

" SIR,—I am directed by His Excellency the Governor General to desire you to take the necessary measures for liberating the state prisoners, now in the gaol of Montreal, without delay, and taking the recognizance and bail required of them respectively. In performing the latter duty, you will have the goodness to explain to the prisoners and to their securities that the Government will have a vigilant eye on their future conduct; that the slighest manifestations of disloyalty, turbulence or sedition will subject the prisoners to the forfeiture of their recognizances, and their friends to that of the securities into which they may have the kindness to enter in their behalf, and that penalty will, on the occurance of any misconduct, be exacted by a sure and summary process. It is, however, His Excellency's hope that the great and unexampled forbearance displayed by the Government in its treatment of these prisoners, will be the more effeatual in preventing any futute misconduct than the terror, of this punishment.

"I am, sir, your obedient servant,
(signed,) CHAS. BULLER,
" To the Attorney General." '" Chief Secretary

Shortly after this letter, we find the following in a Montreal paper :—

" All the state prisoners with the exception of L. M. Viger, T. S. Girouard, Dr. Kimber, W. H. Scott, and Coursolles, have been admitted to bail. For the four last, £10,000 security is required for each which has not yet been received." They were, nevertheless, shortly after liberated on heavy bail, with the exception of Mr. Viger who was detained most unjustly, as many thought, for some time longer.

on the 13th of July. After visiting the principal places in Upper Canada, he arrived at Quebec on the 28th of the same menth.

Sir John Harvey, Lieutenant Governor of New Brunswick, came to Quebec overland from Fredericton, on a visit to the Governor General, shortly after his return from Upper Canada. The visit was short, being it was understood, on public business connected with His Lordship's mission. His visit was followed by the arrival, shortly after, on the Medoa war steamer at Quebec, bringing Lieutenant Governors Sir Colin Campbell and Sir Charles Fitzroy, the former of Nova Scotia,and latter of Prince Edward Island, to confer with the Governor General on the subject of a federal union of the North American Provinces. They re-embarked at Quebec on the 25th August for their respective Governments. Their visit to Canada was immediately followed by deputations named by their three several Executive. Governments of those provinces to Quebec, to confer on that subject with the Earl of Durham.* It was at the time currently reported that the Nova Scotia deputation, as well as that from Prince Edward Island, were in favor of a federal union, but that the gentlemen from New Brunswick were opposed to it.

While Lord Durham was thus engaged in composing the differences in Canada, his political opponents were not unobservant of his movements, nor unwilling, it would seem, to give him annoyance in any shape. Accordingly, shortly after his arrival, it was observed that questions were asked concerning some of those who had accompanied or followed His Lordship to Canada, either as attaches or in the expectation of employment from him, in particular a Mr. Turton, and Mr. Edward Gibbon Wakefield. Against the former, a divorce, for some domestic foible, had been

---

* The names of these gentlemen will subsequently appear in an address to Lord Durham.

it was said, obtained by his lady, and the latter had been convicted and made notorious for the abduction of a Miss Turner.*

* In a report of the debates in the House of Lords, on the 10th July, we find the following by Lord Brougham:—" Why, three days ago, when Lord Durham's appointment of Mr. Turton had been attacked, and when he [Lord B,] endeavoured to excuse it, every member of the Government was silent in Lord Durham's defence—nay, the head of the Government expressed his regret at the conduct of the noble lord, as to whose conduct, forsooth, now not a word was to be said."

Again, on the 6th July, Lord Winchelsea, in referring to those gentlemen, observes that:—" When he had formerly sought information as to this appointment, he entertained no doubt that the individual alluded to had gone out with a view to his becoming a member of one of the highest and most important missions that had ever been sent from this country; and he objected to any such appointment, because he viewed it as being closely connected with the character of the Sovereign. In his opinion, no one should have been employed on such a mission, except his character was free from taint or blemish. He now begged leave to ask the noble viscount a question, namely, whether the individual to whom he had alluded had been recalled?. That was the only question that he meant to ask. He had heard it reported, but he trusted the rumour was without foundation, that the appointment had not been interfered with. It had also been reported that another individual, who had been imprisoned for three years on account of a very grave offence, had left this country with a view to an appointment on the same Commission. He was ready to make all just allowances for the failings of individuals, for the weakness of human nature. He did not mean to say that, in consequence of the unpleasant circumstances in which individuals might place themselves by improper conduct, they ought never to be allowed to hold any appointment under the Government. But this was, in his mind, a most peculiar case, and he must say that the situation which was filled by the person to whom he alluded, ought not to have been conferred upon him, connected, as he repeated that it was, with the character of the Sovereign of the country. If the second report, to which he had drawn the attention of the noble viscount, were fact, then he must say that two persons had been selected for important situations which they were unfit to fill,

This, however, was but skirmishing compared to the onset to which Lord Durham, by his Ordinance No. 1, exiling the eight *detenus* to Bermuda, and purporting to subject them thereat, where he had no jurisdiction, to a restraint in which he was totally unwarranted, had exposed himself. The matter was, on the 7th of August, brought by Lord Brougham under consideration of the House of Lords, and a bill introduced by him to indemnify all those who had issued or acted in putting the Ordinance alluded to in force.* This having been amply discussed by

and from which they ought to be removed. He hoped that the rumour was not true, and to elicit the fact he put the question to the noble viscount."

" Viscount Melborne said that the ministers had very recently received an account of the appointment complained of, and had not yet had time to communicate with the Government abroad. Under these circumstances it would not at present be convenient to state the course which Government intended to persue.

" Here the matter ended."

* The following is from a report of the debates on the subject, in an English paper:—

WEDNESDAY, *August* 7.

" Lord Brougham reverted to the ordinances of Lord Durham, and contended that the powers conferred on him did not justify him in departing from the law relative to the trial of treasonable offenders. Parliament might itself try for high treason, and on the suppression of the rebellion which followed the revolution of 1688, those who were implicated were tried before Parliament instead of being tried before ordinary courts. 'Now mark,' said the noble and learned lord, ' the marvellously incredible absurdity which he was about to point out. They [the Governor and Council] did not begin by declaring what they meant, namely, to pass a bill of attainder, and say that A. B. C. being guilty of high treason, should suffer penalties ; but, without declaring them guilty, these men were sentenced to be banished to the Island of Bermuda ; and if they came away from that place and returned to Canada, then, in that case alone, were they to be treated as being guilty of high treason. So that here was a kind of high treason in suspense—a sort of prospective treason—by which these men were to be pun-

the lords was on the 13th of the same month, on motion of Lord Brougham seconded by the Duke of Wellington finally passed and sent down to the House of Commons. Lord Denman was opposed to the Bill and on the third reading of it observed " that

---

ished, not for any act they committed in Canada, but for having left Bermuda. Now, that ordinance was clearly opposed to the 25th Edward III, which must salutarily limited treasonable offences to a very small number indeed. After noticing the shutting out the murderers of Lieutenant Weir from pardon,' which, from the language used, would, he maintained, tie the hands of the Queen, unless the viceroy over Canada were viceroy over the Quaen also, he proceeded to ask under what authority did the Coercion Act extend to the West India Islands ? ' Now, what said the proclamation ? ' And whereas in the exercise, and in persuance of the extraordinary powers aforesaid, it hath been ordained and enacted by an ordinance of this day, made and passed according to law, intituled, ' An ordinance to provide for the security of Lower Canada', that it shall be lawful for us to transport certain persons named in the same ordinance to the Island of Bermuda during our pleasure.' Now, suppose the Governor and Council to have a right to pass a bill of pains and penalties in Canada, and increase the number of treasonable offences, in opposition to the Acts of Wm. III. and Edward III. still they did not possess the slightest power over the Island of Burmuda." Were Sir Charles Paget to attempt to keep these men under strict surveillance in the Bermudas, he would be liable to an action of false imprisonment. The sooner something were done, by instruction.or bill, to curb the powers so inconsiderately exercised, the better.

"Lord Glenelg admitted that the jurisdiction of the Governor of Canada did not extend to the Bermudas, and he therefore took it for granted that the first ordinance could not be of any avail, though in the exercise of the extraordinary powers vested in Lord Durham, his lordship's justification would be found in the great principles on which he had proceeded to legislate, and having consulted the real and substantial interest of the Province. In the country most affected, he (Lord Glenelg knew that the general feeling was decidedly in favor of the course Lord Durham had taken,"

"Lord Melbourne also gave up that part of the ordinance which relates to the Island of Bermuda,

it would be against common justice to pass it. Yet he must confess that Lord Durham had far exceeded his powers in issuing the ordinance. He acquitted Lord Durham of any improper intention—that noble-

because it is clear that Lord Durham could not advert to places beyond his jurisdiction, but he could say of all other parts, from authority which he could not doubt, and in which he entirely confided, that they were perfectly legal, and warranted by powers committied to Lord Durham. Lord Melbourne protested strongly against the course pursued with respect to Lord Durham. If, said his lordship, you consider that he has exercised powers entrusted to him unfortunately, and in such a manner as to hazard the interests of the country in that part of the empire, it would be unquestionably wise in your lordships to interfere to pervent such a course from being persevered in ; but if you do not see any ground for interfering, then you ought to place some reliance on his judgment, and not be perpetually interrupting the course of his proceedings by comments on his conduct, thus weakening your own authority and the authority of the Government. He added that it was one of the evils pertaining to popular Governments, in consequence of political strife, political attacks, and party and personal dislike,that the enemy of the country has always found the greatest assistance and encouragement in the bosom of Legislative Assemblies."

" Lord Brougham gave notice that he would take the earliest opportunity of bringing the legality of the ordinance before the House. His opinion was, the Act did not give Lord Durham the powers exercised by him, and he thought that the best course would be to introduce a declaratory Act, which he would do on the earliest day, to explain, define and limit the power given to his lordship."

"THURSDAY, *August* 9.

" Lord Brougham moved the second reading of a bill introduced by him, "for declaring the true intent and meaning of an Act passed in the present session of Parliament, intituled, ' An Act to make temporary provision for the Government of Lower Canada ;' and for indemnifying those who have issued or acted under a certain ordinance, made under colour of the said Act., His lordship strongly supported the bill, contending for the illegality of the ordinance."

" Lord Glenelg opposed the bill as inconsistent and uncalled for, although he admitted that the ordinance could

man undoubtedly thought he was doing what would be for the best, but he exceeded all law and justice. He thought a Bill of Indemnity an unconstitutional proceeding. Parliament had no right to say to an injured man that he should not have redress against

not be carried into effect; but he urged that it was requisite for the Government of Canada to adopt some step to exclude certain parties from Canada, otherwise that Government would not have done its duty."

"Lord Lyndhurst condemned the course sued by the Canadian Government and declared the ordinance illegal."

"Lord Melbourne admitted the illegality as regarded Bermuda, but after the support extended to the Act giving extraordinary powers to Lord Durham, he was not prepared to hear censure applied for the exercise of such powers."

"The Duke of Wellington complained of the charge thus conveyed, in return for support of the Government into which he had been 'entrapped;' but though he was willing to strengthen the Government as regarded Canada, he denied that either he or his friends had any part in the responsibility respecting the proceeding done under the Acts. The responsibility of the measure rested with the Government, and he was sure more gross illegality than the ordinance displayed, as far as it concerned Bermuda, could hardly be committed. He denounced the idea of this country permitting banishment without trial.

"Lord Brougham replied.

"Their lordships then divided on the question. The numbers were, for the bill, 54; against it, 46; majority in favor of the bill, 18.

"FRIDAY, *August*, 10.

"Upon the question that the House do go into committee on Lord Brougham's Canada Declaratory Act—

"Lord Melbourne rose and said, before the Lord Chancellor left the woolsack, he would state the course he meant to pursue. He could not express with what feelings of anxiety he had received the decision of their lordships, which would affect very great interests that were now at stake. It was a decision which would be construed in favor of a particular party had lately rebelled against the union with this country. Such was the practical effect of the course that their lordships had adopted He had therefore attempted to dissuade them from it, and he had not been able to conceal the apprehensions with which he look-

his injurer. If the wrongful acts of a public officer were justified by his good intentions, let him be indemnified out of the public purse; but it was not right to prohibit the injured party from seeking redress.

" Lord Brougham admitted the force of what Lord Denman had said, but, unfortunately, there were precedents for the indemnity.

---

ed upon the course taken, especially when, owing to the distance from the scene, it was impossible to say in what condition of feeling these debates and this bill would be received. It appeared to him that it would have been far better to leave ministers to pursue their own course; but as their lordships had decided otherwise, he would now state what he meant to do under that decision. He admitted the informality of that portion of the Ordinance which applied to a district beyond the jurisdiction of the Governor General, and he had also been much struck by the argument that the Government had not the power to disallow a part of the Ordinance, and allow the other part of the same, with respect to a chartered colony, and that, under these circumstances, he ought to advise Her Majesty to disallow the validity of this Ordinance. At the same time, to say that it was all avoid, and that the sentenced parties could be allowed to return, was what he would not naturally have adhered to. It was striking at the root of all authority in that country. For though he admitted there were grave arguments advanced concerning those who had never been taken, yet the character of Lord Durham was too well known for any body not to suppose that that Ordinance was only held out *in torrorem*, and to keep those parties from returning and creating a dangerous state of circumstances. He therefore, had wished their lordships not to interfere. He had, however, under these circumstances, decided, to advise Her Majesty to disallow the validity of the whole of the Ordinance. It was with feelings of great apprehension, but he had been compelled. It followed, almost of course, that the Ordinance being illegal, all that had been done in execution of it was illegal, and those parties who had passed and executed it, were liable to be pursued before courts of justice, and that some provision for indemnity was necessary He would support the indemnity clause. With respect to the first clause, he very strongly objected to it. They had heard much about the prohibition in the Coercion Act, against al-

" The Bill was then possed.

In the House of Commons a very animated debate arose on the bill. The Attorney General Campbell generously vindicated Lord Durham.

" The Earl of Durham had most successfully proceeded in pacifying the dissensions in Lower Canada. His measures were received with satisfaction by both

tering Acts of Parliament. It appeared to him that it would be making the Coercion Act absurd, if that prohibiton was interpreted as meaning any Acts beyond the Act of 1791 and the Tenures Act. It would be absurd to prevent the Governor General from taking measures necessary for the safety of the Province. He understood the prohibition not to interfere with the power of taking measures that might be absolutely necessary, and he should move an explanatory clause to that effect.

" Lord Brougham expressed his satisfaction at this course declaring it to be wise and virtuous, but objected to the clause which Lord Melbourne proposed to introduce. The noble and learned lord proceeded to say, that, after what the Government had determined to do, he had no objection to strike out the declaratory part of the Bill. But he must say, that the noble viscount's proposition to introduce a clause which would arm the Governor General with powers which he did not now possess, was one to be deprecated. The conduct of the Governor General had not been such as to induce him to enlarge his powers. He did not go with the noble viscount in saying, that the Bill relating to Canada gave power to the Governor and Council to pass Bills of attainder or find Bills of pains and penalties. But the noble viscount said that the Governor of Canada ought to have that power. He could hardly consent to give them larger power, because, when they had the doubtful power, they passed bills of attainder illegally, without hearing the accused party. He asked them to leave the law as it stood on the bill. Let it stand, but give indemnity to errors. At the same time he would not deprive certain individuals, who had been illegally used, of their right and action.

" The Duke of Wellington expressed great dissatisfaction with respect to the conclusion of the remarks made by the noble viscount. He would add his sincere desire that the noble viscount be disappointed in his apprehension, that the course taken by the House the preceeding evening, would lead to evils in the Province of Canada, such as the noble

parties in that country. In that country there was no complaint of this Ordinance in any quarters and his firm belief was, that if no objection had been made to it on this side of the water, all would have gone on viscount had described. He was impressed with a conviction that the people of Canada, as well as this country, were looking for justice on this subject, and that they would not be led to believe that the Lords intended, by the course they pursued Thursday night, to effect any other object than justice. With respect to the amendment to be proposed by the noble viscount, he must say, with all the respect he entertained for the noble lord, that he could not be induced to give any public opinion on that subject, until he saw what the amendment was which he intended to introduce. He also begged to submit to the noble viscount that the alteration he proposed was by no means necessary; it was not necessary to adopt this amendment in order to enable the Governor to punish rebellion and treason in the Province. And for this reason ; because he believed that the late Governor General (Sir John Colborne) had acted under the provisions of this very Act of Parliament, and he must have had the power of preventing rebellion and treason under the Act as it existed, without such an alteration as was now proposed by the noble viscount. Under these circumstances he, for one thought that this proposition should not be brought under the consideration of their lordships, inasmuch as he had a sincere desire that this matter should terminate without any further dissension upon it. He felt convinced that the question had now been brought to that stage by which real service had been done to the State, and he hoped also to the Governor of Canada.

" The bill passed through committee.

" On the report.

' Lord Brougham moved some amendments, to the effect that whereas certain acts had been done which could not be justified by law, but which were intended for the security of the Province ; that, therefore, all persons ordaining, or acting under, or in obedience to so much of the ordinance of the Governor General as related to the sending to Bermuda certain persons therein named, should be indemnified ; and that a proclamation should be made of this Act immediately on its reception in the Colonies.

" These amendmrnts were agreed to.

" The report was brought up, and the bill ordered to be read a third time on Monday, the 13th."

smoothly. The object of the Ordinance was clearly to prevent the re-entrance of the persons accused of taking part in the Rebellien into Lower Canada, without the permission of the Governor, until the pacification of the province had taken place. Those individuals would not have thought of entering the province without the permission of the Governor, who might have granted that permission to particular individuals on particular conditions, without any complaint being made by any party; and his belief was, that in a short time the Earl of Durham, who had patriotically undertaken this arduous mission, would have returned to this country covered with complete success. He had hoped that that nobleman would still persevere in the glorious task in which he was engaged : and that he would set at defiance all those who were his distractors and enemies. But it was impossible to disguise that there was great danger that his authority might be shaken by these attempts made to attack the policy which he had pursued. With regard to the bill before the house, he regretted exceedingly that it should ever have been introduced, There existed no necessity for it, for no action ever would have been brought, nor prosecution ever instituted or thought of by the parties named in the Ordinance, if it had not been for the ingenuity of certain lawyers in this country, who had suggested the illegality of that Ordinance. It had been stated by the honorable member for Westminster, and by the honorable member for Lamberth, that the Earl of Durham did not want this indemnity. He agreed with those honorable members that it never would have been required, and that the introduction of such a measure was both officious and insidious. But as it had been introduced, and as the subject had been discussed and the question agitated, and as it did appear to him, on just consideration, that that part of the Ordinance which was to be executed beyond the territory of Lower Canada was not justified by law he had no hesitation in voting for the bill. A bill of indemnity in this case was not at all subject to the objections which had been made against it by the honorable member for Lambert, or by a noble and learned lord elsewhere, because *volenti non fit injuria*. And all those who could have brought actions against persons acting under the authority of this Ordinance had confessed their guilt. " Oh, but," said the honorable member for Westminster, "they did not confess they were guilty of high treason : they only confessed that they were found in arms against the Queen's government, and as the Queen's government was not legal, that act was not high treason." He was sorry that in a house of Parliament such doctrine should be laid down. When it was confessed by these persons that they had openly opposed by force of arms the authority of the state, and when they levied war against the Queen within her realms, was that, or was it not, confessedly high treason ? These persons, then, could have had no cause of complaint at the issuing of the Ordinance ; and if they had instituted a prosecution they would not have been able to have obtained more than one shilling damages. The honerable and learned member admitted that the Governor and his Council had exceeded their authority in that part of the Ordinance which appointed Bermuda as the place for the prisoners. He referred to the acts of Upper Canada having the same object in view with the Ordinance of Lower Canada, and said that these acts could not be distinguished from the Ordinance the legality of which was now disputed. He professed himself ready to take his share of the responsibility which might be incurred by Lord Durham on the subject of this act, believing that he possessed the power which he employed and that he had exercised it wisely and discreetly, and further the noble lord had been fully justified in the departing from the criminal law as it existed in Canada before he went there, and in making it vary from the criminal law in England. He lamented the necessity which existed for a resort to unconstitutional measures in Canada, and trusted the time was not far distant when peace and tranquility would be restored, and the people would return to obedience to the law as it formerly stood."

" Sir Edward Sugden, contended that the Ordinance was illegal and was surprised that the Attorney General after supporting it should consent to its being rescinded, a course in which he saw many difficulties."

" Sir G. Grey saw none of those difficulties which the learned Knight discovered. If the Ordinance and proclamation were annulled the parties affected would be remitted to the situation in which they formerly stood, and he conceived there would be no difficulty in trying these parties after the unqualified admission of guilt they had made. But the Ordinance could not be maintained, and must be got rid of.

The Solicitor General was willing to take his full share of the responsibility with his hon. and learned friend. He cited a precedent, the act prohibiting the Pretender to enter the British dominions, and it might be equally necessary for the public peace that Mr. Papineau should be excluded from Canada.

Lord John Russell said on reflection he had come to the decision that the safer plan would be to pass the Bill as it stood without adding a clause with respect to the future operations of the act that had already passed; and in that opinion he was very much confirmed by the diversity of opinion which he had observed among honorable gentlemen of great legal authority on the other side of the House.

The Bill having passed in the House of Commons received the royal sanction and became law.* Lord

---

* " LONDON, 22d August, 1838.

" MY LORD.—The North American Colonial Association have already expressed, by certain Resolutions transmitted to Lord Glenelg, Lord John Russell, the Duke of Wellirg-

John Russell in course of the debates warmly sustained Lord Durham, expressing his hope that he would still consider himself bound to continue his service to his country in spite of the attacks upon him, and of the obloquy attempted to be thrown upon his conduct.

" The treatment he has received " observed Lord John, " is certainly far different from what he was entitled to expect after his appeal to the generous for-

ton, and Sir Robert Peel, their conviction that the discussions which have been lately raised in Parliament, in regard to Lower Canada, will tend to destroy British power and influence in that Province, by encouraging the disaffected, and disheartening the loyal, and solemnly declared their serious apprehensions that these discussions were calculated to retard the pacification, if they did not cause the loss of these valuable appendages to the British Crown. In these sentiments we fully concur, and being parties deeply interested in the welfare of the North American Colonies, and sincerely desirous to perpetuate their connexion with the Parent State, we feel compelled to address your Lordship and to express our deep regret that certain Ordinance of the Governor in Council should be disallowed, seeing the conflicting opinions expressed in Parliament in regard to them, and that the inhabitants, whether of French or British origin, appreciated these acts of their Governor as best calculated to restore peace and give security and prosperity to the Colony. We, further, cannot but view the recent proceedings as originating in personal disappointment, or elicited by discussion; and in hope that His Excellency will not be driven from the great work he has so well begun, by individuals who were either not aware of the effects which their proceedings might produce or who are regardless of the consequences.

" We do assure you, my Lord,.that we as well as our partners and different correspondents in the Colony, have the fullest confidence in the wisdom, impartiality and lenity of His Excellency the Governor General towards every class of Her Majesty's subjects in those Provinces, and that if His Excellency has in any one instance exceeded the powers given to him by Parliament, it was to save the lives of traitors who would have been justly doomed to death by an English, though in all probability acquitted by a French Canadian Jury.

" The accounts received yesterday from Canada are of a

bearance even of his political opponents. If the Canadian provinces be happily preserved to us; if Lord Durham be able to restore tranquility and good order, without infliction of the punishment of death, and to reestablish a free constitution not only unimpaired but improved, he need care for no violence or invective, for

very favorable nature; His Excellency had visited Upper Canada, and made such dispositions of the force as to ensure tranquility and inspire confidence. He halted at the different cities and towns, seeking information how he could best serve the interests, improve the Province, and rivet their connexion with the mother country. The resident inhabitants took that opportunity of presenting addresses to him of the most satisfactory description, thankful that their Queen had condescended to send them such a man.

"Whatever measure may be ultimately recommended by Lord Durham in regard to the future permanent Government of those Provinces, we cannot but view any change of administration at present with terror and dismay, and we do pray that His Excellency will continue to administer the affairs of these important Provinces until he has matured a system of Government applicable to their peculiar situation, and reconciled all parties to the dominion of the Imperial Government.

We have, &c.

(Signed,)

Robert Gillespie,
Alex. Gillespie, jun.
Nathal. Gould,
Russell Ellice,
George Forsyth,
E. H. Chapman,
Glyn, Halifax, Mills & Co.
Robt. Harrison & Co.
Smith, Payne & Smiths,
W. E. Logan,
A Stewart,
J. Westmoreland,
Fredk. De Lisle,
W. Janvrin,
Wm. Oviatt,
Wm. Pemberton & Co.
Robinson & Co.

W. & J. Benson.
Bowles, Brothers & Co.
R. & B. Brown & Co.
T. Richier, for Phœnix Insurance Company,
W. T. Hibbett,
F. H. Mitchell,
R. T. Maitland,
J. Mackillopp,
A. A. Gowen, Nephews & Co.
Wm. Clarke & Keeling,
W. Crane, of New Brunswick,
James Dowie,
Charles Walton,
Newman Hunts & Christopher.
Carter & Bonas,

To the Right Honorable, Lord John Russell.

no accumulation of charges, for no refinement of sophistry, for no bitterness of sarcasm accompanied by professions of friendship, attempting to disguise, but not succeeding in disguising the petty and personal feeling at the bottom of all these attacks; for he will have deserved well of his country, well of his Sovereign, and well of posterity."

Lord Durham, on the arrival of this news, and learning the fate of his Ordinance, made no concealment of his determination to return to England as early as possible, after being officially notified of the course which the Home Government had taken on the subject. Addresses from all parts in both Canadas pressed in upon him, but none were more gratifying to him, it is said, than that presented by the delegates from the Lower Provinces, then at Quebec.*

LONDON, 24th Aug., 1838.

MY LORD.—We take the, liberty to enclose a letter to your Lordship from parties deeply interested in the North American Colonies, particularly in the Canadas, stating their anxiety lest the late discussions in Parliament may disturb and cause a change in the present Government of these Provinces.

The parties signing the letter have full confidence in the Administration of the Governor General, and we beg to be permitted to express a wish that your Lordship will cause the said letter in duplicate and copies thereof to be transmitted without delay to His Excellency Lord Durham, and would suggest that they may be despatched by the steam ships Royal William and Great Western, the former of which will leave Liverpool about the first, and the latter Bristol, on the 8th proximo.

We are, &c.

(Signed,) ROBERT GILLESPIE.
NATHAL. GOULD.

To the Right Honorable Lord John Russell.

* To His Excellency the Right Honorable the Earl of Durham, Governor General of the British North American Provinces, &c &c.

In approaching your Lordship on the eve of our departure from Quebec, we beg unanimously to offer to your Lordship the expression of our highest respect, and of the deep con-

Besides the commission previously mentioned relative to Crown Lands, another respecting education was announced on the 4th of July. By this, Mr. Arthur Buller, one of the *attaches* or suite of His Excel-

cern with which we heard of your Lordship's rumoured intention to resign the Government of these Provinces.

The duties of the mission with which we have been intrusted by the Lieutenant Governors of Nova Scotia, New Brunswick and Prince Edward Island, and the frankness of communication permitted by your Lordship, have brought us into acquaintance with your Lordship's feelings and views in relation to British North America, and irrosistibly impressed our minds with the conviction that your Lordship cherishes an ardent desire to elevate the Colonies committed to your Government and entertains conceptions calculated to render that desire effective.

In a review of the short period of the Government under your Lordship's personal direction, we behold your Lordship, with that feeling so congenial to Englishmen which turns with repugnance from the shedding of blood on the scaffold, blending mercy with justice; while returning tranquility had already rewarded an administration conducted without the sacrifice of one human life; and we were aware that improved laws and institutions were in preparation, which, under a Government firm, mind, and impartial, gave to the future the reasonable prospect of restored confidence and renovated prosperity.

For the Provinces with which we are more personally connected, we saw in the warm interest, the enlightened and comprehensive views, and the extensive powers of your Lordship, the dawning of vigor and improvement hitherto unknown. With your Lordship's departure those anticipations will we fear fade away; but although it should be our lot to see these Provinces continue feeble and nerveless compared with the condition at which their natural advantages entitle them to aim, yet we shall ever remember with gratitude the stateman who, exalted in the first rank, and treading on the highest eminences of political life in this our common country, hesitated not at the call of his Sovereign, with disinterested zeal, to undertake an office of unparalleled difficulty, and has given to these distant territories the benefit of his enlarged experience and vigorous conceptions. Your Lordship's comprehensive mind has opened to our view the animating prospect of great public improvements advancing our common welfare, and which will ever asso-

lency, was appointed Commissioner, and desired to proceed with the utmost despatch to inquire into and investigate the past and present mode of disposing of the produce of any estate or funds set apart for, or

ciate your Lordship's name with the highest prosperity of the colonies.

We are unwilling to abandon the hope, that your Lordship may yet continue in the administration of your high office. Under any circumstances, we beg to assure your Lordship that our most ardent wishes for the happiness of the Countess of Durham, your Lordship and family, will accompany you through life.

J. W. JOHNSTON, Member of the Legislative Council, Nova Scotia.

JAMES B. UNIACKE, Member for County of Cape Breton and Member of Council.

WM. YOUNG, Member of Assembly for the County of Inverness.   M. B. ALMON.

DEPUTATION FROM NOVA SCOTIA.

CHARLES SIMMONS, Member of the Executive Council, and Speaker of the Assembly of New Brunswick.

HENRY PETERS, Legislative Council.

E. BOTSFORD, Member of Executive and Legislati e Councils

HUGH JOHNSTON, Member of the Executive Council and House of Assembly.

JAMES KIRK.

JOHN ROBERTSON,

DEPUTATION FROM NEW BRUNSWICK.

I. H. HAVILAND, Member of Executive and Legislative Councils.

GEO. DALRYMPLE, Speaker of the House of Assembly.

JOSEPH POPE, Member of Assembly for Prince County.

DEPUTATION FROM PRINCE EDWARD ISLAND.

Quebec, 22d September, 1838.

To which address, His Excellency was pleased to return the following answer:—

It is impossible for me to express to you in language sufficiently strong, the feelings of gratitude and pleasure with which I have received this address.

Representing, as you do so worthly, three Provinces of Nova Scotia, New Brunswick and Prince Edward Island, this proof of your confidence in me, and approbation of the

applicable to, purposes of education in Lower Canada, and into the present means of education enjoyed by, or within reach of, Her Majesty's subjects therein." He was moreover required "to suggest such alteration, modification, and extension of the system of ed-

principles on which my Administration has been conducted is most gratifying to me.

I assumed the Government of the North American Provinces, with the predetermination to provide for the future welfare and prosperity of them all; never doubting that such a provision would be best, nay the only, real security for their permanent connexion with the British Crown. In communications which have taken place between us, and from wh'ch I have derived equal pleasure and information, you have been fully apprised of my views and intentions. These you have appreciated and recognised in a manner for which I can never be sufficiently grateful. I have, indeed had a difficult and laborious duty to perform. The result of my endeavours, however, is one of which I need not be ashamed. In the short space of little more than three months, I havé seen tranquility restored, and confidence reviving. I have caused substantial justice to be administered tempered to mercy. I have carefully examined, with a view to reformation, all the institutions of the Province more immediately committed to my charge; and I was on the point of promulgating such laws as would have afforded protection to all these great British interests which had been too long neglected. I had also, as you well know, devoted the most careful attention to all subjects which could affect the general interests of all the Colonies, and had brought nearly to maturity the plan which I intended to submit in the first instance to the consideration of the Provinces, and eventually of the Cabinet and the Imperial Parliament. In this, I trust useful course, I have been suddenly arrested by the interference of a branch of the British Legislature; in which the responsible advisers of the Crown have deemed it their duty to acquiesce. Under these circumstances, I have but one step to take—to resign that authority the exercise of which has thus been so weakened as to render it totally inadequate to the grave emergency which alone called for its existence.

Be assured, however, of this, Gentlemen, that this unexpected and abrupt termination of the official connexion which united me with the North American Provinces, will not weaken in my mind the feelings of deep interest which

ucation at present prevailing in the Province, and such other management of any estate or funds applicable to such purposes of education as might in his judgment appear likely to promote those objects. In addition to the commission with which Mr. Charles Buller was already entrusted relating to Crown lands, and emigration, he was by letters patent issued on the 23rd of August, invested with another not less important. The letters stated that "whereas it is highly expedient and desirable that the counties, cities, towns,

---

I shall ever take in their fate, or render me less anxious to devote every faculty of my mind, every influence I may possess, to the advancement of their interests, and to the establishment, on the most lasting foundation, of their welfare and prosperity."

The following extract from Mr. Neilson's *Quebec Gazette* express the opinion generally entertained in the Canadas of the treatment which the Earl of Durham had experienced.

"Lord Durham has been ill-used by the House of Peers, and badly supported by Her Msjesty's Ministers. His Lordship, who has frequently enpressed his ardent desire to see the connexion between the United Kingdom and the North American Colonies rendered perpetual, will see the danger of their interests being involved in the political contests which are perpetually going on in the Mother Country. The Ministry, for the time being, is to us, the British Government. If we take a part in their contests, we shall soon, we fear, lose much of our respect for the Home Government, and for the authority of the Sovereign, whose commands must be transmitted through the responsible Ministers of the Crown. Our opposition to the Ministry of the day, would degenerate into disaffection to the Imperial Government, and be productive of the worst consequences.

"Our duty, as well as our interests, combine in respecting the authorities, in whose formation, constitutionally, we can exercise no influence. Fidelity to the Sovereign, to our connexion with the old country, and a determination as much as in us lies to support the established authority, and promote the peace, welfare and good Government of the country, ought to be the main political objects of all its inhabitants. Our own connections on the public affairs will always be quite sufficient to occupy any time we can spare from our private pursuits, without engaging in those beyond the Atlantic."

parishes, and townships, in Lower Canada should respectively enjoy, as extensive a control as may be consistent with their own improvement, and with the general welfare of the Province, over all matters and things of a local nature, to the end that intercourse may be facilitated, industry promoted, crime repressed, education appreciated, and true liberty understood and advanced." His Excellency had appointed him (Charles Buller) "to proceed with the utmost despatch to enquire into the safest and most efficient means of endowing the said counties, &c., with such powers and privileges as to him might seem meet for the effecting of those important ends," and to report thereupon, suggesting by his report "such alterations of modifications of the laws and regulations at present in force, as might appear likely to promote the objects aforesaid." Mr. Buller was authorised to nominate his assistants in the commission, and accordingly he appointed Mr. William Kennedy, one of His Excellency's *attachés*, and Mr. Adam Thom, editor of the *Montreal Herald*, his associates in the commission of inquiry relating to the municipal institutions, which it seems to have been Lord Durham's purpose to establish in Lower Canada. The several reports of those commissioners are, it is presumed, deposited among the public archives of the Province, and to a certain extent have been acted upon, but are too voluminous for reproduction or further notice here. Lord Durham's Report to the Queen, of his mission to Canada, upon his return home, may reasonably be taken as a synopsis of the whole.

Among the remarkable occurrences of the year, attracting public attention, was the trial of Francois Nicholas, Amable Daunais, Joseph Pinsonnault and Gideon Pinsonnault, at the September Criminal Assises in Montreal, for the murder of Joseph Armand dit Chartrand, of St. Johns, on the 27th November last, at Lacadie, as previously noticed. The evidence on behalf of the prosecution seemed to be clear and convincing of the guilt of the accused, but they were, nevertheless, acquitted of this atrocious homicide, by the Jury, who, it was said, dined with the prisoners immediately after accquitting them, in exultation of the circumstance as a party triumph.* A

---

*" Yesterday morning the Honorable Messrs, Chief Justice Reid, Justices Rolland, Pyke, and Gale took their seats on the bench, when François, Nicholas Amable Daunais, Joseph Pinsonnault, and Gideon Pinsonnault, were placed at the bar, charged with the murder of Joseph Armand dit Chartrand, on the 27th of November last. The prisoners had pleaded not guilty. The Attorney and Solicitor General appeared on the part of the Crown and the case was opened by the Solicitor General. The Counsel for the prisoners were Messrs. W. Walker, D.A. Laberge, and Charles Mondlet. We understand that, as we recommended, Nicholas was deprived of his spectacles and enormous mustaches, which it was reported, he had assumed for a disguise, and the want of which gives him a much more civilized appearance than when he was arraigned on the indictment of the Grand Jury.

Mr. D. A. Laberge interrupted the Court several times, and was committed for contempt, to be confined in the common gaol till the last day of the term. The Court was crowded during the whole day. Several witnesses were examined, but as it would not be fair to publish their evidence previous to the conclusion of the trial, we are reluctantly compelled to postpone any report of it till to-morrow. The Court adjourned yesterday afternoon at six o'clock,and will meet again this morning at the usual hour. Sixteen witnesses for the prosecution were examined and cross examined."

The facts as given in evidence at the trial, by an eye witness of this terrible affair, were as follows, according to the *Montreal Gazette*:—

Etienne Langlois, the first witness, deposed—I am a carpenter, residing at Lacaeie, went from home on horseback, on Monday, in the lattes part of November last; was met by one Garant, Gideon Pinsonnault, (one of the prisoners) and others. Was forced to join the party, and accompanied it in the first place to the Inn, in the vicinity, kept by one Surprenant, where we all drank. The party consisted with

bill of indictment was found at the same assizes against Francois Jalbert, Jean Paptiste Maillet, Joseph Pratte, and Louis Lussier, for the murder of Lieutenant Weir, at St. Denis. the trial was post-

myself of fifteen in number, all armed but me. We went from Surprenant's to the house of one Eloi Roy, situated on the Grand Ligne, there we found Bisronet, Nicholas Daunais and the other or Joseph Pinsonault; and there it was that I first heard anything of Chartrand, with whom I was unacquainted. It was declared that Chartrand was at David Roy's whose house was next nearest to us. Nicholas and Eloi Roy, junior, left us for the purpose of going to David Roy's pretending their object was to examine the work going on there. Up to this period, Garant had been leader or captain of the party. After about a quarter of an hour's absence, Nicholas and Garant went to Eloi Roy's. Almost immediately after their return, some one (I believe one Maillou) came to the door and exclaimed. "There he goes, now's the time if you wish to follow him," On going out of the house, saw the man whom I afterwards knew to be Chartrand, He was on the road leading to St. Johns. On observing him, Nicholas and Garant both cried out "Come along my lads," We than ran out, in a direction to intercept Chartrand. We had proceeded more than 15 acres before he was overtaken by four of us. When we so overtook him Nicholas was in the rear. The four alluded to led him back to Nicholas. We were then about half a league from Eloi Roy's house. Nicholas, by signs with his cane directed us to lead Chartrand into the fields, which we did. Nicholas then took the lead, and Chartrand was placed in the centre of the party. We conducted him to a small point of wood, about 20 acres distant from any house; and there stopped. Nicholas then addressed Chartrand, and asked him if it were true, that there were oxen or pigs fit for killing at some certain place, which Nicholas did not however designate; Chartrand replied that he no recollection o having ever said so. Nicholas then asked him some other question having reference to the St. John's volunteers.

Chartrand denied having made the statement. Nicholas replied: You said it, I myself heard you; and added, you may now make your peace with God; then turning to his party, Nicholas asked them if Chartrand did not merit death for having said what he declared to have heard him utter; some of the party cried out "Yes," and thereupon either Nicholas or Beaulieu, (I am positive one of the two)

poned, owing to the absence of necessary witnesses, to the following term, when it took place, but ended as did that of Nicholas, Daunais, and the Pinsonnaults, in their acquittal, the actors in both

---

gave the command to fire, and five of the party, in obedience to the order immediately fired at Chartrand. Beaulieu and Joseph Pinsonnault, were of the number of those who fired. Chartrand fell, and in a few moments afterwards, vainly attempting to raise himself on his side, implored them to finish him: thereupon Joseph Pinsonnault, whose gun had been reloaded by Beaulieu and two others, again fired at Chartrand. He was reluctant to fire the second time, but did so in obedience to orders. We then left the spot, although Chartrand still moved a little. Neither Daunais nor Gideon Pinsonnault had fired. The place where the murder was committed, is situated between two concessions, respectively named Barnier, and Beaujarret; and is about a league and a half from St. Johns. After the party left the spot, we separated: Nicholas went towards Barnier, I returned to Eloi Roy's and the others went home; it was then about sunset. Chartrand wore blue cloth pataloons, a black coat and a blue camlet cloak. He was a tall man, and walked firmly and well, when I saw him pass Roy's.

Cross-examined.—Did not know Chartrand; when I met the party, Garant had the command: they were fourteen in number; Garant addressed me with an air of authority; I accompanied Garant from fear; Garant ordered me to accompany the party. Garant seized my horse by the bridle; the party was going to St. Charles; I understood they were going there to fight; it had already been spoken of in the parish; I had not heard of the battle of St. Charles: I and all accompanying Garant thought we were going to St. Charles; I believe the prisoner thought so likewise. At the Pont de Paradis four or five of the party wanted to go back; the party consisted of unmarried men. At Roy's, reference was at first made to Chartrand. Nicholas lived near Surpenant's; did not near Nicholas enjoin the young men at Surprenant's to forbear committing any crime. Daunais had a gun in his hand; Nicholas left to go to David Roy's. Beaulieu and two others, I believe Giroux and Ouimet, were the most active at the scene of the slaughter; cannot say who gave the word of command to fire. Beaulieu and the two others stood nearest to Chartrand at the time of the second fire. When Chartrand received the second fire, he was dying. Beaulieu ordered Joseph Pinsonnault to re-

J

these atrocious murders, thus escaping for the moment the retribution due them by the laws of God and their country. Nicholas, however, the coolest, most cruel, and guilty of all the murderers, shortly

load; the latter declined, saying he would not fire again. Beaulieu forcibly put the gun in his hand, swearing and ordering him to fire, threatening him if he declined. Witness was with the party, but did not fire; the three reloaded Joseph Pinsonnault's gun and equally urged him to fire. Cannot say that Joseph's last shot struck the deceased. Cannot say if the order to fire on the first occasion was given by Beaulieu or Nicholas; on the second occasion Beaulieu gave the order.

Re-examined. " When Garant commanded, the party only spoke of going to St. Charles; at Eloi Roy's, some spoke of Chartrand, and some of going to St Charles; afterwards the latter idea was abandoned the party being too few in number. When they left Roy's, it was in pursuit of Chartrand. The road they took was not the direct road to St. Charles. After they left the body, they dispersed, and none spoke of going to St. Charles.

Francois Bourassa. "I know Joseph Berthiaume; he has lived with me more than a year; I have a farm on the Beaujarret road in care of a farmer named Ouimet. In the month of November last I was in the house of my farmer, when Mrs Ouimet suddenly said ho! there's Mr. Chartrand passing, adding, it is not long since he passed towards Mr. Roy's and there he is returning very hurriedly; in a minute or two afterwards, the women again exclaimed ah! see all those young men running in the field; and afterwards, ah! there's Etienne Langlois running by with a gun on his shoulder; looking out, I saw as represented and several others also armed; immediately went towards my house apprehensive at what I had seen. On my way home, saw two men about three arpents before me in the road, one of them, a large one, had a dark surtout on and appeared to be making signals; there was a smaller man with him. Knows that neither of them was Chartrand, as he wore a camlet cloak, red sash and grey cap; my farm is in Beaujarret and adjoins Petit Barnier, on a point of which there is a small wood. The man who made the signals, went towards the point where the wood is situated; after that I met two other young men, one of whom at least was armed, but did not take much notice as I was impatient to get home; heard several shots in the wood alluded to, the extreme end of which is

afterwards, as if marked by the divine hand for atonement, suffered the extreme penalty of the law for another offence, as did also, at the same time, Daunais, his comrade in crime.

about twenty arpents from my house; saw the smoke occasioned by the discharges, which were about ten acres from the house ; afterwards heard at least one shot, and enquiring of my neighbour who came up at the time, what was the meaning of the firing, he replied that they had a prisoner and he feared they were shooting him ; saw the young men from a distance, leave the point and disperse going towards Petit Barnier : next day I went alone to the point and saw there the body of Chartrand on the ground, did not approach the body nearer than an acre and a half, but knew him by his cloak and dress; his body was lying in about the middle of the point whence I saw the smoke proceed; told the circumstance to no one but my wife. Next day went to see the Priest and communicated the matter to him ; afterwards attended a meeting at Captain Roy's, and was there told by him that it was reported a dead body was lying in his point; he urged me to go and examine the point, and I agreed to accompany him; found the body lying on its face with its hands clasped beneath the head; afterwards when the body was examined before the Coroner's Inquest, it was found that the deceased had a wound in the lower part of the belly, and another transverse, one immediately under the left breast; believes them to have been made by musket balls.

" Mr. Mondelet, in the most extraordinary and seditious harangue, ever heard within the walls of a temple of justice appealed to the worst passions, and most distorted prejudices of the Jurors, in behalf of his clients, the prisoners at the bar. He contended that the prosecution had been instituted, and was carried on, at the instance of the Executive; that the Government afraid to accuse and try the prisoners before a jury of their fellow countrymen, for alleged political offences, thus sought to gratify their malice and vindictiveness for the state delinquencies of his clients, by compassing their destruction, in a covert and irregular manner. He attempted not to deny their anticipation in the massacre of the ill-fated Chartrand; but contended that the offence imputed to them, was merged and lost, in the greater and more enormous crime of high treason. That the government had not dared to prosecute them for that greater and more comprehensive transgression, and could not now wreak its

Lord Durham having received the official despatches from home, which he awaited respecting his Ordinance for transporting to Bermuda the political exiles whom he had sent thither, issued, on the 8th of October, his proclamation, publishing the Act of Indemnity passed by the Imperial Parliament, together with another porclamation, expressive of his own views on the matter, with his determination to abandon the government. and return to England immediately.*

It being officially known that His Excellency had determined upon leaving the country, fresh addresses from all parts were presented him, expressing approbation of his conduct of the government,

---

vengeance against them, for its commission, by means of the present paltry and obvious subterfuge. That their colleagues in guilt, had dyed their hands in blood at St. Denis, St. Charles and St. Eustache; and by royal proclamation were exempted from the consequences of their temerity or their guilt. That he recognized not the difference in degree of culpability, between the shedding of the blood of one unarmed volunteer, and the taking of the lives of Her Majesty's soldiers by the *hundred*. That the *compatriots* of the prisoners had been exonerated from all punishment for the latter act. and it would be a gross perversion of justice, to convict the prisoners, of a capital felony, for having done the former. That the fault af the whole proceeding, if any fault there were in it, was to be imputed to the Government and to the Government only, in not having preserved and enforced i's authority; and in permitting the country to fall into a state cf anarchy, during the existence of which no man was accountable for his acts, however abhorrent to reason or adverse to justice. We pretend not to cite the language of this most extraordinary forenisie display; but pledge ourselves to the fidelity with which its spirit is recorded. After more than an hour's exertion, to the evident pleasure and conviction of the jurors; and to the no less evident dissatisfactian and disgust of every one present, endowed with reason and judgement, the jury retired ; and in about half an hour, returned into Court, and delivered a verdict of " not guilty," with regard te each and every of the prisoners."

* See at the end of this chapter.

respect for himself personally, and regret at his determination to return to England, particularly the cause of it. These addresses are too numerous for quotation, and if quoted would only express what is in substance here stated, but the answers he gave to those from Quebec, Toronto, and Kingston, are interesting, as explanatory of his views on the subjects touched upon, and are therefore inserted below.*

---

* REPLY TO QUEBEC ADDRESS.

"I request you to accept my warmest thanks for this marked expression of your feelings towards me, and of your generous confidence in my government.

"I most solemnly assure you that no consideration should induce me to leave you, if I thought my presence here could produce the least benefit, or avert the most trifling evil.

"I do not return to England, from any feelings of disgust at the treament I have personally experienced in the House of Lords. If I could have been influenced by any such motives, I must have re-embarked in the very ship which brought me out; for that system of Parliamentary persecution, to which I allude, commenced from the moment I left the shore of England.

"I return for these reasons, and these alone—The proceedings in the House of Lords, acquiesced in by the ministry, have deprived the Government of all moral power and consideration. They have reduced it to a state of executive nullity, and rendered it dependent on one branch of the Imperial Legislature for the immediate sanction of each separare measure. In truth and in effect, the Government here is now administered by two or three Peers, from their place in Parliament. I cannot therefore consistently with what is due to the interests of this Province and my own character, consent to make myself responsible for measures emanating from others, and which in my conscience I consider most injurious to your present tranquility and future welfare,

"In this novel and anomalous state of things, it would neither be for your advantage or mine, that I should remain here. My post is where your interests are really decided upon. In Parliament, I can defend your rights, declare your wants and wishes, and expose the impolicy and cruelty of proceedings, which, whilst they are too liable to the imputation of having originated in personal animosity and party feeling, are also fraught with imminent danger to the wel-

His Excellency, before departing, did an act of justice to a gentleman, James Stuart, Esq., who in the party rage of the times, had been exceedingly ill treated, in deference to the overbearing prejudices

fare of those important Colonies and the permanence of their connexion with the British Empire.

" The restricted limits of this answer will not admit of my entering into the consideration of the various measures which had occupied my attention during my administration of your affairs; not indeed is it necessary; for you will find in the proclamation which I have this day issued, addressed to the North American Provinces under my Government, the fullest information on all matters affecting your interests. I need therefore only assure you that to the last hour of my existence, you will find me your faithful and devoted friend —bound to you by the strongest ties, both public and private, of respect and gratitude.

REPLY TO THE ADDRESS FROM KINGSTON.

" I thank you most cordially for this gratifying proof of your confidence in me.

" You have justly appreciated the principles of that policy which has governed every act of my administration—and which you will find fully, and I hope clearly explained in my proclamation of this day's date.

" You have also correctly described the nature and object of the Ordinance which has been annulled. It was one of mercy and forgiveness, not of tyranny and oppression. I cannot admit its illegality. It is strictly in accordance with the powers and provisions of the Act of Parliament under which I administer the affairs of this Province. I may also remark that transportation to Bermuda has been the constant practice in both the Canadas. As for its policy—recent events have, I think, demonstrated its soundness. The late verdict on the trial of the murderers of Chartrand, shews how fearful is the danger of exposing the sacred institution of Trial by Jury, to the chances of its being abused, under circumstances in which the ordinary considerations of justice, truth and conscience are superseded by the all absorbing power of party feeling.

" Knowing well that such would be the result, if the ordinary forms of judicial procedure were resorted to, I determined on acting on the powers conferred by the Act of Parliament, which I believed to have been passed by the Imperial Legislature not from the abstract love of despo-

of the Assembly, both by the time-serving and truckling policy of Lord Aylmer, Governor in Chief of the Province, and by the Earl of Ribbon, then the Colonial Minister. Mr. Sewell, the Chief Justice,

tism, but from a conviction of the necessity which existed fer supplying the Government here with means proportioned to the exigency of the case, and arming it with weapons sufficient to put down revolt and eradicate treason.

" It has pleased the House of Lords to decree otherwise, and to declare by its enactments, on one day, that the free and representative constitution of a Colony shall be suspended, and a provisional despotism created—and on the next, that the consequences of that Act are not to be followed out, or its powers enforced, even whilst they admit that it would be for the advantage of the public service!

" I bow with submission to their decree, but I never will acknowledge its policy or equity.

" When I had the happiness to meet you, in the course of my visit to the Upper Province, I fully explained to you my views as to the necessity of improving the water communications between the Lakes and the Gulf of St. Lawrence. These I also communicated to Her Majesty's Government, and have the satisfaction of informing you that I have been authorized by them to institute a survey of the whole line from Lake Erie to Quebec. I have applied to the Ordinance Department for the aid of skilful Engineers for this service— and have no doubt that their reports will demonstrate the practicability and the necessity of rendering completely available those great natural means, through which the commerce of the Canadas may be incalculably extended, and their general interests, advanced to the highest pitch of prosperity.

REPLY TO THE ADDRESS FROM TORONTO.

" I beg you will assure the inhabitants of Toronto how sensible I am of their kindness, and of their promptitude in coming forward, with declarations of approbation, and confidence in me, at a moment like the present.

" I well remember the enthusiastic reception which they gave me when I visited Toronto,--in which, happily for me all classes unanimously concurred.

" It is an honest sense of pride to me, to reflect that their feelings have also been shared and exhibited by every one of the North American Provinces—and I shall leave this Continent with the consolatory reflection, that amidst the

being, in consequence of his age and long services, allowed to retire on a pension, from the Bench, Lord Durham conferred the chief justiceship upon Mr. Stuart, whose elevation to the highest position in the

conflict of parties and the collision of interests, a common sentiment has done justice to the rectitude of my intentions and the purity of my motives. I shall preserve the numerous testimonies of regard and confidence, which have been presented to me from all quarters, as documents of which I and my family must be justly proud,—evincing, as they do the unsolicited, unbought, but invaluable proofs of the attachment of so large a portion of my fellow countrymen.

" For the reasons which have induced me to return to England, I must refer you to my proclamation of this day's date in which they are fully set forth and the state and condition of the Canadas amply adverted to. You will, I hope, after giving it due consideration, agree with me in the opinion that I can now be of more service to the North American Colonies in Westminister than in Quebec.

" It is at the same time a great consolation to me to reflect, that notwithstanding my having been so abruptly arrested by the proceedings in the House of Lords, in the arduous task of restoring peace, and providing for your future prosperity,—I have yet done much to justify your confidence and gain your approbation. What was the state of the Canadas when I assumed the Government? Rebellion had been but recently quelled. Martial Law had been proclaimed and the Habeas Corpus suspended. The jails were filled with prisoners, and distrust and apprehension pervaded the minds of all classes. Along the whole line of frontier from Lake Champlain to Lake St. Clair, the most active hostility against the British Government prevailed,—in which Canadian refugees and American borderers equally participated; the communication between the two countries was in a great measure interrupted, and at various points armed incursions took place—life and property were recklessly destroyed, and the chances of preserving peace between Great Britain and the United States daily diminishing.

" In three months what was the change? Martial Law superseded, the Habeas Corpus restored—not a political prisoner remained in confinement in the Lower Province—nor was there any symptom of the existence of any seditious or treasonable movements, until the arrival of the intelligence of the interference of the House of Lords. The state of feeling in the United States with reference to the Canadian question had righted itself. The soundest tone pervaded the

judiciary was an appointment justly popular with the commercial body, and indeed the whole British community in Lower Canada, who with indignation and disgust had a few years before witnessed the injustice done him by a minister of the British Crown, in the unprofitable hope of propitiating a party bent upon extinguishing the authority of the Crown of England in the Canadian Provinces, as demonstrated by subsequent events.

The Earl of Durham sailed for England on the 3rd of November, with his family, in the *Inconstant* frigate, leaving Sir John Colborne in charge of the government. Every Demonstration of regard which

---

expression of public opinion, and I had received from all parts of the States, assurances of confidence in my administration and in my desire, as well as my ability to preserve those amicable relations between the two countries, which they, as well as myself, considered necessary for the welfare of both.

"Whilst I was thus employed, I had also to correspond with the Lieut. Governors of the different Provinces on matters of the highest moment, and am happy of having this public opportunity to acknowledge the cordial and enlightened co-operation which I received from them all. I received, and consulted with, delegates from each Province, and was busily engaged in applying the valuable information I had delivered from them to the formation of a Plan founded on large and comprehensive principles for their general government. I had issued commissions, and received reports on the subject of the Crown Lands and of Emigration—of Municipal Institutions and of general education. I was also preparing measures, to which I have adverted in my Proclamation, for the amelioration of the defective institutions of Lower Canada.

"These, then, have been my acts—this my course of policy, during the limited period of my stay on this Continent. The enumeration of them will, at all events prove my diligence and anxiety to devote my time to the promotion of the great objects of my mission.

"I now bid you farewell! and pray you to believe that from my heart I wish you the constant enjoyment of that happiness, peace and prosperity, to which you are so justly entitled, by your industry, intelligence and Loyalty.

the citizens of Quebec could give, was exhibited on his embarkation, nor did any man in his situation ever leave Canada more deeply and universally regretted than did this nobleman. His application to business was indefatigable, and this, with the sense of wrong from his peers with which his sensitive mind was now chafing, had impared his health, naturally delicate, to a degree threatening his very existence. His style of living in Canada was splendid, beyond that of any of his predecessors, princely and worthy of the sovereign he represented, and his hospitality in keeping with it. By some he was indeed deemed haughty, supercilious and overbearing. To the writer, however, who had occasion to see the late Earl of Durham on business, he seemed unaffectedly, frank, affable, communicative and condescending in fact, all that one could desire. It is universally agreed that his abilities as a statesman were of the highest order. His independence of character, decision, and firmness, none reasonably can question; they are legible and conspicuous in every line of his writing as a public man, and in none more so than in the proclamations he issued on the eve of his departure in relinquishing the government. He no doubt erred in the matter of the Ordinance, but as it certainly was on the side of humanity, the error, was venial, and may well be forgiven for the motive that prompted it. To say that there was absolutely nothing ignoble, sordid, or common in this late nobleman's character would not be enough. He was generous, munificent, and disinterested; of which last quality, in particular, he gave, a few days previous to his leaving Canada, proof, by ordering that the salary and emoluments that had accrued to him as Governor General, should be appropriated to defray the expenses incurred in the repairs of the Government Houses at Quebec and Montreal. The citizens of Quebec are peculiarly obligated to him, and will permanently revere his memory. He threw open and bestowed upon them the site of the ancient Castle of St. Lewis, (destroyed in Lord Aylmer's time), as a public promenade, together with the upper and lower gardens, previously reserved for the use of the inmates of the Castle exclusively, all which ever since have been enjoyed by the citizens, and now are considered the property of the Corporation of the City, though properly appertaining to the military government. He outlived but a short time his brief but eventful perigrination in the Canadian Provinces, where his memory is very generally held in the highest respect.

By HIS EXCELLENCY THE RIGHT HONORABLE JOHN GEORGE, EARL OF DURHAM, Viscount Lambton, &c. &c., Knight Grand Cross of the Most Honorable Military Order of the Bath, one of Her Majesty's Most Honorable Privy Council, and Governor General, Vice Admiral, and Captain General of all Her Majesty's Provinces within, and adjacent to, the Continent of North America, &c. &c. &c.

A PROCLAMATION.

In conformity with one of its provisions, I have this day proclaimed the Act 1 and 2 Victoria, chap. 212, intituled, " An Act for indemnifying those who " have issued or acted under certain parts of a cer- " tain Ordinance made under colour of an Act pass- " ed in the present Session of Parliament, intituled, " *An Act to make temporary Provision for the Gov-* " *ernment of* Lower Canada."

I have also to notify the disallowance by Her Majesty of the Ordinance 2d Victoria, chapter 1, intituled, " An Ordinance to provide for the security of " the Province of Lower Canada."

I cannot perform these official duties without at the same time informing you, the people of British

America, of the course which the measures of the Imperial Government and Legisluture make it incumbent on me to pursue. The mystery which has heretofore too often, during the progress of the most important affairs, concealed from the people of these Colonies, the intentions, the motives, and the very actions of their rulers, appears to me to have been one of the main causes of the numerous errors of the Government, and the general dissatisfaction of the people. Undesirable at any time, such concealment on the part of one entrusted with the supreme authority in the present crisis of your affairs, would be most culpable and pernicious. With a people from whom I have had so many and such gratifying proofs of warm and confiding attachement, I can have no reserve. And my implicit reliance on your loyalty and good sense will justify me in making you acquainted with what it most imports you to know.

It is the more necessary for me thus to act, because, when I first entered upon this Government, I explained to you, in a proclamation issued immediately on my arrival on these shores, the nature of the powers vested in me, and the principles on which it was my intention to exercise them. Now, therefore, that I am about to return to England, I feel it to be my bounden duty to state to you, as fully and as frankly, the reasons which have induced me to lay down powers rendered inadequate to the carrying into effect those or any other principles of government.

I did not accept the Government of British North America, without duly considering the nature of the task which I imposed on myself, or the sufficiency of my means for performing it. When Parliament concentrated all legislative and executive power in Lower Canada in the same hands, it established an authority, which, in the strictest sense of the word, was despotic. This authority Her Majesty was graciously pleased to delegate to me. I did not shrink from assuming the awful responsibility of power, thus freed from constitutional restraint, in the hope, that by exercising it with justice, with mildness and with vigour, I might secure the happiness of all classes of the people, and facilitate the speedy and permanent restoration of their liberties.. But I never was weak enough to imagine that the forms by which men's rights are wisely guarded in that country where freedom has been longest enjoyed, best understood, and most prudently exercised, could be scrupulously observed in a society almost entirely disorganized by misrule and dissension. I conceived it to be one of the chief advantages of my position, that I was enabled to pursue the great ends of substantial justice and sound policy, free and unfettered. Nor did I ever dream of applying the theory or the practice of the British Constitution, to a country whose constitution was suspended,—where all representative government was annihilated, and the people deprived of all control over their own affairs,—where the ordinary guarantees of personal rights had been in abeyance during a long subjection to martial law; and a continued suspension of the Habeas Corpus,—where there neither did exist, nor had for a long time existed, any confidence in the impartial administration of justice in any political case.

To encourage and stimulate me in my arduous task, I had great and worthy objects in view. My aim was to elevate the Province of Lower Canada to a thoroughly British character, to link its people to the sovereignty of Britain, by making them all participators in those high privileges, conducive at once to freedom and order, which have long been the glory of Englishmen. I hoped to confer on an united people, a more extensive enjoyment of free and responsible government, and to merge the patry jealousies of a small community, and the odious animosities of origin, in the higher feelings of a nobler and more comprehensive nationality.

To give effect to these purposes it was necessary that my powers of government should be as strong as they were extensive,—that I should be known to have the means of acting as well as judging for myself, without a perpetual control by distant authorities. It were well indeed if such were the ordinary tenure of government in colonies, and that your local administration should always enjoy so much of the confidence of those, with whom rests the ultimate decision of your affairs, that it might ever rely on being allowed to carry out its policy to completion, and on being supported in giving effect to its promises and its commands. But in the present posture of your affairs, it was necessary that the most unusual confidence should accompany the delegation of a most unusual authority; and that in addition to such great legal powers, the government here should possess all the moral force that could be derived from the assurance that its acts would be final and its engagements religiously observed. It is not by stinted powers, or a dubious authority, that the present danger can be averted, or the foundation laid of a better order of things!

I had reason to believe that I was armed with all the power which I thought requisite, by the commissions and instructions under the royal sign manual, with which I was charged as Governor General, and High Commissioner,—by the authority vested in me and my council, by the Act of the Imperial Legislature—and by the general approbation of my appointment, which all parties were pleased to express. I also trusted that I should enjoy, throughout the course of my administration, all the strength which the cordial and steadfast support of the authorities at home can alone give to their distant officers: and that even party feeling would refrain from molesting me whilst occupied in maintaining the integrity of the British Empire.

In these just expectations I have been painfully disappointed. From the very commencement of my task, the minutest details of my administration have been exposed to incessant cirticism, in a spirit which has evinced an entire ignorance of the state of this country, and of the only mode in which the supremacy of the British Crown can here be upheld and exercised. Those who have in the British Legislature systematically depreciated my powers, and the ministers of the Crown by their tacit acquiescence therein, have produced the effect of making it too clear that my authority is inadequate far the emergency which called it into existence. At length an act of my Government, the first and most important which was brought under the notice of the authorities at home, has been annulled; and the entire policy of which that act was a small though assential part, has thus been defeated.

The disposal of the political prisoners was from the first a matter foreign to my mission. With a view to the more easy attainment of the great objects contemplated, that question ought to have been settled before my arrival. But as it was essential to my plans for the future tranquility and improvement of the colony, that I should commence by allaying actual irritation, I had at first to determine the fate of those who were under prosecution, and to provide for the present security of the Province by removing the most dangerous disturbers of its peace. For these ends the ordinary tribunals, as a recent trial has clearly shewn, afforded me no means. Judicial proceedings would only have agitated the public mind afresh—would have put in evidence the sympathy of a large portion of the people with rebellion, —and would have given to the disaffected generally a fresh assurance of impunity for political guilt. An acquittal in the face of the clearest evidence, which I am justified in having anticipated as inevitable, would have set the immediate leaders of the insurrection at liberty, absolved from crime and exalted in the eyes of their deluded countrymen, as the innocent victims of an unjust imprisonment, and a vindictive charge. –I looked on these as mischiefs which I was bound to avert by the utmost exercise of the powers entrusted to me. I could not, without trial and conviction, take any measures of a purely penal character; but I thought myself justified in availing myself of an acknowledgment of guilt, and adopting measures of precaution against a small number of the most culpable or most dangerous of the accused. To all the rest I extended a complete amnesty.

Whether a better mode of acting could have been devised for the emergency, is now immaterial. This is the one that has been adopted—the discussion which it at first excited had passed away—and those who were once inclined to condemn its leniency, had acquiesced in, or submitted to it. The good effects which must necessarily have resulted from any settlement of this difficult question, had already begun to show themselves. Of these the principal were, the general approval of my policy by the people of the United States, and the consequent cessation of American sympathy with any attempt to disturb the Canadas. This result has been most gratifying to me, inasmuch as it has gone far towards a complete restoration of that good will between you and a great and kindred nation, which I have taken every means in my power to cultivate, and which I earnestly entreat you to cherish as essential to your peace and prosperity.

It is also very satisfactory to me to find that the rectitude of my policy has hardly been disputed at home, and that the disallowance of the Ordinance proceeds from no doubt of its substantial merits, but from the importance which has been attached to a supposed technical error in the assumption of a power, which, if I had not, I ought to have had..

The particular defect in the Ordinance which has been made the ground of its disallowance was occasioned, not by my mistaking the extent of my powers, but by my reliance on the readiness of Parliament to supply their insufficiency in case of need. For the purpose of relieving the prisoners from all apprehensions of being treated as ordinary convicts, and the loyal inhabitants of the Province from the dread of their immediate return, words were inserted in the Ordinance respecting the disposal of them in Bermuda, which were known to be inoperative. I was perfectly aware that my powers extended to landing the prisoners on the shores of Bermuda, but no further. I knew that they could not be forcibly detained in that island without the cooperation of the Imperial Legislature. That cooperation I had a right to expect, because the course I was pursuing was pointed out in numerous Acts of the Imperial and Provincial Legislatures, as I shall have occasion hereafter fully to prove. I also did believe that, even if I had not the precedents of these Acts of Parliament, a Government and a Legislature anxious for the peace of this unhappy country and for the integrity of the British Empire, would not sacrifice to a petty technicality the vast benefits which my entire policy promised, and had already in a great measure secured. I trusted that they would take care that a great and beneficent purpose should not be frustrated by any error, if error there were, which they could rectify or the want of any power which they could supply; finally, that if they found the Ordinance inoperative they would give it effect—if illegal that they would make it law.

This small aid has not been extended to me, even

for this great object; and the usefulness of my delegated power expires with the loss of that support from the supreme authority which could alone sustain it. The measure now annulled was but part of a large system of measures, which I promised when I proclaimed the amnesty. When I sought to obliterate the traces of recent discord, I pledged myself to remove its causes—to prevent the revival of a contest between hostile races—to raise the defective institutions of Lower Canada to the level of British civilization and freedom—to remove all impediments to the course of British enterprize in this Province, and promote colonization and improvement in the others—and to consolidate these general benefits on the strong and permanent basis of a free, responsible, and comprehensive government.

Such large promises could not have been ventured, without a perfect reliance on the unhesitating aid of the supreme authorities. Of what avail are the purposes and promises of a delegated power whose acts are not respected by the authority from which it proceeds? With what confidence can I invite co-operation, or impose forbearance, whilst I touch ancient laws and habits, as well as deep-rooted abuses, with the weakened hands that have ineffectually essayed but a little more than the ordinary vigour of the police of troubled times?

"How am I to provide against the immediate effects of the disallowance of the Ordinance? That Ordinance was intimately connected with other measures which remain in unrestricted operation. It was coupled with Her Majesty's proclamation of amnesty; and as I judged it becoming, that the extraordinary Legislature of Lower Canada should take upon itself all measures of rigorous precaution, and leave to Her Majesty the congenial office of using her royal prerogative, for the sole purpose of pardon and mercy, the proclamation contained an entire amnesty, qualified only by the exceptions specified in the Ordinance. The Ordinance has been disallowed, and the proclamation is confirmed. Her Majesty having been advised to refuse her assent to the exceptions, the amnesty exists without qualification. No impediment therefore exists to the return of the persons who had made the most distinct admission of guilt, or who had been excluded by me from the Province on account of the danger to which its tranquillity would be exposed by their presence; and none can now be enacted, without the adoption of measures alike repugnant to my sense of justice and of policy. I cannot recall the irrevocable pledge of Her Majesty's mercy. I cannot attempt to evade the disallowance of the Ordinance, by re-enacting it under the disguise of an alteration of the scene of banishment, or of the penalties of unauthorized return. I cannot, by a needless suspension of the Habeas Corpus, put the personal liberty of every man at the mercy of the Government, and declare a whole Province in immediate danger of rebellion, merely in order to exercise the influence of a vague terror over a few individuals.

"In these conflicting and painful circumstances, it is far better that I should at once and distinctly announce my intention of desisting from the vain attempt to carry my policy and system of administration into effect with such inadequate and restricted means. If the peace of Lower Canada is to be again menaced, it is necessary that its Government should be able to reckon on a more cordial and vigorous support at home than has been accorded to me. No good that may not be expected from any other Government in Lower Canada, can be obtained by my continuing to wield extraordinary legal powers of which the moral force and consideration are gone.

"You will easily believe that, after all the exertions which I have made, it is with feelings of deep disappointment that I find myself thus suddenly deprived of the power of conferring great benefits on that Province to which I have referred,—of reforming the administrative system there, and eradicating the manifold abuses which had been engendered by the negligence and corruption of former times, and so lamentably fostered by civil dissensions. I cannot but regret being obliged to renounce the still more glorious hope of employing unusual legislative powers in the endowment of that Province with those free municipal institutions, which are the only sure basis of local improvement and representative liberty,—of establishing a system of general education,—of revising the defective laws which regulate real property and commerce,—and of introducing a pure and competent administration of justice. Above all, I grieve to be thus forced to abandon the realization of such large and solid schemes of colonization and internal improvement as would connect the distant portions of these extensive Colonies, and lay open the unwrought treasures of the wilderness to the wants of British industry and the energy of British enterprise.

"For these objects I have laboured much—and have received the most active, zealous, and efficient co-operation from the able and enlightened persons who are associated with me in this great undertaking. Our exertions, however, will not, cannot be thrown away. The information which we have acquired, although not as yet fit for the purposes of immediate legislation, will contribute to the creation of juster views as to the resources, the wants, and the interests of these Colonies, than ever yet prevailed in the Mother Country. To complete and render available those materials for future legislation, is an important part of the duties which as High-Commissioner I have yet to discharge, and to which I shall devote the most anxious attention.

"I shall also be prepared, at the proper period, to suggest the constitution of a form of Government for Her Majesty's dominions on this continent, which may restore to the people of Lower Canada all the advantages of a representative system, unaccompanied by the evils that have hitherto proceeded from the unnatural conflicts of parties; which may safely supply any deficiencies existing in the governments of the other colonies; and which may produce throughout British America a state of contented allegiance, founded, as colonial allegiance ever must be, on a sense of obligation to the parent state.

"I fervently hope that my usefulness to you will not cease with my official connexion. When I shall have laid at Her Majesty's feet the various high and important commissions with which her royal favour invested me, I shall still be enabled as a peer of Parliament to render you efficient and constant service in that place where the decisions that effect your welfare are in reality made. It must be, I humbly trust, for the advantage of these Provinces, if I can carry into the Imperial Parliament a knowledge, derived from personal inspection and experience, of those interests, upon which some persons there are too apt to legislate in ignorance or indifference—and can aid in laying the foundation of a system of general government, which while it strengthens your permanent connexion with Great Britain, shall save you from the evils to which you are now subjected by every change in the fluctuating policy of distant and successive Administrations.

Given under my hand and seal at arms, at the Castle of Saint Lewis, in the city of Quebec, in the said Province of Lower Canada, the ninth day of October, in the year of our Lord one thousand eight hundred and thirty-eight, and in the second year of Her Majesty's reign. By command,

CHARLES BULLER,
Chief Secretary.

By His Excellency the Right Honorable JOHN GEORGE, EARL OF DURHAM, Viscount Lambton, &c. &c., Knight Grand Cross of the Most Honorable Military Order of the Bath, one of Her Majesty's Most Honorable Privy Council, and Governor General of all Her Majesty's Provinces within, and adjacent to the Continent of North America, &c.,

To all to whom these presents shall come—GREETING.

" WHEREAS by the one hundred and twelfth chapter of the statute of the Parliament of the United Kingdom of Great Britain and Ireland, intituled, " An Act for indemnifying those who have "issued or acted under certain parts of a certain " Ordinance made under colour of an Act passed in " the present session of Parliament, intituled, "*An* "*Act to make temporary Provision for the Government* "*of Lower Canada,*" passed in the first and second year of the reign of our Sovereign Lady the Queen, Victoria, it is amongst other things enacted, that the said Act shall be proclaimed in the said Province of Lower Canada by the Governor, or by the person authorised to execute the commission of Governor of the said Province, forthwith after he shall have received a copy of the same from one of Her Majesty's Principal Secretaries of State; And whereas I the said JOHN GEORGE, EARL OF DURHAM, being the Governor of the said Province of Lower Canada, have received a copy of the said Act from one of Her Majesty's Principal Secretaries of State. Now THEREFORE KNOW YE, that I, the said JOHN GEORGE, EARL OF DURHAM, being such Governor as aforesaid, by virtue of the power and authority reposed in me by Her Majesty, and of the said Act of the said Parliament, do, by this proclamation, proclaim the said Act of the said Parliament of the United Kingdom of Great Britain and Ireland, intituled, " An " Act for indemnifying those who have issued or "acted under certain parts of a certain Ordinance "made under colour of an Act passed in the pre- "sent session of Parliament, intituled, " An Act to " make temporary Provision for the Government of " Lower Canada," so that the said Act of the said Parliament, shall and may commence and take effect within the said Province from the day of the date of these presents.

Given under my hand and seal at arms, at the Castle of Saint Lewis, in the city of Quebec, in the said Province of Lower Canada, the ninth day of October, in the year of our Lord one thousand eight hundred and thirty-eight, and in the second year of Her Majesty's reign.

D. DALY,
Secretary of the Province.

The following letter from the exiles at Bermuda, published, on their release, in the "Bermudean," went the rounds of the Canadian papers in November, 1838.

SIR,—Consistently with a line of conduct we had prescribed to ourselves, we have hitherto eschewed all political discussion relative to our country, and forbore taking any notice of many a newspaper article which attached more particularly to ourselves and the position we hold here. But we owe it to our character to relax in some degree from the rigidity of our silence, to ward off the obloquy which the *London Sun*, of the 20th August last, would fain cast upon our measures, in an article which was carefully transferred to the columns of the *Royal Gazette* of these Islands.

Calumniatory as is the article in question, we would not probably have noticed it, were it not apparently clothed with the sanction of Mr. Charles Buller, Lord Durham's Chief Secretary, whose name and official character might give very undue weight to the statements contained therein, were they to remain uncontradicted and unexplained.

To do this, we need but appeal to the documents themselves, upon which the article of the *London Sun* seems founded, to establish its utter disingenuousness and its falsehood. It is false that we ever *petitioned*. It is false that our "deportation," as the *Sun* has it, was our own act. It is false we ever sought for *grace, clemency,* or *mercy,* at the hands of Lord Durham, or any [other. It is false that we *implored* the Goveanor General not to bring us to trial. It is false that the Ordinance under which we were exiled, and which has lately been proclaimed an absolute nullity by the British Parliament, provides for trials on the event of the return of any of the persons thereby expatriated. It is, indeed, an "absurdity" to declare that men shall be hanged without trial, but we, of conrse, are not responsible for it.

It is fit to preface the introduction of the following letters, by stating that the whole negociation originated with John Simpson, Esq., the Collector of Her Majesty's Customs, at Coteau du Lac, who came with a *carte blanche* from Lord Durham's Chief Secretary, to communicate with the state prisoners then within the walls of the Montreal prison.

This gentleman's visit was as unsolicited as it was unexpected. He sought and obtained interviews with the undersigned, to whom, after many prefatory remarks, he produced the draft of a letter to Lord Durham, to which he invited us to affix our names, together with a dozen others. The whole conversation is minuted and authenticated, but it is beside our purpose to divulge more of it at this particular juncture. Suffice to say, that the letter in question was revised, essentially modified, and reconstructed, and in that shape was thankfully accepted by Mr. Simpson, and received the eight signatures it bears.

*Montreal, New Jail, June 18, 1838.

MY LORD,—You came among us with a character not of a class, not of an order, but of yourself—a character that entitles you to our confidence, and we yield it. Do not imagine our minds are subjugated, because our persons are under restraint, or that we seek by an unmeaning compliment to conciliate your favour. We would not, will not, propitiate unworthily to obtain clemency for ourselves. We belong to our country, and make the willing sacrifice on the altar of her liberties.

We rebelled, my Lord---but start not at the avowal. We rebelled neither against Her Majesty's person or her government, but against colonial misgovernment, and we abide the issue—the penalty is ours.

Had your advent been earlier, it had been blessed; it will be blessed. If our efforts have been the cause of your coming, we have effected what we sought to effect—the happiness of our country—and we murmur not.

Had your advent been earlier, misgovernment had ceased; justice would have triumphed; the laws have been administered faithfully and impartially; grievances would have been redressed, and we had happily beheld a government commanding at once the confidence and affection of all.

We remonstrated; we were derided. The press assailed us with calumny and contumely; invective was exhausted; we were goaded on to madness, and were compelled to show we had the spirit of resistance to repel injuries, or to be doomed a captive, degraded and recreant people. We took up arms not to attack others, but to defend ourselves. Did the government put us down, or attempt to put us

---
*The above is the letter referred to in page 160.

K

down? No! if it did not encourage, it tolerated the attempt. We will not say, we will not think, why. The country became excited, the people wretched, and then reckless. Lord Gosford, by his proclamation, invited back to their homes the inhabitants that had fled. Did the magistrates give effect, or offer to give effect to his beneficent views in this respect? No: "the toils were set." Did they not issue warrants indiscriminately against all those who had asked their birthright as British subjects, to canvas public men and measures? Thus, my Lord, we were goaded into resistance, not less by the authorities, than by the violence of that class of the people opposed to us in politics. We wish, however, to forget, as well as to forgive.

You come without limits to your power; with views uncircumscribed—with honour untarnished. High in the councils of your country, and in ours, your voice can reach the throne.

Ardent in the pursuit of civil liberty, you can feel for a people animated by the same principle, but deprived of the same advantage. We felt and we deplored the violation of our constitution. We struggled not for independence: we laboured to maintain the true spirit of the British constitution and British liberty.

We desire not to distract your Lordship's attention from the great and glorious objects of your high mission. We will not occupy your time, by supplications for ourselves; nor embarrass your Lordship with attempts to avert our fate. We desire to avoid all the ceremonies of a trial; convinced, as we are of the impossibility of obtaining an impartial tribunal, before which we should have nothing to fear. We wish to tranquillize the minds of a generous and confiding people. We pray thus to be alowed to establish peace and order. We implore no mercy for ourselves. We would not shock your high and noble mind, by any act unworthy the dignity of men. We have tics, my Lord, that render life as dear to us as to your Lordship: and yet, we cannot ignobly invoke your Lordship's sympathy.

"As a parting prayer, however, we supplicate for the restoration to liberty and to society of the rest of our unfortunate fellow-prisoners, as well as the recall of the fugitives; in the firm conviction, that they will, one and all, shed the last drop of their blood in defence of a government *that can appreciate and uphold the rights of its subjects, however remote their abode from the seat of the empire.*

" We pray God for the success of Your Lordship's peaceful mission—that, worshiping one God, the people may become one people; and, imitating your Lordship's example, in repudiating, as we have ever done, all distinctions of origin, we hope, for the future, our wish, as hitherto our endeavour, may be crowned with success.

We pray, my Lord, that you may be recognised as the saviour of this distracted country; and long enjoy the domestic happiness our fate denies us.

We implore God's blessing on your Lordship; and, *if there be guilt in high aspirations, we confess our guilt, and plead guilty.*

Signed Wolfred Nelson, R. S. M. Bouchette, Bonaventure Viger, S. Marchessault, H. A. Gauvin, T. Goddu, R. Des Rivieres, L. Masson.

To the Right Honourab'e, the Earl of Durham, Governor-General, &c.

The foregoing letter having been presented to Lord Durham, at Quebec, by Mr. Simpson, on the 23rd June; on the 26th following, he returned to Montreal, and having again requested to see the gentlemen who had signed the document, he represented that some supplementary paper would still be requisite to perfect the transaction, and to enable Lord Durham, as he insinuated, to show the magnanimity of his mind, and to give effect to the plan of a general amnesty. He produced a short letter, the sole purpose of which was to *record* an unqualified plea of guilty; to this the undersigned unhesitatingly demurred. We were cordially disposed to facilitate Lords Durham's plans, and quite willing to be instrumental to the liberation of 140 of our captive fellow citizens, and the recall of many more, but we could not do so by an admission of guilt where none was felt, and thereby contradicting the asseveration contained in our previous letter of the 18th. Diffident of our own opinions, where our personal interests felt so deeply involved, we would not entertain the subject but under the guidance of legal counsel; and although the state prisoners had hitherto been denied any resort to counsel, Mr. Simpson,—conceiving himself, no doubt, clothed with sufficient powers from head-quarters,—sanctioned our sending for one of the most eminent advocates of the Montreal bar, who wholly altered the gist of the letter, and made it what it will be found below, pledging his professional reputation at the same time, that it contained nothing derogatory to our character, or calculated to admit our culpability on a charge of high treason. Strong in the opinion of our counsel, we signed this letter:

(COPY)

Montreal Jail, 26th June, 1838.

MY LORD,—We have some reason to apprehend that the expressions used by us in a letter which we addressed to your Lordship on the 18th instant, may appear vague and ambiguous.

Our intention, my Lord, was distinctly to avow, that in pursuit of objects dear to the great mass of our population, we took a part that has eventuated in a charge of high treason.

We professed our willingness to plead guilty, thereby to avoid the necessity of a trial, and thus to give, as far as in our power, tranquillity to the country; but whilst we were thus disposed to contribute to the happiness of others, we could not condescend to shield ourselves under the provisions of an Ordinance passed by the late Special Council of the Province.

Permit us, then, my Lord, to perform this great duty, to mark our entire confidence in your Lordship, and to place ourselves at your disposal without availing ourselves of provisions which would degrade us in our own eyes, by marking an unworthy distrust on both sides.

With this short explanation of our feelings, we again place ourselves at your Lordship's discretion, and pray that the peace of the country may not be endangered by a trial.

We have the honour to be, with unfeigned respect, your Lordship's most obedient humble servants.

(Signed as before.)

It is with great reluctance we give publicity in these Islands to the above documents. We fain would have aided Lord Durham in some wise and just scheme of colonial policy. We sincerely wished him well in the herculean task of quelling the storm conjured up by his predecessors. We believe, however, he has erred, greatly erred, and we deeply lament it.

WOLFRED NELSON.
R. S. M. BOUCHETTE.
Hamilton, Bermuda, 19th October, 1838.

POSTSCRIPT.

The recurrence of the name of Dr. Wolfred Nelson in the foregoing chapter, affords me a suitable opportunity for offering an explanation, and with it, if need be, the *amende honorable* for a *tort* which, in the course of my duty as an annalist, I have unintentionally inflicted it seems on the Doctor. In a work of this nature, it is exceedingly difficult to avoid coming in contact with the self-respect, prejudices, or passions of those, or their surviving friends, who have taken a prominent part in the stirring events of the times treated of. I trust, however, that my cotemporaries will do me the justice to admit that my narrative of events is impartial, consistent with facts as generally understood, and above the suspicion of studied offence to those with whom in politics I may have differed, and differ still. Shortly after the appearance of the forth volume of this work, I received a letter, dated " Montreal, 24th March, 1853," from the Doctor, in which he observes: " if I did not entertain the high respect I do for you, and did not value your opinion, I should not trouble you with any remarks in reference to what you say of me at page 543 in your very useful and interesting History of Lower Canada." He then proceeds. " Even after the order of nature I must ere long render an account to my maker, of my deeds here below; well sir, I fear not to call my GOD to witness, that on the morning of the 23rd November, 1837, I did not order Mr. Papineau, " to desist from his intention of going to join our compatriots to do battle with them against the troops that were coming up," nor did he attempt it, nor had he a gun in his hand." Dr. N. adds: " All that has been said on this subject, I solemnly declare is false. But I freely admit that *previous to that morning*, I told Mr. P. that we did not want him to fight—that we required his presence —that without him, all resistance would be unavailing," &c. This, however, throws no new light upon the subject, leaving, as I understand it, the parties precisely, as previously they were, at issue upon this, to all but themselves, unimportant point.

I had said, in page 543 of the previous (fourth) volume, that down to a certain period, the Doctor had himself warmly vindicated Mr. Papineau against the imputation of having deserted him at St. Denis, by stating that he had done so at his (the Doctor's) special desire, that Mr. Papineau's appearance in public life, which Doctor Nelson thought might prove prejudicial to Mr. Lafontaine, had induced him to give a very different version of the matter; that I believed it was the general opinion that it would have been well in him to have remained silent on this head. Doctor Nelson observes on this: "Had Mr. P's most indiscreet nephew, Mr. D—— not said he had seen me on the morning of the battle wrest a gun from his uncle's hand, and order him to keep away, I should not have been at the pains of proving that he had placed himself, by his gratuitous volunteering to screen Mr. P. in a most reprehensible position, in asseverating a thing that was not. Indeed it is mainly due to this extremely inconsiderate young man, if ever any open breach took place between Mr. P. and myself. I opposed Mr. D. B. Viger in Richelieu, and from that moment D——, young P——, and a few of their friends attacked me in a most scurrilous manner, and attempted to ruin me in my country. Two years after Mr. Papineau's return to Canada, I called upon him, but his reception of me was anything but cordial. Not long after, I had palpable proof that he lent himself to some intrigue to destroy me in the opinion of my electors, and accused me of being the cause of the rising in 1837. It was then only I was compelled to act in my own defence. Yes, all the hostility I met with, even long before his arrival in Montreal, sprung from my having defeated Mr. D. B. Viger at St. Ours.

"When Mr. P. was abused in my presence of cowardice, I did indeed attempt to screen him. I palliated his leaving us all in the lurch. I felt for him as I did for ". General " Brown. I said it was not their fault if nature had not endued them with the qualities of the soldier ; that their views were patriotic, &c., and that they did not know what stuff they were made of, no more than other men, till they were tried. It was not their fault, but their misfortune, if they did not possess the talents for decided action ; and, allow me to assure you, it was not till I was compelled to act in self-defence, that I retorted.

"What I most blamed Mr. P. for, was his silence when called upon in regard to the new rising in 1838, telling his friends ' you know if it is prudent or not to make the attempt.' He would not compromise himself, but had not soul to prevent others from doing a real act of madness—one word from him would have prevented the dreadful events of 1838, here I blame him indeed."

I also observed in the same article that Dr. Nelson's acceptance of office at the hands of Mr. Lafontaine, subsequent to the antagonism that had arisen between him [Doctor N.] and his former leader, Mr. Papineau, had divested the zeal, with which he had assailed his old chief, of the prestige of disinterestedness and patriotism, which at first surrounded it, and subjected the Doctor to the suspicion of venal motives. Such certainly was my opinion, (i. e., that it—the acceptance of office—had subjected him to the *suspicion*, &c., not saying that he actually was moved by such motives), in common with that of many others at the time; but hear what Doctor N., whom it is but proper also to listen to, says on the subject : " You have done me, my dear sir, I dare say unintentionally, a grievous injustice, in stating that I abetted Mr. Lafontaine to the disadvantage of Mr. Papineau. I always thought, and do so at this very moment, that Mr. L. was a sincere, honest, frank man, and not actuated by vile or personal motives; but to say that I ever *paid court to him*, or expected anything from him, or that I was influenced by any personal views, is doing me, I can assure you, with all the candour of a man not given to duplicity, great injustice, nay, cruelty. Heaven knows I owe nothing to Mr. L., nay, not even the *comparatively* trifling position I hold. He never, in the most distant manner, alluded to anything of the kind. Most sincerely, I believe, I owe it to Mr. Hincks, who, with all his imputed faults, is a most warm-hearted and generous man. Indeed I have good reason for being convinced that on *two* occasions I was suggested as a fit person to fill certain high and remunerative offices, and that Mr. L. at once opposed it, saying what will the *tories* say? * * * My sojourn for seven months in the Montreal Jail gave me such a practical knowledge of prison affairs, the accursed abuses that prevailed there, as in all other jails, so far as discipline was concerned, and the uncalled for miseries that were inflicted on the prisoners, as led me to reflect most painfully and deeply on the subject; and, though I may be accused of egotism, it was this which induced me to accept Mr. Hincks' kind offer; and, allow me to assure you, that so far as pecuniary matters are concerned, I have been the loser thereby. My *cash book* proves, that for the ten years I have been in this city, my annual receipts average £850, and that there was np to that moment no diminution of my practice; but this last year my receipts will not reach £600, and this from old accounts mainly, and my practice has much diminished. In good truth, were it not that I do really think that I shall be able to effect some good in our penal institutions, I would resign my present office." [The Doctor's office is Inspector of the Provincial Penitentiary and of Gaols, if I mistake not.]

"I pray you will pardon this most hastily written letter. I have been impelled by a sense of what I owe to myself and my family to express myself as I have done. I may be over sensitive when my motives and conduct are impugned. You will, I am sure, pardon the failing, if it is such."

The Doctor certainly throws a new light upon the subject, by denying all obligation to Mr. Lafontaine, [who however was then Prime Minister]; but how was I to know this until told so by him? His appointment, it was reasonable to presume, was at least with Mr. L.'s consent, he being the leading man in the Cabinet. Being now better instructed, I submit the above most willingly in reparation of any wrong, real or imaginary, involuntarily done Doctor Wolfred Nelson in the passage alluded to by him. The Doctor I do think rather sensitive, but the feeling is honourable, and to be respected. I therefore have much pleasure in placing the matter in the point of view he desires.

R. C.

Quebec, July, 1853.

CHAPTER XLIV.

Indications of another insurrection, and inroads by American "sympathisers" and brigands, under Messrs. Robert Nelson and W. L. Mackenzie—Outbreak begins at Ceauharnois, and simultaneously throughout the District of Montreal—Capture of a party of Patriots by the Caughnawaga Indians—Martial Law again declared—Special Council convoked—Patriots assemble at Napierville under Robert Nelson, who issues a proclamation or declaration of independence—Sir John Colborne moves with a body of troops upon Napierville—Patriots, under Cote and Cazeau, routed at Lacole by the loyal Militia—Nelson falls back from Napierville upon Odelltown—Attacks the Militia, and is defeated—Escapes across the Lines—His narrow escape from the vengeance of his own men—Capture of Hindenlang, a Frenchman—His *expose*—Loyal conduct of Militia in the Eastern Townships—Col. Robert Jones—Operations at Beauharnois, and its recovery from the Patriots—Patriots under Mailhot at Montarville dispersed—Insurrection put down—Sir John Colborne returns to Montreal—Great havock and destruction of property throughout the County of Laprairie—Trials by Court Martial, and examples made of the captive Patriots—Difficulties relating to the Habeas Corpus, and suspension of certain judges in consequence —Remarks, &c.

It was very evident during this summer, from the activity of the fugitive patriots, who had taken refuge in the neighbouring States of Vermont and New York, and the constant intercourse between them and their associates throughout the entire District of Montreal, that another outbreak was in contemplation. Along the whole American frontier from Lake Champlain to Detriot, inclusively, active preparations were only carried on by the Canadian refugees, aided by American sympathisers, with the avowed purpose of invading, at various points. both Provinces.* The departure of Lord Durham seems

* The following General Order was issued about this time in Upper Canada and appeared in a Quebec paper of the 2nd November.

to have been agreed upon as the period for commencing operations, which, so far as they concerned Lower Canada, were to be conducted by Doctor

---

ADJUTANT GENERAL'S OFFICE, Toronto, 23rd Oct., 1838.
MILITIA GENERAL ORDER.
" His Excellency the Lieutenant Governor has received certain information that an extensive conspiracy has been formed by numerous unprincipled and rapacious inhabitants of the neighboring friendly States, with a view to force upon this Province the domination of the said conspirators, and to visit the loyal inhabitants of this province with lawless war, plunder and devastation.

" The Lieutenant Governor, in anticipation of an adequate exhibition of force, and activity on the part of the Government of the United States, who continue to declare a most friendly disposition towards Great Britain, has forborne to call upon the loyal inhabitants of Upper Canada, to prepare to defend in arms their institutions, their families and their homes; but the Lieutenant Governor now conceives that the time is come when it would be unjust to Her Majesty's loyal people to risk the consequence of a failure on the part of the most friendly foreign Government, to preserve peaceable relations towards these Colonies; and therefore, for the purpose of preventing the apprehensions which might naturally arise amongst a peaceable population, in the vicinity of a rapacious enemy, the Lieutenant Governor is induced to call out once more a portion of the gallant Militia of Upper Canada, as a volunteer force, in full confidence and certainty that the wicked and lawless designs of the public enemy will be met by a corresponding exhibition of the loyal and gallant feeling which has always distinguished Upper Canada, when engaged in regular war as well as when threatened with aggression from pirates and brigands.

" The Lieutenant Governor will therefore forthwith issue orders to some distinguished officers to call out a portion of the Militia of the province.

" The Lieutenant Governor assures the loyal inhabitants of the Province, that he is in full possession of the designs of the enemy who have nominally amongst them many who have not forgotten their allegiance to Her Majesty, or their duty to their Canadian brethren, and only appear in the ranks of the brigands at present, to save themselves from insult and violance.

By Command of His Excellency Sir George Arthur,
. RICHARD BULLOCK.
Adjutant General Militia.

Robert Nelson (brother of Wolfred), who, as president of the imaginary republic, into which it was intended by the patriots to erect the Province, assumed, as generalissimo, the command of the so-called patriotic force on the frontiers. Mr. William Lyon Mackenzie, as president of the projected Upper Canada republic, was busy, and continued in command of the brigands collected in the different places along the Lakes Ontario and Erie, for the purpose of making a descent on some weak quarter of that Province.

The commencement of the second insurrection took place at Beauharnois, District of Montreal, on Saturday evening the 3rd of November, by an attack on the steamer "Henry Brougham," which, as usual, on her way from the Cascades to Lachine, had put in at that place, where she was immediately taken possession of by a body of about 400 insurgents, who made prisoners of the passengers, destroying at the same time part of her machinery, to dissable her from proceeding. They surrounded the Manor House, and made prisoners of the inmates, Mr. Ellice (son of Edward Ellice, Esq., M. P. proprietor of the Seigniory of Beauharnois), Messrs. Brown the seigniorial agent, Ross, and Norval, seizing also a small quantity of arms (some 16 stand), in the house at the time. Mrs. Ellice, Miss Balfour, her sister, and two other females, were in the Manor House at the time of the attack, and took refuge in the cellar. It does not appear that they were ill-treated by the assailants. The rising was general throughout the District of Montreal on this same night, no doubt by previous agreement among the patriots. A British inhabitant by the name of Walker, residing at or near La Tortue, a few miles from Laprairie, was during the night, attacked in his own house, and murdered, his wife and family escaping, and making good, on the following day, with several others from

Laprairie and the neighbourhood, their retreat to Montreal. From all parts, north and south of Montreal, the loyal inhabitants of British and Irish origin, as on the previous outbreak, were flocking for refuge into the city, driven from their homes by the patriots, whom the lenity of the Government towards their associates on the former occasion, seemed only to have exasperated, and rendered more unfeeling and furious than ever. A space of the railway between Laprairie and St. Johns was broken, or as to interrupt the communication by the cars. The mail carrier between Montreal and Quebec was stopped at the Bout de l'Isle, but after a short delay, allowed to proceed. Large bodies of unarmed men were at the same time in movement on the Richelieu, and assembling at St. Charles, St. Denis, and St. Ours, where they had been informed they would find arms and ammunition *en depot*, awaiting their arrival. Finding themselves, on reaching these places, disappointed, they at once dispersed, most of them returning to their homes, but many proceeding to Napierville, to join Doctor Robert Nelson, whose head quarters were at that place, in the vicinity of the American frontier line, from which it was separated only by the settlements of River Lacole and Odelltown.*

---

*" MONTREAL, Wednesday, 4 o'clock, Nov. 7, 1838.
" The following is about the correct state of affairs here:
" There are still rebels on the Chateauguay river and in L'Acadie. Mr. Ellice has been sent towards Lake Champlain, and it is said has not been ill treated. Mrs. Ellice and her sister are at the priest's house at Chateauguay. Only Mr. Walker, a farmer has been killed. The steamer Henry Brougham was taken on Saturday night at the wharf at Beauharnois, and is dismantled. This movement was concerted, probably, by the refugees on the frontiers; it commenced at the same time at Chateauguay and St. Jean Baptiste de Rouville, and at Varennes, Vercheres and Contrecœur. The Rouville people moved to St. Charles with sticks and packs on their backs, and were promised that arms were

On Sunday, the 4th November, the day after the occurrence at Beauharnois, noticed above, a Squaw of the Indian Village of Caughnawaga, who was looking for her cow in the bush near the village, perceiving a considerable number of armed men in the woods, apparently in ambush, and ready for a descent, she immediately retraced her steps to the village, and gave notice of her discovery to the Indians, who at the moment were assembled at the church, and attending divine service. Taking the alarm, they immediately seized such arms as were at hand, muskets, tomahawks, axes, and pitchforks, and with the war-whoop, charging the invaders, who were advancing, put them to the flight, capturing also sixty-four of them, whom in triumph they brought prisoners to Montreal that same day. This party had assembled in the morning at Chateauguay, and were expedited thence for the purpose of seizing the arms and stores of the Indians at Caughnawaga. The gallantry of the Indians in this first achievement over the patriots in the second insurrection, had a material effect in damping their ardour, while it inspired the loyal with courage and confidence in themselves.

Sir John Colborne declared by proclamation, dated the 4th November, martial law again in force in the

---

waiting for them there. They found none, and were told to go to St. Denis, where they got none, and were met on their way yesterday returning very dissatisfied. Mailhot, who was wounded with Bouchette, is mentioned as having promoted the rising of St. Jean Baptiste de Rouville. The Varennes people moved to St. Ours, and were also dispersing; but it is said they had a piquet in the woods, eight miles from Sorel, yesterday. If not gone, they would be attacked to-day. The flying artillery and cavalry are just going over the river, and if there is any resistance, there will be little mercy.

"The banks here have been authorised to suspend specie payments till the 1st of June.

District of Montreal.* He had on the previous day summoned the Special Council to meet on the 9th

* By His Excellency Sir John Colborne, Knight Grand Cross of the Most Honorable Military Order of the Bath, Administrator of the Government of the Province of Lower Canada, Lieutenant General and Commander in Chief of Her Majesty's Forces in the said Province, &c., &c., &c.

A PROCLAMATION.

WHEREAS there exists in the District of Montreal a traitorous conspiracy, by a number of persons, falsely styling themselves the destruction of the. established constitution, and government of the said Province; and whereas the said traitorous conspiracy hath broken out into acts of the most daring and open rebellion; and whereas the said rebellion hath very considerably extended itself in so much, that large bodies of armed traitors have openly arrayed themselves, and have made, and do still make, attacks upon Her Majesty's subjects, and have committed the most horrid excesses and cruelties; and whereas in the parts of the said District in which the said conspiracy hath not as yet broken out in open rebellion, large numbers of such persons, so calling themselves patriots, for the execution of such their wicked designs, have planned means of open violence, and formed arrangements for raising and arming an organised and disciplined force, and in furtherance of their purposes, have frequently assembled in great an unusual numbers; and whereas the exertions of the civil power are ineffectual for the suppression of the aforesaid traitorous and wicked conspiracy and rebellion, and for the protection of the lives and properties of Her Majesty's loyal subjects; and whereas the courts of justice in the said District of Montreal have virtually ceased to exist from the impossibility of executing any legal process or warrant of arrest therein; and whereas public safety requires that Martial Law should be exercised; Now THEREFORE, I have thought fit, by and with the advice and consent of Her Majesty's Executive Council of this Province, to issue this proclamation to the end that it be made manifest, that I shall arrest and punish and cause to be arrested and punished, all persons who have been hitherto, or who now are or hereafter may be anywise acting, aiding and assisting in the said Conspiracy and Rebellion, and who hereafter may be anywise acting, or assisting in any other conspiracy and rebellion within the said District of Montreal, according to martial law, either by death or otherwise

of the month at Montreal.* A number of arrests were made, many of them, probably on suspicion only, and the jail at Montreal was soon filled again to overflowing.† The volunteer militia who had served during the previous winter at Quebec and

---

as to me shall seem right and expedient; for the punishment of all rebels in the said District.

Given under my hand and seal at arms, at the Government House, in the city of Montreal, in the Province of Lower Canada, the fourth day of November, in the year of our Lord one thousand eight hundred and thirty-eight, and in the second year of Her Majesty's reign.

By His Excellency's command,
THOS. LEIGH GOLDIE.
Acting Secretary of the Province.

* The Special Council now constituted is as before the arrival of Lord Durham, of the following gentlemen:
It will be seen that Messrs. Debartzch and F. A. Quesnel, who were members of His Excellency's Council, have not been summoned to the present.
The Special Council, which was in session here during the week, consists of the following members. Those marked with an asterisk were in attendance.
* James Cuthbert ; * Toussaint Pothier ; Charles C. De Lery ; James Stuart ; *Peter M'Gill ; Marc P. DeSales Laterriere : Barthelemi Joliette ; *Pierre De Rocheblave ;*John Neilson ; Amable Dionne ; *Samuel Gerrard; *Jules Quesnel *William P. Christie ; Charles E. Casgrain ; *William Walker ; Joseph Faribault ; John Molson ; Thomas Austin ; *George Moffatt ; D. Mondelet ; Etienne Maryrand ; Paul Holland Knoulton ; Turton Penn ; Joseph Dionne.
Among the committals to the gaol yesterday, on political charges, are, Edward Barnard, advocate, of Three Rivers ; Dr. Vallee, Dr. Perrault, and---Berthelot, advocate, all of this city.--Nov. 8.

† In the course of yesterday the following persons were arrested :--

D. B. Viger,   L. M. Viger,
Charles Mondelet,   Dexter Chapin,
L. H. Lafontaine,   François Pigeon,
----Harkin,   ----Labonte,
John Donegani,   J. A. Labadie,
----Goulet,   H. B. Weilbrenner,
----Labelle,   George Dillon,

Montreal, reorganised themselves with the same alacrity as on the previous occasion. The Special Council, on meeting, passed an Ordinance suspending the *Habeas Corpus* law throughout the Province during the rebellion, with power to the Governor to restore it in any or all the districts, by proclamation, when he should see fit.

Doctor Robert Nelson, having fixed, as previously mentioned, his head quarters at Napierville, about half way between Lacadie and the American frontier, was joined by about 2500 patriots from the neighbouring parishes, whom he amused with promises of marching towards Laprairie, and of making thence a descent upon Montreal, after he should have secured forts St. John and Chambly, to be safe in his rear. Here he issued a second proclamation, or rather declaration of independence, similar to one he had sent abroad the year before.*

"In addition to the above we find the following in the Montreal Herald of Tuesday :—

Augustin Racicot, François Xavier Desjardins,
Toussaint Terrett, Henry Budeau,
Louis Courcelles, Cyrile David.
Hiram T. Blauchard, Louis Morin,
William Brown, John Willing.
Joseph Labadie, Jean Bte. Choquette,
Hebert Derome Decareau, Pierre De Boucherville,
François Mencelier dit Morichaud.

" We have heard of some risings in the north ; but have not been able to learn any particulars.

" We would particularly impress upon the minds of our loyal fellow subjects of this city, not to allow themselves to be at all alarmed by passing events. The present crisis could not have arrived at a more favorable juncture ; for we do not really see that any serious danger is to be apprehended if we are only true to ourselves. The energy with which the Government is acting has already had the best effect—2000, at least, of the volunteers, in the course of yesterday, flew to arms.—*Montreal Courier*, Nov. 8.

*CANADA—DECLARATION OF INDEPENDENCE.

" WHEREAS the solemn covenant made with the people of Lower Canada, and recorded in the statute book of the United

Sir John Colborne having previously directed a movement of troops upon Napierville, crossed from Montreal to Laprairie on the 6th of November, to take in person the command. The patriots were

Kingdom of Great Britain and Ireland, as the 31st chapter of the acts passed in the 31st year of the reign of King George III, hath been continually violated by the British Government, and our rights usurped; and whereas our humble petitions, addresses, protests and remonstrances against this injurious and unconstitutional interferences have been made in vain, and the British Government hath disposed of our revenue without the constitutional consent of the local legislature, pillaged our treasury, arrested great numbers of our citizens, and committed them to prison, distributed through the country a mercenary army, whose presence is accompanied with consternation and alarm, whose track is red with the blood of our people, who have laid our villages in ashes, profaned our temples, and spread terror and waste through the land. And whereas we can no longer suffer the repeated violations of our dearest rights, and patiently support the multiplied outrages and cruelties of the Government of Canada.—We, in the name of the people of Lower Canada, acknowledging the divine Providence which permit us to put down a government which hath abused the object and intention for which it was created, and to make choice of that form of government which shall re-establish the empire of justice, assure domestic tranquility, provide for common defence, promote general good, and secure to us and our posterity the advantages of civil and religious liberty.

SOLEMNLY DECLARE:

" 1. That from this day forward, the people of Lower Canada are absolved from all allegiance to Great Britain and the political connexion between that part and Lowe Canada is now dissolved."

" 2. That a republican form of government is best suited to Lower Canada, which is this day declared to be a republic.

" 3. That under the free government of Lower Canada all persons shall enjoy the same rights : the Indians shall no longer be under any civil disqualification, but shall enjoy the same rights as any other citizens of Lower Canada.

" 4. That all union between church and state is hereby declared to be dissolved, and every person shall be at liberty

still in possession of Beauharnois, but of these he made light, leaving them to the Glengary Militia, two regiments of whom, under the command of Lieut· Colonels McDonald and Fraser, were on their route thither, with a detachment of the 71st Regiment. The force under Sir John's immediate command consisted of the 15th, 24th, 71st, 73rd, and part of

freely to exercise such religion or belief as shall be dictated to him by his conscience.
" 5. That the feudal or seigniorial tenure of land is hereby abolished as completely as if such tenure had never existed in Canada.
" 6. That each and every person who shall bear arms, or otherwise furnish assistance to the people of Canada in this contest for emancipation, shall be, and is, discharged from all debts, dues, or obligations, real or supposed, for arrearages in virtue of seigniorial rights heretofore existing.
" 7. That the *Douaire Coutumier* is for the future abolished and prohibited.
" 8. That Imprisonment for debt shall no longer exist, excepting in such cases of fraud as shall be specified in an act to be passed hereafter by the legislature of Lower Canada for this purpose.
" 9. That sentence of death shall no longer be passed or executed, except in cases of murder.
" 10. That mortgages on landed estate shall be special, and to be valid, shall be enregistered in offices te be created for this purpose by any act of the legislature of Lower Canada.
" 11. That the liberty and freedom of the press shall exist in all public matters and affairs.
" 12. That trial by jury is guaranteed to the people of Lower Canada in its most extended and liberal sense, in all criminal suits and in civil suits above a sum to be fixed by the Legislature of the state of Lower Canada.
" 13. That as general and public education is necessary, and due by the Government to the people, an act to provide for the same shall be passed as soon as the circumstances of the country will permit.
" 14. To secure the elective franchise, all elections shall be had by ballot.
" 15. That with the least possible delay the people shall chose delegates according to the present division of the country, into counties, towns and boroughs, who shall con-

the 93rd regiments, the Dragoon Guards, the Hussars, a body of 400 Indians, and about 500 Volunteers from Montreal, with a party of Royal Artillery and eight field pieces, presenting in all an imposing force.*

---

stitute a convention or legislative body, to establish a constitution according to the wants of the country, and in conformity with the disposition of this declaration, subject to be modified according to the will of the people.

"16. That every male person of the age of 21 and upwards shall have the right of voting as herein provided, and for the election of the aforesaid delegates.

17. " That all *Crown Lands,* also such as are called *Clergy Reserves,* and such as are nominally in possession of a certain company of landholders in England, called the " British North American Land Company," are of right the property of the state of Lower Canada, except such portion of the aforesaid lands as may be in the possession of persons who hold the same in good faith, and to whom titles shall be secured and granted by virtue of a law which shall be enacted to legalize the possession of and a title for such entitled lots of land in the townships as are under cultivation or improvement.

18. " That the French and English languages shall be used in all public affairs.

" And for the fulfilement of this declaration, and for the support of the patriotic cause in which we are now engaged with a firm reliance on the protection of the Almighty, and the justice of our cause, we by these presents solemnly pledge to each other our lives, our fortunes, and our most sacred honor.

By order of the Provisional Government,
ROBERT NELSON, President.

* Sir John Colborne had written on the 1st Nov. to Lieut. Col. Turner, at Cornwall, on special service as follows :—

Quebec, Nov. 1. 1838.

" SIR.—I request that you will explain to the officers of the militia in the District in which you are stationed, that Canada being threatened with an attack from the American frontier by a horde of rapacious brigands, every man that can bear arms, I am persuaded, will not hesitate to join his regiment, and prepare to repel the wicked and unprovoked invasion with which the Provinces are threatened, and which no doubt, will be immediately attempted. The loyal inha-

The occurrences in the vicinity of Nelson's head quarters previous to the advance of the Commander of the Forces, are to be noticed. Dr. Cote and his colleague, Gagnon, were at Rouse's Point, within the United States, at the foot of Lake Champlain, attended by a number of patriots, and busy in securing munitions of war provided by American sympathisers, and supplies necessary to enable Nelson to organize and arm his force at Napierville, some twenty miles distant within the Canadian territory, and but a short distance west of Isle aux Noix, in the River Richelieu.* The loyal Militia volunteers of Odelltown had on the outbreak turned out, and organizing themselves, a party of them had been placed at the Lacolle Steam Mill; by which the communication between Nelson and the patriots at Rouse's Point, in his rear, was intercepted. This it was necessary to keep open in case of a retreat. Cote accordingly determined upon attacking this post to dislodge the occupants, and keep the communication clear. On the evening of the 5th of November, a small schooner which had come down the lake, anchored at Rouse's Point, and landed a small cannon and 250 stand of arms for the use of the patriots. In the course of the night a body of 400 Canadians came over from Alberg, on the opposite (eastern) side of the Richelieu, where they had previously re-assembled, and took up their quarters

---

bitants may be assured that the mother country will no longer suffer these Provinces to be kept in a state of suspense and alarm to which they have been lately exposed; but that the strength of the empire will be exerted fully to put an end to the disgraceful proceedings on the frontier. I have the honor to be, &c.

    (Signed,)   J. COLBORNE,
        Commander of the Forces.

* It is said that the patriots while at this place, took away, by direction of Cote, the iron chest, containing at the time £327 11s, belonging to the church.

in some houses on the road between Champlain and Odelltown, and thence to Lacolle and Napierville. This body, led on by Cote and Gagnon, advanced at nine o'clock next morning to dislodge the guard at the steam mill. They at first succeeded in driving in the small biquet of volunteers on the outlook for them, but not without an opposition and loss that considerably cooled their fervour, and which moreover afforded time to Colonel Odell, who commanded the volunteers, to notify Major Schriver, of the Hemmingford Militia, in his immediate vicinity, of what was going on, and who at once reinforced him by a body of the Hemmingford Militia. The arrival of this volunteer reinforcement decided the fate of the day. They gallantly charged the patriots, carried their gun, and put them to flight, leaving in possession of the victors 400 stand of arms and a quantity of ammunition. Of the patriots, eleven were killed and eight made prisoners; a number were wounded, but effected their escape over the Lines. Two of the volunteers were killed and two wounded. Captains March, Weldon, and Fisher, with their companies of militia-volunteers, shared in this affair, which reflected the highest credit upon those loyal and brave men.

Nelson, finding his situation becoming more and more precarious, his rear occupied by the militia, and his retreat intercepted, while Sir John Colborne was advancing, resolved upon falling back upon Odelltown. He accordingly, on the morning of the 9th November, entered that place at the head of 800 men armed with firelocks, and 200 with pikes. The volunteer militia opposed to them did not exceed 200, but providentially Lieut. Col. Taylor, posted on special service at Caldwell Manor [east bank of the Richelieu], on the frontier line, having just then crossed from that side, arrived at the moment when the patriots were entering, and took the command of the volunteers. The action that took place will be best explained in his despatch on the subject:—

Odelltown, November 9, 1838.

SIR,—I have the honour and the satisfaction to report to you, for the information of His Excellency the Commander of the Forces, the successful result of an affair with the rebels, which took place this morning. The insurgents mustered one thousand strong, under the personal command of Dr. Nelson. They attacked my advanced guard at Captain Weldon's, at about a quarter to eleven, A. M.; upon which, I immediately directed the concentration upon Odelltown Church, of the small force of 200 men, under my command.

The enemy extended around us, and kept up a sharp fire, which was as sharply answered. After an action of about two hours and a half, during which several brilliant sallies were made by the volunteers, the insurgents retreated, leaving fifty dead, and carrying off several wounded.

I regret to say that Captain M'Allister and four men have fallen, and that Lieutenant Odell and nine men have been wounded—none of the latter, however, are seriously injured.

When I arrived at Caldwell Manor, at daybreak, I learnt the great disparity of force which existed; I heard, also, that the loyalists were much worn out by constant watching and harrassing duty. I accordingly wrote Captain Grattan, at the Isle aux Noix, asking him if he could, consistently with the safety of the fort, give me any aid. That officer promptly replied, by coming in person with a detachment, but unfortunately he reached Odelltown too late to participate in the engagement.

A reinforcement from Hemmingford, under Major Schriver, arrived also after the retreat of the rebels.

It is my intention to advance and take up a new position at Lacolle to-morrow morning.

After the above plain recital of events, it were needless for me to say, that I have every reason to speak in the highest terms of approbation of the gallantry and conduct of the volunteers under my orders. I have the honor to be, sir, your most obedient humble servant,

CHAS. CYRIL TAYLOR,

Lieut.-Colonel.

Lieut. Griffin,

Dy. Asst. Adjt. Genl.

While the patriots were endeavouring to carry the position of the volunteers, the appearance of 100 militia from Caldwell Manor, under Captain Vaughan, who hearing the report of the fire-arms, had crossed the Richelieu, and reached the scene of action, utterly disconcerted them, and they immediately fled in all directions. The militia volunteers were in possession of the small cannon taken a few days before from Cote, and on this occasion, turned it with dreadful effect against its former owners. When the patriots were advancing in compact order up the road to the church in which the volunteers had taken post, a discharge of grape in their midst did fearful havoc, clearing a space of some feet wide through the moving mass. It was, however, discharged but thrice, the volunteers being, by the overwhelming numbers of the assailants, obliged to retire within the church, but in the frequent efforts of the patriots to get possession of the gun, such a destructive fire was kept up from the windows as to render all their attempts abortive, though never fought patriots with greater bravery and perseverance than did these men while there was a prospect of success. The gun, so useful on the occasion, was served but by two regulars, a sergeant

L

and a private, whose gallantry was noticed by the Commander of the Forces in general orders.*

Sir John Colborne, with a part only of his force, entered Napierville on the morning of the 29th, but, as mentioned above, the patriots had left it for Odelltown that same morning, and he consequently found all quite at that place. Dr. Robert Nelson, immediately after his defeat at the church, effected his escape on foot over the frontier line, reporting as he went that he had gained a victory over the volunteers at Odelltown, which he had left, he said, in possession of the

HEAD QUARTERS, Montreal, Nov. 17th, 1838·
*GENERAL ORDER,
No. 1.—The Commander of the Forces has the greatest satisfaction in expressing and recording his admiration of the gallant conduct of the volunteers on the Lacolle Frontier, under the command of Colonel Odell, Captain March, the late Captain M'Allister, Major Schriver, Captain Vaughan, and others, who notwithstanding the disparity of their numbers, defeated the traitors and invaders near Rouse's Point and Odelltown; and he avails himself of the earliest opportunity of offering his cordial thanks for the heroic perseverance and devotion to the service of their country, which they have displayed from the first moment of this second revolt.

His Excellency also begs that Colonel Davidson and the Huntingdon Volunteers, will accept his best thanks for their conduct and bravery in attacking the rebels at Beauharnois.

The prompt assembly and movements of the brave Glengary Regiments, under Colonels M'Donnell and Fraser, and of the Stormont Militia, under Col. Æneas M'Donnell, and their march to Beauharnois, has had the effect of entirely dispersing the rebels in that quarter:

The great activity and judgment which has been evinced by Lieut. Col. Taylor, in his defence of the post of Odelltown, and by Colonels Carmichael, Campbell, and Phillpots, in Beauharnois, reflect the highest credit on these officers.

The gallantry of Serjeant Beattie, of the Royal Regiment, who worked the captured gun during the attack on Odelltown, has been brought under His Excellency's notice. Such examples, and the determined spirit which animates the volunteers of the whole Province, cannot fail to give confidence in every section of the country.

(Signed,)   JOHN EDEN,
(True Copy,)   D.A.G.
E. J. GRIFFIN, D A.A.G.

patriots, and procuring a horse rode full speed towards Plattsburgh under pretence of seeking medical aid for his wounded. Several of the unfortunate patriots were taken while making their way for the line, and within a very short distance of the scene of their defeat, and among them Nicholas, the sanguinary miscreant, who had superintended the murder of Chartrand. Nelson, it is to be observed, had previous to this action very narrowly escaped the vengence of his own men. He was in the act of visiting one of his outposts at Napierville, when having incurred, it would seem, the suspicion of some of his co-patriots of an intention to desert them, he was seized and, his arms being pinioned by them, put into a cart, with the intention of delivering him up as a propitiatory offering to Sir John Colborne. The party in possession of him had proceeded with this intention a short distance on their way, when mistaking the road, they accidently met some of their own party, among whom were Nicholas and another influential man by the name of Trudeau, by whose intercession he was brought back to the bivouac of the patriots, whe.e after some deliberation he was released, and restored to the command. The argument used by Nicholas and Trudeau to induce their comrades to bring back the impounded patriot general to his people was ingenious and just in principle: "You suspect your general of treachery and an intention to desert the patriotic cause—if so, it is for the patriots to try him—not Sir John Colborne, who of course will approve of the intended treachery, and in consequence of it, very possibly, may set him at liberty."

Among the captives secured after the action at Odelltown, was a young Frenchman by the name of Hindenlang recently from France, and who had just joined the patriots, among whom he bore the rank of general. He sent shortly after his capture a statement to Sir John Colborne of the occurrences that had taken place among the patriots during his short service with them.* He was a mere youth,

* The following narrative is rather long and prolix, but nevertheless interesting, from the lively description it gives of the " getting up" of an insurgent or " patriotic" army, its organisation, discipline, &c., and especially the opinions entertained by the " generals" for each other and the cause, the army once scattered, and the melancholy day of reckoning at hand. This unfortunate young man evidently contemplated his doom with dismay, and intended, by the abuse he lavished upon his late leader and comrades, to atone for his error, and conciliate the Commander of the Forces, who however deemed him a proper subject for an example, and he accordngly suffered.

From L'Ami du Peuple.

" Voluntary confession of Mons. CHARLES HINDENLANG, brigadier general in the rebel army.

" We publish the account given by Mr. Chs. Hindenlang, the French officer, whom the rebels had decorated with the title of general. The short and simple narration of a man so cruelly deceived by the rebels, ought to open the eyes of all those Canadians who will read it without prejudice.

" (The prisoner gives an account of his birth, parentage and first steps in life, from which it appears that he was born at Paris, in 1810, of parents holding a respectable situation in mercantile life ; that being ambitious of a military life, he enlisted in the 5th regiment of Light Infantry, in which he obtained the rank of a subaltern officer. Seeing that promotion was not likely to follow as rapidly as he wished, he quitted the army, and came to New York, intending there to engage in mercantile pursuits, and was waiting, he says, the arrival of goods which were to be sent to him in the spring, when he was solicited by Mr. Duvernay, through several channels, amongst others an Italian refugee named Faliere, whom the rebels also wished to engage as an officer. A. M. Von Schoultz, calling himself a colonel, and who was recruiting officers and men for a regiment to serve in Upper Canada, likewise made proposals to him ; but he was led in an evil hour, to engage with the Lower Canada rebels)

The narrative continues :

" Mr. Duvernay, acting in the name of and for Dr. Robert Nelson, made fair proposals and tempting offers to myself and another French officer who had served in the 1st Lancers of the Anglo-Spanish Legion, in the rank of Lieutenant or

without experience in military affairs, and suffered for his indiscretion in joining the patriots, being one of Captain; these were made in presence of a merchant named Bonnafous. A duplicate copy, transcribed in my hand writing, I put into the hands of an officer at Lacolle. It contains the details of the preliminary reciprocal engagement proposed to me. After having consulted with my friend, we refused to sign till we had made ourselves better acquainted with the situation of Canada, of which we were both equally ignorant. The better to deceive us, we were assured that it was only necessary to go to St. Albans, to form keleton regiments for the organization of the army : we were told also by Mr Duvernay and others to whom we addressed ourselves, that we need not provide ourselves with arms. Not only were the people of Canada rising, *en masse*, but the troops, and above all the English officers, were tired of a service which kept them at a distance from home, and would be glad of the opportunity of getting rid of it. They added further that the immense expense to which the Crown of England was put, every year, by these Colonies rendered Queen Victoria, as they knew from a good source, indifferent to retaining them.

" We decided to satisfy ourselves further as to the truth of all this. We were then directed to Burlington where we were received by M. Dufort. Here the same language and the same promises were held out to us. We were strictly prohibited from conversing during our journey with any one about our affairs, this, it was pretended would be for our own advantage, but the sequel has proved to be. that it it was from the fear of our learning the truth, that we were so instructed. M. Dufort forwarded us to Plattsburg, where we found horses and were conveyed, by a person they called a *Hunter*, to Champlain, where we were lodged by a Mr. Desmarais, who kept us concealed as if he was hiding the most notorious criminals. 1 have remarked throughout, in all the agents I have had to do with, in this affair, a pusillanimity which bordered upon weakness, to speak of it in the most favorable terms. We required to be conducted, according to promise, to St. Albans ; we were taken across the river in a boat, where we found Dr. Nelson and a person, who I supposed to be a guide. That very night, the Canadians who had risen, were according to the infamous and miserable Nelson, to have thronged to the banks of the river, to receive him and congratulate him on his disembarkation. Two hundred and fifty muskets had been brought and deposited in the boat by an American, Col. Burton ! We

of those, of whom it was deemed neccesary to make
examples, and who accordingly suffered shortly after
at Montreal.

pushed off, and dropped down the river as far as Vitman's
whaif. The party consisted of the Doctor, his guide, the
boatmen, myself, and my companion., We arrived in dreadful weather. There was not a single man to receive the
famous President of the *Provisional Government*; and it was
only after a full hour's search, and much trouble, the guide
returned with five or six men to land the arms. We were
immediately furnished with three horses, and set off for
Napierville. There, Dr. Cote, at the head of 2 or 300 men,
received Dr. Nelson and proclaimed him President of the
Republic of Lower Canada. Nothing was omitted in the
farce which was then played; speeches and promises on one
side and on the other were made in due form. We were
presented to a crowd, speedily collected, as two French officers, but we said nothing on our parts; we stood more in
need of a good fire than of empty compliments. This was
on Sunday morning.

" During three days, Dr. Nelson and his colleagues were
chiefly occupied in sending messages to hasten the arrival of
men. On Monday, Touvrey, a French officer, set out with
fifty men to feel his way, and scour the environs of our position. I have not seen him since.

" I have been informed that Dr. Cote forced M. le Cure,
of the place, to give him up a considerable sum of money,
the property of the parish: and similar attempts were made
upon certain tory individuals; even a bed and pillow were
seized from an aged invalid prisoner. I was requested by a
lady to order them to be returned. I did so, and on my return to quarters, reported the circumstances, as I thought
it my duty to do, to Dr. Cote. Whereupon he took me aside
and said 1 had no orders to receive from him, for I was a
brigadier. At these words, I opened my eyes, and had my
companion been present, I have not the smallest doubt we
should have extricated ourselves from the vortex we were
plunged in. To make a general of one who enlisted a private soldier, was a jest that I laughed at, as did many
others.

" The next day, Dr. Cote marched with 50 or 60 armed
men, and a detachment was sent to reinforce that commanded by Mons. Touvrey. I have since learned that the arms
Dr. Cote wished to bring in had been seized, and that be
himself was repulsed by the Queen's troops, leaving a field
piece in their hands. During these three days, Canadians
armed and unarmed, urged by the messenger of Dr. Nelon's,

During these occurrences, the militia in the Eastern Townships, and in the county of Missisquoi where the inhabitants were particularly exposed to the forces, came to Napierville, to the number, I should think, of 2.500 men,—the whole that could be mustered at that place. During all this time, my occupation was (according to the orders of Dr Nelson,) to divide the force Into companies of 50 men each, forming five divisions of 9, each commanded by a non-commissioned officer. On Tuesday, Dr. Nelson ordered the advance upon Odelltown; six hundred men, armed, and all the officers accompanied him. I recollect only the names of some of the officers. He stopped our march at Odelltown, where we passed the night: and there, under pretext of going to bring in a distant post, 150 men, under the command of a man named Dupuis and another captain, the miserable poltroon, Nelson, having possessed himself of all the money he could lay his hands on, endeavoured to make his escape. He was seized, tied, manacled, and on the point of being given up by the Canadians; he was only saved by the prayers and intercession of Captains Nicholas and Trudeau.

"He returned to Lacolle, where, by the most solemn oaths, he succeeded in again persuading the rebels of his honest intentions, and then decided on an attack on Odelltown, to be conducted by himself, in person, on the following day.

" For the sake of truth, and in order to do justice to some unhappy beings, I declare, upon my honor, that many persons were forced by the menaces and precautions taken by the cowardly Nelson to join in these movements. They were told they must declare themselves, and be either *patriots* or *bureaucrats*. Fear made many of them patriots despite of themselves. The affair of Odelltown is the only one at which I was present, and I was in a situation to satisfy myself of the truth of what I advance, when I say that many men marched forward only from sheer fear. On arriving on the open ground fronting a fortified house, the greater part of the force spread itself in a field, to the right and to the left; there was only a handful of men, more brave than their fellows, who sheltered themselves behind a barn and opened a fire. The greater part of the Canadians kept out of the range of shot; threw themselves on their knees, with their faces buried in the snow, praying to God, and remaining as motionless as if they were so many saints, hewn in stone. Many remained in that posture as long as the firing lasted: Oh! pity upon such men! those who could lead such recreant mortals to revolt must have been most adroit deceivers. It

inroads of American sympathisers and brigands, acting in connection with Cote, Gagnon, and other refugee patriots, acquitted themselves with the most

is certain that if many of them were asked what they sought to gain and what they hoped for they would not know what to answer.

" I now became convinced that Dr. Nelson was no better than a cowardly, vile instigator of trouble,—a shameless robber who fled with the money, leaving the people to be butchered, who, but for his perfidious insinuations would have been safe in their cottages, of which the ground they covered is now only to be seen. I never had any fire arms, and I bent under my feet the sword with which I was armed; my determination was taken, to save those unfortunate people if I could ; I traversed the field amidst the flying bullets, asking on all sides what had become of Dr. Nelson.

" Hundreds of men were about to suffer for the guilt of one. The wretch had taken advantage of the moment, when his troops were engaged, to regain the frontier, by a circuitous path. I remained a quiet spectator of the action, waiting for the opportunity of surrendering myself and treating for the safety of these unfortunate men. But presently some twenty *bureaucrats* appearing from a wood, struck such terror into the Canadians, that forthwith the little army was, like a flock of sheep, flying as fast as legs could carry them. On foot, and surrounded by some horsemen, I wished only to wait till we should be pursued, and then to stop and surrender myself; but we were allowed to fly without molestation. I was amongst the last that reached Napierville. The officers were there assembled, and were busily occupied in posting guards. I then declared openly, that having been deceived, and being now able to judge for myself of the stupidity of such an enterprize, having neither bound myself by oath, nor by receipt of money, not even so much as my own necessary disbursements, I considered myself entirely free to act as I pleased, and in no way mixed in the cause, of the unfortunate Canadians. I invited the officers present to do as I did, and it was decided we should separate.

We set off, a dozen of us together, and took to the woods to avoid the picquets of our people who would have stopped us, and, at break of day I left the party near Champlain, in company with one man whom I hardly knew by sight. I came out of the wood and went to surrender myself to a young man whom I saw at a distance, armed with a gun. I wished to ask him immediately, to conduct me before a superior officer, but not being able to speak a word of Eng-

exemplary loyalty. Lieutenant Colonel the Honorable Robert Jones, commanding in that quarter, was indefatigable, and with his loyal companions were

lish, I could not make myself understood. I was taken from post to post. At length, at Lacolle, I asked some officer for permission to write to His Excellency. They gave me permission but as I was still in handcuffs, it was not till the present time, that, here in Montreal, I have been able to bring under the eye of His Excellency all that I know. In doing so, I am animated by a hatred and profound contempt for Dr. Nelson and his accomplices.

" I could not see, without emotions of the most painful anger, one man meditating in cold blood, and that with full knowledge of what he was doing, the ruin of a whole people and from motives of the basest self-interest. I have it from Nelson himself, that the city of Montreal alone sent him upwards of 20,000 dollars. What has he done with the money? Churches have been plundered; individuals have been ransomed, parish funds have been carried off. Such a man deserves to be proscribed and attainted by the laws, in whatever country he may seek refuge. Nothing can authorise theft and violence.

" Besides Touvrey and myself, there are, remaining on the frontier, some French and some Polish officers who have been deceived as we were. Some of these I know, and hope I may be allowed to undeceive them, that my example may warn them, and I shall feel eternally grateful to His Excellency.

" Let me be permitted to use the medium of the American and French journals at New York, to expose these traitors and cowards who have raised the present difficulty. They contrive by their lies and their false appearance of devotion to the cause. to excite sympathy; in New York, I know a number of merchants. I have done my duty as a man of honor. I did not turn my back under the fire of the Government, I remained in spite of the repugnance I felt. I am not an adventurer; I belong to a respectable family; I shall be believed, for my conscience tells me I have nothing to reproach myself with. I know many editors of French journals; I will make them speak out so that these traitors may be every where exposed.

" For five days I saw myself in the ranks of the enemies of a Government, the ally of my country. That is my offence,—I shall think nothing painful by which I may make reparation; it was for this reason that rather than save myself like a coward, I preferred to remain and trust myself.

honored by the thanks of the Commander of the Forces.*

Simultaneously with the disappearance of the patriot host from Napierville, and its dispersion at Odelltown, disappeared also that at Beauharnois. A body of a thousand Glengary men, accompanied by a detachment of the 71st Regiment, crossing from the north shore of the St. Lawrence, landed early in the morning of the 10th November, near the

---

to the generosity of a Government. I shall not be obliged to cast down my eyes and blush when I am spoken to upon this unhappy affair. I have prevented as much mischief as I could; but this is not sufficient, let me be employed in the good cause, and I engage, on my sacred honor, to make reparation, by every possible service that may be required of me, for the error of a few days.

" Would that my situation could be rightly understood, I have my head still stunned with the misery I have witnessed; I am worn down by fatigue. This narrative is, no doubt, very incomplete; many things have been omitted; but except the repugnance I feel at denouncing persons whom I do not name, my conscience in imposing upon me the duty of communicating all that may prevent misery to the vanquished prevents me also from being as exact in my details as I wish to be. If any other information I may be able to give, may become necessary, I again repeat that it will cost me nothing to disclose it.

" I declare upon my honor, and before God, that all that I have written is true, that if there is any error in my statements, of which I am not aware, it can only be in what I have related upon hearsay, and not where I speak as an eye witness.

" I swear also, to be for ever the enemy of Dr. Nelson; to follow him and reproach him before the whole world, were it possible, with the infamy of his actions.

Done in the Prison of Montreal this 14th November, 1838
CHAS. HINDENLANG.

Acknowledged before me, in the Prison }
of Montreal, this 14th Nov. 1838.   }
P. E. LECLERE. J. B.

*BEDFORD, Nov. 12, 1838.

SIR,—I have the pleasure to acquaint you that His Excellency Sir John Colborne, considering the insurrection, which commenced the week before last, as put down, he loses

village af Beauharnois upon which they immediately marched.* They took possession of it after a shew of resistance by the patriots, whom they drove from the village. Messrs. Ellice, Brown, Norval, and others, in the power of the patriots during the previous week, were released by them on their learning the defeat of Nelson. Mrs. Ellice and her sister had been treated with civility, residing during

---

no time in restoring the militia of this part of the country, to the comfort of their homes and families. In doing so, he desires me to convey to you, and the officers and men of your regiment who are under arms, the high sense he entertains of their zeal, activity and loyalty, on this occasion.

" Connected, as I am, with the district, it is a grateful duty to be the medium of conveying thanks so well merited; and I feel confidently assured, that in making known His Excellency's further pleasure, that they should hold themselves in readiness to turn out on the shortest notice, the Missisquoi Militia will be up and ready at a moment's warning. I have the honor to be, sir, your most obedient, humble servant,

W. F. WILLIAMS, Lieut. Col.
Commanding the Missisquoi Rouville Frontier.
To Lieut. Col. the Hon. R. Jones,
Commanding the Missisquoi Militia, &c., &c., &c.

*BEAUHARNOIS, 10th November, 10, P.M.
"SIR,—I have the honour to acquaint you, for the information of His Excellency the Commander of the Forces, that in conjunction with Colonel Phillpotts, a detachment of one officer of Engineers, twenty-two Sappers and Miners, one captain, three subalterns, four sergeants, two buglers, and one hundred and twenty-one rank and file, 71st Regt., with upwards of one thousand Glengarymen, were landed at Hungary Bay this morning, marched, and took Beauharnois, rescued all the prisoners, with the exception of Messrs. Ellice, Brown, Norman, Ross, Norval, Bryson, Houndslow and Surveyer supposed to be at Chateauguay—with the loss of one man killed, and three wounded, of the 71st Regiment.

" The men are much fatigued, and we wait here for orders.
" I have the honor to be, sir,
Your most obedient humble servant.
L. CARMICHAEL,
Colonel P. S.
" Major Hall, Assistant Quarter Master General.

the week the patriots were in possession of the
village, at the presbytere, or parsonage house, as
guests, of the parish priest of Beauharnois, whose
hospitality and kindness to the ladies, and indeed to
all those captured in the steamer Henry Brougham,
could not be exceeded.*

A body of about two hundred patriots, under the
guidance of Mr. Mailhot, during these events, had
taken possession of the Manor House and mills of Mr.
Bruneau, at Montarville Mountain, about midway between
Boucherville and Chambly, and were intrenching
themselves with the view of making a formidable
resistance. This was the only assemblage of patriots
now remaining to be disposed of. A detachment of

---

*EXTRA.

RELEASE OF THE PRISONERS TAKEN BY THE RE-
BELS—TAKING OF BEAUHARNOIS.

"Messrs. Brown, Ellice, Norval, and other persons taken
at Beauharnois by the rebels on Saturday night the 3d instant arrived in town this morning from Laprairie. After
their capture at Beauharnois, they were, as we mentioned
before, taken to Chateauguay, where they were detained
several days. It was afterwards determined by the rebels
to convey them inland, it is supposed to Napierville; but
last night, when they reached La Pigeonniere, in the Seigniory of St. George, the rebels there heard of the occurrences at Napierville, and abandoned their charge. Mr. Ellice
and the other prisoners then got conveyances for Laprairie,
to which they travelled during the night, and arrived in
Montreal this forenoon about ten o'clock.—*Montreal Gazette*.

"BEAUHARNOIS, 10th November, 1838.

" We, the undermentioned passengers, on board the *Henry
Brougham*, captured at Beauharnois on the 4th instant, are
very desirous, before separating to express Our feelings of
sincere gratitude to you, for the extremely kind and hospit-
able treatment we have received from you, since we have
been kept prisoners at your house by the insurgents.

" Your sincere sympathy with us, and the unremitting attention with which you endeavoured to procure for us all
the comforts which circumstances admitted of, will ever be
most gratefully remembered by us, and must, in after life, be

two companies of the 66th Regiment, then at William Henry, was sent against them, and on the approach of this small force they abandoned the post, leaving three small pieces of ordnance, a considerab'e quantlty of arms and ammunition, and some individuals whom they had made prisoners.*

---

a source of satisfactory reflection to yourself. As we believe that your anxiety to discharge a Christian duty was the motive which actuated you, and as this consciousness must be your best reward for services, for which no pecuniary compensation could be an equivalent, we shall offer none, but shall request your acceptance of a piece of plate, as a small memorial of our gratitude and sincere wishes for your welfare and happiness. We are, sir, your obedient servants,

Sarah Ussher, Anna Maria Griffin.
B. Colelough. Hyde Parker. Lieut. R. A.
D. M'Nicol. James Campbell, M. D.
N. Carman, Amos Lister, D. A. C; G.
R. Young J. M'Dougall.
Edward Griffin, U. C. Poultney.
D. E. M'Intire, M. D. Duncan M'Donell.
Thos. M'Mahon H. N. Clarke.
A. Farewell.

Messire Quintal, Cure of Beauharnois.

"The reverend gentleman made an appropriate reply, thanking the parties for their intended gift, which, we understand, has since been prepared by Messrs. SAVAGE & Son, of this city, for the donors."—*Montreal Gazette.*

*CHAMBLY, Nov. 15. 1838.

"SIR,—I have the honor to acquaint you, that on my arrival here yesterday evening, I learned that the camp in the Boucherville mountain had broken up, and that Mailhot had crossed over at the ferry to Point Oliver: I also heard of some threatened disturbances at St. Mary's. on the opposite side of the river. I ordered an officer and 30 men of the 15th, accompanied by some loyal persons, acquainted with the inhabitants, to leave this at five o'clock this morning, and to go there to look for arms not without hopes of taking Mailhot. Some arms were taken, and two leading agitators were brought in, who remain for examination to-morrow. I also learn from the cure of this place, (who has been most praiseworthy in his exertions to restrain his flock from participating in the rebellion, and in bringing to justice the agi-

This put an end to the insurrection, and Sir John Colborne re-entered Montreal on the 14th November, being enthusiastically received by the citizens or his landing from the steamer Princess Victoria, in which he crossed from Laprairie. During the expedition to Napierville, different reconnaissances were made by the cavalry, volunteers, and light troops attached to it, by whom it was ascertained that nearly the whole adult male population in the various parishes they visited were absent from their homes, and therefore supposed to be in the patriot ranks. Great destruction of property was wantonly made by the burning of farm houses and barns of suspected patriots in the different parishes on the route of the

---

tators and those who had coerced the peaceably disposed,) that he had learned that three guns and a considerable quantity of arms and ammunition were in the mill near the lake in the centre of the Boucherville mountain; that he had sent a young ecclesiastic of the name of LeFevre, to recommend to his parishioners for their own interest, the voluntary surrender of all those warlike stores immediately to him, to be, by him delivered to me, and I hourly expected them.

"As they did not arrive last night, I patroled this morning to the mountain with twenty dragoons, and on arriving at the wood, about eleven o'clock, met Major Johnston, with the 66th and two guns. proceeding to make the seizure. After making some visits for arms, and sending home the patrole, I joined Major Johnston, at the mill, and found him in possession of three guns, ten or a dozen casks of powder some thirty muskets, and a great many pikes—also, a good deal of ammunition made up, particularly artillery catridges with bags containing some dozen of musket balls attached to each.

"Major Johnson was to return to Beloeil, for the night, with his capture, the particulars of which he will, no doubt himself detail; but I write this, as I have a more direct means of communication.

I have the honor to be, sir,
Your most obedient humble servant,
GEORGE CATHCART,
Lieutenant Colonel K. D. G.

To the Military Secretary, &c., &c., &c.

troops to Napierville, and indeed throughout the County of Laprairie, greatly however to the annoyance of Sir John Colborne, who had given the most positive orders to avoid all excesses of the kind. They were attributed, probably with reason, to the exasperation of the irregulars accompanying the troops, whose passions roused by the ill treatment their fellow subjects of British origin, and perhaps many of themselves personally, had experienced from the patriots in those places, they availed themselves of the opportunity to retaliate, which they certainly did with unscrupulous rigour, spreading devastation on all sides to an extent much to be regretted; and of which to this day that part of the country has scarcely recovered.

From the lenity shewn by the Government towards those who, during the previous rebellion, had been foremost in it, a notion very generally prevailed among the patriots and their friends, that the Executive would not bring those, who on the present occasion were taken, to trial, from a conviction that no jury impartially chosen, would find them guilty. The verdict of the jury in Nicholas and Daunais' case was exultingly alluded to as in point, and not a few pretended that the Government, even if convictions were by any means obtained, would not dare to make examples. It was deemed necessary to remove this error. The loyal inhabitants of the province were exasperated, having twice in the course of a twelvemonth been driven to arms in defence of the Government and of their property and lives, some of which had been cruelly sacrificed, and the circumstances of all injured more or less, by the crisis and the long agitation that had preceeded them. Sir John Colborne accordingly determined upon vindicating the laws and to make an example of some of the most guilty of the insurgents. A general Court Martial for their trials was ordered, which commenced its sittings at Montreal on the 20th November.* Messrs. C. D. Day and Dominic Mondelet, of the Montreal Bar, were retained by the Government to conduct the prosecutions on the part of the Crown. A number of the patriots were tried, and being found guilty were sentenced, some to death, others to transportation. Twelve of these unfortunate men suffered the extreme penalty of the law, pursuant to sentences of the court martial. An exception to the legality of the court was made by the counsel for the prisoners, but the court overruled it.†

---

* President, Major General John Clitherow.
Lt. Col. Sir John Eustace, 2nd Bat. Gren. Guards.
Lt. Col. Henry Bernard, do. do.
Lt. Col. James Crawford, do. do.
Lt. Col. John Grierson, 15th Regiment.
Major Arthur Biggs, 7th Hussars.
Major H Townsend, 24th Regiment,
Major John Lloyd, 73rd do.
Capt. Augt. Cox. Grenadier Guards.
Capt. Geo. Cadogan, do.
Capt. H. Mitchell, do.
Capt. Wm. Smith, 15th Regiment,
Capt. Robert March, 24th do.
Capt. Edward Muller, Royal Regt. Dy. Judge Advocate

† Joseph N. Cardinal and Joseph Duquette were the first who suffered, being executed on the 22rd December, 1838. They headed the party taken by the Caughnawaga Indians, upon whom they had made a descent from Chateauguay. The former, a public notary, had been a member of the House of Assembly, the latter had been his clerk or student, as a notary, and being a youth, much sympathy was expressed by all classes at his unhappy fate. They had both it seems, been deeply implicated in the former rebellion, but generously forgiven, they had forgotten the mercy shown them, and it was probably for this reason deemed necessary to make examples of them. Decoigne, Robert, the Sanguinets brothers, and Hamelin, suffered on the 18th January, following--and finally on the 15th of February, Lorimier, Hindenlang, Narbonne, Nicholas and Daunais were executed. Much sympathy was expressed for Mr. Lorimier, being a young gentleman highly esteemed and of good family; Hindenlang,

Sir John Colborne had effectually put down the insurgent patriots who had taken to the field, but he had yet to contend with difficulties from a quarter whence they were little expected—the judiciary—into which, in pursuance of the conciliatory policy prevalent of late years, some of the chiefs of those constituting that class of politicians now in the field, had been introduced, and who it was but natural should sympathize with their former associates, whom they had familiarised with the notion that sooner or later their pretensions must be decided by arms. It was in fact contended by some of the judges that the Ordinance recently passed by the Governor and Special Council suspending the *habeas corpus*, was unconstitutional, inasmuch as they had not, it was urged, the necessary authority by the Act under which they were constituted, to do so, and consequently that it was an illeged stretch of power. Several inidviduals were apprehended in Quebec, known to be in connexion with the insurgent patriots, and, on suspicion of treasonable practices, committed to the common gaol. From this they were, immediately after commitment, transferred for better safe keeping to the Citadel. An application on behalf of one of the prisoners Mr. Teed for a writ of *habeas corpus*, being made to Messieurs the Justices Panet and Benard, in chambers, it was granted, and the keeper of the common Gaol Mr.

---

ae previously noticed, was a Frenchman, serving as a general with the patriots of Odelltown, where he was taken, Nicholas and Daunais, had been princ:ples in the murder of Chartrand, at Lacadie, during the first rebellion, and died exhibiting sincere contrition and repentance for the offences they had eommitted. The time, let us hope, is for ever gone bye for putting men to death in cool blood for political offences, or indeed any other crime. Such barbarous exhibitions are disgraceful to governments, to civilization, and to humanity. The solitude and confinement of the Penitentiary or exile, atonement for any crime, and will supersede, it is to be hoped, capital punishment.

Jeffrey,) ordered to produce the man. This, as the individual in question was not in his custody, having been removed from it to the Citadel, by superior authority, before the service of the writ upon the gaoler, he could not do. Accordingly, on return of the writ before Messrs. Panet and Bedard, (the Chief Justice Stuart being absent at Montreal on duty, and Mr. Justice Bowen, absent either from indisposition, or not choosing to attend in so nice a matter, in which on one side or the other he might find himself compromised,*) the gaoler certified that he had no such person as John Teed, mentioned in

---

* It was ascertained afterwards that he took a different view of the subject, from his *conf eres* Judges Panet and Bedard, but he was freely and much spoken of at the time, whether justly or not, I cannot say, for " shirking" the question. Considering, however, the pliancy to popular clamor and obsequiousness, almost to servility, of some of the late Governors to the ruling demagogues, it need not have surprised anybody that one, in Mr. B's, position, threatened with impeachment by the late Assembly, most of it's members instigators, and several of them actors in the existing rebellion and that threat still hanging over his head, should have quailed on the occasion. Men of ordinary nerves in his station, particularly those who by indiscretion may more or less have been compromised, are in times of agitation and public disturbance, something worse than mere nuisance. It was only to such a man as Chief Justice Stuart, whose extensive and profound knowledge of the laws, fearless spirit and iron nerves were equal to any emergency, that the people could look up with confidence, as in fact they did universally, in matters of law. Lord Durham in appointing him to the Chief Justiceship writes to the Colonial Minister (Lord John Russell.) " In the place of Mr. Sewell I have not hesi-
" sated a movement to appoint Mr. James Stuart. Public
" opinion with so universal a consent, points out this gen-
" tleman as the ablest lawyer in the province, that there
" cannot be a doubt that it would be injustice and folly to
" place any other person in the highest judicial office
" of the province. It is especially necessary that in times
" like these, the capacious understanding, sound knowledge
" and vigorous decision of Mr. Stuart should be employed in
" the public service."

the writ, in his charge. This return being deemed by the two judges insufficient and evasive, the gaoler was ordered into custody of the sheriff, to be confined, of course, within the walls of his own domicile. A writ of attachment for contempt was at the same time also ordered by the judges against Colonel Bowles of the Coldstream Guards, then quartered in the Citadel, whereof he was Commandant, but which by his keeping within the fortress, with closed gates, it had been impossible to serve upon him. The discussion of this matter here would be idle; it, moreover, is a subject to which the writer is incompetent, involving as it does legal subtleties beyond his ken. The main grounds, however, upon which the two judges took their position and insisted that the *habeas corpus* in force notwithstanding the Ordinance purporting to suspend it, were briefly and in substance,—that the statute of the British Parliament, 14 Geo. 3, ch. 14, introducing the criminal laws of England into Canada, brought with them also as part of those laws, the Habeas Corpus Act, (31 Charles 2) and that it therefore formed part of the laws of this country. That the Act 1 Vict., c. 9, suspending the Constitution of Lower Canada, restricts the Council from passing any law repealing or suspending any act of the Parliament of Great Britain. The Ordinance passed by the Administrator of the Government and the Special Council on the 8th instant, suspending this Act of the British Parliament, is therefore invalid. This, it is believed, is substantially the argument as given by the judges.

The error of the two judges who took cognizance of the case, consisted, according to several of the best jurists in the country, in the assertion that the English Habeas Corpus Act made part of the criminal law, and was therefore introduced with it, whereas it had subsequently been brought into force by an Ordinance of the Governor and Legislative Council of the Province of Quebec, in the 24th year of the reign of George the Third, which, however, the judges in question seemed to view as a supererogatory Act.*

---

* Taking a common sense view of the subject, it certainly would seem that the Habeas Corpus law is an appendage to the English criminal law, and to secure the liberty of the subject against abuses under it. But it appears that some of the best opinions in England were taken previous to the passing of the Ordinance of the Governor and Legislative Council of the Province of Quebec, by which it was formally ushered into existence in Canada. The following notices of the matter, taken from some of the newspapers of the day, are interesting as explanatory of it:

SIR JOHN COBOROE'S ORDINANCES.

"The following opinion of Mr. Maseres, the first Attorney Generel of this Province after the capture of the country, upon his examination before the House of Commons, in Committee on the 14 Geo. III. cap. 83, is interesting at the present crisis:—

"This reasoning may perhaps be just. It is so new to me that I cannot undertake just at present to form a judgment of it. But though it should be just, and, in consequence of it, the use of *lettres de cachet* should not be legal, yet I cannot help thinking that, if they were used, the subjects against whom they were employed would be without any legal remedy against them. For if a motion was made on the behalf of a person imprisoned by one of them in the Court of King's Bench in the province, for a writ of habeas corpus, or any other relief against such imprisonment, the judges would probably think themselves bound to declare that, as this was a question concerning personal liberty, which is a civil right, and in all matters of property and civil rights they are directed by this Act of Parliament, to have resort to the laws of Canada, and not to the laws of England, they could not award the writ of habeas corpus, or any other remedy prescribed by the English law, but could only use each methods for the relief of the prisoner as were used by the French courts of justice in the province during the time of the French Government, for the relief of a person imprisoned by the Independant or Governor, by a *lettre de cachet* signed by the King of France. And such relief would, I imagine, be found to be none at all. Therefore, if it is intended that the King's subjects in Canada should have the benefit of the ha-

But the matter did not remain as we left it above. A habeas corpus was now issued by Mr. Justice Panet, directed to Thomas A. Young, Esq., the Police Magistrate under whose warrant Mr. Teed was apprehended. Mr. Young, not having the prisoner in his custody, nor in fact any control in the matter, made default to return the writ, and an order was therefore given by the judge for his imprisonment in the common jail of the district, until such time as he should make a proper return.*

---

beas corpus Act, I appreh·nd it would be most advisable, in order to remove all doubts and difficulties upon the subject to insert a short clause for that purpose in this Act."—*Mr. Neilson Quebec Gazette.*

Mr. Maseres was a constitutional lawyer of the first order, and a man of integrity, and a firm and rational patriot. His suggestion, however, was not embodied in that act, but the habeas corpus was shortly after introduced into the Province by Ordinance of the Governor and Legislative Council in 1782, 24 Geo· III. chap. 1.

* The following remarks are from the *Quebec Mercury*:
" Mr. Justice Panet delivered judgment immediately. The sentence was T. A. Young, Esq., be imprisoned in the common gaol of this district until he made a proper return to the writ of habeas corpus served upon him. His honor the judge prefaced this judgment by reading a very lengthy harangue which was, probably, the most extraordinary that ever emanated from a legal functionary in his judicial capacity. Having alluded to the former proceedings respecting the babeas corpus, in defence of the decision, which had been rendered by him and Mr. Justice [Bedard, his honor proceeded to comment on the " singular party spirit" which hod beeen manifested on this subject. The observations which had been made on his conduct by a press sold to power, fell on his head with no effect. Partial and corrupt judges were not to be found in this country ; and the observations which had been made respecting his (Mr. Justice Panet's) suspension—hanging even—were as nothing. The judges were immoveable by popular clamour ; that clamour proceeded from the veutal press to which he had aliuded." His honor also animadverted in strong terms on the "scandalous example of insubordination to legitimate authority," which had been set by the officers of the Government of Her

Mr. Young kept out of the way, by secluding himself, until the judges Panet and Bedard were suspended from their functions, which took place shortly after this.* Mr. Justice Vallieres, the resident

Majesty ; and more particularly by the Superintendent of the Police, who had rendered himself guilty of a most unheard of flagrant contempt of the Queen herself, through one of her courts of justice. Mr. Justice Panet's emotions of the deference due to his mandates, under existing circumstances when the very existence of the Queen's authority was at stake, and her forces out in the field in support of it, were it must be acknowledged, rather absolute; if really he made the extravagant epilogue imputed to him —R. C.

* THE HABEAS CORPUS CASES.

" We are far from being disposed to find fault with the alleged tardiness of Government, or to urge it, by clamour, to hasty proceedings. We know that every government, to be deserving of the name. must proceed with deliberation, so as to conform with law and justice, and encounter that high responsibility which is imposed on all those who exercise power over their fellow men. This responsibility lies heavily on Governors of British Colonies of all times, but particularly in times like those, which prevail in the Canadas. No one who has a proper sense of justice, who does not share in their resp nsibility, would hurry them into steps for which they alone are responsible, but would rather wish that all their acts were founded on the dictates of their own mind. Still less would any person having such a sense endeavour in any way to prejudge their conduct, or bring them into public disrespect, because that conduct does not happen to coincide with his view of things, which must frequently be founded on very imperfect knowledge

" It is not wonderful, however, that in times when every one feels peculiarly interested in the management of public affairs, there should be a feverish impatience ; that people should be ever ready to set up their own judgment over those in authority, and approve or condemn according as suits their inclinations and their confidence in their own capacity, which is generally the most absolute and noisy where incapacity is the greatest.

" The good citizens of Quebec are getting impatient at the conflict of authority, which has been going on for the last ten days, between two of the judges of the Court of King's Bench on the one side, and the Legislative authority

Judge at Three Rivers, coinciding with his confrères Panet and Bedard, issued, about the same time with the above, a habeas corpus to the gaoler at that place to produce the person of Celestin Houde, confined on a charge of sedition and treasonable practices, and whom, on being brought up, the judge liberated on bail. It was generally understood that the Chief Justice Stuart, and all the other judges, were of a different opinion from those three.* Mr. Justice Rolland, of the Montreal Bench, was sus-

---

on the other. These, in all well regulated communities, act in harmony for the common weal, the legislature making the law, the executive causing it to be executed, and the judiciary applying it in contested cases. Here the contest has risen, from two of the judges having agreed to nullify the law altogether, consequently rejecting the authority of the legislative body, and depriving the executive of its assistance. We have arrived at the period, if efficient measures be not epeedily taken to put an end to the present conflict, when the truth of the saying will be woefully exemplified: 'A house divided against itself cannot stand.'

" The first duty of every government is to maintain its authority. All history cries out against rulers who have let power slip out of their hands to be succeeded by anarchy or faction. The weakness and faults of men in power have indeed produced more real and extended evils than despotism itself. The powerful *can* be just, but the weak, *never*. Power, supported by justice, securing peace, order and public prosperity, is the only foundation on which any Government can stand

" It is not for us to suggest what steps ought to be taken in the present extraordinary state of things at Quebec; but although we may not partake in the impatience, or participate in the apprehensions of some, we, equally with them, look to the Government for decisive measures, and we look to it with confidence.--Mr. Neilson's *Quebec Gazette.*

* In reply to some questions from Mr. Leader. (House of Commons:) " Lord J. Russell stated that, in consequence of the disturbed state of Lower Canada, the Government of that province has been compelled to suspend the operation of the habeas corpus Act until August next, and that it was not intended to apply for a bill of indemnity, as these proceedings were within the Act of Parliament.

pected of a leaning towards the decision of the patriot
judges, now so called, and is said to have, rather
uncautiously, expressed himself to that effect in a
private correspondence with Mr. Bedard, in which
he approved of the course taken by Mr. Panet.
His views of the matter, as expressed by himself
subsequently from the bench, were not however
such, unless he tergiversed, which indeed, in a French
journal published in Quebec, has, with many bitter
reproaches on the subject levelled at Mr. Rolland,
been not long since boldly asserted, and without any
public denial by that gentleman or his friends. He
probably had pondered on the subject, and obtained
new lights affording him a better view of it, and
perhaps also may have counted the costs.

Whatever may be thought of the bias of those
judges, from their former connexion with the patriots,
they no doubt believed the law to be as they expounded
it. It is indeed possible that the wish, by no means
unatural in them, considering their antecedents, may
have been father to the belief, and in truth many deemed it so. But the law, if it were such, besides placing
the Government in a false position, really stood in the
way of the public safety, a consideration, however, with
which, it must be admitted, the judges had nothing
to do their duties being merely to expound the laws
as they stood.* The emergency being extraordinary
required at the hands of those entrusted with the
common safety extraordinary energy, and happily
Sir John Colborne was the man to grapple with it.†
He accordingly, with characteristic resolution and

---

*" An Ordidnance of the Governor in Special Council was
passed declaring the English Habeas Corpus Act never to
have been in force in Lower Canada, and the proceedings
of the three Judges a nullity·

† " The following remarks from the *Quebec Gazette*, by
Mr. Neilson, appeared a day or two after the suspension of
the three judges.

wisdom, did not hesitate to use his authority in suspending the three judges, Messrs. Panet, Bedard, and Vallieres, from their judicial functions, a stroke that put down this insurrection on the bench, as the

THE HABEAS CORPUS CASE.

" The Montreal papers remark that much sensation was caused at Quebec by the recent decision, of two Judges here of the nullity of the Ordinance of the Special Council of the 8th November, instant, suspending the *habeas corpus* till the 1st June next.

" This decision naturally excited some sensation. It was hardly expected that nullification could have taken root in the cold climate of Quebec; but the town is nevertheless as cool as usual, and likely to remain so.

" The two Judges in question, it must be presumed, decided according to the best of their judgment. One of them however, (Bedard,) appears to have been a volunteer in the service. Upon the whole, we fancy that the correction of the error of the temporary legislature might as well have been left to the authority from which its legislative power is derived. This authority alone, we presume, has a right to nullify the legislative acts of its creature. We suppose that it never occurred to those concerned in this nulification that they were not only placing themselves *above* the legislative power in the colony, but also above the Imperial Parliament, and nullifying their power: for it is manifest that if there is a power in the Province that can declare null and void the laws enacted under its authority, Parliament had as well resign all pretensions to delegate legislative power in the colonies.

" The result of the whole, however, is, that the Suspension Act will remain in force till disallowed or repealed, and those who are imprisoned under it, will remain imprisoned, till discharged according to its provisions or by its expiration."

The following from the newspapers is illustrative of some of the matters previously noticed.

" It appears that the Judges awarded the writ, on the ground that the Habeas Corpus Act, of the 31st Chas. I cap. 2, is in force in this Province.

" But this is not the case. The act in question was never in force in this Province; and forming no part of the criminal law of England, it was not introduced by the Imperial Statute of 1774. It was not till 1784 that the habeas corpus was enforced in this Province, by the Ordinance now suspended, which is a clear proof that this ordinance forms

M

matter was popularly termed, raised, it was said, by the patriot judges in support of their compatriots in the field. The course he took, though arbitrary, is generally admitted to have been necessary under the circumstances of the day. Mr. Bedard, immediately after receiving notice of his suspension, left Quebec for England, via New York, to lay his case, and those of his two suspended brethren, before the home Government. A voluminous correspondence took no part of the criminal law. The conduct of the Quebec Judges, therefore, appears to us to be founded on the most erroneous principles : and we trust some further notice may be taken of so extraordinary a decision.

" We understand that when the writ thus granted was served upon Colonel Bowles Commandant at Quebec, in whose custody Teed is, the Colonel wrote a letter to the judges, explaining the reasons which induced him to decline to give up the body of the prisoner; but that his explanatory letter was so far from giving satisfaction to their honours, that they immediately issued a warrant for the apprehension of Colonel Bowles, for a contempt. In proceeding to execute this warrant the Sheriff found that Colonel Bowles was in the citadel barracks, the gates of which have been since closed day and night. The gaoler was committed for permitting Teed to be conveyed from prison to the citadel; and the affair has occasioned very great and unusual excitement at Quebec.—*Montreal Gazette.*

[There were two writs issued on the 21st instant, the one directed to the keeper of the common gaol for the District of Quebec and the other to the Commander of the Garrison. The former writ is marked as having issued under the authority of the 31st Chas. II., c. 2. The latter purports to be under the Provincial Statute, 52 Geo. III. c. 8 which authorizes judges in vacation to award writs of *habeas corpus* upon complaint made by any person restrained of his liberty otherwise than for some criminal, or supposed criminal matter —The return made of the gaoler was in the following terms :--" My return to this writ is, that I have no " such person within my charge, possession, custody or " power, and that at the time of the issuing of the within " writ, or at the time of coming of the within writ to me, " I had not, nor have since had the body of the within named John Teed in my custody." For this return the gaoler has been visited with the penalties upon persons wilfully neglecting or refusing to make a return, or pay obedience to a writ of *habeas corpus* O. Q. G.

place, it seems, between Mr. Bedard and the Colonial Minister, but as it has not been published, the precise views entertained by the law officers of the Crown in England, to whom most probably the matter was referred, have never been ascertained. The three judges remained suspended from the exercise of their functions until a short time previous to the union, when they were reinstated by Lord Sydenham, who also allowed them their salaries for the time they had been suspended, nearly two years.

The *Canadien*, published in Quebec by Mr E. Parent, having commented with considerable freedom upon the suspension of the judges, Mr. Neilson, in the *Quebec Gazette*, made the following remarks upon that gentleman's course :—

" The *Canadien* still appeals to, and promotes these dissensions. Does he mean to continue in the same course till it is proved to all the world, that the inhabitants of the colony, under the influence of the prejudices and passions connected with these distinctions, are utterly incapable of having any share in their Government? He cries aloud against " military power," and has long actually laboured, and is still labouring, to render it *necessary* in Lower Canada.

That the suspension of the two judges is an act of "military power," (*pouvoir militaire,*) is one of the frequent misrepresentations of the Canadien. It is the lawful exercise of the undoubted prerogative of the Crown, by the person to whom its authority has been delegated. The independence of the judges, indeed! The three judges have taken care to justify the committee of the House of Commons of 1828, in refusing to recommend that measure prayed for by the 87,000 petitioners of that year. That committee was of opinion, that for the present, it would be imprudent, seeing the qualifications of persons too frequently appointed to the bench in the colonies, to invest them with so much power. The excessive liberality of the Home Government, however, three years afterwards, recommended the measure, which, after being passed by both branches, again approved of by the British Government, passed a second time by the Council, and was *finally rejected by the House of Assembly*, till the Legislative Council should be rendered elective! These, who then formed and supported the majority of the House of Assembly, will have an ill grace to talk of the "*Independance des Juges.*"

The suppressal of the rebellion had driven a horde of fugitive patriots to the American border, near Lake Champlain, whence, to the annoyance of the inhabitants upon whom they had quartered themselves, destitute as they were of the means of subsistence; they kept the inhabitants on the Canadian frontier in a state of incessant alarm during the winter, making occasionally nocturnal incursions upon them, and committing, in the spirit of brigands, the most brutal outrages upon the families and property of those within their reach, who by their loyalty and zeal in aiding to put down the insurrection, had incurred the resentment of the patriots.* The

---

* "It is believed certain that Government has received reports of collections of vagabonds on the Champlain frontier: probably persons who have suffered in the late stupid attempts, and do not know what to do with themselves. They are nearly in the position of those malefactors who have lost their character and means of subsistence by vices and crimes, and are *forced* to continue in them in lieu of any other.

"There have, no doubt, been many dupes engaged in the late proceeding in Canada. The Government suffered the deception and demoralizing proceedings of a few factious leaders, to be carried on too long not to produce some effect on honest but ill-informed persons throughout the country. The sooner the laws are put in execution against the leaders, and the rest pardoned, and restored to their families and their country, the better. The good conduct of the inhabitants of ' French origin,' on the Detriot frontier during the inroads and acts of piracy and murder in Upper Canada by the brigands from the United States, acting under the direction of Mr. Mackenzie, in that quarter, though in connexion with the rebellion in the Lower Province, are not, as not coming within the purpose of this work detailed in it. That is an undertaking which it is to be hoped some Upper Canadian will in due time take up. The same loyalty and spirit that had characterised the Lower provinces of New Brunswick and Nova Scotia on the rebellion in 1837, again manifested themselves in those truly patriotic provinces upon the renewal in 1838 of that ill-advised and most absurd experiment, with a view to establish a French-Canadian *nationalite* in the centre of British North America, as the pivot upon which such of the other provinces as should think proper to follow in subordination the example set them by their co-subjects of French origin, might turn.

The reports of the Constitutional Associations of Quebec and Montreal at the close of the year give interesting synopses of the state of the country and its affairs, and will be found in the Appendix.

---

recent attack, and their acknowledged loyalty in Upper Canada and the Lower Provinces, shews that their feelings of national origin have been most shamefully acted upon in Lower Canada, to produce so much disaffection among them.

"It is not very creditable to the press that most of those engaged in the late disgraceful attempts at rebellion and invasion in the Canadas were connected with the press. *McKenzie, O'Callaghan, Dunernay Bouvhelle,* and several others were Printers or Editors in Canada. *Van Rensselear* was formerly concerned in, command at Prescott, and lately executed at Kingston, was a printer in the same office. *Sutherland* and several others whose names we do not recollect were alse printers. Most of those named were bankrupts in fortune and character, with minds excited and corrupted by the constant political and acrimonious discussion, and agitations of which the press is the chief instrument."
—*Neilson,s Quebec Gazette*

From the Supplement to the London Gazette of Friday November 30.

Colonial Office, Downing Street, Dec. 3, 1838.

Despatches, of which the following is an extract and a copy, have been received from Lieutenant General Sir John Colborne, G. C. B. Commander of the Forces in Canada, dated Montreal, the 5th and La Colle, the 11th Nov. 1838 :—

Extract of a Despatch from Lieutenant General Sir John Colborne, G. C. B, to Lord Glenelg, dated Head Quarters, Montreal, Nov. 5, 1838.

The information which Lord Durham has communicated to your lordship will have prepared you for the movement of the rebels, which has now taken place in all counties of the Richelieu. and in the section of this district from the left bank of that river to Beauharnois and the south of the St. Lawrence.

The *habitants* are collecting in large bodies at St. Ours, St. Denis, St. Charles, Acadie, Chateauguay, and Beauharnois.

The general movements of the rebels commenced on the 3rd. They made an attack on the Indians of the village of Caughnawaga, on Sunday, the 4th instant, who sallied out of the church where they were assembled for divine service, repulsed the rebels, from the village, and captured seventy prisoners.

I am prepared to march against the rebels in Acadie. Our troops occupy Laprarie, Chambly and St. Johns.

HEAD QUARTERS, ODELLTOWN,
Seigniory of Lacolle, Nov. 11. 1838.

MY LORD,—With reference to my despatch of the 5th inst. I have the honor to acquaint you that the habitans between the Yamaska and Richelieu rivers who quitted their villages the night of the 3rd, to take up arms against Her Majesty's government, assembled at St. Ours, St. Charles and St. Michel. Those from the westward of the Richelieu, from Contrecœur, and Vercheres, at Belœil ; the greater part of the rebels. however, of the Richelieu, on finding that the depots of arms and ammunition which had been promised them, where not at the points of rendezvous ready to be delivered to them, returned to their homes on the 4th and 5th instant.

The inhabitants, generally of Beauharnois, Laprairie, and L'Acadie, also were in arms on the night of the 3d ; attacking all the loyal subjects residing in their neighbourhood, and either drove them from their homes or made them prisoners. At Beanhauois, Chatearngnay, and Napiervile, the rebels assembled in great numbers; about four thousand of them were concentrated at Napierville, under the command of Dr. Robert Nelson, Dr. Cote add Gagnon, between the 3d and 6th instant. Under these circumstances, I ordered the corps under the immediate command of Major General Sir James Macdonell and Major General Clitherow, to march to L'Acadie, and St. Johns, with the intention of attacking Napierville on the 9th; but the unfavorable weather and the very bad state of the roads prevented the troops from reaching the vicinity of Napierville till late in the evening and they did not enter the town till the morning of the 10th. The rebels hearing of the approach of the Queen's troops, dispersed during the night of the 9th, and the following morning. When the rebels first established themselves at Napierville, they endeavored to open a communication with the United States by Rouse's Point, with a view of bringing in supplies of arms and ammunition from their friends in the States of New York and Vermont, but the brave, persevering and loyal Volunteers of Lacolle, Odelltown, Hemmingford and Sherrington, who from the first moment of the revolt, had posted themselves on the frontier, attacked four hundred of them on the march, from Lacolle, to Rouse's Point two miles from the frontier line, defeated them, and took one field piece, three hundred stand of arms, and drove them across the frontier. On the 9th, being reinforced from Sherrington, the volunteers took possession of the Church of Odelltown, and defended their post with the greatest bravery against an attack of nine hundred of the rebels on their march from Napierville, under Dr. Nelson, and compelled them to retire with great loss.

I had directed Colonel Taylor (employed on particular service,) to proceed to the frontier, to inform the volunteers of the march of the Queen's troops. This officer arrived at Odelltown about half an hour before the volunteers were attacked, and was of the greatest use to them in directing the defence of their position.

As soon as I received information of the revolt in Beauharnois, I despatched Major Phillpots, R. E., with orders to Major Carmichael (particular service), to pass Lake St. Francois from Point au Baudet, near Lancaster, to the south bank of the St. Lawrence, with a detachment of the 71st regiment, on the route from Upper Canada, and two battalions of the Glengarry militia, under Colonels M'Donnell and Fraser, and to march on Beauharnois. This movement was promptly carried into effect by the exertions of Major Phillpots, Major Carmichael, and the Colonels of the Glenry militia, on the 10th inst. Four or five men of the detachment of the 71st regiment were killed and wounded in driving the rebels from Beauharnois. I shall take an early opportunity of conveying to your Lordship a more correct account of these occurrences, and of forwarding the reports of the officers commanding the volunteers posted on the frontier. Their loss has been severe, but several valuable officers and loyal subjects have fallen ; and I entreat that their families may be provided for by Her Majesty's Government. On every occasion, since the commencement of the revolt, the British population have come forward with the greatest zeal and activity.

No doubt now exists that the leaders of this revolt have been actively employed in organizing this second attempt to establish a republic in Canada since June, and that a secret oath, which has been extensively administered to the habitans, was taken by a large portion of the disaffected in July and August; but it is certain that a large portion of the habitans who appeared in the ranks of the rebels, were forced to join them, or have their properties destroyed. Several hundred prisoners have been taken. and among them a French officer, who had a command at Napierville. I enclose two proclamations issued by Dr. Nelson,

I have, &c.
(Signed.) J. COLBORNE.
The Lord Glenelg.

HEAD QUARTERS, Montreal, 12th January, 1839.
GENERAL ORDER.

The Commander of the Forces has much satisfaction in publishing the following extract of a communication from the Secretary of State for the Colonies.

DOWNING STREET, 10th December, 1838.

SIR,—I had the honor to receive your despatches, reporting your assumption of the Government of Lower Canada; the breaking out of the insurrection in the country bordering on the Richelieu; the Proclamation of Martial Law in the District of Montreal; and the entire dispersion of the insurgents.

Your late despatches report the invasion of Upper Canada near Prescott, by persons from the American bank of the St. Lawrence,—the gallant resistance opposed to them, by the force under Major Young, and their final defeat and capture by the troops under the command of Lieutenant Colonel Dundas.

Having had the honor to lay these despatches before the

Queen, I am commanded by Her Majesty to express her deep regret that the peace of Her Canadian Provinces should have been again disturbed by the attempts of lawless and unprincipled men.

While Her Majesty sincerely deplores the events which have recently occurred in that part of her dominions, Her Majesty has contemplated with the greatest satisfaction the zeal, promptitude and gallantry with which her loyal subjects in both Provinces, have come forward, for the suppression of the insurrection and the defence of their country. The steadiness and valour displayed by the militia and volunteers, both in Upper and Lower Canada, are deserving of the highest praise; and I am commanded to convey to them through you Her Majesty's sense of their valuable services.

Her Majesty has observed, with sincere gratification, the unqualified success which has attended Her Majesty's troops whereever they have been engaged, and Her Majesty relies with proper confidence, on their discipline and gallantry, aided by the loyal and generous courage of her faithful subjects in the Canadas, for the defeat of any future attempt either to invade the Provinces from without, or to excite internal insurrection, I have the honor, &c. &c.

(Signed,) GLENELG.
Lieut. General Sir John Colborne, G. C. B. &o. &c.

JOHN EDEN,
Dep. Asst. Adjt. Genl.

The following interesting article relating to the habeas corpus question raised by the Judges Panet and Bedard, is from *Mr. Neilson's Quebec Gazette* of 27th November, 1838, and is, I believe from the pen of the late Andrew Stuart, one of the best informed and ablest lawyers of his day in the country:

THE HABEAS CORPUS ACT.

At all times, particularly in such time as these, the firm and able exercise of the legislative and executive authority is essential to the maintenance of the government and the protection of life and property. Not less so is the exercise of judicial power, the power not of the judge, but of the law : the judge is but the mouthpiece, the organ of the law he must know the laws and enforce its execution. If it be erroneously administered, in dangerous times, in relation to political offences above all others, the danger to the state becomes imminent, the executive authority becomes paralyzed, it is liable to be thwarted at every step, it has to contend with enemies from without and provide against its own

essential weakness. It cannot take any one step without fear of falling into error. The lively interest which the public mind has taken in the decision rendered by their Honors Judges Panet and Bedard yesterday, has led to these observations, applicable if their decision be wrong, inapplicable, if it be right. The case is not a difficult one. The existing legislature has suspended the *habeas corpus* act for a limited period, During this period, while treasonable practices are rife within this district, and rebellion prevails over a large section of the country, an individual applies for a writ of *habeas corpus* and to be admitted to bail, upon the ground that the existing legislature, the Governor and Council, have transcended limits of their anthority; that althongh the Imperial Legislature has constituted a Special Council for the affairs of Lower Canada, to make such laws or ordinances for the peace, welfare and good government of the Province as the Legislature of Lower Canada, as hitherto constituted was empowered to make this Imperial Legislature has curtailed that power by enacting " that " it shall not be lawful for the said Governor and Council " by any such law or ordinance to repeal. suspend, or alter " any provision of an act of the Parliament of the United " Kingdom, or of any act of the legislature of Lower Canada " as now constituted, repealing or altering any such act of " Parliament." The point that has been decided is, that the *habeas corpus* act of Charles II. of Great Britain, is a statute of the Imperial Parliament introduced into this country. Is this decision legal or is it not? The answer depends upon the legal enactments related to the writ of the habeas corpus. The first enactment upon this subject, is the Provincial Statutes 24 Gee. 3 cap, 1, commonly called in this country, the *habeas corpus* act, the first clause to the preamble of which is as follows :—" Whereas it has gracious-
" ly pleased the King's Most Excellent Majesty, in his in-
" structions to His Excellency the Captain General and
" Governor of this Province, to commit to the Legislature
" thereof, the consideration of making due provision for the
" security of the personal liberty of his subjects therein, and
" to suggest for that purpose, that the Legislature could not
" follow a better example than that which the common law
" of England has set, in the provision made for a writ of ha-
" beas corpus, which is the right of very British subject in
" that Kingdom ; be it declared and enacted by, &c., that
" from and after the passing of the publication of this ordi-
" nance, all persons who shall be, or stand committed or de-
" tained in any prison within this Province, for any crimi-
" nal or supposed criminal offence, shall of right, be entitled

"to demand, have and obtain, from the Court of King's Bench in this Province or from the Chief Justice thereof, or from the Commissioners for executing the office of Chief Justice respectively, or from any Judge or Judges of the said Court of King's Bench, the writ of habeas corpus, together with all the benefit and relief resulting therefrom, at all such times, and in as full, ample, perfect and beneficial a manner, and to all intents, uses, ends and purposes, as His Majesty's subjects, within the realm of England who may be or stand committed or detained in any prison within that realm, are there entitled to that writ, and the benefit arising thereform, by the common and statute laws thereof."—This statute, in its very terms, enacts that which did not exist before, viz : that this country should be governed by the same law relative to the habeas corpus as the people in England were goverued by. Its enactments are clearly prospec·ive not retroactive. His Majesty not having dissallowed this act, it has always been publicly and notoriously acknowledged, by judicial authority in and throughout the Province, as the authority under which the writ of *habeas corpus* could be allowed : it has been so acknowleged since 1784, a period of fifty-four years, until the circumstances under which the country has been most unfortunately placed have led to the innovation sanctioned by the above decision —The ground assigned by the senior *puisne* Judge, in rendering his judgment to the above purport is, as I have understood, that there is to be found in the Provincial Statute, another provision of an act passed in 1812, extending the provisions of the above act, 24 Geo. III, which is to this effect :

" And be it further enacted that the several provisions " made by this act, &c . shall extend to all writs of *habeas* " *corpus* awarded in pursuance of a certain act passed in the " 31st year of King Charles the Second, intituled, An Act " for the better securing the liberty of the subjuct, and " for prevention of imprisonment beyond seas, and of a cer" tain ordinance," &c., viz : the Provincial Ordinance above cited. From the proviso last cited, Judge Panet said, that he had no doubt the Statute of Charles the Second had been introduced, and formed part of the law of this country. This may be true in one sense, viz : that the provisons of that act have been introduced, that is, its substance, as an independent enactment, by these two Provincial Statutes, but it is untrue, in another sense, viz : that it has a binding effect in this country as a law of the Imperial Parliament. The two Provincial Statutes are in their provisions essentially Provincial, enacting, in substance, the provision of the Imperial

Statutes. They are in words, names and substance provincial acts, embodying in them the provisions of an Imperial Statute, a Statute binding in another country. It cannot be inferred from these that the Statutes of Chas. II, has been introduced as an Imperial act any more than a modern provision of the law of France embodied in the law of this country since the conquest, could be considered as an enactment of the kingdom of France binding on this country. The above mentioned acts being then Provincial enactments, and not Imperial Statutes, the law of Sir John Colborne's Council suspending their operation, for a limited " period, is not " a *law repealing, suspending, or altering* any provision of any " act of Parliament of Great Britain, or of the Parliament of " the United Kingdom, or any act of the Legislature of " Lower Canada as now constituted, repealing or altering " any such act of Parliament,"—This construction appears to be founded, too, on common sense. The Provincial Parliament has, in many other instances, incorporated the Provisions of Imperial acts in its enactments, and if the Council were to search for these whenever it undertakes legislation for fear of trenching upon Imperial Legislation, there would be no end to difficulties. From these reasons, it appears to me that the opinion of the learned Judge is untenable---it is one that invites discussion, as our security depends upon its being right or wrong, and upon the question being decided at once. In support of the Council we have the implied sanction of the Imperial Legislature, as a similar bill of last Session was not found fault with in England, when Lord Durham's Ordinances were annulled. Whether right or wrong, the authorities are in an awkward dilemma ; one result is certain. the Supreme Legislature within the Colony, or the Supreme Judicial Authority, has committed a gross error, one which must be fraught with evil consequences. The moral influence of the one or the other must suffer, not only in our small community, to which it is so deeply interesting, but in the Mother Country, and in all the other countries which are anxiously watching the progress of events amongst us.--*Neilson's Quebec Gazette.*

CHAPTER XLV.

Sir John Colborne appointed Governor General—Inroads by brigands on the bordres—Bearing of the United States Government---Generals Scott and Worth, of the United States Army---Court Martial sits at Montreal for trial of patrio's---Consequences---Opinion of the Chief Justice Stuart as to the ordinances suspending *Habeas Corpus*—Militia disbanded---Lord John Russell gives notice in Parliament of certain resolutions relating to a reunion of the Canadas—Bill introduced and discussed, but postponed to next session---Resolution on the subject by the Assembly of Upper Canada---trials of Jalbert and others for the murder of Lieut. Weir—Bill of indictment for treason found by Grend Jury at Montreal against Mr. Papineau and others ---Incidental observations relating to these gentlemen and Mr. Lafontaine---Mr Poulett Thomson named Governor General---Arrives at Quebec, and assumes the Government --Sir John Colborne sails for England, and is raised to the peerage under the title of. Lord Seaton---His character---Varieties.

SIR JOHN COLBORNE received in January a letter commission from home appointing him Governor General, and on the 17th of the month he took the oath of office as such. The forces in Canada were during the present, as in the preceding winter, reinforced, the 11th Regiment of foot marching in January through the portage of Madawaska from New Brunswick to Quebec, in three divisions, and with them detachments for the 65th and 93rd regiments, which arriving on the coast too late in the season to reach Quebec by the St. Lawrence, had been landed at Halifax.

The fugitive patriots from Lower Canada who had sought refuge on the borders of Maine, Vermont, and New York, gave much uneasiness to the loyal inhabitants on the Canadian frontier. Several marauding incursions being made during the winter by bands of those ruffians upon different settlements in the neighbourhood of Lake Champlain. One or two instances of their atrocious acts will suffice to characterise them. On the morning of the 30th December, 1838, the dwelling house and barn of a farmer (Mr. Gibson) at Caldwell Manor, near the line, and the dwellings of his three next neighbours, were attacked by a party of those brigands, in sleighs, from Alberg, an adjacent township in the State of Vermont, who, after brutally dislodging and maltreating the occupants, set fire to the buildings, which, with the barns and outhouses, were entirely destroyed. A still more brutal attack was made on the family and dwelling house of another farmer (Mr. Vosburg) of the same place, and residing within half a mile of the line, on the morning of the 3rd of February following, the circumstances of which are thus related by the Stipendiary Magistrate for the District, D. K. Kinnear, Esq., since and still, the well-known and able editor of the *Montreal Herald*:

" Vosburg states himself to be an American, of Dutch descent. He is sixty-two years of age, and has lived with his family for forty-three years, on the farm where he nearly met his death; from his conversation, I should think him an intelligent and industrious man, and such is the character he has always borne among his neighbours. He has himself taken no part in the late troubles in the country, but his son, a married man, who, with his wife and three children, lived with his father and mother, has served, during this winter, as a loyalist volunteer. The family consisted of the father and mother, the son his wife and three children, a grown-up unmarried daughter, a widowed friend and her child—making two men, four grown-up women and three children. It appears that the neighbourhood has, for some time, been in a great state of alarm and fear of night attacks, in consequence of information received from Alberg, Champlain, Swanton and other villages on the American side of the frontier, and they seldom ventured to retire to bed, but spent the night in watching.

"Between two and three o'clock on Saturday morning, the family were these watching, with their clothes on, when without warning of any sort, the windows were violently stove in, and the house entered by a party of twelve or fourteen men, well armed with muskets and bayonets. The Vosburgs made no attempt at defence, but merely begged that they would spare their lives. The marauders demanded money, and ten dollars being all the money in the house, was given to them. They then bound the two men with cords, and having placed the women and children in the kitchen, took the men with them into the other rooms of the house, helping themselves to everything portable and destroying that which they could not remove—they then entered the kitchen, and a party of them seized some fire brands from the hearth and ran towards the barn, they took one pair of valuable horses, and having yoked them to a sleigh, set fire to the buildings—three horses, nine cows and eight calves perished in the flames—a large quantity of hay was also destroyed—they brought the double sleigh to the house and having loaded it, and two sleighs they had brought with them, with plunder, they commenced firing the dwelling house by throwing the fire about in all directions; the women and children, as I have stated, were in the kitchen, while the two men were detained in another part of the house, which was now burning in various parts. A party of ruffians pushed Vosburghs, father and son, still bound with cords, into the room with the women, and commenced butchering them. The only man the family recognised was a Canadian lad of between eighteen and nineteen years old who had formerly been a servant in the family, and who doubtless acted as guide in the attack. His face was blackened, but both husband and wife can swear to his identity—this man commenced the attack by trusting his bayonet into Vosburg the younger's side. Although his hands were tied, he continued to seize the bayonet, and struggle with his assailant, and although thrice wounded, succeeded in wrestling the bayonet from the musket, and rushed through the door—the ruffians fired two shots after him, but without effect—he escaped. Another of the party then thrust his bayonet into the father, who, also succeeded in wresting the bayonet from the top of the musket—the leader or officer of the party then drew his sword and cut the old man down, inflicting a wound on his head and face, he fell, and states that the first circumstance he remembered before becoming sensible, was seeing the first ruffian seize his musket by the barrel and endeavour to knock his brains out with the breach while he lay on the ground—from the first blow on the head, he became insensible. You will keep in mind that the women were all spectators of this scene, and corroborated the evidence of old Vosburgh.

"You will observe that I mention an officer, or leader of the party as having drawn his sword, and cut down the elder Vosburg—this man was minutely described to me—he was of middling stature, dark complexion and black whiskers, was the general spokesman and although the Vosburghs seemed to think he was a Frenchman spoke good English—he was evidently a man in the better classes of society, and swore, "that he would hang as many God damn Tories, as the Government have hung of our friends" —this he said when the women were praying for mercy.

"When the ruffians thought they had killed the elder Vosburgh, they left the place in their sleighs—on crossing the lines they gave some shouts of triumph, which alarmed four American farmers who lived close to the lines—these men arose, and seeing the flames from the barn, came to the assistance of the Vosburghs, and ultimately succeeded in putting out the flames, and saving the dwelling house. In the meantime, however, Vosburgh had recovered from his swoon, and his family taken refuge in the house of a neighbour.

"The only one of the marauding party recognized by the Vosburghs was the servant lad—Michel dit Peter Bruiette.

"The object of the attack seems to have been partly for the sake of plunder, and partly for the sake of a general revengeful retaliation for the execution of the convicted rebels."

The United States Government, whatever its disposition might have been towards the patriots at the previous insurrection, did its best to save at least appearances on the present occasion, by depriving the brigands assembled on its frontiers of the means of annoyance which they possessed in arms, including several field pieces, as well as muskets, rifles, and various other munitions of war, with which, through the zeal of American sympathisers, they were provided. Generals Scott and Worth, of the United States army, were employed on this service by the general government, the district of the former extending from Ogdensburgh westward to Buffalo and Detriot, and that of the latter from Ogdensburg to Lake Champlain, and thence eastward along the frontier, and it must, in justice, be admitted that the exertions of those gentlemen were unremitting, and essentially contributed to frustrate the mischief contemplated by the brigands and their sympathising associates against the loyal inhabitants along the Canadian frontier. The brigands (they are no longer, in the new mode of warfare to which many of them were now recurring, to the injury and ruin of offenceless individuals, worthy of the name of patriots], had formed themselves into lodges, banded together, by an oath, and recognizing each other by manual signs, in imitation of free masons, under the denomination of "HUNTERS," for the alleged purpose of releasing the Canadas from colonial bondage, and realising their independence as a republic, but more correctly speaking, to harass and to rob the loyal inhabitants on the Canadian border, burn and destroy their property, and murder such of them as those banditti should single out for destruction.

The suspension of the Judges Panet, Bedard, and Vallieres, for issuing writs of habeas corpus, in disregard of the Ordinance of the Governor and Special Council suspending the habeas corpus law, has been mentioned. It was generally understood that the Chief Justice Stuart and the other judges did not coincide with them, but their opinion had not been judicially expressed. To obtain this, another application was made to the Chief Justice and Mr. Justice Bowen, on behalf of Mr. Teed, still immured in the Citadel of Quebec, for a writ, but both these judges deemed themselves restrained, by the Ordinance in question, from issuing writs of habeas corpus in favour of persons committed for treasonable practices. Mr. Teed was, however, soon after this, along with several others, who for some months had been confined with him in the Citadel, set at liberty without being subjected to a trial.

The Court Martial which had been ordered to sit at Montreal for the trial of those implicated in the late insurrections, continued its sittings during a great portion of the winter. Many of the prisoners were convicted, and some sentenced to the extreme penalty, [twelve of whom, as previously mentioned, suffered], others to transportation, and a few acquitted. Sixty-eight of those who had been so convicted, together with eighty-three political convicts from Upper Canada, in all 151 individuals, were on the 26th September, embarked at Montreal in a steamer for Quebec, from which they were on the following morning transhipped on board a transport, the Buffalo, despatched for the purpose from England, and which on receiving her unfortunate guests, made sail for her destination, New South Wales, where she safely arrived after a short passage.* The whole of those, and the exile patriots generally, were in less than five years after this, humanely released, chiefly through the intercession of members of the Legislative Assembly of Canada, and allowed to return to their homes.

The militia corps embodied in consequence of the

---

* "We understand that twenty-seven of the prisoners convicted of high treason have been pardoned, four of them on condition of leaving the country and not coming within a stated distance of the frontier of Upper and Lower Canada. The other twenty three have a free pardon on finding sureties for good behaviour. All were found guilty of high treason and condemned to death. Twelve were executed last winter. Such is but a small part of the melancholy results of the late rebellions.—*Quebec Gazette*, 27th *Sept*. 1830.

"Yesterday afternoon, fifty-eight of the Canadian rebels under sentence of death were shipped on board the steamer British America, to be re-shipped on board the transport Buffalo, in which they will be transported to Botany Bay for life. They were chained in couples and escorted to the steamer by a guard of the 24th Regt. The Upper Canada rebels and brigands, whose sentence of death were commuted to transportation for life, arrived yesterday evening by the Lachine Canal; and were shipped on board the steamer St. George, and are destined to share the fate of the other rebels. Both steamboats sailed as soon as they had received their cargoes. We are told that the parting scene between the convicts and their relations was distressing in the extreme, and caused tears to flow from eyes which witnessed it. Twenty-five prisoners are to be released on giving satisfactory security that they will leave the Province in forty-eight hours after their liberation, and never come to it again; two others, named Levesque and Prieur, are to enter into a similar arrangement, with this difference, that they are to remove six hundred miles from the Province.—*Montreal Paper*.

last insurrections, were pursuant to a general order, of the 4th of April, disbanded on the first of May.† The Special Council which had been in session two months was also adjourned by His Excellency on the 13th of April. The Ordinances passed by this body during the session, amounted to sixty-seven, some of them making important and very beneficial innovations upon the previous laws.*

---

†By a General Order, dated the 4th instant, the following corpus, now embodied for general service, are placed on the sedentary footing from the 15th instant, but will receive pay and gratuity to the 30th instant:—
 1. Hemingford Loyal volunteers.
 2. 1st Company St. Johns Volunteers
 3. Odelltown Loyal Volunteers.
 4. Blairfindie Loyal Volunteers.
 5. Missisquoi Borderers.
 6. Noyan Loyal Volunteers.
 7. Henryville Loyal Volunteers.
 8. Clarenceville Rangers.
 9. Barnston Volunteer Company.
 10. Queen's Mounted Rangers.
 11. British American Rifle Company.
 12. Sherbrooke Troop of Cavalry.
 13. Hatley Loyal Volunteers.
 14. Stanstead Volunteer Company.
 15. Huntingdon Loyal Volunteers.
 16. Chateauguay Loyal Volunteers.
 17. Beauharnois Loyal Volunteers.
 18. St. Eustache Loyal Volunteers.
 19. Eastern Townships Loyal Volunteers.
 20. Coteau Volunteer Rangers.
 21. Queen's Volunteers.
 22. Quebec Volunteer Artillery.
 23. Quebec Highland Company.
 24. St. Anns Troop of Cavalry.
 25. Three Rivers Loyal Volunteers.
 26. Kennebec Volunteer Rangers.

We understand that the present local force stationed on the frontier, consisting of the Montreal Volunteer Cavalry, Queen's Light Dragoons, and Col. Dyer's battalion, is to be retained on active service for another year.—*Montreal Gazette.*

* Among them was an Ordinance relating to the St. Sulpiciens, at Montreal, respecting which, Sir John Colborne

Lord John Russell gave notice in the House of Commons, on the 3rd of June, of certain resolutions which he intended to submit, relating to the projected union of the Canadas. He was, however, induced, on the suggestion of Sir Robert Peel, to waive them, and at once to introduce his Bill for the purpose. In doing which, he stated it to be his intention to carry it only through a second reading,

---

writes on the 13th April, to the Colonial Minister of follows :

My Lord,—I beg leave to state to your Lordship, that I am persuaded that the most important remedial measures required in the present situation of the country are those which would tend to the reconstruction and enlargement of the judicature, to the establishment of registry offices, to the commutation or abolition of the lods et ventes, particularly in towns, and the other oppressive incidents of the feudal tenure, to the continuation and completion of local improvements, and to the introduction of a well regulated system of district police.

With returning tranquillity it is justly expected that the measures to which I advert will be speedily carried into effect, preparatory to the changes of a more difficult nature which may be proposed for the parmanent government of this Province. Lord Durham, I am aware, appointed commissioners to report upon several of the subjects in question, and, I believe, framed Ordinances for the consideration of Her Majesty's Government to authorize a commutation of the lods et ventes in Montreal, and the establishment of registry offices; but I imagine that the reforms which he was desirous of introducing were not finally determined on, and I have therefore requested the Executive Council to collect such information as will enable me neither to promote the views of my predecessor, or to propose measures for reconstructing the Court of Appeal and the judicature of the Province, if the alterations which may be suggested can be effected through the legislative power granted to the Special Council.

* * * * * * * * *

Sir John had previously (21st January, 1839,) written to the Minister, as follows :

The Ordinance to incorporate the Ecclesiastics of the Seminary of St. Sulpice, to confirm their title, and to provide for the general extinction of seigniorial rights and dues within their fiefs and seigniories, I trust will be sanctioned

in order that it might undergo discusssion, but that having received a strong protest on the part of Upper Canada against the intended union, he did not deem it advisable to legislate that session finally upon the subject. The protest alluded to came, it was thought, from the Chief Justice of Upper Canada, Mr. Robinson, then in England, and who, it was known, was strongly opposed to the union of the two provinces. The Bill was discussed in Parliament and very favourably received, but postponed on motion of the minister, to the following session. The measure was popular in Upper Canada, the Assembly thereof, then in session, having in committee of the whole on the state of the province, declared, that " in the opinion of this house, a union of the two provinces, having in view the permanent security of British interests, would remedy those glaring evils," (previously detailed), " and place Canada in that elevated position contemplated by the Earl of Durham, with the least delay, and least difficulty." An Act was passed by the Imperial Parliament to remedy a defect in that which had the previous session been passed for suspending the constitution of Lower Canada. It received the royal sanction on the 17th of August, and was intitled, " An Act to amend an Act of the last session of Parliament for making temporary provision for the Government of Lower Canada.

The trial of François Jalbert for the murder of

---

by Her Majesty's Government as soon as possible, and be authorized by an Imperial Act, to be continued in force till repealed or revoked by competent legislative authority in the province. The provisions of this Ordinance appear to give satisfaction generally to the inhabitants of Montreal, and also to the Superior and Ecclestiastics of the Seminary, but certainly demand the confirmation of the Imperial Parliament with reference to the extensive interests which would be affected by any doubt as to the permanency of the arrangements proposed.

Lieutenant Weir took place at Montreal, in the September assizes. The jury was mixed, consisting of nine persons of French and three of British origin. The prosecution was conducted by the Attorney General Ogden, assisted by the Solicitor General, Mr. Andrew Stuart, Messrs. Walker and Charles Mondelet being the prisoner's counsel. The trial lasted some days, but the jury disagreeing as to the verdict, two only being for finding him guilty, and the term expiring without coming to a verdict, the whole consequently fell through. It was at first intended to subject him at the following term to another trial; but, on further consideration, as it was the general opinion that no jury of his compatriots, however clearly his guilt might be proved, would, in the feeling of the times, find a verdict against him, it was wisely determined to set him at liberty |without further proceedings, and he was accordingly released. Thus did this most atrocious murder, the particulars whereof as given on the trial by some of the eye witnesses of it, are inserted below,* escape the retribution it so justly deserved. Jalbert it is said however was not the most guilty man.

---

*COURT OF KING'S BENCH—MONTREAL.

CRIMINAL TERM.

The Queen vs. François Jalbert.

The indictment is read, after which the Solicitor General opens the case by addressing the Jury.

The following witnesses are then called on behalf of the Crown.

Dr. Carter—I was a Captain of Militia in November, 1837. I met Lieutenant Weir at Sorel on the evening previous to the outbreak at St. Denis. He came there on horseback and asked where the barracks were. I went with him, and he asked the sergeant of the guard if his sword, &c., had arrived. He was informed that all the baggage of the 32nd had gone on. Lieutenant Weir then got a caleche to take him to St. Denis, in the hope of overtaking his regiment. I saw him leave. He was dressed in a blue surtout, I believe, and seemed very much fatigued; he seemed surprised that the

The horror and grief of Dr. Wolfred Nelson, on learning the assassination of this unarmed, pinioned, and defenceless gentleman, by those to whose custody he had committed him for conveyance to the

troops had gone on; he left, I am sure, with the intention of overtaking the troops.

Cross-examined—The troops left, I believe, about half past seven, and Lieutenant Weir left in the said caleche about 9 or ten o'clock. His dress to all appearance military, but he had no weapons.

2d Witness, Andrew Lavalle—I am a carter, a,d was at Sorel in November, 1837, I remember about that time being engaged to conduct a person to a distance of about three leagues. The person was Mr. Weir, as I understood. He was dressed in dark clothes, and was in a hurry to get on. He left about 11 at night, and his object was to overtake the troops, as he expected to find them at Jones' Mills, about two leagues distant from Sorel. I drove Lieut. Weir to St. Denis, and when about 15 or 20 arpents from it, we were stopped by a guard. We said we were going to Chambly, on which four persons on horseback took us to Dr. Wolfred Nelson's house in the village. Lieut. Weir was taken into a room and I was sent into the kitchen: I remained there about an hour, and I then left to go home. When I was leaving the house I saw Dr. Nelson, Lieut. Weir and another person at the breakfast table.

Cross examined—I understood perfectly that Lieut. Weir left to join the troops. I speak a little English. We did not meet any person until we encountered the guard. I could not tell that Lieut. Weir was a military man. When we arrived at St. Denis, Dr. Nelson with others came to the door of his house, and spoke to Mr. Weir in a gentlemanly manner, receiving him as such. When I left, I saw the table laid for breakfast. The number of the guard was considerable. When we said we were going to Chambly, only four of them came with us. No person spoke. They appeared to be all armed, and I know that those who came with us were so. There were a number under arms in the village, and they appeared prepared to make a defence. I did not hear that they expected the troops, but from my observation they appeared to me to be anticipating something. It was not quite daylight when I left Dr. Nelson's. I returned by the same route (along the banks of the Richelieu) and met many armed men, but no troops.

Pierre Guertin—I was at St. Denis on the 23rd Nov.,

head quarters of the insurgents, under Mr. Brown, at St. Charles, has already been noticed, and is confirmed by the evidence given on the trial of Jalbert.

1837, and was ordered to take charge of an officer who was a prisoner at Dr. Nelson's---This was between 5 and 6 A. M. I remained there in charge of the prisoner until 8 o'clock; Jalbert was there armed with a sword or bayonet; I did not receive any orders from him. The officer was put on board of a waggon---He was dressed in a fearnaught coat. We were going to St. Charles; when I left Dr. Nelson's with the prisoner it was eight o'clock or more, there were several persons about the house, I saw one Migneau, but I cannot say if I saw Jalbert or not, Migneau held the strap with which the officer was tied; I was armed with a gun and went with them a little distance, when I was ordered to get out because the roads were very bad and the others in the waggon said they could guard the prisoner. They had gone on some distance when I heard a noise; the officer had fallen down and was lying among the wheels. Malliot could not have struck the officer because he was lying among the wheels, both his arms were raised when I turned round; the cries seemed to proceed from a person in great distress, and were intermingled with cursing. I then ran off and was ordered into the large house of Madame St. Gormain. I received orders from Jalbert to take charge of Weir, it was then dark; I was not the only person ordered to take him in charge. Shortly after Migneau arrived we left. Lieut. Weir had his hands tied, but afterwards they were unloosed.

Cross-examined---I did not hear any insolence offered to the officer when he was in the waggon. I do not recollect having seen any person on horseback near it, I did not see Jalbert, when I left or as I returned, nor at Madame St. Germain's; I entered that house by the front door. I do not recollect having heard the bells ringing.

Emilie Plante---I was at St. Denis when the soldiers first came there in 1837. On the morning of their arrival I saw an officer there in a waggon along with Malliot and Migneau the postmaster. The officer was not bound but had a string round him; Migneau was alongside of him; the waggon was close to the house where I was I saw the officer jump out of the waggon. Malliot who was behind him struck a blow, but I cannot say what it was at; he broke his sword; the officer's face was toward the ground, and his hand was on his head which had blood upon it he was near dying. I saw Jalbert on horseback after the officer was dead, he had a drawn sword on his shoulder, and he came over to our

A riot was apprehended on the conclusion of Jalbert's trial, from the indignant and highly excited feelings of the multitude in attendance day after day in and near the court, and had not effectual

house to ask for a pistol; the sword was stained with blood. I did not observe whether it was fresh or dry; this was after the officer was killed but not along after; Jalbert did not dismount; the house I was in belonged to Joseph Pratt; Jalbert asked my father-in-law about the pistol; this was before the firing began; it was a good while after I saw Malliot break the sword that I saw Jalbert; this was after the officer was dead. I was at my prayers, and when I saw the officer was dying I did not look until I had finished, so I cannot say what occured during that interval. Some time elapsed from the period I saw blood until the officer was dead; I remained in the kitchen at my prayers after seeing the blow until the time I saw Jalbert.

Cross-Examined—I am 17 years of age; I was at that time a good deal alarmed, and therefore I cannot tell precisely what took place, though I have related as nearly as I could what passed. The waggon was in the road and I was in the gallery beside it; the road is wide When I saw Capt. Jalbert I am sure the officer was dead. It was long after I saw the officer dead that I saw Jalbert; I did not see the officer dying but I saw him dead; Jalbert was on horseback and going towards Dr. Nelson's—I saw the sword on the right side going down the river; I was quite close to Jalbert, and I am quite sure it was blood I saw, I did not drink brandy or any kind of liquor; I was greatly agitated.

Francois Migneau—I live at St. Denis, where I have been postmaster and innkeeper for many years. I know the prisoner Jalbert. On the 23rd November, 1837, an officer arrived at St. Denis about 8 or 9 o'clock, a. m. I was ordered to go to Dr. Nelson's and from thence to conduct the officer to St. Charles. I found a waggon ready at Dr. Nelson's door, and saw Nelson himself who told me I was the fittest person to take the officer to St. Charles, I asked if the officer was armed. His hair I believe was fair, and he wore a blue surtout, but put-on an over coat before going out. I was driving the waggon. I told Guertin to get out because the roads were bad. The officer's hands were tied, but I untied them, seeing that they were becoming discoloured. I gave him my gloves and told him he was under my protection. After I untied his hands a strap was put round his middle, and on proceeding a little distance the officer jumped out and from the position of the strap, fell on his knees. Malliot

precautions been taken by calling out the military, violence towards the prisoner and jury would very probably have taken place, the masses being but too well disposed to administer summary justice upon

had a sword in his hand about a foot and a half or at most two feet long. He struck the officer two blows and the sword broke. I do not think that he inflicted grevious wounds. The officer got up. The waggon might have gone on about 40 or 50 feet before I could stop it. The officer was making for the troops whose advanced guard was about 7 or 8 arpents off. Malliot called out for assistance. I then saw Joseph Pratt striking the officer with a large cavalry sword. When I got there he must have struck 10 or 12 blows, for the officer was dreadfully mangled. I then raised him and saw that some of his fingers were cut off, and that there were great cuts in his head. There were many persons there. The officer had lost a great deal of blood: I spoke to him. Jalbert had not come up at this moment. I said to the officer, in broken English. "I am afraid my protection is too late. I am afraid somebody shot you in a minute, I can't help you." I meant to say one would shoot him in a minute. I pushed Pratt away. Several persons in the crowd cried "let us finish him, let us finish him." At this moment Jalbert came up on horseback with a sword at his side and a pistol, which was in his saddle, I think, and he probably might have commanded to finish him. I knew Jalbert before. He could not come into the crowd, being on horseback. Captain Jalbert said "finish him, finish him," I heard the words "achevez le, achevez le.". Jalbert was an officer. Louis L'Hussier came up with a gun which he levelled at the officer, but it snapped thrice; some one then came up with a pistol, and I then left, for I was very much afraid, because they insisted on my finishing the officer, and threatened to do as much for me if I did not do so; I was very much overcome, but what I have related occurred before I was so overcome. I did not hear the report of a pistol. When I again returned, Pratt was still striking with his sword. I asked them to assist me to remove the officer, for he had been barbously used. One of them then helped me to take him between two houses. I only heard Jalbert say "finish him, finish him;" I did not see him strike; his sword was by his side. I had my back turned towards Jalbert; I was endeavouring to help the officer. All that I have stated, you will learn from other witnesses, When I returned I did not see Captain Jalbert. Previous to Jalbert's coming up, I heard persons say "finish

them. The following remarks on the subject, about the most temperate to be found in the Montreal papers of the day, are descriptive of the asperities that prevailed.

"On Tuesday night about half-past eleven o'clock, him;" Jalbert said so probably; 1 believe he did so, I have no doubt but that he did so.

Cross-examined—I saw the officer in the room on the left hand as you enter Nelson's house, and I recollect perfectly what Nelson said. He told every man to treat the officer like a gentleman. The officer told Dr. Nelson that he was Lieutenant Weir of the 32nd Regiment, and Dr. Nelson told me so. The officer had apparently breakfasted with Dr. Nelson. There was no one on horseback with us. Firing had commenced farther down when we left Dr. Nelson's. No insult was offered to the officer, and he understood that he was under my protection. He wanted to see the soldiers, whose firing we heard, but Malliot would not let him. Mr. Weir then leaped abruptly from the waggon; he had passed his word that he would not attempt to escape; he had not asked to have his hands untied but he gave his word and I untied them; Malliot struck him as soon as he leaped and continued to do so. I am positive that Jalbert was not there when Malliot and Pratt struck; Mr. Weir's head and fingers were cut and he was all besmeared with blood. I thought he could not have more than five or six minutes to live. There were a great many people there, and they were in great agitation. When I came up I heard people crying out "finish him," and I tried to push through the crowd. Jalbert arrived just as I came up; he might have said "finish him," but the crowd had said so before. I stopped the waggon and ran up with the intention of saving the officer. Before Jalbert arrived there might have been ten or twelve who cried out "finish him, finish him." It might have been four or five minutes after I first came and when the head and arm of Mr. Weir was so much cut that I heard the cry of "finish him." Jalbert stood on the outside of the crowd being on horseback. There was a crowd between him and the officer who appeared to be almost dead. I think motives of humanity prompted many to cry out "finish him." I believe that Jalbert said "finish him"—the cry was general, and I have no doubt but that Jalbert joined; it might be that I could not discover Jalbert's voice. The condition of the officer was such that immediate death was desirable. Jalbert remained there five or six minutes perhaps ten, but not a quarter of an hour. Jalbert was a church-warden

the court, which h id adjourned in the afternoon, resumed its sitting, and the prisoner Jalbert was placed in the dock. The jury were then introduced, and were asked if they were agreed upon a verdict. The answer being in the negative, the court continued in session until midnight, when it declared its session to be closed. The jury then became dis-

and had been Captain of Militia for several years; he was on the frontier during the late war, I have always known him to be a brave and humane man. I was quite overpowered at the beginning of the affair.

J. *M'Gregor, Surgeon, 32nd Regiment*—I knew the late Lieut. Weir, well.—(The witness relates precisely the same circumstances as Mr. Griffin did yesterday as to the finding of the body.) The arms were pinioned. I took his watch out of his pocket. I had seen it before. One Mason who has been a witness on this occasion, assisted us. We brought the body to Montreal where the examination took place. On the left side of the neck there was a large sabre wound about five or six inches in length which alone was sufficient to produce death. Forming an angle with this wound there was another nearly as large which had exposed the windpipe. On the front of the head there was a great sabre cut; also sufficient to cause death. This wound was evidently inflicted by a very sharp instrument. The blow described by last witness as having been given by Jalbert, would have produced such a wound as this. On the left shoulder blade there was a gunshot wound; also several stabs. I removed the bullet. The wound on the skull of which I have spoken appeared to have been inflicted by a person higher than the deceased when standing. There was also a gunshot wound on the left groin. Two shots must have been fired, for I extracted one ball from the body lodged between the two orifices. The fingers on the left hand were completely hacked. There was another wound from the ear to the forehead.

Cross-examined—I saw two or three sabre wounds on the head. There were other wounds on the body which might have caused death. The profuse bleeding arising from all these wounds would have produced death.

Dr. *Arnoldi, Jun.*—(Heard and corroborates the evidence of the last witness.) The blow as descrioed by Cadieux to have been struck by Jalbert, if it produced the wound on the forehead of the deceased was sufficient to cause death. The wound seemed to have been inflicted by a person above the deceased.

charged by necessary course of law; and the judges had no sooner quitted the Bench than the excitement of the multitude, which crowded the court to excess, broke out into noisy threats and an active assault on the jury, whom they considered, with only two exceptions, as having violated their oaths, and refused justice, under the influence of a preconcerted party combination.

"It was to be feared that, under all circumstances of the case, this movement would hardly terminate but in some fatal result, deeply to be deplored; the precautions which had been wisely taken, to meet and curb any explosion of popular indignation, sufficed to rescue the twelve from their perilous situation in the jury box, where the benches saved them from many a hearty blow; and where they suffered only some contusions upon their obdurate heads, which will make most of their hats a tight fit, for some days to come. They are deeply indebted to the activity of the police, who dragged forth several of their number, during an auspicious moment and conveyed them away in safety. The two jurymen who were understood to have adhered to the dictates of their own conscience, and of justice, were raised upon the shoulders of the populace, and borne away amid loud cheers; the one to the St. Lawrence Suburb, and the other to Mack's Hotel.

"Now all this was quite natural, although we cannot assert it was right; for men's natural feelings and impulses very often urge them to do what is wrong. It furnishes a just anticipation of what may be expected to arise in this colony, where, as things now stand, "it is not in the power of the government, if indeed it be so disposed, to protect the property, or lawfully avenge the murder of loyal British subjects." The scene of Tuesday night furnishes a most useful lesson, if it be promptly and impressively imparted to the British Government. Few occasions appear to us to have called so loudly for a general meeting of the British population to set forth the fact that the law has become a solemn mockery—and that the consequent insecurity to their lives and their properties, is what cannot and will not be tolerated."—*Montreal Transcript.*

Bills of indictment had been laid at the late assizes at Montreal before the grand jury, against various persons concerned in the late rebellions. The grand jury returned on the last day (10th of September), of the term, true bills against several of those supposed to have been active in the predatory incursions upon Caldwell Manor and the Eastern Townships.* True bills for high treason were found against L. J. Papineau, Robert Nelson, E. B. O'Callaghan, T. S. Brown, and several others, at this time absent from the province, having taken refuge in the United States. They all were allowed, however, after tranquillity was restored, to return to Canada. The indictment found against Mr. Papineau, (who, from the United States had with his family gone to France, where he was hospitably received), remained pending, until the appointment of Mr. Lanfontaine as attorney General during the Bagot administration. Mr. Lafontaine, although an antagonism had arisen between him and Mr. Papineau on public matters previous to 1837, generously insisted, upon his nomination to office, if he did not even make it a condition previous to his acceptance of it at the hands of Sir Charles Bagot in 1842, that all proceedings against M. P., as well as others indicted for treason, should be stayed, and that they should be free to return home when they pleased. Sir Charles Bagot, there is reason to believe, had no insuperable objections to forget the past, and pass a sponge over the late

---

* Viz.: Celestin Beausoleil, Bonaventure Viger, Helary Viger, Henry Newcomb, Jaques Langlois, and Michel Brouillet, on charges of arson.

events, but his death occurring soon after Mr. Lafontaine's appointment to office, it became necessary to consult his successor, Sir Charles Metcalfe, on the subject, whose views were opposed to Mr. Papineau's return, and consequently to an abandonment of the legal proceedings that had been taken against him. He, however, finally yielded to the instances of the Attorney General, whom he allowed to fyle a *nolle prosequi* to the indictments against that gentleman and others for political offences.*

---

* I avail myself here of the *a propos*, to correct an error in a previous part of this work (Vol. IV., page 523,) where it is stated that the *nolle prosequi* was entered by permission of Sir Charles Bagot. In this, I find myself corrected by an article in the *Minerve* of Montreal of the 16th April, 1853, to which, in correction of the error, I willingly give insertion. The permission was from Sir C Metcalfe. The article alluded to is as follows:—

"En lisant de nouveau la " Revue parlementaire" du *Journal de Quebec*, numero du 7 avril, nous avons remarque le passage suivant :

" Est-ce que M. LaFontaine considerait les *autres questions*
" quand il disait, en 1842, au Gouverneur-General *Sir Charles*
" *Bagot* de douce memoire :

'Ou il me sera permis de mettre fin aux poursuites judicia-
' ires qui pesent sur *M. L. J Papineau*; ou je me retire de
' vos conseils.'

" Ces paroles que l'auteur de la " Revue," non sans raison, attribue a *M LaFontaine*, annoncent qu'il y a eu lutte, et lutte serieuse, entre lui et *un* gouverneur, au sujet de *M. Papineau*, alors absent du pays sous accusation de *haute trahison*.

" Nous avons plus d'une raison de croire, et les debats de 1849 sont la pour nous justifier ; nous avons raison de croire, disonsnous, qu'en effet cette lutte a eu lieu entre *M, LaFontaine* et un gouverneur. Ce gouverneur n'est pas *Sir Charles Bagot*, mais bien *Sir Cahr'es Metcalfe*, l'homme *a la volonte de fer*, comme on l'a appele dans le temps. Eh bien! ce gouverneur, *a la volonte de fer*, a ete oblige de ceder, apres plusieurs refus, il est vrai, a la demande de *M. LaFontaine*, de lui permettre d'enregistrer un *nolle proseqai* sur l'indictment rapporte contre *M. Papineau* pour haute trahison ; en d'autres mots, pour etre mieux compris de nos lecteurs, de permettre a *M. Papineau* de revenir au pays. Ce *nolle prosequi*,

Mr. Papineau returned to Canada in 1844, af.er an absence of seven years, spent principally in France, and received in 1846, by vote *nem. con.* of the Legislative Assembly, on recommendation of Lord Cathcart, the Governor General, £4500 for arrears of Salary as Speaker of the Assembly of Lower Canada, some palliative to his crosses, and the seven years of exile he had undergone, short,

---

nous avons raison de croire, a ete enregistre au terme de la cour criminelle, tenu a Montreal vers la fin du mois d'aout 1843, c'est-a-dire plus de trois mois apres la mort de *Sir Charles Bagot.*

" Il nu faut pas conclure de cette circonstance que *Sir Charles Bagot* de *douce memoire*, ainsi que l'auteur de la " Revue" l appelle, mu par un sentiment qui fait honneur a son cœur, sentiment honorable que le Bas-Canada a deja exprime avec la plus vive reconnaissance; il ne faut pas conclure de cette circonstance, disonsnous, que *Sir Charles Bagot* etait oppose a une amnistie, meme a une amnistie generale. Les debats qui ont eu lieu en Parlement a ce sujet en 1849, ont prouve le contraire, a la honte meme de celui qui, sans pudeur, s'etait montre assez *lache*, et assez *ingrat*, pour provoquer de pareils debats.

" En reportant a *Sir Charles Bagot* ce qui a eu lieu sous *Sir Charles Metcalfe*, l'homme *a la volonte de fer*, il est evident que l'auteur de la " Revue" a ete induit en erreur, par la note relative a ce sujet, qui se trouve a la page 523 du 4e volume de l'Histsire du Canada, de *M. Christie.*

" Dans cette note, *M. Christie*, qui s'est cru *assez fort* pour ecrire *impartialement*, quant aux individus qu'il met en sc n', l'histoire des dernieres quinze annees, rend compte de la " lutte en question." Nous avons raison de savoir que, si, dans cette note, M. Christie s'est trompe sur plusieurs faits incidents ou de details, faits que pour le m ment nous ne sommes pas appele a rectifier, il ne s'est point trompe sur le fait principal, celui de la " lutte" entre *M. LaFontaine* et un gouverneur, au sujet de *M. Papineau*, *M. Christie* a dit *juste.* Seulement, il a attribue cette lutte a *Sir Charles Bagot* lorsqu'il aurait du l'attribuer, *ce qui est la verite*, a l'homme *a la volonte de fer.* Et comme, nous l'apprenons avec plaisir, *M. Christie* se propose d'a jouter un cinquieme volume a son histoire du Canada, nous esperons qu'il voudra bien rectifier l'erreur qu'il a commise " It accordingly stands rectified. —R.C.

however, of the sum accrued and due him at the suspension of the constitution, unless the difference were withheld by way of mulct for his participation in the spirit and agitation of the times, a presumption scarcely consistent, with the fact that the past was to be forgotten, and a total absolution of all offences, real or supposed, of a political nature, the consequence

It is not probable that any such unworthy consideration can have influenced the Government, of which Mr. Papineau's brother, the Hon. D. B. Papineau, was at the time a member, as Commissioner of Crown Lands.*

Reports of the appointment of Mr. Poulett Thomson, President of the Board of Trade, as Governor General, reached Canada in September. He arrived on the 17th October at Quebec in H. M. S. Pique, Captain Edward Boxer, where, after taking the customary oath of office, on the 19th, he issued his proclamation, notifying that he had assumed the government.† Sir John Colborne being relieved,

---

*See note on this subject at the end of the chapter.

† By His Excellency the Right Honorable Charles Poulett Thomson, one of Her Majesty's Most Honorable Privy Council, Governor General of British North America, and Captain General and Governor in Chief in and over the Provinces of Lower Canada, and Upper Canada, Nova Scotia, New Brunswick, and the Island of Prince Edward, and Vice Admiral of the same.

The Queen having been graciously pleased to appoint me to be Governor General of British North America, I have this day assumed the Administration of that office. In the exercise of this high trust it will be my desire, no less than duty, to promote to the utmost of my power the welfare of all classes of Her Majesty's subjects—To reconcile existing differences—to extend and protect the trade, and enlarge the resources of the colonies entrusted to my charge—above all to promote whatever may bind them to the Mother Country by increased ties of interest and affection, will be my first and most anxious endeavour. In the pursuit of these objects I shall ever be ready to listen to the representation of all,

sailed with his family for England in the Pique, on the 23rd of October, having, a few days previous to

whilst I shall unhesitatingly exercise the powers confided to me to repress disorder—to uphold the law—and to maintain tranquility.

The suspension of the Constitution in Lower Canada places in the hands of the Executive Government powers of an extraordinary nature, the necessity for which is deeply to be deplored, and which can be justified only by the circumstances of the Province. One principal object of my mission will be to determine in what manner, and at what time, this state of things may most safely be brought to a close, and the full benefits of British Institutions be restored to Her Majesty's Lower Canadian subjects.

In Upper Canada the loyalty and courage of the inhabitants have preserved her Constitution, and maintained the powers of the law through difficulties of the most trying nature. Their exertions during the last two years have been viewed by Her Majesty with the highest satisfaction, and have commanded the applause and admiration of all classes in the Mother Country. It would appear however that in that Province causes of embarrassment are not wanting. Her trade is said to be cramped,—finances deranged and the development of her resources impeded. To devise measures by which these evils may be removed, in a manner satisfactory to the inhabitants, will be one of the objects to engage my earliest attention, and I shall rely upon the patriotism of the people and the wisdom of the Legislature to aid me in the effort.

"Animated by the most anxious desire to promote the welfare of these important Provinces---to uphold the rights of the Crown, by whose confidence I have been honoured, and to advance the true interests of the people to whom I am sent, I confidently call on all those to whom the prosperity of British North America is dear, to unite with me in the work I have undertaken, and laying aside all minor considerations, to afford me that assistance and co-operation which can alone enable me to bring my task to a successful end.

Given under my hand and seat at arms, at the Castle of Saint Lewis, in the city of Quebec, in the said Province of Lower Canada, the nineteenth day of October, in the year of our Lord one thousand eight hundred and thirty-nine, and in the third year of Her Majesty's reign.

By His Excellency's command.

T. W. C. MURDOCH,
Chief Secretary.

his departure, been invested, at Quebec, with the insignia of the Grand Cross, of the most noble Military order of the Bath, transmitted him by Her Majesty, the ceremonial of investiture being performed by Sir James McDonnell, of the Guards, in the presence of a few guests, the heads of military departments and officers of the garrison. He received from all quarters in both Canadas the most flattering addresses previous to his departure, and shortly after his return to England was elevated to the peerage, by the title of Lord Seaton. The following general order may be considered his farewell address to the country.

HEAD QUARTERS, Montreal, Oct. 12, 1839.

"The Governor General and Commander of the Forces cannot leave these Provinces, without requesting the Officers commanding volunteer corps, to convey his thanks to the Officers and men of their respective districts for the important services they have performed in defending their country, and the institutions under which they live, from the combined attack of desperate rebels, and marauders from the United States. Deeply sensible of the arduous nature of those services, of the hardship and personal suffering consequent on them, and but too well acquainted with the misery inflicted on the inhabitants of the frontier, who have been incessantly exposed to predatory and incendiary excursions from the States of New-York, Vermont, and other frontier States, during two successive winters, His Excellency avails himself of this opportunity of recording his opinion, that the forbearance which, under circumstances of unprecedented provocation, has marked the conduct of the Volunteers, (and which, he is confident, will be continued,) does them honour as soldiers, and ensures them respect from every civilized nation, and that the fearless zeal with which a peaceful and industrious population, imperfectly armed and equipped, came forward to crush the first attempts at rebellion, must be ever gratefully remembered by the empire which they represent, and by the Government which they have upheld.

By command,

JOHN EDEN
Dept. Adjt. Gen.

The *Quebec Mercury* on his departure observes:—

"Sir John Colborne has now taken leave of Canada and probably of public life, to enjoy that easy retirement in the bosom of his family which his long and tried services have abundantly won for him. The administration of the civil government of this Province was, in a manner, thrust upon him by circumstances, but the prudence and firmness with which he acquitted himself during the critical period it remained in his hands, justly entitle him to the praise and gratitude of all who desire to support Her Majesty's Government and to maintain the connexion with the parent state; his firmness, foresight, and integrity have achieved what men of more brilliant talents might have failed to accomplish; and we feel assured that he bears with him the respect of the loyal population in both Canadas and their warmest wishes, that he may long wear in his native land, those honours which have been acquired during a life honorably and constantly devoted to the service of his country.

The following amounts of the Revenues received in Lower Canada, in each of the years, 1833,-4,-5-6,-7, and 1838, and of the Public Expenditure during the same years, are copied from returns printed by order of the House of Commons.

	Gross amount received...	Net amount for Lower Canada after deducting expenses of collection and proportion for Upper Canada.	Expenditure.
	£ s. d.	£ s. d	£ s. d.
1833	212,971 13 8	147,712 0 0	134,621 8 8
1834	150,470 11 10¼	101,360 17 4½	127,793 10 8
1835	153,969 13 2½	126,672 11 3¼	67,448 11 6
1836	162,629 14 4½	107,518 9 8	173,753 6 5
1837	142,726 1 5	92,832 5 8	141,164 9 10
1838	146,079 14 9¼	95,547 17 8	224,050 1 5

NOTE.—The foregoing statement shows the amount of payments during each of the years stated but not the expenditure for those years respectively, as, in consequence of the regular supplies being withheld by the House of Assembly since 1832, the payments were made irregularly, as funds could be procured for the purpose ---On a calculation it appears that deducting the expense of the commission of inquiry and of the police in 1838, there will be found a mean expenditure of about £143,5'0 and this includes a sum of £14,251 paid, in the years 1833-4 and 6, for wages to Members of the House of Assembly.

Comparative statement of arrivals and tonnage at the Port of Quebec for the years 1838 and 1839 :

```
              VESSELS.                TONNAGE.
Sept 29th, 1838,  930  ............   287,786
Sept. 29th, 1839, 966  ............   304,426

Increase this year, 36 vessels,       16,640 tons.
```

OFFICE OF THE CHIEF AGENT FOR EMIGRATION.
Quebec. 21st October, 1839.
Statement of number of emigrants arrived at the Por of Quebec during the week ending the 18th instant.—

From England.......................... 6
Ireland 64
Scotland....................... 16
                                      ——
                                      84
Previously reported................ 7,261
                                    ——
                                    7,347
To corresponding period last year... 3,239

Shewing increase in favour of 1838....4,108 souls.
A. C. BUCHANAN, Jun., Chief Agent.

ARTICLE REFERRED TO IN PAGE 30.

It is but justice to remark, here, that if Mr. Papineau were to be paid the like full amount of salary accrued to him as Speaker of the Assembly of Lower Canada, as paid to the Speaker of the Legislative Council (Mr. Sewell)—and why not?—there would still be due him £1000, which, sooner or later, when the asperities of our times shall have passed off, he, or his, will no doubt recover, as a debt of honour due him by the country. The reader who takes an interest in this matter may consult to advantage a report of the Committee on Public Accounts of the Legislative Assembly of Canada in 1850. (Appendix (N. N.) to the Journals of that year.)

Whatever may be thought of Mr. Papineau's course in politics at the period alluded to, and his evasion to avoid the consequences, it is always certain, that constitutionally, the Assembly not having been dissolved, he was, down to the day upon which the Constitution was suspended (27th March, 1838,) the Speaker of that House. To urge, that the members of it were all, or nearly so, more or less concerned, and he, more than any of them, in bringing on the rebellion, were now merely idle, and nothing to the purpose The Government wisely having consigned the whole to oblivion, there remains naught in law, equity or sound policy to bar him of his rights. This, with the unconditional discontinuance, at the instance of Mr. Lafontaine, then Attorney General, in 1848, of the legal proceedings against him for high treason, freed him, it may reasonably be concluded, of all penal liabilities for his participation in the events of 1837, yet to withhold from him £1000 of the salary appertaining to the distinguished post he occupied, (Mr. Sewell of the other branch, being, as its Speaker, paid to the very utmost farthing of his salary down to the 31st March, 1838, four days after that, 25th March, 1838, on which the Constitution was suspended, to say nothing of the heavy salary he also enjoyed as Chief Justice,) looks certainly very much like mulcting him of so much for his politics and the troubles of those times with which he was mixed up, and is indeed unworthy of a government, which in passing a sponge over the past should also, as I at least humbly opine, honourably have settled his account, and paid him to the last denier of his dues.

The justification with some for paying Mr. Sewell his salary in full, to wit, his loyalty and adherence to the Government, and in withholding a portion of Mr. Papineau's for an opposite reason, is more specious than sound There are many in Canada whose opinions are entitled to much respect, who maintain that the principles and policy of the late Chief Justice Sewell, and his partisans, actually had more to do in producing the disastrous events of 1837 and 1838 than those of Mr. Papineau, whose exertions they contend were roused by the misgovernment of the "family compact," constituted of that gentleman and his friends, then virtually ruling the Province; and that the object of M. Papineau was rather the legitimate one of obtaining a responsible and better system of colonial government, than of imme-

diately severing the connexion with Great Britain, an
event, however, which he looked, and I presume, still
looks forward to as ultimately certain. Be this as it may,
the Government, by its course towards Mr. Papineau,
has replaced him, whether it intended so or not, on a
perfect equality with his brother Speaker, Sewell, as to
his claim of full payment for the entire period during
which he was Speaker, and in the full and entire possession of all his civil, legal and other rights without
reserve, precisely, in fact, in the position he would have
been, had there been no rebellion, or he not concerned
in it; or else he has not been wholly, but only partially
forgiven. To withhold from him any portion of the
salary that had accrued to him, looks like punishing him
for what the Government professes to have amnestied,
forgiven and forgotten, and is scarcely logical or consistent with the justice and fair dealing which every just
government should, and would exhibit, particularly in
cases of this nature, which to be well and gracefully
done, should be done thoroughly. Either Mr. Papineau
ought never to have been allowed to return to Canada,
or, returning to it with leave, none of his rights having
been declared forfeited, the right of recovering his
pecuniary claims upon the public treasury to the full
amount, seems to follow as a matter of course.

It was justly remarked by Mr. Lafontaine (who was
not then of the Government) in his place in the Assembly, when, in 1846, the sum of £4,500 for arrears was
voted Mr. Papineau, " that as the Executive had deemed
" it just to entertain Mr. Papineau's claim for arrears
" of salary due him as Speaker of the late Assembly of
" Lower Canada. it ought in justice, to have proposed
" payment in full of the amount accrued to him in that
" quality, which he apprehended the vote in question
" would not cover ; the sum really due him being larger,
" he believed, than that now proposed." But the real
secret, for not proposing a vote in full was, I have no
doubt, an apprehension on the part of the Draper and

Daly administration then in office, but on the wane, that in the prejudices still subsisting against Mr. Papineau, it might not be prudent at that juncture to call for a larger sum, lest it might risk the whole, as, voting on that question myself, and knowing the feeling on this matter of many of the members, I think it indeed very possible, might have been the case.

Having said this much on the subject, it may not be amiss to refer to official documents. Mr. Papineau, sometime after his return to Canada from france, submitted, by letter dated 4th March, 1846, to Lord Cathcart, then administering the Government, his "just "claim for the payment of arrears of salary due him as "former Speaker of the Assembly of Lower Canada." Pursuant to this, His Lordship, shortly after, without consultation it seems with Mr. Papineau, sent down to the Assembly, then in session, a message recommending a vote of £4,500, being as he said " advised that this debt is due in point of law" to Mr. Papineau, stating further, that " if the House concur in this opinion and " shall be pleased to make provision for the payment of ". it, the Administrator of the Government is authorised, " in such case, to signify his willingness to accede to Mr. " Papineau's application." The sum recommended was accordingly voted *nem con*, on the strength of its being due " in point of law." Now it may very fairly be asked why, in point of law, was not the whole sum £5,500 due, as well as the part, £4,500, for which the vote was recommended? If he were by law entitled to the latter, he was by the same rule equally so to the former, or how came Mr. Speaker Sewell to be paid that amount? the law being no more in favor of the one than the other, the only difference between the two men being that Mr. Sewell was in a position, during the suspension of the constitution, to cause himself to be paid out of the public treasury, and took care to do it, whereas Mr. Papineau was not in such a position, and I do him the justice to believe, would not, had he been so, have taken the advantage of it, nor accepted even of his just dues, otherwise than through the free votes of the representatives of the people; such at least has always been his policy.

In the session of the Legislative Assembly of Canada, in 1850, a question on this subject having incidentally arisen, it was referred to the Committee on public Accounts, before which an inquiry took place. Mr. Papineau on being questioned stated: "When I made "this demand I knew not what was the sum due to me, "referring it to the Government to establish, by a correct "examination of public documents, what it might be. "If through a mistake they have named a less sum that "unintentional error impairs in no manner a just claim."

" The unanimous vote of the Assembly, on the 29th "day of May, 1846, was in these words, "Resolved, that "there is now due to the Honorable L. J. Papineau, "Late Speaker of the House of Assembly of Lower Ca- "nada, the sum of £4,500, currency, and that for the "papment of the said sum there be granted to Her "Majesty, out of the consolidated revenue, the said sum "of £4,500, currency."

"This," observes Mr. Papineau, "was all true, but "not the whole truth, as more than that sum was due. "When it was voted," he adds: "the Honorable Mr. "Lafontaine correctly stated, that since Government "was to pay Mr. Papineau they ought to do it in full, "and that he thought the sum due him larger than the "one proposed to be voted. It was thus that I learned "that there had likely been an error made in the amount "demanded, and that I was led to ask my brother if "there was time to correct it, to which he answered "that it was too late, and that business so crowded at "the close of a session that there remained no time to "search and find it out; nor was it of moment, as if "there was an error, it could readily be corrected in "another session.

"Party spirit," says Mr. Papineau in course of the

" inquiry alluded to, " heaped through the press
" against me, and other public men, many extra legal
" incriminations, much of abuse and slander, for the
" part which they, or I, may have taken in our intestine
" discussions. The proceedings neither of the Govern-
" ment nor of this house, ought to be influenced in the
" least by such statements. I left the country after a
" large sum had been promised for my apprehension. I
" might have returned to it, much sooner than I have
" done, the Government having long before cancelled
" the procedure begun against me; but besides, and
" before that step, many respectable gentlemen and
" friends in this country and abroad, influential near the
" home Government, had kindly offered to make interest
" near it, to facilitate my earlier return to my native
" country; I had declined their obliging offers. I have
" come to it when it suited me from my own free deter-
" mination, after having loudly proclaimed that I re-
" pented not of any act of my public life.

" It is neither the right, the duty, nor inclination of
" this house, to investigate for praise or censure, for
" remuneration or punishment, into the acts of public
" men in 1837. In establishing what is the amount of
" my claim, it will be guided by the consideration of
" what was the desire of the Province of Lower Canada,
" as expressed by the Acts of its Legislature and the
" votes of its representatives, as to what were to be the
" salaries attached to the high and honourable station of
" the Speakers of the Houses of Parliament. Referring
" to the Public Accounts, it will be found that the
" Speaker of the Legislative Council has been paid £500
" currency for the six month's salary ending on the 31st
" of March, 1838. If this payment has been correctly
" made, there is presumptive evidence that the same
" ought to be made to the Speaker of the House of
" Assembly." It had been urged, it seems, that the
sum recommended by the Executive and voted by the
Assembly to Mr. Papineau was in pursuance of an

"amicable arrangement on the part of the Government
" and Parliament." This he totally repudiated. "There
" was neither in the Government nor in Parliament, nor
" with me, any bargaining for an " amicable arrange-
" ment." I did not then, as I do not now, and as I
." hope I never shall do, ask a favor from any man, or
" set of men for any thing done by me in public life."

Mr. Joseph Cary, the Deputy Inspector General of
Public Accounts being examined before the Committee,
stated, that the Constitution of Lower Canada ceased
on the 27th March, 1838. That the Honorable Jonathan
Sewell was paid his salary as Speaker of the Legislative
Council to 31st March, 1839, in common with the other
officers of the Legislative Council, and no longer. The
other officers of that body were placed on pensions from
that date. Being asked " to what period were the
Speaker and other officers of the House of Assembly
of Lower Canada paid their salary? He answered,
" These were all in like manner, except Mr. Papineau
" paid to the same period, viz: to 31st March
" 1838." And finally, " the last payment to Mr. Pa-
" pineau, on account of his salary as Speaker of the
" House of Assembly of Lower Canada, was in 1846,
" the sum of £4,500 currency being voted by the Le-
" gislature in the session of that year, being the amount
'' of his salary at the rate of £1000 per annum from 1st
" October, 1832, to 21st March, 1837, the several war-
" rants for that salary having been issued from time to
" time in his favor in the same manner and time as the
" warrants issued for salaries of other public function-
'' aries, but Mr. Papineau declined taking them up.
" On the political troubles breaking out in the fall of
" 1837, these warrants in favor of Mr. Papineau were
" destroyed. I believe by order of Government. There
" would be due him, if paid to the same time to which
" Mr. Sewell was paid, £1000 for one year's salary from

" 1st April, 1837, to 31st March, 1838." This sets "the matter in a very clear light.

Many, however, I must also observe, think Mr. Papineau fortunate in recovering arrears to the extent mentioned. This may be very true, but is no bar to his recovery of the residue legally and justly due him, which will, I have no doubt, sooner or latter, be recognized.—*Fiat justitia, ruat cœlum.*

July, 1853.

CHAPTER XLVI.

Favourable reception of Mr. Poulet Thomson at Quebec—Proceeds to Montreal—Convokes the Special Council—Proceedings of this body---Vote for the Union--Governor General proceeds to Upper Canada---Meets the Legislature—Lord John Russell's despatch relating to tenure of office---Resolutions of both branches in favour of a re-union of the two Provinces--Address to Her Majesty in consequence---Amendments proposed to the resolutions relating to the re-union---Address relating to Responsible Government.—Governor's answer—Prorogation and speech---Act of re-union passed by the Imperial Parliament—Proclamation declaring it in force—The Cunard Line of Steamers, Memoir of the late Sir James Stuart, Bart.

THE appointment of Mr. Poulett Thomson, who had resided many years at St. Petersburg, and been concerned in the trade of Russia, (a rival commerce to that of Canada), with England, was not very acceptable to the British and commercial population of the Canadas, to whose interests they deemed him, from his former connexion with the Baltic timber trade, if not opposed, at best but a lukewarm friend. He was, nevertheless, on his landing in Quebec, warmly received by the British public, on account of the important mission on which he had been sent, namely to effectuate the terms upon which the intended union of the two provinces should be made.

The magistrates residing in Quebec, and the merchants constituting the committee of trade in this city, presented him on his landing separate addresses of congratulation on his arrival. In the address of the former it was observed:—"We have no doubt but that your Excellency is fully aware that the city of Quebec, from the earliest periods, has been fixed upon in consideration of its strength and central position as the seat of government of all the

countries which now form the Provinces of British
North America. There have been provided, at great
expense, fortifications for the safety of the city and
port, appropriate places of deposit for the public
archives collected from all the Provinces, and suitable buildings for the convenience of the public departments, civil and military, and here is the sole and uninterruptible channel of communication, with the metropolis in the season of navigation, and the safe resort
of her fleets and armies for the Canadas. Should circumstances permit that your Excellency should establish your residence amongst us, we trust that in the
magistracy, and among all classes of our fellow citizens, your Excellency will find a ready disposition to
promote the beneficent views of Her Majesty's Government, and the peace, welfare, and permanent connexion
of this Province with the other dominions of our most
Gracious Sovereign,"

To this he answered that he fully appreciated the
political and commercial importance of the city of
Quebec. That it would afford him sincere satisfaction at all times to contribute to its prosperity, and
when circumstances permitted, by residing within its
walls, to cultivate the good feelings and regard to its
inhabitants.

The committee of trade in their address observed:
"Merchants ourselves, and representing the mercantile community of this city, it is, we assure your
Excellency, with no small degree of pride and satisfaction that we see the government of the country
entrusted to one who himself has been a merchant,
and notwithstanding that the opinions understood to
have been entertained by your Excellency in regard
to a most important branch of the trade of this country,
differ very materially from ours, we have never
doubted but that from the moment of your undertaking the Government of these Colonies, your strenuous and unbiassed efforts would be directed to the

promotion of their interests commercial as well as political. We are fully persuaded that the withdrawing of that protection hitherto afforded to the timber trade of the British North American Colonies, would be, not only fatal to their prosperity, by destroying their great staple trade, weakening the bonds that now happily unite them to the Mother Country, but also highly injurious to the empire at large. We therefore confidently hope that when your Excellency's mind shall have been more particularly applied to this subject, you will be satisfied that it involves the question of supporting or abandoning those important elements of national strength and greatness, " Ships, Colonies and Commerce."

His Excellency thanked them sincerely for their address. "Bred," said he, "a British merchant myself, the good opinion of those who follow the same honourable career is to me naturally and justly dear. You may rely upon my attention to the great interests you represent. Whatever acquaintance with commercial subjects I may have acquired by my early pursuits, or through my later duties, will be earnestly and zealously devoted to the consideration of all that relates to the trade of the Colonies, and with an honest endeavour to promote their prosperity as connected with that of the British Empire."

The Governor General made no stay at Quebec, but proceeded immediately to Montreal, where he convoked his Special Council, and which accordingly met in that city on the 11th November.* We find

---

* It consisted of the following gentlemen :
The Chief Justice, Messrs. Cuthbert, Pothier, De Léry, Moffatt, M'Gill, De Rocheblave, Neilson, Gerraid, Quesnel, Christie, Walker, Molson, Harwood,* Hale, (Sherbrooke,) Wainwright,* Taché, and Hale, (Portneuf.)

Those to whose names a * is added, were appointed to the body since its adjournment in April last.—*Quebec Mercury.*

the following proceedings recorded in the journals of the Special Council :

"His Excellency proposed to the Council for consideration and adoption, the following Ordinances, which were severally read for the first time :—

"An Ordinance to continue for a limited time, a certain Ordinance relative to the seizing and detaining for a limited time, of gunpowder, arms weapons, lead and munitions of war.

"An Ordinance further to continue for a limited time, a certain Ordinance relative to persons charged with high treason, suspicion of high treason, misprision of high treason and treasonable practices.

"An Ordinance to Incorporate the Ecclesiastics of the Seminary of Saint Sulpice of Montreal, to confirm their title to the Fief and Seigniory of the Island of Montreal, the Fief and Seigniory of the Lake of the Two Mountains, and the Fief and Seigniory of *Saint Sulpice,* in this Province; to provide for the gradual extinction of Seigniorial rights and dues, within the Seigniorial limits of the said Fiefs and Seigniories, and for other purposes.

"His Excellency was then pleased to name the Honourable the Chief Justice (Mr. J. Stuart) of the Province, to preside at the Council table, during His Excellency's absence.

"The Governor General called the attention of the Special Council to Her Majesty's gracious message to both Houses of Parliament, of the third May last, relative to the Legislative re-union of the Provinces of Upper and Lower Canada.

"His Excellency explained to the Council the views entertained by Her Majesty's Government upon this subject, and the anxious desire felt by Parliament and the British people, that a settlement of the questions relating to the Canadas should be speedily arrived at, by which an end might be put to the present suspension of the Constitution in the Lower

Province, the resources of both might receive their full development, and the peace and happiness of all Her Majesty's Canadian subjects might be effectually secured.

His Excellency stated that it was with this view that Her Majesty's advisers proposed the re-union of the Provinces to Parliament and were prepared to proceed with that measure.

"Mutual sacrifices were undoubtedly required, mutual concessions would be demanded, but His Excellency entertained no doubt that the terms of union could be adjusted by the Imperial Legislature, with fairness to both Provinces, and with the utmost advantage to all within them.

"His Excellency requested to be favoured with the opinion of the Council on this important subject.

On the day following, (12th November), "According to order, the Council was put into a committee of the whole to take into consideration the communication made yesterday by His Excellency the Governor General, and entered on the journals, in reference to the re-union of the Provinces of Lower and Upper Canada.

"After some time the Council was resumed, and Mr. Hale, of Sherbrooke, reported from the said Committee, " That they had come to several resolutions upon the said communication," which he delivered in at the table.

The resolutions were as follows:

"1. *Resolved*, That under existing circumstances, in order to provide adequately for the peace and tranquillity, and the good, constitutional and efficient Government of the Provinces of Upper and Lower Canada, the re-union of these Provinces under one legislature, in the opinion of this Council, has become of indispensable and urgent necessity.

"2. *Resolved*, That the declared determination of

Her Majesty, conveyed in her gracious message to Parliament, to re-unite the Provinces of Upper and Lower Canada, is in accordance with the opinion entertained by this Council, and receives their humble and ready acquiescence.

"3. *Resolved*, That among the principal enactments, which, in the opinion of this council, ought to make part of the Imperial Act for re-uniting the Provinces, it is expedient and desirable that a suitable civil list should be provided for securing the independence of the judges, and maintaining the executive government in the exercise of its necessary and indispensable functions.

"4. *Resolved*, That regard being had to the nature of the public debt of Upper Canada, and the objects for which principally it was contracted, namely, the improvement of internal communications alike useful and beneficial for both Provinces, it would be just and reasonable in the opinion of this Council, that such part of said debt, as has been contracted for this object, and not for defraying expenses of a local nature, should be chargeable on the revenues of both Provinces.

"5. *Resolved*, That the adjustment and settlement of the terms of the re-union of the two Provinces, may, in the opinion of this Council, with all confidence be submitted to the wisdom and justice of the Imperial Parliament, under the full assurance that provision of the nature of those already mentioned, as well as such others as the measure of re-union may require, will receive due consideration.

"6. *Resolved*, That in the opinion of this Council, it is most expedient, with a view to the security of Her Majesty's North American Provinces, and the speedy cessation of the enormous expense now incurred by the parent state for the defence of Upper and Lower Canada, that the present temporary legislature of this Province should, as soon as practicable, be succeeded by a permanent legislature, in which the people of these two Provinces may be adequately represented, and their constitutional rights exercised and maintained.

The first and second of the above being, on the 13th of November, read, and the question put on each, the divisions were as follows:

Yeas.—The Honble. the Chief Justice, Messrs. Pothier, De Léry, Moffatt, McGill, De Rocheblave, Gerrard, Christie, Walker, Molson, Harwood, Hale of Sherbrooke.

Nays.—Messrs. Cuthbert, Neilson, Quesnel.

So they were carried in the affirmative.

The third of the said resolutions, being again read and the question being put thereon, the Council divided on the same:

Yeas.—The Honble. the Chief Justice, Messrs. Cuthbert, Pothier, De Léry, Moffatt, McGill, De Rocheblave, Gerrard, Quesnel, Christie, Walker, Molson, Harwood, Hale of Sherbrooke.

Nay.—Mr. Neilson.

So it was carried in the affirmative.

The fourth, fifth, and sixth of the said Resolutions being again read, and the question being separately put thereon, the Council divided upon each:

Yeas.—The Honble. the Chief Justice, Messrs. Pothier, De Léry, Moffatt, McGill, De Rocheblave, Gerrard, Christie, Walker, Molson, Harwood, Hale of Sherbrooke.

Nays.—Messrs. Cuthbert, Neilson, Quesnel.

So they were carried in the affirmative.

On motion of the Honble. Mr. Moffatt, seconded by the Honble. Mr. McGill,

Resolved, That an humble address be presented to His Excellency the Governor General, submitting to His Excellency the foregoing resolutions.

Mr. Moffatt moved the next day an address in the following terms:

"To His Excellency, the Right Honorable Charles Poulett Thomson, one of Her Majesty's Most Honorable Privy Council, Governor General of British North America, and Captain General and Governor in Chief in and over the Provinces of Lower Canada and Upper Canada, Nova Scotia, New Brunswick and the Island of Prince Edward, and Vice Admiral of the same.

"MAY IT PLEASE YOUR EXCELLENCY.

"We, Her Majesty's dutiful and loyal subjects, the Special Council for the affairs of Lower Canada, at a meeting convened by your Excellency, under the authority, and in pursuance of the statute in this behalf provided, beg leave respectfully to return to your Excellency our thanks for your considerate care of the interests of this Province, in having called our attention to Her Majesty's gracious message to both Houses of the Imperial Parliament, relative to the re-union of the Provinces of Upper and Lower Canada, upon which important subject your Excellency has been pleased to desire the opinion of the Special Council.

"In conformity with the desire of your Excellency, we have applied our deliberate consideration to the various complex interests and objects involved in the measure of re-uniting the two Provinces, and we most heartily express our humble gratitude to Her Majesty, for having granted her high sanction to a measure which from our local knowledge and the experience we have had of the Government of these Provinces, and of their past and present political state, we deem to be essential to their future peace and welfare, and for the good, constitutional and efficient government of them, under the protecting care and authority of Her Majesty; and the adoption of which we are intimately convinced has become of indispensable and urgent necessity.

In considering the contemplated measure, we have directed our attention to a few of the more prominent and important provisions fit, as we conceive, to be embraced in it, and the views entertained by us on them as well as on the measure itself, we have embodied in certain resolutions, which we have now the honour humbly to submit to your Excellency, as containing our opinion on the important subject, respecting which it has pleased your Excellency to consult us.

The Honble. Mr. Moffatt moved, seconded by Mr. Gerrard,

That the address to His Excellency the Governor General, now submitted, be adopted by this Council.

The Council divided on the motion :

Yeas.—The Honble. the Chief Justice, Messrs. Pothier, De Léry, Moffatt, McGill, De Rocheblave, Gerrard, Christie, Walker, Molson, Austin, Harwood, Hale of Sherbrooke.

Nays.—Messrs. Neilson, Quesnel.

So it was carried in the affirmative, and resolved accordingly.

On motion of the Honble. Mr. Moffatt, seconded by the Honble. Mr. Neilson,

Ordered, That the said address be presented to His Excellency the Governor General, by the whole Council, and that three of its members do wait on His Excellency, humbly to know when His Excellency will be pleased to receive the same.

Ordered, That the Honbles. Messrs. Pothier and Moffatt and Mr. Gerrard, be the said members.

The Council was adjourned during pleasure.

After some time the Council was resumed.

The Honble. Mr. Moffatt reported, " That the Honble. Mr. Pothier, Mr. Gerrard and himself had, according to order, waited on His Excellency the Governor General, humbly to know at what time His Excellency would be pleased to be attended by the whole Council with their address, and that His Excellency had been pleased to say that he would receive the same immediately after the passing of the Ordinances."

The Council was adjourned during pleasure to wait on His Excellency the Governor General with their address.

After some time the Council was resumed.

The presiding member, reported that the Council had presented their address to His Excellency the Governor General, to which His Excellency was pleased to return the following answer:

Gentlemen,

I thank you for the prompt attention you have given to the important subject on which I desired to consult you.

It will afford me great satisfaction to convey to Her Majesty's advisers the opinions which you have recorded, and I can assure you that they will receive from the Imperial Legislature and from the Government, the consideration which is so justly due to them.

My best attention will be devoted to the important suggestions contained in your resolutions, and it will be most gratifying to me to promote the accomplishment of your wishes.

The presiding member then stated, that he had received the command of His Excellency the Governor General to inform the Council, that the affairs for which the Council was convened having been concluded, the present meeting is closed, and the members discharged from further attendance.*

---

* These Ordinances were passed during this short Session of the Special Council, viz:

An Ordinance to continue, for a limited time, a certain Ordinance relative to the seizing and detaining for a limited time of gunpowder, arms, weapons, lead and munitions of war.

An Ordinance further to continue, for a limited time, a certain Ordinance relative to persons charged with high treason, misprison of high treason, and treasonable practices.

Thus was this important matter settled, as far as Lower Canada was concerned, by vote of the Special Council, consisting solely of nominees of the crown, expressing, no doubt, the wishes of the population of British birth and origin in the Province, but the very reverse of those of French descent, who in fact were not consulted on the subject, a course justifiable only by the necesssity which recent events had imposed on the Imperial Government. The Governor General addressed the following letter to Lord John Russell:

"GOVERNMENT HOUSE,
Montreal, Nov. 18, 1839,

"MY LORD.—I have the honour to inform your lordship, that having summoned the Special Council by proclamation, to meet on Monday, the 11th instant, I then submitted to them the question of the re-union of the two Provinces of Upper and Lower Canada, and solicited their opinion respecting it.

"On Thursday, the 14th inst., I received from that body the address, of which, and my answer, I have the honour to enclose copies; and I likewise transmit an extract from the journals, from which your lordship will learn their proceedings.

"I beg your lordship to remark, that the members compo ing the Special Council remain the same as during the administration of my predecessor. It may

---

An Ordinance to incorporate the Ecclesiastics of the Seminary of Saint Sulpice of Montreal, the fief and seigniory of the Lake of the Two Mountains, and the fief and seigniory of Saint Sulpice, in this Province; to provide for the gradual extinction of seigniorial rights and dues, within the seigniorial limits of the said fiefs and seigniories and for other purposes.

☞ The two first are continuations, till June, 1840, of Acts of last session; the Seminary Bill is Cap. L. of last session, with the omission of the sixteenth clause, which sought the authority of the Imperial Parliament to make it permanent—a power not possessed by the Special Council.—*Quebec Gazette.*

be necessary hereafter, in the exercise of my discretion, to make some alterations, with a view to increase the efficiency of that body; but I felt that, as the opinions of Her Majesty's Government in regard to the union are well known, it was extremely desirable that I should if possible, submit the consideration of that important question to a council in whose selection I had myself had no voice.

"It appeared to me that to secure the due weight in the Mother Country to the judgment of a body so constituted, it was indispensable to avoid even the possibility of an imputation that I had selected for its members those only whose opinions coincided with my own.

"I had moreover every reason to believe, from the motives which guided my predecessor in his choice that the Council contains a very fair representation of the state of feeling in the different districts of the Province.

"For these reasons I determed on making no alteration whatever; and it is with great satisfaction that I can now refer to the opinions of this body, adopted almost unanimously. Their views as to the urgency of the union and the advantages likely to result from it to the Province, are set forth in their address in terms so forcible, as to leave me nothing to say with reference to their opinion. But I must add, that it is my decided conviction, grounded upon such other opportunities as I have enjoyed since my arrival in this country, of ascertaining the state of public feeling, that the speedy adoption of that measure by Parliament is indispensable to the future peace and prosperity of this Province.

"All parties look with extreme dissatisfaction at the present state of Government. Those of British origin, attached by feeling and education to a constitutional form of government, although they acquiesced at the time in the establishment of arbitrary power, as a refuge from a yet worse despotism, submit with impatience to its continuance, and regret the loss, through no fault of their own, of what they consider as their birthright. Those of the French Canadians who remained loyal to their Sovereign and true to the British connexion, share the same feelings; whilst among those who are less well affected or more easily deceived, the suspension of all constitutional rights affords to reckless and unprincipled agitators a constant topic of excitement.

"All parties therefore, without exception, demand a change; on the nature of that change, there undoubtedly exists some difference of opinion.

"In a country so lately convulsed, and where passions are still so much excited, extreme opinions cannot but exist; and accordingly, while some persons advocate an immediate return to the former Constitution of the Province, others propose either the entire exclusion from political privileges of all of French origin, or the partial dismemberment of the Province, with the view of conferring on one portion a representative system, while maintaining in the other a despotism.

"I have observed, however that, the advocates of these widely different opinions have generally admitted them to be their aspirations, rather than measures which could practicably be adopted, and have been unable to suggest any course except the union by which that at which they aim, namely, constitutional government for themselves, could be permanently and safely established.

"There exists, too, even amongst these persons, a strong and prevailing desire that the Imperial Legislature should take the settlement of Canadian affairs at once into its own hands, rather than that it should be delayed by reference to individual opinions, or to be put forward by different sections of local parties.

"The large majority, however, of those whose

opinions I have had the opportunity of learning, both of the British and French origin, and of those, too, whose character and station entitle them to the greatest authority, advocate warmly the establishment of the union, and that upon terms of perfect fairness, not merely to the two Provinces, but to the two races within these Provinces. Of the extent to which this feeling with regard to the Upper Province is carried, your lordship will find a most conclusive proof in the resolution of the Special Council respecting the debt of Lower Canada. By this resolution a large sum, owing by that Province on account of public works of a general nature, is proposed to be charged on the joint revenues of the United Province. Upon other details of the arrangement, the same feeling prevails. It would be, however, useless for me to trouble your lordship with respect to them, until I have had the opinions entertained by the people of Upper Canada. If, however, as I trust, the principle of re-union should meet with their assent, I am of opinion that it can only be in consequence of demands of an unwarrantable character upon their part, that difficulty will arise in settling the principal terms. I have, &c.

C. POULETT THOMSON.

His Excellency having thus accomplished his purpose, in so far as Lower Canada was concerned, immediately posted for the Upper Province to meet also the legislature there. He received on his way to Toronto at all the principal p'aces the most complimentary and encouraging addresses. On his departure, Sir Richard Downes Jackson, as the senior officer commanding the forces, assumed the Government of Lower Canada, issuing his proclamation, dated at Montreal, 18th November, to that effect. The Governor General reached Toronto on the 21st, and superseding temporarily Sir George

Arthur, the Lieutenant Governor, assumed the Government on the 22nd November. His installation is thus noticed in a paper of that city:

"This day at 12 o'clock, His Excellency the Governor General proceeded in state to the Executive Council Chamber, accompanied by the Lieutenant Governor, and attended by the officers of His Excellency's staff. His Excel ency was received by a guard of honour of the 32nd Regt., with the customary formalities. In the Council Chamber the members of the Council—the lord bishop—the vice chancellor and judges—the crown officers—the mayor and corporation—the college of physicians and surgeons—the principal of U. C. College, and the Heads of Departments generally were waiting for His Excellency's arrival. His Excellency having taken his seat, his Commission of Governor General was read by the Provincial Secretary, the Honorable Mr. Tucker, after which the oaths were administered to His Excellency by the President of the Council, the Hon. Mr. Sullivan, at the conclusion of which ceremony, a salute of 21 guns was fired from the Royal Artillery stationed in front of the public buildings—His Excellency the Governor General then administered the oaths to the members of the Executive Council—and finally, the Lieutenant Governer placed in the Governor's hands the public seal of the Province—His Excellency having been introduced to the public functionaries assembled, the ceremonies were concluded.

"This business having been dismissed, His Excellency the Governor General received the mayor and corporation, who presented him with an address, which, with His Excellency's reply, we give below.

"We, Her Majesty's loyal subjects, the mayor, aldermen, and commonalty of the city of Toronto, influenced by the respect due to the representative of our gracious Sovereign, beg leave to congratulate your Excellency on your arrival in this city.

"Amidst the doubts and incertitude which the frequent changes of Governors and Lieutenant Governors of these Provinces, and of the policy of the Imperial Government with regard to them, have created in the minds of the loyal and well-affected inhabitants, we would fain hail the arrival of your Excellency as the advent of a more certain, permanent and prosperous condition of our commercial, social and political relations, which will restore prosperity to the commerce and agriculture of the Province—give a new impulse to internal improvements, and encourage the emigration of our loyal fellow subjects from the mother country to this important appendage to the British crown.

"Having understood that one of the principal objects of your Excellency's visit to this Province, and of your assuming the government thereof, is to ascertain the state of public opinion upon the question of the proposed legislative union of the Provinces of Lower and Upper Canada, we beg respectfully to express our conviction, that any legislative union which shall not be predicated upon the ascendency of the loyal part of the inhabitants, or which shall give to that portion of the population who, from education, habits and prejudices are aliens to our nation and to our institutions, and to that part of it more particularly which has been engaged in open rebellion or treasonable conspiracy against the Government, the same rights and privileges, with the loyal British population of the Provinces who have adhered so zealously and faithfully at the risk of their lives and property, to their Sovereign and constitution, would be fatal to the connexion of these Provinces with the parent country.

"Faithful in our allegiance to our Sovereign, and calmly but earnestly determined as far as depends upon us, the highest municipal body in the Province, to perpetuate the connexion with the parent state, your Excellency may confidently rely on our cordial support in whatever measure you may think it advisable to adopt tending to uphold the cherished constitution under which we live, and which we are firmly resolved to the ntmost of our power to preserve inviolate and unchanged.

"JOHN POWELL, Mayor.
Council Chamber, Nov. 18, 1839."

His Excellency's Reply.

"Gentlemen,—I thank you for your congratulations on my arrival in this Province.

"I trust that the information which I shall acquire during my stay here may enable me to recommend such measures as may promote the agricultural and commerical interests of this important Province: among these measures the re-union of Upper and Lower Canada appears to me the most essential, and you have been rightly informed that one principal object of my mission is to determine in what manner it can most safely and most advantageously be carried into effect; that measure is recommended by Her Majesty's government from a deep conviction that it will cement the connexion between the colonies and the parent state, which it is the firm determination of Her Majesty to maintain inviolate, but to be of permanent advantage, it must be founded upon principles of equal justice to all Her Majesty's subjects.

"For this, and for all other measures having in view the advantage of these Provinces, I shall confidently rely upon the support and co-operation of the people of Upper Canada."

The legislature of Upper Canada met at Toronto on the 3rd December, and the Governor General opened the session with the speech following:

"*Honourab'e Gentlemen of the Legislative Council, and
Gentlemen of the House of Assembly:*

"In discharge of the duties of Governor General of

British North America, confided to me by our Gracious Sovereign, I have deemed it advisable to take the earliest opportunity of visiting this Province, and of assembling Parliament.

"I am commanded by the Queen to assure you of Her Majesty's fixed determination to maintain the connexion now subsisting between Her North American Possessions and the United Kingdom, and to exercise the high authority with which she has been invested, by the favour of Divine Providence, for the promotion of their happiness, and the security of her dominions.

"It is with great satisfaction I can inform you, that I have no grounds for apprehending a recurrence of those aggressions upon our frontier which we had lately to deplore, and which affix an indelible disgrace on their authors.

"If, however, unforeseen circumstances should again call for exertion, I know from the past, that in the zeal and loyalty of the people of Upper Canada, and in the protection of the parent state, we possess ample means of defence, and to those I should confidently appeal.

"I earnestly hope, that this state of tranquillity will prove favourable to the consideration of the important matters to which your attention must be called during the present Session.

"It will be my duty to bring under your consideration, at the earliest possible moment, the subject of the legislative re-union of this Province with Lower Canada—recommended by Her Majesty to the Imperial Parliament. I shall do so in the full confidence that you will see, in the measure which I shall have to submit, a fresh proof of the deep interest felt by the Queen, in the welfare of Her subjects in Upper Canada; and that it will receive from you that calm and deliberate consideration, which its importance demands.

"The condition of the public departments in the

Province, will require your best attention. In compliance with the address of the House of Assembly of last session, the Lieutenant Governor appointed a commission to investigate and report upon the manner in which the duties of those departments are performed. The commissioners have already conducted their enquiries to an advanced stage; and the result of them will be communicated to you as soon as they shall be completed.

"I am happy to inform you that Her Majesty's Government have concluded an arrangement for opening a communication by steam between Great Britain and the British possessions in North America. In the completion of this arrangement, Her Majesty's Government have allowed no consideration to interfere with the paramount object of conducing to the public advantage and convenience. I feel confident that the liberality with which the parent state has assumed the whole expense of the undertaking will be duly appreciated by you.

"The answers of Her Majesty to various addresses, adopted by you during your last session, and Her Majesty's decisions on the bills passed by you but reserved for the signification of her royal pleasure, will be made known to you without loss of time.

"*Gent'emen of the House of Assemb'y.*

"The financial condition of the Province will claim your early and most attentive consideration. To preserve public credit is at all times a sacred obligation; but in a country so essentially dependent upon it for the means of future improvement, it is a matter no less of policy than of duty. It is indispensable, then, that measures should be at once adopted, for enabling the provincial revenue to fulfil its obligations, and to defray the necessary expenses of the Government. It will be my anxious desire to co-operate with you in effecting this object; and I feel confident that, by the adoption of measures calculated to promote the full development of the resources of this fine country, the difficulty may be overcome. The officer by whom, under your authority, these obligations have been contracted, will be able to afford you every information ; and I shall direct a statement of your financial condition to be immediately submitted to you.

" The estimates for the ensuing year will be prepared with every regard to economy, compatible with the due execution of the service of the Province.

" It is with great satisfaction I find, that notwithstanding commercial difficulties which prevail in the neighbouring States, the banks of this Province have resumed specie payments; and I congratulate you upon the guarantee thus afforded of the greater security and stability of our pecuniary transactions—a circumstance which cannot fail to be attended with the most beneficial results.

" I am commanded again to submit to you the surrender of the casual and territorial revenues of the crown, in exchange for a civil list; and I shall take an early opportunity of explaining the grounds on which Her Majesty's Government felt precluded from assenting to the settlement, which you lately proposed. They are of a nature which lead me to anticipate your ready assent to their removal, and to the final settlement of the question.

" *Honourable Gentlemen and Gentlemen.*

" In assuming the administration of the Government of these Provinces, at the present time, I have not disguised from myself the arduous task which I have undertaken. The affairs of the Canadas have, for some years back, occupied much of the attention of the Imperial Parliament, and of the Government; and their settlement upon a firm and comprehensive basis, admits of no other delay.

" To effect that settlement, upon terms satisfactor to the people of these Provinces, and affording so curity for their continued connexion with the British Empire, will be my endeavour; and I confidently appeal to your wisdom and to the loyalty and good sense of the people of this Province, to co-operate with me for the preparation and adoption of such measures as may, under Divine Providence, restore to this country, peace, concord and prosperity."

The Governor General's speech was well received in Upper Canada, and favorably responded to by the Assembly which had already pledged itself to the proposed union, indeed solicited it. A day or two after the opening of the session, an important circular despatch from Lord John Russell, the Colonial Minister, to the Lieutenant Governor of Upper Canada, relating to the tenure of office in the Province, appeared in the *Upper Canada Gazette.* It appeared by the public prints that the Lieutenant Governors of the Lower Provinces (Nova Scotia and New Brunswick), had also received similar circulars.*

---

* DOWNING STREET, 16*th October*, 1839.

"SIR.—I am desirous of directing your attention to the tenure on which public offices, in the gift of the crown, appear to be held throughout the British Colonies. I find that the Governor himself, and every person serving under him, are appointed during the royal pleasure, but with this important difference,—the Governor's commission is in fact revoked whenever the interest of the public service are supposed to require such a change in the administration of local affairs,—but the commissions of all other officers are very rarely indeed recalled, except for positive misconduct. I cannot learn that during the present, or the two last reigns, a sing'e instance has occurred of change in the subordinate colonial officers, except in case of death or resignation, incapacity or misconduct. This system of converting a tenure at pleasure, into a tenure for life, originated probably in the practice which formerly prevailed, of selecting all the higher class of colonial functionaries from persons who at the time of their appointment were resident in this country, and amongst other motives which afforded such persons a virtual security for the continued possession of their places, it was not the least considerable that, except on these terms they were unwilling to incur the risk and expense of transferring

It had the effect of reconciling to the union some of the officials seated in the Assembly, who otherwise, it was believed, wou'd have opposed the measure.

The following message was transmitted on the 7th of December by the Governor General to the Assembly, a similar one being in like manner sent to the Legislative Council :

---

their residence to remote and often to unhealthy climates. But the habit which has obtained of late years of preferring as far as possible, for all places of trust in the colonies persons resident there, has taken away the strongest motive which could thus be alleged in favour of a practice to which there are many objections of the greatest weight. It is time, therefore, that a different course should be followed; and the object of my present communication is to announce to you the rules which will be hereafter observed on this subject, in the Province of Upper Canada.

" You wil understand, and will cause it to be generally known, that hereafter the tenure of colonial offices, held during Her Majesty's pleasure, will not be regarded as equivalent to a tenure during good behaviour; but that not only such officers will be called upon to retire from the public service, as often as any sufficient motives of public policy may suggest the expediency of that measure, but that a change in the person of the Governor will be considered as a sufficient reason for any alterations which his successor may deem it expedient to make in the list of public functionaries--subject, of course, to the future confirmation of the sovereign.

" These remarks do not extend to judicial officers, nor are they meant to apply to places which are altogether ministerial, and which do not devolve upon the holders of them duties, in the right discharge of which the character and policy of the government are directly involved. They are intended to apply rather to the heads of departments than to persons serving as clerks or in similiar capacities under them ; neither do they extend to officers in the service of the Lords Commissioners of the Treasury. The functionaries who will be chiefly, though not exclusively affected by them, are the Colonial Secretary ; the Treasurer, or Receiver General ; the Surveyor General ; the Attorney and Solicitor General ; the Sheriff, or Provost Marshall ; and other officers who, under different designations from these, are entrusted with the same or similar duties. To this list must also be added the members of the Council, especially in those colonies in which the Legislative and Executive Councils are distinct bodies.

"In pursuance of the intention expressed in his speech from the throne, the Governor General desires now to bring under the consideration of the House of Assembly, the subject of the re-union of this Province with Lower Canada, recommended by Her Majesty in her gracious message to both Houses of Parliament on the third of May last.

" For several years the condition of the Canadas has occupied a large portion of the attention of Parliament. That they should be contented and prosperous—that the ties which bind them to the parent state should be strengthened—that their administration should be conducted in accordance with the wishes of the people, is the ardent desire of every British statesman—and the experience of the last few years amply testifies that the Imperial Parliament has been sparing neither of the time it has devoted to the investigation of their affairs, nor of the expenditure it has sanctioned for their protection.

" The events which have marked the recent history of Lower Canada, are so familiar to the House of Assembly, that it is unnecessary for the Governor General further to allude to them. There, the constitution is suspended, but the powers of the Government are inadequate to permit of the enactment of such

---

" The application of those rules to officers to be hereafter appointed, will be attended with no practical difficulty. It may not be equally easy to enforce them in the case of existing officers, and specially of those who may have left this country for the express purpose of accepting the offices they at present fill. Every reasonable indulgence must be shown for the expectations which such persons have been encouraged to form. But even in these instances, it will be necessary that the right of enforcing these regulations should be distinctly maintained in practice as well as in theory, as often as the public good may clearly demand the enforcement of them. It may not be unadvisable to compensate any such officers for their disappointment, even by pecuniary grants, when it may appear unjust to dispense with their services without such an indemnity. I have, &c.,

(Signed,)   JOHN RUSSELL.

permanent laws as are required for the benefit of the people.

"Within this Province the finances are deranged—public improvements are suspended—private enterprise is checked—the tide of emigration so essential to the prosperity of the country and to the British connexion, has ceased to flow—while by many, the general system of Government is declared to be unsatisfactory.

"After the most attentive and anxious considerations of the state of these Provinces, and the difficulties under which they respectively labour, Her Majesty's advisers came to the conclusion, that by their re-union alone could those difficulties be removed. During the last session of the Imperial Legislature they indeed refrained from pressing immediate legislation, but their hesitation proceeded from no doubt as to the measure or its necessity. It arose solely to ascertain more fully the opinions of the Legislature of Upper Canada, and to collect information from which the details might be rendered more satisfactory to the people of both Provinces.

"The time then is now arrived beyond which a settlement cannot be postponed. In Lower Canada it is indispensable to afford a safe and practicable return to a constitutional government, and so far as the feelings of the inhabitants can be there ascertained, the measure of the re-union meets with approbation.

"In Upper Canada it is no less necessary, to enable the Province to meet her financial embarrassments, and to proceed in the development of her natural resources. There are evidently no means in this Province of fulfilling the pecuniary obligations which have been contracted, but by a great increase in the local revenues. But so long as Lower Canada remains under her present form of Government, neither Province possesses any power over the only source from which that increase can be drawn. Nor even, were it possible to restore a representative constitution to Lower Canada, unaccompanied by the union, would the position of this Province be much improved; since past experience has shown the difficulty of procuring assent to any alteration of the customs laws suggested from hence.

" This Province has engaged in undertakings, which reflect the highest honour on the enterprise and industry of her inhabitants. The public works which she has completed or commenced, have been conceived in a spirit worthy of a successful result. But additional means are indispensable to avert the ruin of some, and secure the completion of others. Nor will that alone suffice; Lower Canada holds the key to all those improvements. Without her co-operation, the navigation for which nature has done so much and for which this Province has so deeply burthened itself, must remain incomplete, and a barrier be opposed to the development of those great natural resources which the hand of Providence has so lavishly bestowed on this country.

" With a view to remove all those difficulties: to relieve the financial embarrassments of Upper Canada: to enable her to complete her public works and develop her agricultural capabilities: to restore constitutional government to Lower Canada: to establish a firm, impartial, and vigourous government for both: and to unite the people within them in one common feeling of attachment to British institutions and British connexion, the union is desired by Her Majesty's Government; and that measure alone, if based upon just principles, appears adequate to the occasion.

" Those principles, in the opinion of Her Majesty's advisers, are, a just regard to the claims of either Province in adjusting the terms of the union—the maintenance of the three estates of the Provincial Legislature;—the settlement of a permanent civil list for securing the independence of the judges and to the executive government that freedom of action which is necessary for the public good, and the establishment of a system of local government adapted to the wants of the people.

"It was with great satisfaction then that Her Majesty's Government learnt, that upon the question of the union itself the House of Assembly had pronounced their decided judgment during their last session; and it will only remain for the Governor General now to invite their assent to the terms upon which it is sought to be effected. Their decision was indeed accompanied by recommendation to which the government could not agree; but the Governor General entertains no doubt that, under the altered circumstances, they will no more be renewed. It will be for the Imperial Parliament, guided by their intimate knowledge of constitutional law, and, free from the bias of local feelings and interests, to arrange the details of the measure.

"The first of the terms of re-union, to which the Governor General desires the assent of the House of Assembly, is equal representation of each Province in the united legislature. Considering the amount of the population of Lower Canada, this proposition might seem to place that Province in a less favourable position than Upper Canada; but, under the circumstances in which this Province is placed, with the increasing population to be expected, from immigration, and having regard to the commercial and agricultural enterprise of its inhabitants, an equal apportionment of representation appears desirable.

"The second stipulation to be made is the grant of a sufficient civil list. The propriety of rendering the judicial bench independent alike of the Executive and the Legislature, and of the furnishing the means of carrying on the indispensable services of the government, admits of no question, and has been affirmed by the Parliament of Upper Canada in the acts passed by them for effecting those objects. In determining the amount of the civil list, the House of Assembly may be assured that the salaries and expenses to be paid from it will be calculated by Her Majesty's Government with a strict regard to economy and the state of the provincial finances.

"Thirdly, the Governor General is prepared to recommend to Parliament, that so much of the existing debt of Upper Canada, as has been contracted for public works of a general nature, should, after the union, be charged on the joint revenue of the United Province. Adverting to the nature of the works for which this debt was contracted, and the advantage which must result from them to Lower Canada, it is not unjust that that Province should bear a proportion of their expenses.

"On these principles, the Governor General is of opinion that a re-union of the two Provinces may be effected—equitable and satisfactory in its terms, and beneficial in its results to all classes. He submits them to the consideration of the House of Assembly, in the full conviction of their importance, and in the hope that they will receive the assent of that House. Fortified by the expression of their opinion, Her Majesty's Government and Parliament will be able at once to apply themselves to the full development of the scheme, and to the consideration of the provisions by which it may be carried into effect with the greatest advantage to the people of both Provinces.

"If in the course of their proceedings, the House of Assembly should desire any information which it is in the power of the Governor General to afford, they will find him ready and anxious to communicate with them frankly and fully, and to aid, by all the means in his power, that settlement on which he firmly believes that the future prosperity and advancement of these Colonies mainly depend."

The following resolutions on the subject were carried in the Legislative Council by a large majority:

"*Resolved*, 1—That the events which have lately marked the history of Lower Canada—the consequent necessity for a suspension of her constitution, and the inadequacy of the powers of Government existing there, for the enactment of permanent laws, such as are required for the benefit of the people, present a state of public affairs in the sister Province, deeply to be deplored by this house, as well from a disinterested anxiety for the welfare of a people so nearly connected with Upper Canada, as in consideration of the injurious consequences resulting to this community, from a continuance of the unsettled political condition of the Lower Province.

"*Resolved*, 2—That the present derangement of the finances of Upper Canada—the total suspension of her public improvements—the paralyzed condition of private enterprise—the cessation of immigration, and the apparent impossibility of the removal of these evils, without the united efforts of both the Canadian Provinces—make the adoption of some great measure necessary, which will restore prosperity to the Canadas, and renew confidence at home and abroad in the stability of their political institutions.

"*Resolved*, 3—That considering the hopelessness arising from past experience, and from a view of the political condition of Lower Canada, of ever realizing, in separate legislatures, the unity of feeling or action in measures effecting equally the interests of both provinces, on which the prosperity or safety of either may essentially depend, a re-union of the Provinces of Upper and Lower Canada has, in the opinion of this house, become indispensable for the restoration of good government within these colonies, and for the preservation of their institutions in connexion with the parent state.

" *Resolved*, 4—That for these urgent reasons, the assent of this house be expressed to the enactment of the important measure of re-union of the Provinces of Upper and Lower Canada, recommended by Her Majesty to both Houses of Parliament, and to the houses of the Provimcial Legislature by His Excellency the Governor General ; and that such assent, on the part of this house, be given on the following terms :

First—That there be an equal representation of each Province in the United Legislature.

Secondly—That a sufficient permanent civil list be granted to Her Majesty, to enable Her Majesty to render the judicial bench independent alike of executive power and popular influence, and to carry on the indispensable services of government.

Thirdly—That the public debt of this Province, contracted for public works of a general nature, shall, after the union, be charged on the joint revenue of the united Province.

" *Resolved*, 5—That in yielding this ready concurrence to the measure of the re-union of the provinces, strongly recommended by Her Majesty, the Legislative Council of Upper Canada rely upon the wisdom and justice of their most gracious Sovereign, and of Her Majesty's Parliament, for devising the details of the plan of re-union, and for the establishment of such a system of Government in the united Province, as will tend to the development of its natural resources, and enable it, with the blessing of Divine Providence, to pursue steadily, and free from distractions by which the country has lately been divided, the course of prosperity and happiness, which the best interests of the people of Canada, and of the empire, alike require not to be longer impeded."

An address in conformity with these was presented to His Excellency by the Legislative Council.

An address having been sent by the Assembly to the Governor General, shortly after the transmission of his message relating to the union, requesting to be informed whether His Excellency was possessed of any information that he could communicate to the house relative to the terms of the measure intended to be proposed to the Imperial Parliament for the reunion of the Canadas, he sent down (14th January 1840) the following answer:

"In answer to the Address of the House of Assembly of the 11th instant, the Governor General has to state, that by his message to both Houses of the Provincial Legislature, he has already explained the principles upon which Her Majesty's Government desire to effect the reunion of the Province with Lower Canada, and the terms upon which it can, it his opinion, be established.

"In accordance with the wish of the House of Asembly, the Governor General transmits a copy of the bill introduced into Parliament last session by Her Majesty's Government, and which was afterwards withdrawn; but he must, at the same time, state to the House of Assembly, that as one of the Principal objects of his mission was to procure information upon which to enable Her Majesty's Government to submit a new measure to Parliament better calculated to effect the object of good government in these Provinces, this bill cannot be considered as embodying the provisions which may hereafter be adopted.

"It will be the duty of the Governor General, acting upon the information he shall have acquired, to make many important suggestions for that purpose, in conformity to the principles and terms laid down in his message, and he is already prepared to state, that it is his intention to recommend to Her Majesty's Government, in the new measure which must be introduced, to adhere as much as possible to existing territorial divisions for electoral purposes, and to maintain the principle of the Constitutional Act of 1791, with regard to the tenure of seats in the Legislative Council.

"If as the Governor General confidently hopes, the House of Assembly should think proper to assent to the terms proposed by him in his message, and should hereafter offer any recommendations upon matters connected with the measure, it will be his duty to transmit them for the consideration of the Government and the Imperial Parliament; and he begs to assure the House of Assembly that they will receive the most respectful attention."

The House of Assembly having in committee of the whole taken into consideration the subject, adopted the following resolutions:

"Resolved,—That the House of Assembly, at its last session, declared that, in their opinion, a United Legislature for the Canadas, on certain terms, was indispensable,. and that further delay must prove ruinous to their best interests, and that His Excellency the Governor General, by his message to this house, has announced, that with a view to remove the difficulties of these Provinces, to relieve the financial embarrassments of Upper Canada, to enable her to complete her public works, and develop her agricultural capabilities, to restore constitutional government to Lower Canada, to establish a firm, impartial, and vigorous government for both, and to unite the people within them in one common feeling of attachment to British institutions and British connexion; the legislative union of Upper and Lower Canada has been recommended by Her Majesty to the Imperial Parliament; and His Excellency the Governor General has invited the assent of this house to certain specified terms, upon which the union may be established. It, therefore, becomes the duty of the representatives of the people of this Province carefully to consider the provisions by which this measure may be carried into effect, with the greatest security to their future peace, welfare, and good government, and the permanent connexion of these Colonies with the British empire.

Yeas, 47 : Nays, 6 :

"*Resolved*,—That this house concur in the proposition that there be an equal representation of each province in the United Legislature.

Yeas, 33 : Nays, 20 :

"*Resolved*,—That this house concur in the proposition, that a sufficient civil list be granted to Her Majesty, for securing the independence of the judges' and to the Executive Government that freedom of action which is necessary for the public good. The grant for the person administering the Government, and for the Judges of the several Superior Courts to be permanent, and for the officers conducting the other departments of the public service, to be for the life. of the sovereign, and for a period of not less than ten years.

Yeas, 43 : Nays, 8 :

"*Resolved*,—That the public debt of this Province shall after the union, be charged on the joint revenue of the United Province. Unanimous.

An address to Her Majesty in accordance with these was voted, and transmitted through the Governor General in the following terms :

MOST GRACIOUS SOVEREIGN :

" We your Majesty's most dutiful and loyal subjects the Commons of Upper Canada, in Provincial Parliament assembled, beg permission to approach your Majesty with renewed expression of our unwavering attachment to your Majesty's royal person and government.

" During the present session of your Provincial Parliament, a subject more important than any that has ever engaged the attention of the representatives of the people, has been brought under their consideration in pursuance of the commands of your Majesty, by your Majesty's Governor General of these Provinces, namely, the legislative re-union of Upper and Lower Canada. In the message of His Excellency to the two branches of the legislature, they are informed that "after the most attentive and anxious consideration of the state of these Provinces, and of the difficulties under which they respectively labour, your Majesty's advisers came to the conclusion that by their re-union alone could these difficulties be removed: that during the last session of the Imperial Legislature they refrained from pressing immediate legislation, but their hesitation proceeded from no doubt as to the principle of the measure, or its necessity; it arose solely from the desire to ascertain more fully the opinions of the legislature of Upper Canada, and to collect information from which the details might be rendered more satisfactory to the people of both Provinces."

"The House of Assembly deeply feel this additional proof of your Majesty's solicitude for their happiness and prosperity; and it will ever be held by them in grateful remembrance.

"In pursuance of the message referred to, the House of Assembly lost no time in taking into consideration three distinct propositions submitted by your Majesty's Governor General as the basis on which the re-union might be established, namely: First—equal representation of each Province in the United Legislature:—Secondly—the grant of a sufficient civil list;—and thirdly—that the public debt of this Province be charged on the joint revenue of the United Province.

"In the discussion of these propositions, it happened that some of the members of this house apprehending the greatest danger to our civil and political institutions, and even to our connexion with the parent state, were opposed to the union on any terms, while of those who supported the measure, there were many who were not wholly free from apprehensions as to the result, and who regarded it as a hazardous experiment, unless in addition to terms submitted by the Governor General, certain details calculated to secure their connexion with the Imperial crown, should accompany their concurrence with the terms proposed A majority, however, gave their unconditional assent to the propositions above mentioned, in the fullest confidence, that your Majesty, in calling the attention of the Imperial Parliament to the union, would at the same time recommend the adoption of every necessary safeguard to the maintenance of British interests and British supremacy. It is in this confidence that we now humbly submit to your Majesty's most gracious consideration the following propositions, which in the opinion of this house, are calculated to secure the great end, in expectation whereof the assent to the union was given:

"And first, we respectfully entreat your Majesty, that the use of the English language in all judicial and legislative records be forthwith introduced; and that at the end of a space of a given number of years, after the union, all debates in the Legislature shall be in English. And as a matter of justice to your Majesty's subjects in Upper Canada, we earnestly and confidently appeal to your Majesty, to admit their right to have the seat of the Provincial Government established within this Province. It cannot be denied to the people of this Colony, that if favour is to be shewn to either Upper or Lower Canada. their claim stands pre-eminent; independent of which, the moral and political advantages of the concession are too obvious and undeniable to admit of dispute.

"It is with the most sincere satisfaction that this house has received from your Majesty's representative the assurance that the bill introduced into the House of Commons during the last session of the Imperial Legislature, is not to be " considered as embodying the provisions which may hereafter be adopted by the Imperial Parliament." And, " that it is His Excellency's intention to recommend to Her Majesty's Government, in the new measure that must be introduced, to adhere as much as possible to existing territorial divisions for electoral purposes, and to maintain the principle of the constitutional act ot 1791, with regard to the tenure of seats in the Legislative Council."

" We would further respectfully submit the necessity of providing that the members of the legislature should possess a stake in the country equal to that now required by the laws of this Province, that, to the call of public duty, that of private interest may be added, as an inducement to wise and careful legislation ; and for this purpose we trust that a sufficient qualification in real estate will be required from any person holding a seat in the legislature.

" We would also respectfully suggest to your Majesty the paramount subject of emigration from the British isles, which we consider the best calculated to render the United Province British in fact as well as in name. No time, in our humble opinion, should be lost, in the establishment and vigorons prosecution of a well organized system of emigration, calculated to afford every possible facility to the settlement of that extensive domain, the proceeds of which have been proposed to be surrendered to the control of the Provincial Legislature, upon certain terms and conditions, which in Upper and Lower Canada is at present in right of the crown, at your Majesty's disposal.

" We have no desire to interfere unnecessarily in questions of detail, which more immediately affect the sister Province ; but we cannot omit respectfully soliciting your Majesty's attention to the introduction of a system of municipal government into Lower Canada, in order to provide for local taxation, and under local management, on the same principles as have obtained in Upper Canada, where the system established by the Provincial Legislature, after repeated and careful revision, has in its operation proved highly satisfactory to the people.

"We would, lastly, desire humbly to assure your Majesty, that to the principles on which our constitution has been established, to the representative mode of government under a monarchy, and to a permanent connexion with the British empire, and a dutiful allegiance to our Sovereign, the people of Upper Canada most faithfully and firmly adhere.

"It is only from apprehensions of danger on these most important matters, that doubt or difficulty has been felt in assenting to the union; and we therefore now humbly trust that your Majesty, fully acquainted with our situation, will not confine your royal consideration to the claims that are referred to in this address, or in any other proceeding of this house, but that continuing to us that gracious and generous protection we have hitherto experienced from your Majesty and the British nation, your Majesty will add such future safeguards as in your wisdom may be thought necessary and desirable to protect your faithful subjects in the peaceful enjoyment of their laws and liberties, and to perpetuate their connexion with your Majesty's crown and empire.

ALLAN N. MACNAB, *Speaker.*

13th January, 1840.

In the report of the debates which took place in the Assembly on the passage of the four resolutions quoted above, the following occurs:

"Mr. Sherwood, in a speech of great force and eloquence, contended that Upper Canada was intitled to the numerical preponderance in the new legislature, and gave notice that he would move an amendment to the resolution of the last session, which limits the number of members to be elected for Lower Canada to fifty and leave the representation of this Province as it is, by which a preponderance of about fifteen members would be secured.

Mr. Sherwood accordingly moved in amendment to the proposition, " that there be an equal representation of each Province in the united legislature" —that the whole, be expunged, and the following substituted:—" That this house cannot concur in the proposition that there be an equal representation of each province, but are of opinion that the number of members to be returned to serve in the House of Assembly of the united legislature be as follows· From Lower Canada, fifty members; from Upper Canada, as at present." On division this was lost —yeas 19, nays 36. The Attorney General Hagerman next explained his views on the subject: He stated that he was aware that the report had been industriously circulated, that if any officer of the Government, who had opposed the union of the Provinces formerly, should continue their opposition now, that it was what was termed a Government measure, he would be dismissed, and that he must choose between abandonment of principle and loss of office—he took occasion to say, and he was happy to have it in his power to declare, that ao such degrading proposition had been made to him, and that he wholly denied that any such scheme of coercion had been contemplated,—that in all the communications he had with the Governor General he had plainly stated his own opinions, and he had been met with a frankness of communication on the part of His Excellency, for which he could not be too thankful, and that he took the opportunity now, as he had done on various occasions, public and private, to declare that the system of Government which His Excellency had stated it to be his determination to carry out, was in the highest degree satisfactory, and such as to entitle him to the confidence of the house, and of the people of the Province generally.

"The Attorney General then stated that his opinions with respect to the Union, remained unchanged—that he was as much opposed to it now as he had ever been—and that he was as ready to vote in opposition to the measure now as he was last year; but that if the resolution in favour of the Union was persisted in, its friends must not calculate on his endeavouring, under present circumstances, to evade it by concurrence in any unjust or unreasonable condition. Whatever might have been his disposition on a former occasion, it was impossible for him now, that the measure was brought under the notice of the Legislature, by *command of the Sovereign*, to meet it otherwise than in a plain straight-forward and intelligible manner,—the question must be met by a direct affirmative or negative—if in the affirmative, then unaccompanied by matter inadmissible. The latter course might be justified by parliamentary tactics, so long as the discussion arose voluntarily within the House; but not so when brought under their notice by command of the Sovereign. He intimated that an equality of members for each province was as much as could be expected, and as much as, upon view of the population and condition of the respective Provinces, we had a right to claim. That the pretensions set forth in the resolution of last year were inadmissible, and amounted to a virtual rejection of the proposed Union, and in that light he was well aware several members regarded them, and on that account voted for them. He stated that the propositions contained in the Message were such as were fair and reasonable in themselves, and as favourable as could be expected for Upper Canada, and that if the vote in favour of the Union was persisted in, he would vote for them, adding, however, such stipulations with respect to the place of the Seat of Government, language to be used in the Legislature, and, above all, for a continuance of the Constitution as it at present existed, as he was convinced the Legislature would feel it their duty to contend for.

On motion of the Solicitor General, Mr Draper, that an humble address be presented to the Governor General, transmitting to His Excellency the resolutions of the House, on the subject of an union, it was moved in amendment by Mr. Cartwright :

" *Resolved*,—That this House having thus far concurred in the proposition of Her Majesty's Government, are bound, by a sense of justice and duty to their constituents and the Province at large, to declare further, what provisions they consider as essentially necessary to obtain from the Union those results which can alone justify its adoption, and in the expectation of which this House alone consents to the measure. That in order to secure to the deliberation of the United Legislature all possible freedom from the influence of origin and institutions derived from a foreign country, and of the associations arising from the deplorable events which have happened within the last two years in the Sister Province, the seat of Government should be fixed at some place in Upper Canada, and that English alone should be the language of the United Legislature, as this provision will, in the opinion of this House, be found an indispensable auxiliary to the amalgamation of the people, and to the gradual assimilation of the institutions of Upper and Lower Canada, and that this House desire to recommend to the consideration of Her Majesty's Government the propriety of introducing into any law for uniting these Provinces, a clause requiring a real property qualification for Members of the House of Assembly, and that saving such exceptions as the foregoing resolutions may render necessary, this House desires to see the principles of the constitution of 1791 maintained and preserved inviolate, and they rejoice to perceive that among the principles recognised by Her Majesty's Ministers as forming the basis of the Union, is to be found, the maintenance of the three estates of the Provincial Legislature, by which this House clearly understand, that the constitutional prerogative of the Crown will be upheld, that the principles upon which the Legislative Council was created will not be departed from, and that the rights and liberties of the people and privileges of their representatives will be guarded and sacredly preserved."*

The Assembly, it is to be observed, did not on this as on previous occasions, when voting for an union of the two provinces, insist as a condition of their consent to the measure, that the seat of government and of the legislature should be within Upper Canada. This was probably to avoid the semblance of interfering with the royal prerogative, but there is cause for believing that the members, individually, received the assurance of the Governor General that the seat of the legislature should permanently remain within the limits of Upper Canada, and as far as it depended upon him, the promise was accomplished,

---

* On which the yeas and nays were taken as follows:

Yeas.—Messrs. Bockus, Boulton, Burritt, Burwell, Cartwright, Detlor, Elliott, Hunter, Lewis, Malloch, McGrae, McDouell of Northumberland, McLean, Murney, Richardson, Ruttan. Rykert, Shade, Sherwood, Solicitor General, Thomson —21.

Nays.—Messrs. Attorney General, Caldwell, Chisholm of Halton, Chisholm of Glengarry, Cook, Duncombe, Dunlop, Ferrie, Cowan, Hotham, Kearnes, Manahan, Marks, McCargar, McDonell ef Glengarry, McDouell of Stormont, McIntosh, McKay, McMicking, Merritt, Morris, Parke, Powell, Robinson, Shaver, Small, Thorburn, Wickens, Woodruff.—29.

the first parliament, of which there were three sessions, being held at Kingston.

The Assembly addressed, early in the session, His Excellency, requesting he would be pleased to inform the house whether any communications had been received from Her Majesty's Principal Secretary of State for the Colonies on the subject of responsible government, as recommended in the report of the Earl of Durham, or as suggested in any other manner, and if any such despatches had been received, or any by which the opinion of Her Majesty's Government upon that subject could be collected, His Excellency would cause copies of the same to be transmitted for the information of the house.

To this he replied that he would answer by message, which accordingly came down a few days afterwards as follows :

"In answer to the address from the House of Assembly of the 13th December, respecting communications received from her Majesty's Principal Secretary of state on the subject of Responsible Government, the Governor General regrets that it is not in his power to communicate to the House of Assembly and despatches upon the subject referred to.

"The Governor General has received Her Majesty's commands to administer the Government of these Provinces in accordance with the well understood wishes and interests of the people, and to pay to their feelings, as expressed through their representatives, the difference that is justly due to them.

"These are the commands of Her Majesty, and these are the views with which Her Majesty's Government desire that the administration of these Provinces should be conducted; and it will be the earnest and anxious desire of the Governor General to discharge the trust committed to him, in accordance with these principles."

Having carried his measures, the Governor General prorogued the legislature on the 10th February, 1840, with expressions of his satisfaction at the result:

Honorable Gentlemen of the Legislative Council; and,
Gentlemen of the House of Assembly:

" In relieving you from further attendance in Parliament, I desire to express my deep sense of the zeal and assiduity which have distinguished your discharge of your duties during this, perhaps the most eventful session of the Upper Canada Legislature; and I am anxious to offer you my own acknowledgments for the ready attention which you have given to the consideration of the important business which it was my duty to bring before you.

" Your willing acquiescence in the proposed reunion of this Province with Lower Canada, upon the terms, and according to the principles suggested by me, has afforded me the most lively satisfaction; and I look forward with confidence to the completion of that measure, under the direction of our gracious Sovereign, and of the Imperial Parliament, as the means by which the peace, happiness and good government of the inhabitants of the Canadas will be permanently secured.

" By the Bill you have passed for the disposal of the clergy reserves, you have, so far as your constitutional powers admit, set at rest a question which, for years past, has convulsed society in this province. In framing that measure you have consulted alike the best interests of religion, and the future peace and welfare of the people, for whose service you are called upon to legislate; and I rely on your efforts proving successful, nothwithstanding any attempt which may be made to renew excitement, or to raise opposition to your deliberate and recorded judgment.

" The care and attention which you have bestowed

on these important subjects, and the calmness and dignity which have marked your deliberations on them cannot fail to give additional weight to your decisions before that tribunal to which they are now necessarily referred.

"I have given my assent with great satisfaction, to different bills which you have passed; and I shall transmit, without delay, such others as, from their nature, it is my duty to reserve, in order that Her Majesty's pleasure may be signified thereupon.

"Amongst the latter is a bill for payment of "losses by the rebellion or invasion." To this bill I should have been ready to assent, but as I observe that the House of Assembly have addressed Her Majesty, praying that the losses may be defrayed by the Imperial Treasury, I have considered it to be more for the interest of the parties concerned, that the bill should be reserved, in order that the address may be considered by Her Majesty's Government, before the Provincial funds are finally charged with this payment.

Gentlemen of the House of Assembly:

"I thank you for the readiness with which you have voted the supplies for the public service.

"The decision to which you came respecting the future settlement of the civil list, under the proposed union, rendered it impossible for me to submit to you any renewed proposal for the surrender of the revenues of the crown, in exchange for a provision for the expenses of the civil government of this Province; but in transmitting your resolutions to Her Majesty's Government, I have not failed to draw their attention to this subject.

"I lament that the circumstances in which this Province is placed, have necessarily prevented you from adopting measures by which its financial difficulties could be permanently removed; but this can only be effected when the obvious and easy means of augmenting the revenue, through the customs duties, with little comparative inconvenience to the people, shall be placed within your control. In the meantime, it will be my anxious desire to use the powers with which you have entrusted the executive government, to relieve, as far as possible, the most pressing demands upon the public faith; and I shall devote myself to the consideration and recommendation of measures, by which the credit of the Province may be sustained, and its future prospects improved.

Honorable Gentlemen ; and Gentlemen :

"On your return to your different districts, I earnestly hope that it will be your endeavour to promote that spirit of harmony and conciliation, which has so much distinguished your proceedings here. Let past differences be forgotten—let irritating suspicions be removed. I rejoice to find that already tranquility and hopeful confidence in the future, prevail throughout the province. Let it be your task to cherish and promote these feelings; it will be mine cordially to co-operate with you; and by administering the government in obedience to the commands of the Queen, with justice and impartiality to all, to promote her anxious wish, that her Canadian subjects, loyal to their Sovereign, and attached to British institutions, may, through the blessing of Divine Providence, become a happy, an united and a prosperous people."

The Imperial Parliament being at this time in session, a bill for uniting the Canadas was introduced by Lord John Russell, immediately after receiving the official account of the proceedings and determination of the Parliament of Upper Canada. The bill was framed by chief justice Sir James Stuart, (created a baronet of the United Kingdom on the recommendation of the Governor General, as well for his services, as in reparation of the wrongs he had experienced through the accusations of the Assembly of Lower Canada, from the home government, or rather Lord Goderich, the Colonial Minister), and contained clauses for the creation of district councils or municipalities throughout the united province. These clauses being objected to in the House of Commons, as relating to local institutions, which it was thought ought to be left to the Provincial Legislature, Lord John Russell consented to omit them, and they were accordingly struck out of his bill, which, having passed both houses, received, on the 23rd July, 1840, the royal sanction, and become law. Owing, however, to a suspending clause, it did not take effect until the 10th February, 1841, when in virtue of a proclamation, dated the fifth of that month it came into force, and Lower Canada thereafter ceased to be a seperate province, the two provinces being united under the name of Canada, the Act of union wisely making provision for the support of the civil government thereof by a permanent civil list, to prevent agitation in future on, at least, this head, which in the Lower Province had been so prolific of evils. The following was the proclamation issued on the occasion.

Victoria, by the grace of God, of the United Kingdom of Great Britain and Ireland, Queen, Defender of the Faith.

To our loving subjects whom these presents may concern;—Greeting:

Whereas for the good government of our provinces of Upper Canada and Lower Canada, and for the security of the rights and liberties and the preservation of the interest of all classes of our subjects within the same, it is, by an Act of Parliament of the United Kingdom of Great Britain and Ireland made and passed in the fourth year of our reign, intituled an "Act to reunite the Provinces of Upper Canada and Lower

Canada and for the government of Canada," amongst other things enacted that it shall be lawful for us, with the advice of our privy Council to declare or to authorise the Governor General of our said two Provinces of Upper and Lower Canada, to declare that the said two Provinces, upon, from, and after a certain day, in such Proclamation to be appointed, such day being within fifteen calendar months next after the passing of the said Act, shall form and be one Province under the name of the Province of Canada, and thenceforth the said Province shall constitute, and be one Province under the name aforesaid. upon, from and after the day so appointed as aforesaid ; and whereas in pursuance and exercise of the powers so vested in us by the said recited Act, we did on the tenth day of August, one thousand eight hundred and forty, with the advice of our Privy Council authorise the Governor General of the said two Provinces of Upper and Lower Canada, to declare by proclamation, that the said two provinces upon, from and after a certain day, in such proclamation to be appointed, such day being within fifteen calender months next after the passing of the said Act, should form and be one Province under the name of the Province of Canada,

" Now know ye therefore, that our right trusty and well beloved Councillor, Charles. Baron Sydenham, our Governor General of our said two Provinces of Upper and Lower Canada, hath in pursuance of the provisions of the said recited Act, and under and by virtue of the power and authority by us granted to him as aforesaid, determined to declare, and it is, by this our royal proclamation declared that the said Provinces upon, from and after the tenth day of Canada, of which all our loving subjects, and all others concerned, are to take notice and govern themselves accordingly.

" In testimony whereof, we have caused these

our letters to be made patent and the great seal of our said Province of Canada to be hereunto affixed. Witness our right trusty and well beloved, the Right Honorable Charles Baron Sydenham, of Sydenham, in the County of Kent, and Toronto in Canada, Governor General of British North America, and Captain General and Governor in Chief in and over our Provinces of Lower Canada and Upper Canada, Nova Scotia, New Brunswick, and the Island of Prince Edward, and Vice Admiral of the same; at our Government House, in our city of Montreal, in our said Province of Lower Canada the fifth day of February, in the year of our Lord one thousand eight hundred and forty-one, and in the fourth year of our reign. By command,

D. DALY,
Secretary of the Province.

Copy of a Despatch from Lord John Russell to the Right Honorable C. Poulett Thomson.

Downing Street, 4th Oct. 1839.

"Sir,—It appears from Sir George Arthur's despatches that you may encounter much difficulty in subduing the excitement which prevails on the the question of what is called 'Responsible Government.' I have to instruct you, however, to refuse any explanation which may be construed to imply an acquiescence in the petitions and addresses upon the subject I cannot better commence this despatch than by reference to the resolutions of both Houses of Parliament, on the 28th April and 9th May, in the year 1837.

" The Assembly of Lower Canada having repeatedly pressed this point, Her Majesty's confidential advisers at that period thought it necessary not enly to explain their views in the communications of the Secretary of State, but expressly called for the opinion of Parliament on the subject. The Crown and the two Houses of Lords and Commons having thus decisively pronounced a judgment upon the question, you will consider yourself precluded from entertaining any proposition on the subject.

" It does not appear, indeed, that any very definite meaning is generally agreed upon by those who call themselves the advocates of this principle; but its very vagueness is a source of delusion, and if at all encouraged, would prove the cause of embarrassment and danger.

"The constitution of England after long struggles and alternate success, has settled into a form of Government in which the prerogative of the Crown is undisputed, but is never exercised without advice. Hence the exercise only is questioned, and however the use of the authority may be condemned, the authority itself remains untouched.

"This is the practical solution of a great problem. the result of a contest which from 1640 to 1890 shook the monarchy and disturbed the peace of the country.

"But if we seek to apply such practice to a colony, we shall at once find ourselves at fault. The power for which a minister is responsible in England, is not his power, but the power of the Crown, of which he is for the time the organ. It is obvious that the executive councillor of a colony is in a situation totally different. The Governor, under whom he serves, receives his orders from the Crown of England. But can the colonial council be the advisers of the Crown of England? Evidently not, for the crown has other advisers for the same functions, and with superior authority.

"It may happen, therefore, that the Governor receives at one and the same time instructions from the Queen and advice from the Executive Council, totally at variance with each other. If he is to obey his instructions from England, the parallel of constitutional responsibility entirely fails; if, on the other hand, he is to follow the advice of his Council, he is no longer a subordinate officer, but an independent sovereign.

"There are some cases in which the force of these objections is so manifest, that those who at first make no distinction between the constitution of the United Kingdom and that of the Colonies, admit their strength. I allude to the question of foreign war and international relations, whether of trade or diplomacy. It is now said that internal government is alone intended.

"But there are some cases of internal government in which the honor of the Crown, or the faith of Parliament, or the safety of the state, are so seriously involved, that it would not be possible for Her Majesty to delegate her authority to a ministry in a colony.

"I will put for illustration some of the cases which have occurred in that very Province where the petition for a Responsible Executive first arose—I mean Lower Canada.

"During the time when a large majority of the Assembly of Lower Canada followed Mr. Papineau as their leader, it was obviously the aim of that gentleman to discourage all who did their duty to the Crown within the Province, and to deter all who should resort to Canada with British habits and feelings from without. I need not say that it would have been impossible for any Minister to support, in the Parliament of the United Kingdom, the measures which a ministry, headed by Mr. Papineau, would have imposed upon the Governor of Lower Canada; British officers punished for doing their duty—British merchants discouraged in their lawful pursuits, would have loudly appealed to Parliament against the Canadian ministry, and would have demanded protection.

"Let us suppose the Assembly as then constituted to have been sitting when Sir John Colborne suspended two of the judges. Would any councillor possessing the confidence of the Assembly have made himself responsible for such an act? And yet the very safety of the Province depended on its adoption. Nay, the very orders of which your Excellency is yourself the bearer, respecting Messrs. Bedard and Panet, would never be adopted or put in execution by a ministry depending for existence on a majority led by Mr. Papineau.

"Nor can any one take upon himself to say that such cases will not again occur. The principles once sanctioned, no one can say how soon its application might be dangerous or even dishonourable, while all will agree that to recall the power thus conceded would be impossible.

"While I thus see insuperable objections to the adoption of the principle as it has been stated, I see little or none to the practical views of Colonial Government recommended by Lord Durham, as I understand them. The Queen's Government have no desire to thwart the representative assemblies of British North America in their measures of reform and improvement. They have no wish to make those Provinces the resource for patronage at home. They are earnestly intent on giving to the talent and character of leading persons in the Colonies advantages similar to those which talent and character employed in the public service obtain in the United Kingdom. Her Majesty has no desire to maintain any system of policy among her North American subjects which opinion condemns. In receiving the Queen's commands, therefore, to protest against any declaration at variance with the honour of the crown and the unity of the empire, I am at the same time instructed to announce Her Majesty's gracious intention to look to the affectionate attachment of her people in North America as the security for permanent dominion.

"It is necessary for this purpose that no official misconduct should be screened by Her Majesty's representative in the Provinces; and that no private interests should be allowed to compete with the general good.

"Your Excellency is fully in possession of the principles which have guided Her Majesty's advisers on this subject; and you must be aware that there is no surer way of caining the approbation of the Queen, than by maintaining the harmony of the executive with the legislative authorities.

"While I have thus cautioned you against any declaration from which dangerous consequences might hereafter flow, and instructed you as to the general line of your conduct, it may be said that I have not drawn any specific line beyond which the power of the Governor on the one hand, and the privilege of the Assembly cn the other, ought not to extend. But this must be the case in any mixed government. Every political constitution in which different bodies share the supreme power, is only enabled to exist by the forbearance of those among whom this power is distributed. In this respect the example of England may be well imitated. The sovereign using the prerogative of the crown to the utmost extent, and the House of Commons exerting its power on the purse, to carry all its resolutions into immediate effect, would produce confusion in the country in less than a twelvemonth. So in the Governor thwarting every legitimate proposition of the Assembly, and the Assembly continually recurring to its power of refusing supplies, can but disturb all political relations, embarrass trade, and retard the prosperity of the people. Each must excercise a wise moderation. The Governor must only oppose the wishes of the Assembly, where the honour of the Crown, or the interests of the empire are deeply concerned; and the Assembly must be ready to modify some of its measures for the sake of harmony, and from a reverent attachment to the authority of Great Britain.

J. RUSSELL.

This year (1840) commenced running between England and North America the magnificent and hitherto unrivailed sea-going steamers constituting the "CUNARD LINE," and which have brought, with wonderful precision, the old and new worlds within ten days of each other, an enterprise of itself worthy of a Columbus, attended also, as it has been with admirable safety and success, owing as well to the great care and attention to the navigation, as to the construction and outfit of those match'ess ships—and chiefly, if not entirely, due to the enterprise and public spirit of the Hon. Samuel Cunard, a native of Halifax, Nova Scotia,—a gentleman of whom the land of his birth, indeed Great Britain, even may be proud, as one of her most patriotic and distinguished subjects. Mr. Cunard has rendered not only to British North America, but to this continent generally, by the splendid line of steamers bearing his name, more important service than any other man of his day, and posterity will justly rank him among the most eminent benefactors of the new world. This successful achievement of the safe, regular and constant navigation of the Atlantic at all seasons by steamers, as already (1854) evinced by a practical trial of fourteen years, constitutes an epoch.

The following letter from Captain John McDougall, claiming to have been the first who actually crossed the Atlantic solely by steam, and this in the " ROYAL WILLIAM," a steamer built at Quebec, and launched in 1832, intended to run between this port and Halifax, an enterprise, however, that failed, will be found interesting:

SAINT FOY, 10th *August*, 1853.

Robert Christie, Esq., M.P.P.

DEAR SIR,—I lately found some papers connected with the Royal William steamer, which brought to my recollection my promise to furnish you with a brief sketch of her history while I was attached to her, from the 19th of April, 1833, to the 1st of January, 1838.

I took charge of her at Sorel after she was sold by Sheriff's sale, from Capt. Nicolas, and was employed during the month of May, towing vessels from Grosse Isle, and afterwards made a voyage to Gaspe, Pictou, Halifax, and Boston in the United States, being the first British steamer that entered that port. On my return to Quebec, the owners

Q

decided on sending her to London to be sold, and I left for London, via Pictou, on the 5th of August, and was detained at Pictou until the 18th, repairing the engines and boilers, and receiving coals. I then started for London, and was about twenty days on the passage, having run six or seven days with the larboard engine, in consequence of the starboard engine being disabled, and was detained at different times, about a week laying too repairing the boilers, which had become very leaky.

About the latter end of September, the Royal William was sold by Messrs. Geo. Wildes & Co., (the agents to whom the was consigned,) to Mr. Joseph Somes, she ship owner of Radcliff, through Messrs. Willcox & Anderson, for £10,000 sterling, and chartered to the Portuguese Government to take out troops for Don Pedro's service, and on my arrival in Lisbon offered to them for sale as a vessel of war, but rejected by their admiral, Count Cape Saint Vincent, the present admiral Sir Charles Napier.

I then returned to London with invalids and disbanded soldiers from Don Pedro's service, and laid her up off Deptford Victualling Office. In July, I received orders to fit her out to run between Oporto and Lisbon, and made one trip between these ports and a trip to Caniz for specie for the Portuguese Government, and on my return to Lisbon, I received orders to dispose of her to the Spanish Government, through the Spanish Ambassador at Lisbon, Don Evanston Castor da Perez, which was completed on the 10th September, 1834 and her name was changed to Ysabel Segunda, being the first war steamer the Spaniards ever possessed, and Commodore Henry hoisted his broad pennant on board as Commodore of the first class, and Commander in Chief of the British Auxiliary Steam Squadron to be employed on the north coast of Spain against Don Carlos. I joined the Spanish service under him with the rank and pay of a commander, but with a special agreement by which I was guaranteed £600 sterling per annum, and under a contract to supply the squadron with provisions from Lisbon. We proceeded to the north coast of Spain, and about the latter part of 1834 returned to Gravesend for the purpose of delivering her up to the British Government to be converted into a war steamer at their dock yard, and the crew and officers were transferred to the Royal Tar, chartered and armed as a war steamer, with six long thirty-two pounders, and named the Reyna Governadoza, the name intended for City of Edinburg steamer which was chartered, and then fitting up as a war steamer, to form part of the squadron. When completed she relieved the Royal Tar and took her name.

The Ysabel Segunda, when completed at Sheerness dock yard, took out General Alava, the Spanish Ambassador and General Evans and the most of his staff officers to Saint Andero and afterwards to Saint Sebastian, having hoisted the commodore's broad pennant again at Saint Andero, and was afterwards employed in cruizing between that port and Fuenti Arabia, and acting in concert with the Legion against Don Carlos, until the time of their service expired in 1837. She was then sent to Portsmouth with a part of those discharged from the service and from thence she was taken to London, and detained in the city canal by Commodore Henry, until the claims of the officers and crew on the Spanish Government were settled, which was ultimately accomplished by bills, and the officers and crew discharged from the Spanish service, about the latter end of 1837, and the Ysabel Segunda delivered up to the Spanish Ambassador, and after having her engines repaired returned to Spain and was soon afterwards sent to Bordeaux in France to have the hull repaired.

But on being surveyed it was found that the timbers were so much decayed, that it was decided to build a new vessel to receive the engines, which was built there and called by the same name, and now forms one of the Royal Steam Navy of Spain, while her predecessor was converted into a hulk at Bordeaux. She is justly entitled to be considered the first steamer that crossed the Atlantic by steam, having steamed the whole way across, while the Savannah American steam ship, which crossed in 1822 to Liverpool and Petersburg, sailed the most part of the way going and returning. I remain, dear sir, your most obedient,

JOHN McDOUGALL.

THE LATE CHIEF JUSTICE SIR JAMES STUART, BART.

THE recent death of this most able and eminent Judge as well as an] excellent man, of whom, as a native colonist, (born during the American revolutionary war, in a neighbouring British colony, now one of the United States,) we of that ca'egory may well be proud, in some sort imposes, upon me the melancholy yet pleasing obligation towards departed worth, of sketching a short memoir of him, which, imperfect as it must be, being thrown together at the moment from memory merely, may nevertheless, be interesting until superseded by a better from some abler pen.

Sir James Stuart, Baronet, died suddenly at Quebec, on the 14th July, 1853, in his 74th year, in the bosom of his family, after a short but not alarming illness of a few days, —universally respected and regretted by all classes and from which, far from anticipating his death, enjoying, as he did, a robust frame and hale constitution, they believed him to have recovered, so far, at least, as to be out of danger and nearly able to appear abroad. He leaves a reputation second to none of his predecessors, if not superior to that of the best and ablest of them all, and a blank on the bench which all seem to admit, without undervaluing any of those who aspire to his post, there is no man living of equal science, ability, and experience in the jurisprudence, civil and criminal, of this country, to fill in his stead. He possessed, in an eminent degree, most of the qualities that constitute or lead to human greatness. With a mind highly cultivated, and of the highest intellectual powers, combined with a presence at once prepossessing and inspiring respect, he was also, in the fullest sense of the terms a learned and profound lawyer, and though but a provincial barrister, nevertheless as a jurist, a celebrity of his day, who would have been an ornament and an honour to the judicature of any country. In the duties of his situation he was impartial, just, and proverbially laborious and indefatigable. His eloquence was magnificent in its very simplicity. There was nothing in it redundant, far-fetched or studied. It might, truly be said of him as of one Homer's heroes, but in the noble language of Pope, in this justance equal at least if not superior, to that of the blind old Bard himself:—

"When Atreus' son harangued the listening train,
Just was his sense and his expression plain;
His words succinct, yet full, without a fault,
He spoke no more than just the thing he ought."

His reasoning was lucid, powerful, and convincing. Quick and clear in his perception of matters the most intricate, he was equally happy in his exposition of them, and of the law applicable thereto. Above the hair-splitting habits, and suphistry too common with the legal profession, it was his custom to bring out the main points upon which his judgments were based, so clearly, as to make them intelligible, and bear conviction in every understanding. None who have heard any of those thrilling bursts of oratory delivered by him in the legislature, of which he was several years a distinguished member, on momentous cocasions when his powers were called forth, but must have felt the supremacy of his master mind. As a logical and powerful debater, he would indeed have commanded attention,and excelled in the House of Commons, had Providence cast his lot there. He in fact felt himself in a field too limited for the full exercise of the great and extraordinary powers he unquestionably possessed, though there was absolutely nothing of the boastful or vain glorious in his character. Well has it been said, in a short but elegant obituary in the *Quebec Mercury* of Sir Jas. Stuart's decease, that,—" Whoever succeeds to his seat will have a position of no ordinary difficulty, for he will sit in the shadow of a great man, and on his slightest sin of omission or commission will come down the heavy visitation of *comparison*. The vulgar and the learned alike will say, it would not have been so were Sir James Stuart alive." Be who may his successor he indeed will be fortunate if he does not suffer from comparison. Sir James Stuart was of an aristocratic turn of mind, and some will have it that he was haughty in bearing towards his brethern of the bench and bar. Occasional differences in opinion with his brother judges, in matters of law, seasoned, perhaps with a little warmth on either side, may possibly have given rise to the notion, but this, I apprehend, was all. He no doubt however was conscious of his superiority. As to the bar, we know that the frowardness and squabbles frequently occurring there, especially among the tyros of the profession, are such as would exhaust the patience of an angel, and, to be checked require a strong hand, and such assuredly, was Sir James Stuart's, and in his position he needed it to uphold and enforce the decency and respect due by some of the junior, and perhaps a'so unruly among the elder practitioners in the Court. As to his natural disposition, no man in existence could be more placable than the late Chief Jastice in case of difference with a friend or acquaintance. He was, it is true, hasty, and for the moment highly resentful; but like most men of that temperament, without rancour, easily conciliated, kind-hearted and generous, seeming always happy to meet more than halfway any approach to conciliation on the part of those with whom he may have had any misunderstanding. When he took, however, a dislike, from whatsoever cause, he was, it must be admitted, at no pains to conceal it; but the whole world do him the justice to believe that no personal or private motive ever had the least influence upon any of his judgments. Though Sir James had, as a judge, for several years renounced all active interference in politics, he nevertheless felt a deep interest in them, and was in principle a liberal conservative. He certainly augured unfavourably of the present state of things in the country, considering it one of transition, and if not leading to immediate anarchy, anything but stable or satisfactory. Such, if I have not widely misunderstood them, were h s views of public matters, and which, from his long experience and discernment are entitled to consideration. His anticipations of the recurrence of stormy, times, it is to be feared, from all we see and hear, may soon be realized. But time will tell.

Sir James Stuart was born on the 4th March, 1780, at a place called Fort Hunter, in, as I understand, the then British Province, now State of New York, but the precise locality whereof, or by what name now known, I have not been able to ascertain. and was the third son of the late Rev. John Stuart, D. D., subsequently Rector of Kingston and Bishops Official for Upper Canada, by Jane, daughter of George Odill, Esq., latterly of Philadelphia, and originally of Liverpool, England, in the neighbourhood of which place at Lee Hall, the Okill family had long been seated.

Doctor Stuart emigrated at the close of the revolutionary war as an U. E. Loyalist, with his family to Upper Canada. The young Stuart (with his elder brother George, now the Venerable Archdeacon of Kington) was educated at King's College, Windsor, Nova Scotia, under the Rev. William Cochran, D.D., then principal of that establishment, since erected by Royal Charter into an University, where the writer well remembers him as a student, some fifty odd years ago, retaining also a perfect recollection of some of the feats of his boyhood. He entered, on his return to Canada, upon his studies at law, in the first place with Mr. Reid, Prothonotary of the Court of King's Bench at Montreal, but finished his clerkship at Quebec, under Mr. Sewell, then Attorney General. On being admitted to the bar, he very soon gave promise, by his diligence and attention to business, as well as by his talents, of rising in his profession. Lieut Governor, Sir Robert Shore Milnes, perceiving his talents, took him by the hand and appointed him, some time before the expiration of his clerkship, his Assistant Secretary, naming him, very shortly after being called to the bar, Solicitor General. This latter post he retained until some time after the advent of Governor in Chief, Sir James Henry Craig, who, for some cause not generally understood, taking a pique at Mr. S uart, gave him the go-by, on the advancement of the Attorney General Sewell to the Chief Justiceship, by appointing a junior barrister (Mr. Bowen) Attorney General over his head. This of course, was felt and resented by Mr. Stuart as a *passedriot* and injustice to him, and who about this time having obtained a seat in the Assembly, sided with the party in opposition to the executive, which afforded the Gover or a pretext for dismissing him from the office of Solicitor General, which he conferred on Mr. Stephen Sewell, brother to the chief justice

Mr. Stuart. nothing disconraged, however, at this "*contretemps,*" but diligently pursuing his profession at Montreal, where from the time of his appointment as Solicitor General, he resided, attained to eminence, and was accumulating wealth. War coming on in 1812 with the United States, he took, in the legislature, a course in opposition to the Government and of which many of his friends disapproved as unpatriotic, and indeed factious, but which was more than counterpoised by a resolute and successful stand against the doctrine asserted by Sir George Prevost, the Governor in Chief, of his right to lay at pleasure, if he should see fit, the Province under martial law, a right—Mr Stuart leading the debates on the subject—denied him by the Assembly, unless with the authority of the Provincial Parliament. Happily, however, owing to the loyalty and zeal of both Canadas, there was no necessity for such a measure. He also caused, towards the close of this administration (Sir George Prevost's) the Chief Justice Sewell and Monk, to be impeached by the Assembly, the result whereof is noticed in a previous volume, and which it is unnecessary to expatiate upon further than to observe that he was finally abandoned by his party, from, as it was generally believed at the time, pusillanimous, or as some would have it, mercenary motives, in his endeavours to follow up the impeachments with effect against those functionaries, which so disgusted him as to induce him to retire from Parliament and indeed public life. The impeachments of the Chief Justices, although they escaped unscathed, had, nevertheless, a most salutary effect in checking the overbearing tendencies, then too frequently observable, indulged in from the Bench and of teaching the Judges a proper respect for public opinion, which occasionally some of them seem'd to think they might disregard with impunity.

Mr. Stuart, after a retirement of several years from public life, confining himself entirely to the practice of his profession, was again induced, in 1822, when, the spirit of the British population in Lower Canada being roused, the proposed Union of the Canadas was, for the first time, seriously stated, to take an interest and an active part in public matters. He drew up the petition on this subject, to the Imperial Government, as forwarded from Montreal on the occasion, and was deputed by the uuonists as the bearer of it. This brought him into immediate communication with Earl Bathurst, the Colonial Minister, who could not fail to notice the superior endowments of the man before him, representing as he ably did, nearly the entire mass of the inhabitants of British birth or descent in Lower Caunda. Nothing however, with respect to the union, being done in England in that or the following year, Mr. Stnart returned to Canada. He again visited England in 1824, by desire it was believed of Lord Bathurst, at which time Lord Dalhousie also was on a visit to England on leave of absence. His Lordship though entertaining the highest personal regard for his Attorney General, Mr. Uniacke, whose private qualities were estimable, long had felt that he was not the man for that important office but would not remove him unless in the way of promotion. A vacancy on the Bench at Montreal by the retirement of Chief Justice Monk and promotion of Judge Reid in his stead occurring at this juncture, while his Lordship abd Mr. Stuart, were in England, enabled the former to get over the inconvenience he long had wished to obviate, and Mr. Uniacke being now placed upon the Bench, Mr. Stuart was appointed his successor (2nd Feburary, 1825,) and elected in his stead as representative in the Assembly, for the Royal Borough of William Henry, which brought him once more into parliament, much it is believed against his own wish, but it seems to have been the desire of the government that he should have a seat in that house as the chief organ therein of the government. But things since his last appearance in parliament had materially changed, and so had his position. All his influence, vast and unbounded as it once had been, had vauished. He was then leader of the opposition, popular to idolatry, and carrying all before him. He was now the organ of the Government, but his voice in the assembly like that of '' one crying in the wilderness,' was unheard and absolutely lost. In the spirit that prevailed he could accomplish nothing in the assembly, and indeed he frequently acknowledged to his private friends that it were better he were not there, seeing that he was contending against the current of the then po-

pular feeling and to no other purpose than that of braving
"*a pure perte,*" as he himself used to say, the hostility of the
demagogues of the day. The parliament having been dissolved in 1827, the Attorney General again, by desire of the
Governor, Lord Dalhousie, came forward as a candidate for
William Henry, where he was successfully opposed by Doctor
Wolfred Nelson. The inquiry and impeachment that arose
out of the contest at this election, and Mr. Stuart's suspension from his office of Attorney General, by Lord Aylmer,
in 1831, pursuant to address of the Assembly, have been
fully noticed and need not be dwelt upon here. Mr. Stuart
lost no time in repairing to England to defend himself against the accusation of the assembly, and though, as evident
by his correspondence with the colonial minister, he triumphantly refuted every charge against him in the most masterly and conclusive manner, he was nevertheless most unjustly sacrificed by Lord Goderich, evidently for the time
serving double purpose of propitiating an anti-British party
in the province, which however not long afterwards broke
out in open rebellion, and of screening Lord Aylmer from
the heavy responsibility towards Mr. Stuart, to which by his
suspension of that gentleman from his office without just
cause, he had subjected himself in the law courts at Westminister, where he might be held to account for it before a
jury of his country, upon his return to England. The minister in fact. however strange it may seem, and it certainly
was strange enough, absolved Mr. Stuart of every article
against him in the impeachment, dismissing him nevertheless
upon a charge of his own finding, but of which there was no
impeachment before him. nor in reality cause for impeachment, viz : for receiving certain fees on the renewal of commissions to public notaries, which by reason of the demise
of the crown some of them had deemed a necessary precaution to prevent cavilling at any future time as to their *actes*,
or their authority to act as notaries,—fees recognised by the
government, and for duties it had imposed upon him. Never
did minister or man in the character of a gentleman, make
a more pitiful, indeed lamentable figure than did the colonial minister, Lord Goderich (now Ripon) and his under
Secretary Lord Howick, (now Grey) as did also, subsequently, Mr. Spring Rice, (now Lord Monteagle), when colonial
minister, in their correspondence with Mr. Stuart in consequence of the iniquitous dismissal of this gentleman on assumed and false grounds, the injustice and odium of which
Mr. Stuart pointed out in the strongest possible light.

    Mr. Stuart, after fruitlessly spending three and a half years
in England, in the expectation of righting himself, returned

in 1834 to Canada, the office of Attorney General in the meantime having been conferred upon Mr, Ogden, by direction of Lord Goderich, at the solicitation it was supposed, of Lord Lynhurst, with whom, by marriage, Mr. Ogden, was connected. On Mr. Stuart's return to Canada. still in his vigour, enjoying as a lawyer largely the confidence of the public, mere so indeed than any other professional man in the Province, and unsubdued by the crosses and illtreatment he had experienced, he resumed at Quebec, where he had resided since his appointment as Attorney General, with his wonted ability and dilligence, his practice, which seemed, from the general confidence reposed in him by the public, to increase, in ratio of the injustice and injury done him Not long after his return, Lord Aylmer, wounded by a remark made touching him by Mr. Stuart in his correspondence with the minister, while in England, addressed him a letter, calling his attention to the passage at which he had taken offence, and desiring he would recall it, as injurious to his Excellency's public character. This, however, Mr. Stuart not only formally refused, but reiterated his remarks, insisting upon their truth, and his readiness to meet the consequences in any shape. Mr. Stuart had stated in a letter to Lord Goderich, of the 25th February, 1833, in reference to his suspension from the office of Attorney General, that Lord Aylmer had taken that step "under a singular misapprehension of his duty, real or feigned, and upon grounds upon which he either did or ought to have known the insufficiency." In his letter to Mr. Stuart on the occasion, dated "Quebec, 14th December, 1833," he observes: "The correctness of my judgment might perhaps have been called in question, but not the integrity of my character. But what I do complain of, or rather that against which I do now most decidedly protest, is this, that in adverting to an act performed in the discharge of my public duty, as Governor of this province, you should have gone out of your way to assail my private character, for if it were true that I were capable of feigning misapprehension of my duty or of acting upon grounds the insufficiency of which I was acquainted with, for the accomplishment of any, no matter what purpose, I must not only be unworthy to associate with men of honor, but I must in that case be so totally devoid, even of common honesty, as to deserve to be banished from society altogether. I cannot therefore permit myself to doubt upon a calm review of the expressions quoted above from your letter to Viscount Goderich you will explicity disavow the extraordinary imputations affecting my character as a member of society which these expressions convey."

This letter, through some delay not accounted for only came to Mr. Stuart's hand, in Nov, 1834, while on a visit at Montreal, to which immediately on his return to Quebec, he answered (21st November) with characteristic manliness— The substance of his answer is expressed in the following quotation—" Where a tortuous deceptive course of action is pursued in a high official situation, persons injuriously affected by it are not likely to mistake its character. I never entertained a doubt of the motives by which you were actuated in suspending me from my office * * * * * *—I do believe that your real motive for suspending me was a desire to secure for yourself the favour and support of a few leading demagogues in the House of Assembly whom you knew to be most anxious for my destruction, and in fulfilment of this motive you were willing to sacrifice me to gratify their malignity by suspending me on grounds which you know to be insufficient. This continues to be my deliberate opinion and I hold myself responsible for it in any and every form." Mr. Stuart also in this letter calls in turn upon his lordship for an explanation of a strange piece of double-dealing he had evinced towards him in relation to a petition from a Mr. L., in which he deemed his character to have been injuriously and wrongfully reflected upon.

"Having thus disposed of the subject of your letter, your lordship will permit me to solicit your attention to a matter connected with the proceedings of the Assembly, as to which, cause for explanation, from your lordship, has been afforded to me. I advert to the petition of Mr. Lampson, presented to your lordship, on the 21st December, 1830, in which unfounded imputations and insinuations, injurious to my character, are contained. In a letter from me to Lieutenant Colonel Glegg, of the 30th December, 1830, having relation to this petition, I express a desire to be made acquainted with any charge or imputation, affecting my character, that might have been conveyed, in this form, and solicit an investigation of it. In your lordship's answer, transmitted through Lieutenant Colonel Glegg, dated the same day, your lordship assures me, that *no* insinuation affecting my character had reached you. It is, nevertheless, a matter of fact, that the petition now referred to did contain false imputations and insinuations prejudicial to my character; and it is also true, that your lordship subsequently communicated this petition to the House of Assembly, by which it was made a ground of false accusation against me, and even transmitted a copy of it to His Majesty's Secretary of State for the Colonies, without ever having made me acquainted with its contents. Upon these facts, I am justified in requesting from your lordship an explanation of the circumstances which induced you to assert, while you were in possession of this petition, that *no* insinuation affecting my character had reached you, and also led you to withhold from me the knowledge of the contents of this petition, although you communicated it to the House of Assembly, to be made a ground of accusation by that body, and subsequently transmitted it to the Secretary of State, as a part of the evidence in support of their accusation."

Lord Aylmer in acknowledging Mr. Stuart's letter, merely observes, that " what measures it may be necessary and proper that I should adopt in protecting my character, assailed by you in its very foundation, must remain for my consideration hereafter."—declining at the same time to enter into any explanation as desired by Mr. Stuart " in relation to the petition of Mr. L., or in relation to any other matter connected with my administration of the Government of this Province.'

Mr. Stuart in reply to his lordship's letter remarks:
"On that part of it which relates to the supposed cause of offence afforded by me, I will only remark, that it is to be presumed that your lordship's protracted reflections will ultimately conduct you to that recourse which usage has sanctioned in such cases. On the subject respecting which some explanation has been requested by me, I cannot but express surprise that your lordship should decline compliance with a request, in itself so reasonable and proper, involving also, as it does, your lordship's personal veracity and honour. The facts stated in my letter of the 21st November, verified by public documents, establish, that an untrue assertion was made by your lordship injurious to me in its consequences, and followed by acts of your lordship, inconsistent with fair dealing towards me, as a public officer. On this head I requested explanation;—you refuse it. Under these circumstances, there can, I apprehend, be but one inference, drawn from your lordship's refusal, which it is unnecessary for me to specify. When your lordship shall have descended from the eminence you now occupy, and become subject to the responsibilities acknowledged in civilized society, I shall deem it necessary to call your attention again to this matter, and should hope with better success."

This in fact was an invitation to a hostile meeting, which the correspondence being published in the newspapers, occasioned considerable speculation at the time ; but which, however, his lordship very properly decl ned as of a nature to compromise the high position he occupied, and by no means from cowardice, of which no man with a shadow of reason could suspect Lord Aylmer. He moreover received the commands of his superiors at home to decline a hostile meeting. Lord Aylmer certainly stultified himself in the opinion of all the world by this very unnecessary appeal for reparation to the man he had so deeply injured, and upon whom by such a step, after all that had occurred, he was now heaping insult; nor was Mr. Stuart, though without doubt most grievously wronged, and generally admired for his spirit on the occasion, thought justified, considering upon whom he made the call; most right thinking men being of opinion, that he had better have dispensed with it, the enlightened public sympathising with him, as it certainly did, in the wrongs done him.

Lord Goderich's final determination and unworthy treatment of Mr. Stuart was the more surprising as, on this gentleman's arrival in England, he was told at the Colonial Office that he had given himself unnecessary trouble in crossing the Atlantic, as, had he remained in Canada, the order for his reinstatement in office would have been then on its way to this country. His dismissal was notoriously the result of an after thought, with the view of screening Lord Aylmer.

Before leaving England for Canada, Mr. Stuart had the satisfaction of being offered the Chief Justiceship of Newfoundland by Mr Stanley, (now Earl of Derby,) who having succeeded to the Colonial Office, entertained a widely different view of Mr. Stuart's merits from that of Lord Goderich, but Mr. Stuart not only deemed the indemnity offered inadequate to the wrong done him, but he had a still higher motive,and though grateful to Mr. Stanley, with a very commendable feeling, declined the offer, principally on the ground that as the injustice done him had been in Canada, it was there also that it must be repaired, if reparation were to be made him at all. This happily was realised not long afterwards by the Earl of Durham who shortly after his arrival in Canada with extraordinary powers as Her Majesty's High Commissioner and Governor General, allowing the Chief Justice Sewell to retire upon a liberal retiring pension, appointed Mr. Stuart in his stead, with the universal approbation of the British public, and indeed of all parties, the former asperities, having in the lapse of time and course of events since his return from England, almost entirely disappeared. The baronetcy, as mentioned in the proceeding chapter, was conferred upon him (Lord John Russell being Colonial Secretary at the time) at the instance of Mr. Poulett Thomson (Lord Sydenham,) to whom he rendered important assistance in his management of affairs in the Canadas preparatory to their union, digesting for him, with a multitude of other matters, the Union Bill, with clauses, which were struck out in its progress through the Imperial Parliament, providing for the establishment of Municipal Councils throughout the United Province, and which it was deemed advisable to leave to the Provincial Parliament. He also prepared the Judicature and Registry Ordinances, passed by the Special Council previous to the Union; the latter of which, amended in certain respects by certain acts of Canada, still stands on the statute book, and the former after being repealed some years ago during the Lafontaine Baldwin Administration, has been in a great measure recently re-enacted, and incorporated in the existing Judicature Act.

From his intense application to public business, and his studious habits, Sir James was somewhat of a recluse, mixing little in society, and indulging in very few or no intimacies, which indeed even in his earlier days, he is said to have been cautions in forming. He affected nothing either before or after his elavation to the bench, or advancement to the baronetcy, in the way of " style," living in an unostentatious manner though in due keeping with, and befitting his station. As a barrister, he was like most of the class, eager in amassing wealth, but he also was liberal of his purse, in particular towards those of his confreres who may have met with misfortunes, or were overtaken by indigence. Distinction and honour in his profession rather than wealth were however his predominant aspirations and the ruling passion of his soul. In all his domestic and social relations, whether as husband, father, friend, neighbour or citizen, he was, in one word, perfect.

Finally, Sir Jas. Stuart, the day's work by providence allotted him being over, now sleeps in an honoured grave. He has descended, ripe in years, though not absolutely from age to his last resting place, covered with honour by his sovereign---respected and regretted by his country, leaving a name and reputation of which his descendants, justly may feel proud. He leaves three sons and a daughter, issue of his marriage, the 17th March, 1818, which Elizabeth, only surviving daughter and heiress of the late Alexander Robertson, of Montreal, Esquire, of the Robertsons of Foscally Perthshire, He is succeeded in the [Baronesctey by his eldest, son, now Sir Charles Stuart, Bart., M. A., of University College, Oxford, and of the Honourable Society of the Inner Temple, Barrister at Law—born at Montreal, in January, 1824 consequently, now in his thi.tieth year.—*Cui omnia bona ac fuusta.*"

Quebec, 30th July, 1853.

The following resolutions of the respective bars at Quebec and Montreal express the sense justly entertained by these bodies of this highly distinguished member of the profession. (Quebec.)

At a meeting of the members of the bar, of this section, held in their rooms, on Friday, the 15th inst., the following resolutions were unanimously adopted:

Resolved,—That the members of the bar have learned with the deepest sorrow the death of the Hon. Sir James Stuart, Baronet, Chief Justice of the Chief Justice of the Court of Queen's Bench for Lower Canada, and as such the head of the profession therein: and feel it right to record their high estimate of his abilities and character and their profound sense of the loss which the profession has sustained by his decease.

Resolved,—That throughout the long period of more than 50 years, during which Sir James was a member of the profession, and during a very great portion of which he held the highest professional rank and office, his great and varied learning, his profound legal research and attainments, his unwearied industry, and his inflexible integrity, have placed him among the foremost of the jurists of his day, and marked him as one of whom our country may be justly proud.

Resolved,—That in testimony of the respect of this bar for his memory, the members thereof do attend his funeral, and wear mourning for one month.

Resolved,—That the Secretary communicate to the family of Sir James Stuart a copy of these resolutions, with the expression of the sincere and respectful sympathy of this bar.

"At a meeting of the Montreal section of the bar of Lower Canada, held at the Council Rooms in the Court House of this city, on the 18th of July, 1853, in order to adopt measures expressive of respect for the memory of the late Sir James Stuart, Chief Justice of the Court of Queen's Bench and Appeals, in Lower Canada the following resolutions were adopted:

Resolved,—That the members of the Montreal section of the bar have received with emotions of deep regret the intelligence of the death of the late Chief Justice Sir James Stuart, who for several years past has occupied the position of head of the judiciary in this section of the province.

Resolved,—That his acknowledged abilities and deep learning in his profession obtained for him the respect of the bar whilst his integrity in his judicial office secured for him the confidence of the public generally.

Resolved,—That the members of this section tender to the

family of the deceased Chief Justice the expression of their sympathy and condolence.

Resolved,—That they will wear the usual badge of mourning for one month, in testimony of their respect.

Resolved,—That a copy of these resolutions be transmitted to the family of the deceased, and the other bar sections of Lower Canada."

The foregoing short memoir of the late Sir James Stuart, Bart., having appeared in the *Quebec Mercury* of the 2nd August, 1853, and subsequently in other public prints, in anticipation of the present volume, for which, in the plain shape of a note, hastily thrown together, it was solely intended, a passage in it, I regret to find, as will be seen by the following letter, has been misapprehended, as implying a reflexion upon Mr. Ogden. I do not, indeed, see that the passage alluded to, carries the inference which Mr. Ogden attributes to it, but it is to me sufficient that he thinks so, to induce my unqualified disavowal of such intention. There certainly is nothing in it to imply a belief or suspicion of any intrigue on his part, " to supplant" Mr Stuart in his office of Attorney General, unless it be the supposed interest of Lord Lynhurst, (distinctly denied, however, by Mr. O.), in favour of Mr. Ogden, which very naturally might be presumed, considering the relationship between his lordship and this gentleman then Solicitor General, for the office of Attorney-Gen., on its become vacant by the removal of Mr. Stuart, an office which in fact Mr, Ogden, as Solicitor General, was almost of right entitled to, and which accordingly it seems was spontaneously conferred upon him by the Colonial Minister.

It were nothing, certainly, supposing it to be true, to Mr. Ogden's prejudice. that so distinguished a man as Lord Lynhurst, should have taken an interest in his behalf. The protest, however, is only directed against the apprehension which he infers may be drawn from a passage in the foregoing memoir, that he intrigued or endeavoured in any respect " to suppliant" his predecessor, and I may add in support of his protest, that I have too long and well known Mr. Ogden to believe him capable of anything of the kind.

To the Printer of the Quebec Mercury.

Sir,—In the memoir of the lamented Chief Justice, the late Sir James Stuart, Bart., published in the *Mercury* of the 2nd of August last, the following statement is made:

" Mr. Stuart, after vainly spending three and a half years in England, in expectation of righting himself, returned in 1834 to Canada, the office of Attorney General in the mean time having been conferred upon Mr. Ogden, by direct'on of Lord Goderich, at the solicitation, it was supposed, of Lord Lyndhurst, with whom, by marriage, Mr. Ogden was connected."

Were it not that the foregoing supposition in regard to the manner of my appointment to the office of Attorney General of Lower Canada involved the inference that whilst my colleague Mr. Stuart, was in England, defending himself against the imputations cast upon him by the Assembly, I sought to supplant him in his office, I should not have thought it necessary to advert to it. As it does, however, convey that impression to my mind I feel that I owe it to myself and to my friends in Canada, to relieve myself from the imputation the paragraph is calculated to fasten upon me, and accordingly I avail myself of the earliest opportunity the receipt of your paper has afforded me, to declare that I neither by myself, or by or through any person, either directly or indirectly, or in any manner or way whatever, at anytime, either before, or during, or subsequent to Mr. Stuart's suspension from the functions of his office of Attorney General, sought or applied for promotion to that office; and I further declare that no application for that office was ever made by Lord Lyndhurst: and, lest it might be supposed that Lord Aylmer may have recommended me for the office, I take leave to add, that when His Excellency placed in my hands the royal mandamus, directing my appointment to that high office, he distinctly stated that *he had not done so, as he had determined from the moment of Mr. Stuart's suspension from office, to do no act which could in the slightest degree be considered as expressing an opinion on the merits of the Assembly's comp'aint against him.*

As I understand, "the memoir" has been published in anticipation of its appearance in the forthcoming volume of Mr. Christie's History of Lower Canada, I purpose transmitting a copy of this letter to that gentleman, in the hope that he will correct the statement referred to, and I have to request that you will in the meantime give publicity to the same in the *Mercury.* I am sir, your obedient servant,

C. R. OGDEN.

Kirby, 15th September, 1853.

The following documents were intended to be included and make part of the 6th volume, which I had promised as an APPENDIX to this work: but as some time may elapse before the promised volume can make its appearance, and there is in the present volume some room to spare, I give them, by anticipation, insertion here, in the belief that they will be highly interesting to readers curious to know the opinions on public matters of those who, at the dates they respectively bear, ruled the country. The views in particular of such men as Sir James Craig and Chief Justice Sewell, who in their day filled no small space in the public eye, are worthy of purusal:—

EXTRACT of a Despatch from the Right Hon. Lord Hobart to Lieut. Governor Milnes, dated Downing-street, 9th January, 1804.

"It is highly proper that you should signify to the Catholic Bishop the impropriety of his assuming any new titles, or the exercise of any additional powers, and it will be right that you shou'd intimate to him, that although no express orders have been issued upon the subject, it is expected that if any such have been recently taken up, that they should not be persevered in. The French emigrant priests should also be reminded that their residence in Canada only is upon sufferance, and it is therefore the more incumbent upon them to observe the utmost circumspection in all their proceedings, as they must be aware the indulgence with which they have been treated by the British Government is liable to be withdrawn, if they should render themselves undeserving of it, by anything questionable in their conduct."

A LA TRES EXCELLENTE MAJESTE DU ROI.

L'humble requêtte de Pierre Denaut, Evêque de l'Eglise Catholique Romaine.

Lequel prend la liberté de s'approcher du trone de votre Majesté pour remontrer très respectueusement—

Que la religion Catholique Romaine ayant été introduite en Canada avec ses premiers Colons sous l'ancien gouvernement de France, l'Evêché de Québec fut érigé en mil six cent soixante-quatre, et a été successivement rempli par des evêques, dont le sixième est mort en mil sept cent soixante, époque de la conquête de ce pays par les armes de votre Majesté.

Que depuis cette date les Catholiques, qui forment plus des dix-neuf vingtièmes de la population de votre province du Bas-Canada, ont continué, par la bonté de votre Majesté, d'avoir des evêques, lesquels, après le serment d'allégeance prêté entre les mains des représentans de votre Majesté en cette province en conseil, ont toujours exercé leurs fonctions avec la permission de votre Majesté, et sous la protection des différens gouverneurs qu'il a plu à votre Majesté d'établir pour l'administration de cette province, et que votre suppliant est le quatrième evêque qui conduit cette eglise depuis que le Canada est heureusement passé à la couronne de la Grande-Bretagne.

Que l'extension prodigieuse de cette province, et l'accroissement rapide de sa population, exigent plus que jamais que l'Evêque Catholique soit revêtu de tels droits et dignités que votre Majesté trouvera convenables pour conduire et contenir le clergé et le peuple, et pour imprimer plus fortement dans les esprits ces principes d'attachement et de loyauté envers leur souverain et d'obéissance aux lois dont les Evêques de ce pays ont constamment et hautement fait profession.

Que cependant ni votre suppliant, qui conduit depuis huit ans cette eglise, ni ses prédécesseurs, depuis la conquête, ni les curés des paroisses, n'ont eu de la part de votre Majesté cette autorisation spéciale dont ils ont souvent senti le besoin, pour prévenir les doutes qui pourraient s'élever dans les cours de justice touchant l'exercice de leurs fonctions civiles.

Ce considéré, qu'il plaise à votre Majesté de permettre que votre suppliant approche de votre Majesté, et la prie très humblement de donner tels ordres et instructions que dans sa sagesse rayale elle estimera nécessaires pour que votre suppliant et ses successeurs soient civilement reconnus comme Evêques de l'Eglise Catholique Romaine de Québec, et jouissent de telles prérogatives, droits et émolumens temporels que votre Majesté vondra gracieusement attacher à cette dignité.

Pour plus amples détails, votre suppliant prie votre Majesté de s'en rapporter aux informations que Son Excellence Sir Robert Shore Milnes, Baronet, le lieutenant gouverneur de votre Majesté en cette province, veut bien se charger de donner a votre Majesté.

Et votre suppliant continuera d'adresser au ciel les vœux les plus ardens pour la prospérité de votre très gracieuse Majesté, de son auguste famille et de son empire.

(Signé,) † PIERRE DENAUT,
Evêque de l'Eglis Catholique Romaine.
Québec, 10 juillet 1805.

The following document addressed to Sir Jas. H. Craig is without date, but there is reason to believe it was written at the beginning of 1810 :—

MAY IT PLEASE YOUR EXCELLENCY,

You have been pleased to call for my sentiments upon the present situation of Canada, and I have now, the honor to submit them to your consideration and superior judgment.

The poliical evils which we labour under arise in my apprehension, from two principal causes, 1st from French predilections in the great mass of the inhabitants: and, 2dly, from want of influence and power in the Executive Govenment. From the former arises that distinction between the Government and the people which is daily and too visibly productive of mutual distrust, jealousies, and even enmity, and from the latter a total inability to produce the means of which the effects of that distinction may be counteracted. What must be the result, if things remain as they are, is obvious; no hopes can be entertained, that French predilections can be obliterated from the minds of His Majesty's Canadian subjects, and if they be not counteracted will continue to augment until by some crisis force will be required, and the future state and condition of Canada will then be decided by a recourse to arms.

The great links of connection between a Government and its subjects are religion, laws, and language, and when conquerors profess the same religion, and use the same laws and the same language as the conquered, the incorporation of both into one political body is easily effected; but when they are at variance on these points, experience seems to have demonstrated in Canada, that it cannot at all be effected while this variance subsists. Obedience may be rendered by conquered subjects under such circumstances, but it is the obedience of a foreigner to a government which in his estimation is not his own; and as he views it as an alien power, there is no attachment, no affection in his mind towards it, and consequently no disposition to unite with those who constitute the government or its natural subjects. Every favour conferred is considered to be no more than what is due to him, or as a matter obtained from persons who would not have conceded so much if it had been possible for them to retain it. No confidence exists and he is in continual belief, that more is meditated by the government, in every of its measures, than meets his eye. At the conquest of Canada, the conquerors were Englishmen and Protestants; they spoke the English language, and no other; they were attached to English law, and fostered in their minds a national antipathy against Frenchmen. The English subjects of the present day who are settled in Canada, having no cause to be dissatisfied with the religion, the language, or the laws of their mother country, and having no cause to be better pleased with France than their forefathers, are now, precisely what the conquerors of Canada were. On the other hand, the people of Canada at the conquest were Frenchmen and Roman Catholics, they spoke the French language, and no other; they were attached to French laws, and fostered in their minds, a national antipathy against Englishmen. Since that period, by the Statute 14 Geo. III, c. 83, the laws of France have been enacted, and declared, to be the laws of Canada, and the Roman Catholic Religion has been established in the Province; and as it has not been thought advisable by any Act of Parliament, or other means, to attempt the general introduction of the English language, the French tongue universally prevails, even in the Courts of Justice and in the Legislature; the Canadians therefore in these several respects are also precisely what they were at the conquest: they are still Frenchmen, their habits (the fruits of their Religion, and their laws,) are still the habits of Frenchmen, and so much in opposition to the habits of our own people, that there is no intercourse between them. I fear I may add with truth, that the antipathy of Canadians and English subjects against each other, is mutually as great as ever.

It seems, sir, to me impossible that the incorporation of two such extremes can ever be effected; and to this I add, that no change in the laws or religion of the country can be even expected until the majority of its inhabitants are Englishmen in principle: and that while the number of English settlers remain so small in comparison to that of the Canadians, a change in language cannot be looked for; yet the Province must be converted into an English Colony, or it will ultimately be lost to England.

I am led from these considerations in the first instance to conceive it indispensably necessary to overwhelm and sink the Canadian population by the introduction of a greater population of English Protestants, and this I believe to be practicable. I do not mean that subjects can or ought to be procured from England to the extent required for this purpose, but they may, and I think ought, to be procured from the neighbouring States; for although it may be feared by some that they would not be good subjects, I have myself no such fears. I believe that once settled in the Province they would have no wish to return to their former system of Government, an expectation justified by the conduct of those who are already settled in the country. It is besides in the case only of a war with the Northern States of America, that the disaffection of such settlers is to be dreaded, and this is an event to be contemplated probably as a remote contingency. We should also remember, that the great fear of the Northern States is the existence of a nation of Frenchmen upon their borders, and that in all probability the introduction of other settlers, by appeasing this apprehension, by increasing our connections with them and particularly our commercial intercourse, would have a tendency to preserve the good understanding which subsists at present for a longer course of years than otherwise might be expected, and possibly until the original settlers shall be succeeded by a new generation of British-born subjects. But let the weight of these observations be what it may, such settlers it is certain would be the descendants of Englishmen, profess the same religion, and speak the same language, and would therefore be more easily assimilated and become better subjects than those which we now possess: and if to people the country with such characters is to incur a risk, the risk incurred will be less than that which we must incur by suffering the Province to remain in its present state. The waste lands of the Crown afford sufficient means for the accommodation of a much greater number of settlers than is required, but their dispersion through the settled parts of the country is desirable upon many accounts, and to effect this would require the aid of Parliament. All the grants of the French Government were made under the feudal system, and all the lands so granted, are now so held by the Lords of the several seigneuries in Canada, and their respective tenants: to such tenures all Englishmen and Americans have an utter aversion, and the consequence is that all the seigneuries in the Province are entirely settled by Canadians, most of the Seigneurs however would be glad, to take a fixed price for the fee simple of their farms, and in consideration of that price to exonerate them from the payment of all rents, mutations, fines and other feudal burthens for ever; but as the law now stands this cannot be done, and an act of Parliament for this conversion of tenures similar to the act which was formerly offered to the consideration of the Provincial Legislature would be required, and as such an act must necessarily proceed upon the principle of a mutual agreement between the lord and the tenant, and provide for the payment of the king's quint upon the purchase, it is evident that no injury could accrue to the tenant, to the lord or to the Crown.

In the present state of the Legislature of Canada, three-fourths of the House of Assembly are Canadians and of that proportion, the whole nearly of the lowest class; the fruits of universal suffrage. Four-fifths of the whole also are Roman Catholics, and under the guidance of a priesthood, which is established by law, but denies that the right of supremacy is or can be vested in the sovereign. From such a House laws calculated in principle to counteract French predilections, or to increase the power or influence of the crown must not be expected, and almost any alteration in it must necessarily be for the better. The introduction of English settlers of itself will increase the number but the augmentation of their number would be greatly promoted by an act requiring a qualification as well for members as for electors. The character of the Canadians is idleness and inactivity; of the English settlers industry and perseverance. The Canadians also divide their real property among their children in equal proportions *ad infinitum*, while the English settlers observe an opposite conduct, and almost universally place their younger sons upon new lands, reserving the patrimonial estate to the eldest. Generally speaking, therefore, the English settlers will possess property of greater value than the Canadians, and if qualifications comparatively high are required, the nomination of the members to the Lower House will, ultimately rest with the English settlers; the number also of persons qualified to be members will increase among them, while among the Canadians it will be diminished.

The present exigencies of the Colony, however, require measures more immediately calculated to produce a change in the Legislature than those to which I have alluded, and in my mind, none would be more efficacious than an incorporate union of the two Provinces of Upper and Lower Canada, under one Governor General, and one legislature; leaving to the Uppe

Province its present Executive Government, but rendering it subordinate, and liable to the control of the Governor General, and to both, all laws in force in each respectively at the time of the union, subject to such alterations and regulations, from time to time as circumstances to the Parliament of the United Kingdom or to the Provincial Legislature of the United Provinces may appear to require. By the addition of the representatives of Upper Canada to the Legislature of this Province, the English interest in the House of Assembly would be much increased and it might be made to preponderate by diminishing the number of the representatives for the Lower Province and augmenting the number for the Upper Province. The importance, the respectability and the weight of the Legislative Council would be materially augmented; the influence of the Roman Catholic Priesthood in the Legislature would be annihilated, the strength, the power, and the resources of both Provinces would be consolidated, the commercial jealousies and dissatisfactions which have arisen from the peculiar geographical situation of the two Provinces, from the independence of their respective Legislatures, and the danger of their acting in opposition to each other, with their consequences (to this time prevented by temporary compacts between the two) would effectually be done away; the influence of the Governor General would be augmented by patronage, (which ought to be increased by every means,) and the designs of the Imperial Government would be more easily carried into execution in both Provinces, because there would be but one Legislature to consult.

It is obvious if a Union of the two Provinces should be adopted that some alteration in the Courts of Justice would be necessary, but as detail in the several matters upon which I write would carry me far beyond the bounds to which I am limited in a letter,

I refrain from it in the present instance. As this, however, is a subject immediately within my own department, I shall beg your Excellency's permission to refer to a report upon the Courts of Justice in this Province, submitted by me when Attorney General, to Sir Robt. S. Milnes, and dated   and to add that if it be thought expedient to erect a Court of King's Bench in this Province with the powers there pointed out, it would, in my opinion, be right to vest in the same court, a control, to a certain extent, over the courts of the Upper Province.

Among the means to be adopted for increasing the power and influence of the Crown, I know of none which, after those which I have mentioned, would be so immediately efficacious as to increase the patronage of the Governor by resuming and exercising the king's right to appoint incumbents to all the Roman Catholic livings in Canada under the sanction of a declaratory act of the Imperial Parliament; but as his Majesty's right to make such appointments may be doubted, because antecedent to the conquest, that right was vested in the then Roman Catholic Bishop of Quebec, I shall beg leave to lay before your Excellency the grounds upon which, in my opinion, it is now vested in his Majesty.

At the erection of the Bishopric of Quebec in 1670, after great contestations between the Courts of Versailles and of Rome, it was determined that the Bishop of Quebec should hold of and be dependent upon the See of Rome, with the title of "Vicaire du Saint Siege Apostolique,"* and in consequence of this agreement, though the Bishop was nominated by the King of France, he received from him no

---
*Charlevoix 4 to. Vol. 1, p. 400.
Repertoire de Jurisprudence. vol. 23, p, 512.
Letters patent of Sept., 1713, confirming the chapter of Quebec Secretary's Office, Register of the Superior Council D. fol. 1.

commission. His powers were derived to him entirely from the Pope, and given by his Bull, upon which he was admitted to take the oath of allegiance, and installed in his Bishopric by Royal Letters Patent.*

By the 6th Article of the Capitulation of Quebec, "the Bishop was to exercise his functions with decency "*untill the possession of Canada should be decided,*" and in the same spirit, by the 29th the 30th and the 31st Articles of the Capitulation of Montreal, and the answers, every demand made for the continuation of the Bishop's authority were rejected. Under the Capitulations, therefore, the exercise of the Episcopal Functions could not be claimed after the treaty of 1763, by which the possession of Canada was decided.

The treaty of 1763 permits the Canadians to "profess the worship of their religion according to "the rites of the Church of Rome, as far as the laws "of Great Britain will permit;" and the statute 14 Geo. III, cap. 83, declares, that they may have, hold, exercise, and enjoy the free *exercise* of the religion of the Church of Rome, subject to the King's supremacy, declared and established by the Statute, 1 Eliz. cap. 1. Since, therefore, the titular Roman Catholic Bishop of Quebec, according to the original creation of the See of Quebec, "holds of and is dependant upon the See of Rome," and at this moment, as heretofore, derives his entire authority from the Pope, without any commission or power whatever from His Majesty, it is most clear that the Statute of Eliz., which is formally but unneccessarily recognized by the Statute 14th Geo. III., cap. 83, to be in force in Canada, has annihilated, not only his power, but his office, the 16th section having especially prohibited all exercise of the Pope's authority, and of every authority derived from him, not only in England, but in all the dominions which the

---

* See the proceedings upon the appointment of Bishop Pontbriand in 1741. Edicts and Ordinances, Vol. 1. p. 516.

Crown then possessed or might hereafter acquire. Yet, upon a point of so much importance, I am desirous of strengthening my own opinion by that of others, and with your Excellency's permission will cite a paragraph from the Report of the Advocate General, (Sir James Marriet,) to His Majesty, in the year 1773, upon the affairs of Canada. It is in these words, "that the benefices, (in Canada,) " heretofore in the gift of the Bishop, are vested in " your Majesty only, cannot be doubted in law, " because there being no Bishop by law, the patronage " of the said benefices is devolved to your Majesty's " Crown, of course."

I must state as alarming facts, that the education of all the Canadian youth of the country, male and female, and of a considerable proportion of the English, is entirely in the hands of Roman Catholic conventual institutions; that in the Seminary of Montreal, every teacher is a native born subject of France, and a member of the brotherhood of Saint Sulpice,—and that in the Seminary of Quebec, the late superior was, and the present is, also a native of France!—Such institutions in every country are nurseries of bigotry and of aversion to the civil power; with us, in addition to these evils, they are the foster parents of French predilections and of a national antipathy against England and her "heretical" government.

Of these establishments, by far the most important and most extensive, is the Seminary of Montreal, whose entire property, most unquestionably, has been vested in the Crown since the period of the conquest. It is not, however, necessary for me to enter into any proof upon this point, or to state the means by which this property can be resumed, because it is not in my power to add anything to a Report upon this subject submitted by me to Sir Robert Milnes, dated 2nd July, 1804, nor will I trespass upon Your Excellency's time by any remarks upon the advantages to be derived from the influence of government in the education of the rising generation. I have only to observe, that I may enumerate the resumption of this property and the application of its rents and issues to the purposes of education throughout the Province, under masters appointed by the Crown, among the means by which French predilections may be prevented and the power and influence of the Crown eventually increased.

In the course of this letter I have hitherto had the honour of offering to your Excellency's consideration those objects only which constitute, in my view, the greater alterations and amendments in the constitution and government of the Province, more immediately and indispensably necessary; and a further detail of the whole, with the measures which, in my humble judgment, it will be right to adopt in the execution of all or any of them, I shall be ready to lay before your Excellency, if at any time you should be pleased to direct me so to do.

I beg leave to add, that much injury to His Majesty's government and to the public peace and tranquillity of the Province may be prevented by an Act of the Imperial Parliament to regulate printing and printers in Canada, similar to the English Statute of the 38th of Geo. III, cap. 78.

I have the honor to be, with perfect respect,
Sir,
Your Excellency's most obedt, and most humb. serv.
   (Signed,)   J. SEWELL.
His Excellency Sir J. H. Craig, K. B.,
  Governor in Chief, &c., &c., &c.

COPY OF A DESPATCH from Sir James H. Craig, Governor in Chief, to Lord Liverpool.

QUEBEC, 1st *May*, 1810.

MY LORD.—If my short despatch No. 2, which I transmitted by way of New-York, has reached your Lordship, you will be in some degree prepared to receive the Report on the state of this Province, which I conceive it to be my particular duty, under the events that have lately taken place, and the impression to which these have given rise in my mind, and in that of very many of the best informed persons here, to lay before His Majesty's Government.

Aware of the important matters that must press upon His Majesty's Ministers at this eventful crisis, and extremely unwilling to trespass upon them beyond what I feel to be indispensably necessary, it is with great regret that I perceive the extent to which my Reports is likely to run; I am fearful, however, lest under any more contracted form, it should fail of conveying that complete view, which I am desirous of submitting to Your Lordship, but even in this desire, it shall be my endeavour to confine it more particularly to those objects, by which the safety, the internal tranquility, and, above all, the political relation of the Province as dependant on the British Empire, may be influenced.

In the consideration which may be given to the various objects, which I may feel myself called on to submit to Your Lordship, I must request, that the particular situation in which this Province stands, *as being a conquered country*, may never be put out of view and I claim that it may always be recollected that I speak of a colony, the population of which is usually estimated at 300,000 souls, and which, calculating upon the best data in our possession, I myself believe to exceed 250,000. Of these 250,000 souls, about 20,000, or 25,000 may be English or Americans, the remainder are French—I use the term designedly, My Lord, because I mean to say, that they are in language, in religion, in manners and in attachment completely French—bound to us by no one tie, but that of a common Government, and on the contrary, viewing us with sentiments of mistrust and jealously, envy, and I believe I should not go too far, were I to say with hatred.

This is the first point of view in which,. whatever may have been the opinion hitherto, I do not hesitate to present them, though under so perfect a consciousness of the consequences that might possibly ensue from it, I feel a moral obligation dwelling on my mind on the occasion, from which I should shudder, if I did so without a conviction of its being well founded.

So complete do I consider this alienation to be, that on the most careful review of all that I know in the Province, there are very few whom I could venture to point out as not been tainted with it. The line of distinction is completely drawn between us; friendship and cordiality are not to be found, even common intercourse scarcely exists between the French and English. The lower class of people to strengthen a term of contempt, add Anglais, and the better sort, with whom there did formerly exist, some interchange of the common civilities of society, have of late entirely withdrawn themselves: the alleged reason is, that their circumstances have gradually declined in proportion as ours have increased in affluence. This may have had some effect, but the observation has been made also, that this alteration has taken place exactly in proportion as the power of the French in Europe has become more firmly established.

Next to this first and most important point of view, that which presents itself as the prominent feature in the picture of the Canadian people, is their extreme ignorance arising from a total want of education; this exists, I believe, in as high a degree as among any people in the world advanced beyond the savage state: it is scarcely necessary to add that it is attended with its usual share of credulity and superstition.

With respect to the moral character of the Canadians, as far as my own observation goes, it seems pretty much the same as that of other people not better instructed or informed in their duties. If on the one hand I do not perceive any very great or predominant vice, except one, so on the other, those who would hold them up as models of purity and innocence, unquestionably see them with very partial eyes: the vice to which have I alluded, is drunkenness; to this they are very generally addicted, and they are brutal and quarrelsome when in a state of ebriety. Like other people who are suddenly freed from a state of extreme subjection, they are apt to be insolent to their superiors. They are totally unwarlike and averse to arms or military habits. though vain to an excess, and possessing a high opinion of their prowess: they have indeed been flattered and cajoled so much upon their conduct in the year 1775, that they really believe they stand as heroes in history, whereas no people, with the exception of a very few individuals, ever behaved worse than they did on that occasion.

Among the objects which I deem it necessary to bring to Your Lordship's view, it is impossible for me to overlook the Clergy and the religious establishment of the country. The Act of the 14th of His present Majesty, by which the free exercise of the Roman Catholic religion is granted to the Canadians, expressely adds the condition, *that it shall be subject to the King's supremacy*, as established by the Act of the 1st of Elizabeth, but neither has this, or one article of His Majesty's instructions to the Governors ever been attended to. The appointment of the Bishop seems to have been conducted loosely, and with very little ceremony: the Council books offer no other document on the occasion, than that the person has taken the oath pointed out by the Act of the 14th of Geo. III, in lieu of the oath required by the Statute of the first year of the reign of Queen Elizabeth, but without even mentioning of what account he takes it. He has of late, on that occasion, been designated as Roman Catholic Bishop of Quebec; formerly he was only called Superintendent of the Romish Church.

Although it does not appear upon the records of the Council Board, or by any other document, His Majesty does nominate the Coadjutor, but this nomination appears to have been verbal. I observe on the return of the offices of emolument of this colony lately made to Your Lordship's Office, the Bishop says it is *cum futura successione*; how that can be, when it does not appear to be under any written document of any sort, I do not know, unless it be in the Pope's subsequent confirmation, which always takes place; it is, however, of such weight that the succession of the Coadjutor to the Bishopric seems to be considered as a matter of course, at least there is no appearance of there ever having been any interference on the part of His Majesty's Government.

This Bishop, though unknown to our Constitution, and confirmed if not appointed, by a foreign power, has been suffered to exercise every jurisdiction incident to the episcopal functions; he nominates to all the benefices in the Province, and removes at his pleasure, from one living to another, and it is not an unfrequent circumstance for an offence, or a supposed offence, to be punished by a degradation from a good cure to one of lesser emolument. His patronage is at least equal to that of the Government, and it is so perfectly at his pleasure, that Government has no other notice of it, than that he usually once a year delivers to the Governor a list of such changes as have taken place during the preceding twelve months. So complete does the Bishop consider his independence to be, and so cautious is he not to perform any act *which might be construed into an acknowledgment of His Majesty's rights*, that if a proclamation is issued for a fast or thanksgiving, or any other object which involves in it an act of the Church, he will not obey it as an emanation from the King, but he issues a "mandat" of his own to the same effect, indeed, but without the least allusion to His Majesty's authority, or the proclamation which the Government has issued.

In truth, the Catholic Bishop, though not acknowledged as such, exercises now a *much greater degree of authority than he did in the time of the French Government*, because he has arrogated to himself every favor which was then possessed by the Crown relative to the Church.

The Arms of Great Britain are nowhere put up in the Churches.

With the Curés themselves, no direct communication from the Government exists in any shape: a numerous and powerful body dispersed through every corner of the country, and certainly possessing a very considerable weight and influence with the people, scarcely know and are hardly known to the Government. No one act of Government since it has been under my direction, has ever been addressed to a Curé, nor has any one instance of communication from a Curé ever reached me, and perhaps an exception to the first part of this observation might be brought, in my having, in the desire of circulating the speech that I made to the Parliament, when I dissolved it, directed a copy to be sent to each of the Curés: this circumstance, however, will furnish no exception to the second part, for there did not occur a single instance of a Curé even acknowledging the receipt of it.

It is now a system of their Church, I know not why I confess, to chose its members from among the lower orders of society; very few, indeed, are of the better families of the Province; the Bishop is the son of a blacksmith, the Coadjutor is among the few who are of a somewhat better family, though still of what is called a new family, which has risen in the law; he is the brother of the leading demagogue of the democratic party, who is himself an advocate. Indeed there is a wonderful connection between the two bodies. Your Lordship will observe that the *avocats* here are Attornies as well as Barristers.

As to the principles of the Curés in general, they are not to be depended upon. It is, of course, not to be supposed that they should do otherwise than profess sentiments of loyalty to the Government to which they are aware that they owe it: even their professions, however, are but feeble, they are never produced spontaneously, and are only drawn from them by the occasion; and whenever that occasion will admit of it, they do not hesitate to shelter themselves under the plea of their religious duties, and their consequent unfitness to enter into the affairs of the world. It is not to be doubted that their religion renders them our secret enemies; the most liberal professors of the most unbounded toleration, (I confine the observation to those residing here, and who see what passes daily) admit this. Their attachment to France is equally undoubted, and it is now even supposed to be not a little directed to the person of Bonaparte, who, since the *concordat*, is considered among them as the restoror of the Roman Catholic religion.

Of the Legislative Council, it is not necessary to

say much; it is certainly composed of every thing that is respectable in the Province, and I believe the members to be on all occasions, animated by the best intentions towards His Majesty's service and the public good. It is an object of great jealousy to the Lower House, who seem anxious to seize every opportunity of showing the little respect in which they hold it. It is thought that an increase of members would add to their weight; at present, they seldom exceed five or six in the House. To a people circumstanced as I have described these to be, ignorant and credulous in the extreme, having no one common tie of affection or union, viewing us with jealousy, mistrust and hatred, having separate and distinct interests, it has been thought proper to give a share in the Government of the country, by a House of Representatives, in which they must ever have the majority. It is very far from my intention to question the liberal views on which the measure was originally founded, but it is my business to point out the consequences that have ensued from it.

Your Lordship is aware that, though the Constitutional Act has established a qualification for the electors, there is none required in the representative, I mean with respect to property. The number of English in the House has never exceeded fourteen or fifteen; in the two last Parliaments, there have been twelve; in the present, there are ten. Some of them have of late come from a pretty low step in the scale of society, but in general, they are composed of two or three *avocats*, about the same number of gentlemen possessing landed property, and the remainder of merchants of character and estimation. Upon the first establishment of the House, the few Canadian gentlemen that exist in the country stepped forward, and some were elected, but they soon found that nothing was to be gained by it; on the contrary, that their absence from home and attendance at Quebec during three months of the year, was given at an expense that very few of them could afford, and they gradually withdrew; now that some of them have attempted to resume the stations they abandoned, they have found it impossible; but at all times, their numbers were inconsiderable; the House has ever been as it is now, in great proportion as to the Canadian part, filled up with *avocats* and Notaries, shop-keepers, and with the common *habitants*, as they are called, that is, the most ignorant of labouring farmers: some of these can neither read nor write. In the last Parliament, there were two who actually signed the roll by marks, and there were five more whose signatures were scarcely legible, and were such as to show that to be the extent of their ability in writing.

I know not whether the excessive ignorance of the people be not more prejudicial, than even any malevolence could be, with which they could be supposed to be actuated. In the latter case, one might at least expect that there would sometimes be division amongst them, but at present they are completely in the hands of the party that leads the House. Debate is out of the question, they do not understand it; they openly avow that the matter has been explained to them by such and such persons, and they invariably vote accordingly. It is in this manner, at their nightly meetings, which are held for the purpose, that every question is decided, and it is impossible that these people can ever be set right, for those who judge right never meet them out of the House; they do not associate with them. There was lately in the House, a *habitant* who uniformly voted on every occasion against the prevailing party; but with this single exception, I do not believe that during the three Sessions that have been held since I came here, there has been an instance of one of the members of that class voting otherwise than with the general mass—that is, as directed. I mentioned this in order to point out the complete subjection in which these people are held, for if they made use of their own judgment, it is impossible, but that during so long a period some question must have arisen, on what there must have been a difference of opinion.

In such a House of Assembly as I have described, your Lordship will easily perceive that it is impossible that Government can possess any influence. They are certainly the most independent assembly that exists in any known Government in the world, for a Governor cannot obtain among them even that sort of influence that might arise from personal intercourse. I can have none with blacksmiths, millers and shop keepers, even the *avocats* and Notaries, who compose so considerable a portion of the House, are generally speaking such as I can nowhere meet, except during the actual sitting of Parliament, when I have a day in the week expressely appropriated to the receiving a large portion of them at dinner.

Of the party which lead the House, I have already had occasion to speak in a former despatch, and have been induced to enter into the characters of a few of them. They consist mostly of a set of unprincipled *avocats* and Notaries, totally uninformed as to the principles of the British Constitution or Parliamentary proceedings, which they, however, profess to take for their model: with no property of any sort, having everything to gain and nothing to lose by any change they can bring about, or by any state of confusion into which they may throw the Province. That *the sepeople have gradually advanced in audacity in proportion as they have considered the power of France as more firmly established* by the successes of Bonaparte in Europe, is obvious to every one, and that they are using every endeavour to pave the way for a change of dominion, and a return under that

Government, is the general opinion of all ranks with whom it is possible to converse on the subject. Even the very few of the better sort of Canadians themselves, who have sufficient information to be aware of the misery that would ensue on such an event, while the present Government exists in that country, and who, notwithstanding their national affection toward *what they still consider as the mother country*, would shrink from a return under its rule at this moment, nevertheless confess the obvious tendency of the proceedings that are going on here. Unfortunately, the great mass of the people are completely infected; they look forward to the event, they whisper it among themselves, and I am assured that they even have a song among them which points out Napoleon as the person who is to expel the English. With them the expectation is checked by no sort of apprehension, they are completely ignorant of the nature of the French system: they have not an idea that a change of rulers would produce any change in their situation; they are ready to admit that they are happy and in a state of prosperity as they are, they do not conceive that they would not have been equally so, had they remained subject to France.

It is scarcely possible to conceive the influence that the ruling party in the House has acquired among the people, or the lengths to which they have been carried by that influence. Without the possibility of pointing out one act, by which they have been either injured or oppressed, they have been taught nevertheless to look to His Majesty's Government with the utmost jealously and distrust; they avow it, and they publicly declare that no officer of the Crown is to be trusted, or to be elected into the House. These, together with all the English in general, and their own *Seigneurs* are entirely *proscribed*, it is only in the cities and boroughs that they have my chance. There are only two instances, where long possession of very extensive property has enabled the holders to retain their seats, though it has been in both cases, with the utmost difficulty. It is now to *la Chambre*, which is the usual expression, for they never even mention the Council, that the people look up as the Governors of the country, and yet such is the extraordinary effect of old impressions, that *de par le Roi* at this moment, would I believe, be followed by immediate compliance, without once reflecting whether the order were warranted by Act of Parliament or contrary to it.

The great vehicle of communication between the leaders and the people, has been a paper called *Le Canadien*, which has been published and industriously circulated in the country for these three or four years. The avowed object of this paper has been to vilify and degrade the officers of Government under the title of *gens en place*, and to bring into contempt His Majesty's Government itself under the affection of the supposed existence of a *Minister*, the conduct of which was held as open to their animadversions, as is that of His Majesty's Ministers at home.

Every topic that is calculated to mislead and influence the people has at times occupied the pages of this paper—nothing has been omitted. The various circumstances that brought on the abdication of James the Second, have been pointed out with allusions, as applicable to the Government here, inferring a similarity in the occurrences of the present day, and as if to inspire them with that confidence, that might be necessary in asserting their rights, when the occasion should call for it, several members were employed in narrating the actions of the wars of 49 and 56, in which Canadian prowess was held up in a very conspicuous point of view, and their advantages and victories dwelt upon in an emphatic manner: it need scarcely be added that the history was drawn from a very partial and exaggerated source.

In considering the probability of these people having in view their return to their old Government, it may be urged that they have hitherto been quiet and faithful subjects during the long lapse of fifty years, in which it would rather be to be supposed that their old attachment should have gradually decreased, so that there should be the less likelihood of their assuming now a disposition of which they have hitherto shown no indication; to all this, however, it may be replied that no circumstances whatever has occurred to weaken their attachment to their mother country, nor have any pains ever been taken to produce such a change. Their habits, language and religion have remained as distinct from ours as they were before the conquest. Indeed it seems to be a favorite object with them to be considered as a separate nation. *La nation Canadienne* is their constant expression; and, with regard to their having been hitherto quiet and faithful subjects, it need only be observed that no opportunity has presented them any encouragement to show themselves otherwise. From the year 1764 to '75, the country was in a state of poverty and misery that would not for a moment admit of a thought of revolt, in which they could expect no assistance; but even during that period there was a constant intercourse with France. Young men who sought to advance themselves went to France, not to England, and some are now in the Province who, during that period, served in the French army. During the American rebellion, it was a contest whether they should remain attached to the Crown of Great Britain, or become a part of the American Republic, and to say the best for them, their conduct did not manifest a very strong affection for the former, though the force the Americans had in the Province, was never such as to encourage them in an open display of any predilection for the latter, which, however, I do not believe they entertained; their object was to remain quiet. The French never turned their views this way. In the year 1794, a strong Jacobin party showed itself, and was with difficulty kept under; but during all this period to which I have hitherto alluded, they had no foreign assistance to look to, nor any head to direct them. To France they now direct their view for the former, and I am pointing out those who, I fear, are preparing to offer themselves for the latter, and certainly under the most formidable shape, under which a head could be found.

But, independent of every view which may exist, as to a change in their political relation with, as a dependent on the British Empire, the composition of the House of Assembly as it now stands, is to be considered, as it affects the public good and the general prosperity of the Province—and these, I fear, my Lord, can never be promoted to any extent by it. Religious prejudices, jealousy and extreme ignorance all forbid the expectation, and these, I am afraid, must prevail among the Canadian part of it, for a long period to come.

Questions directly of a nature to affect either the Protestant or the Roman Catholic religion have indeed never been brought before the House, but there are many that appear to be perfectly unconnected with the subject, but which are nevertheless viewed by them, either as affecting some temporal right of their Clergy, or as having some remote tendency to promote the establishment of the Protestant interest, and to such it is vain to expect that they should for a moment listen. This has been exemplified in some remarkable instances, and that even in the Legislative Council, where, in the case of a Bill brought into that House, which did not seem to have the slightest relation to religion, Canadian gentlemen, otherwise I am sure, most perfectly disposed to promote the public welfare, and who admitted the beneficial tendency of the proposed Act, nevertheless acknowledged, they were withheld from giving their concurrence by what they conceived a paramount duty; and it is to be remarked that this question could by no construction whatever be supposed to affect any right of the Catholic Bishop or Clergy.

How the Act for the establishment of public schools was permitted to pass, has always been matter of surprise; indeed the present Bishop once observed, in a very serious and official conversation, " You say that our Church never sleeps—-you will " allow, however, that we were asleep, and very " profoundly, too, when we suffered that Act to " pass." It is observable that the carrying the Act into effect has very generally met with the opposition of the *Cure* of the parish in which it has been proposed to establish a school.

The great object of their jealousy at this moment is the progress of the Townships, that is in fact, the introduction of settlers of any denomination but Canadians, as having a tendency which of all others, they are most anxious to avert, to impede the complete establishment of a Canadian nation. These Townships are generally settled by Americans, a portion of whom are Loyalists, who were under the necessity of quitting their country on the peace of 1783, but by far the greater number are Americans who have come in and settled upon those lands since that event. How far it may be good policy to admit settlers of this description is another question. The Canadians, however, are loud in their clamours against it, the circumstance of their being Americans, and the principles generally attributed to those, afford them the pretext, while, the truth is, it would be equally repugnant to the idea they entertain of their own interests, and they would just have the same feelings upon it, were the tracts in question, in a progress of settlement from Britain and Ireland, though in the latter case, it is probable they would not venture openly to complain. As it is, the subject has been mentioned in the House of Assembly, once under the idea of introducing an Act relative to it, and at another time, under that of addressing the King upon it. This jealousy has increased much since they became more systematic in their operations, and will now prevent any measure that may be proposed for the benefit of that part of the country. Two years ago they passed an Act for the establishment of a turnpike road through a part of it; at present hopes are entertained of getting them to consent to another, though it would be highly beneficial to the City of Quebec, endeavours are therfore using to carry it into effect by other means.

The common people, as may be supposed, understand nothing of the nature of the Constitution that has been given them, or that of the House of Assembly for which they elect members, except inasmuch as they begin to look up to them as the Governors of the country. It is a fact that in one part of the Province, whole parishes have constantly declined giving any votes at all; they say they do not understand it, but they suppose it is to tax them in the end. The cry of many of them now is, they wish *la Chambre* (the usual expression) at the devil, they were very well before and they have never had a moment's peace since that took place.

I must repeat, my Lord, my regret at the great length to which this dispatch has run, but it has occurred to me that it has been indispensably necessary that I should support the opinions I am offering on the state of the Province by arguments and, above all, by a detail that would be inexpedient on any other occasion. It may not be useless, in order to bring the whole under one view, that I should now present a summary of the various objects, which it has been my intention to submit to the consideration of His Majesty's Ministers, and to the support of which, the arguments and details to which I have alluded are meant to lead. They are:—

1st. That this is already a powerful Province in so far as depends upon numbers of inhabitants; and, that in the short period of twenty-five years, these will probably exceed half a million.

2nd. That the great mass of the population, indeed that proportion that admits of no balance from the other part, so far from being united to us by any bond of affection, views us with mistrust, jealousy, and hatred.

3rd. That they are, and consider themselves as, French, attached to that nation from identity of religion, laws, language, and manners. This is general, and runs through all ranks and descriptions, the exceptions, as I believe, being very few.

4th. That this people, immersed in a degree of ignorance that is scarcely to be exceeded, and credulous in the extreme, are particularly open to the arts and delusions that may be practised on them by factious and designing men.

5th. That they are at this moment completely in the hands of a party of such factious and designing men.

6th. That the whole proceedings of this party are calculated to alienate the people from any attachment they might be supposed to entertain for a government, under which they cannot but confess they have enjoyed the most perfect security, liberty, and prosperity, and to pave the way for their return to their ancient connection with that which they esteem their mother country.

7th. That there is reason to fear that they have been successful in their attempts, and that the people do look forward to a change in their government.

8th. That the clergy, under the general influence of attachment to France, are further from religious motives decidedly our enemies, and so will they continue till His Majesty, by his representative, takes upon himself the exercise of the patronage of the Romish Church.

9th. That the party who have the lead in the country have also the complete command of the House of Assembly, and are therefore placed in a situation particularly favourable to their views, and of consequence in the same proportion dangerous to His Majesty's interests.

10th. That from the composition of the House of Assembly it is likely that it will ever be in the hands of any party who may have a view in taking the direction of it; and that government possesses no influence, by which such view, whatever it may be, can be counteracted.

11th. That from prejudice, jealousy, and ignorance, it is little to be expected that the House as at present constituted will accede to the measures that may advance the real prosperity of the Colony.

12th. That the government is equally destitute of all influence over the clergy, with whom it has scarcely a connection, and that this influence is entirely in the hands of an individual who holds his power under the confirmation, at least, of a foreign authority, which authority is now under the complete direction of our inveterate enemy.

Having thus, my Lord, given you a report on the actual state of this Province, such as it appears to me, with the fidelity that I consider my duty to call for, and permit me to add, with the frankness that I hope will not be thought otherwise than in that duty, it may perhaps be looked for that I should assume an infinitely more difficult task, in the attempt to point out a remedy for the evils, which I foresee as likely to result from that state, as I have represented it. Upon this, my Lord, I must proceed with extreme hesitation, and I must earnestly request that anything I venture to advance on the subject may be received as offered with the utmost deference to the very superior judgment and wisdom to which it is submitted.

The first and most obvious remedy that presents itself, is to deprive them of their constitution, as they term it; that is, of that representative part of the government which was unquestionably prematurely given them. Neither from habits, information, nor assimilation with the Government of England were they prepared for it; nor was this circumstance of their unprepared state unforeseen by many of the best informed of the Canadians themselves, who opposed its being granted to them. It was in fact brought about by the English part of the inhabitants, who in their enthusiasm for the constitution which they so justly esteemed, as it exists in their own country, could not conceive that any inconvenience, or anything but happiness and prosperity, could result from its establishment elsewhere. The (since) Catholic Bishop, Dinaud, a very worthy man, observed at the time to an English gentleman, who was very warm on the subject, though now quite the reverse: "You do not know my countrymen; they are not at all prepared for the constitution you wish to give them; once let them run loose, and be assured they will never know when to stop."

I am perfectly aware, my Lord, of the delicacy of such a measure as that here alluded to, and of the possible difficulty that might attend it. It is not, however, I assure your Lordship, without giving the subject the utmost consideration in my power, or without giving due weight to the importance of such an opinion, that I venture to say, that nothing short of that measure will afford just grounds of hope of retaining the Province under the subjection of Britain, or of the preservation of its tranquillity, and the furtherance of its prosperity. The first object will always be, to a certain degree, precarious. Two hundred and fifty thousand people, decidedly animated by a foreign attachment, must always be subjects of doubtful continuance. Time may possibly alter that foreign attachment, but religion is one great bar to the hope, and no one step has ever yet been pursued that could foster the expectation; but however precarious our hold may be, is it not incumbent on us to do away with a measure, of which the consequence certainly was not foreseen, but from which every facility and every advantage are given to deprive us of that hold? That spirit of independence, that total insubordination among them, that freedom of conversation by which they communicate their ideas of government, as they imbibe them from their leaders, all which have increased wonderfully within these five or six years, owe their origin entirely to the House of Assembly, and to the intrigues incident to elections: they were never thought of before. In the Assembly, too, the leaders of any party who may have a revolution in view, will always be found, and from them faction will ever spread. The people are already taught to look up to the House on every occasion, and to consider it as the tutelary genius that watches over the welfare of the country. They will very soon consider obedience as a duty, and will be led to mutiny before they are aware that they are guilty of a crime.

 Having already observed to your Lordship, that I am aware of the delicacy and difficulty of the measure alluded to, I have only on that head to add, that here I do not think it would meet with much of the latter. The English are decidedly for it; among the Canadians themselves it is considered as far from improbable, nor is it without its partisans. That it would, however, occasion considerable clamour, and that attempts might be made to create disturbances upon the occasion, I have no doubt; but for the latter, the people are at this moment unprepared, and a very little previous precaution would be sufficient to prevent serious danger.

Next to this great measure, that which is most generally looked up to, is the reunion of the two Provinces, so as to balance the Canadian party in the House. Of the success of this measure, I confess, I have doubts. It would produce a heterogeneous mixture of opposite principles and different interests, from which no good could be expected, and if it did not avert, I apprehend it might accelerate, the evil. I am more inclined to keep the Province of Upper Canada as a foreign and distinct population, which may be produced as a resource against that of this country, in case of necessity. It must always be interested in opposing revolution of every sort here. The great distance and general poverty of the people appear to me further obstacles to such a measure, scarcely to be overcome.

It has been suggested that by a new division of the Province, new counties might be formed in that now distinguished by the general name of the Townships, from whence members might be furnished with the same view of balancing the Canadian party. This seems to me more practicable at least than the proposed reunion of the Provinces, besides being in itself a measure that is in some sort required in justice to the inhabitants, who begin to complain of not being represented. The Canadian part of the electors so infinitely outnumber them, that though confined to a much less extent of country, they can never succeed. The only reception is the County of Bedford, which is almost entirely composed of townships, and from this county, till the present election, an English member has usually been sent: on this occasion it is a Canadian member. With this exception, not one Canadian member has ever been returned from this very large tract.

But without the intervention of the Imperial Parliament, conferring on the Governor and Council the powers of altering the existing division of the Counties, and making a fresh one in proportion to the numbers of inhabitants, it will be impossible to effect even this measure. No consideration could, I am convinced, be offered to induce the present House, or any House that can be formed, to entertain the proposal for a moment.

Short of the decisive step of taking away the House altogether, one or other of these two measures, either that of reuniting the Provinces, or of *forming a new division of the Counties*, seems to offer the only opinion, from which a hope can be entertained of rendering that House less capable of doing mischief; when I say this, I mean, as offering the only expectation of even effecting a balance to the Canadian party; but under any shape in which it may be thought proper to continue the House, the enactment of a qualification with respect to the representatives, seems to be indispensably necessary. It really, my Lord, appears to me, an absurdity that the interests of certainly not an unimportant Colony, involving in them those also of no inconsiderable portion of the commercial concerns of the British Empire, should be in the hands of six petty shopkeepers—a blacksmith, a miller and fifteen ignorant peasants, who form part of our present House, a Doctor or Apothecary, twelve Canadian Avocats and Notaries, and four, so far respectable people, that at least they do not keep shops, together with ten Englishmen, complete the list. There is not one person coming under the description of a Canadian gentlemen amongst them.

The qualification that I think best adapted to the circumstances of the Country, would be *one hundred pounds currency*, clear annual revenue arising from land, actually the property of the person presenting himself, for twelve calendar months previous to the day of election; or two thousand pounds currency, in personal property clear of all debts or demands.

With respect to a qualification for the electors, though I am clear that such would be advantageous and that the present one as established by the Constitutional Act, is of little use, yet I feel much greater difficulty in proposing an alteration. Forty shillings yearly value of their lands, scarcely excludes one farmer in a thousand; in fact, nearly every head of a family possesses a farm, and every farm is of a value exceeding that amount. The farms in general run so nearly of the same value, or vary only on account of being in a more or less favorable part of the Province, that any qualification under the general average would leave the right of suffrage very near where it now is, and if it were established at a higher rate it might perhaps narrow the right below its fair limits. It undoubtedly would be desirable that the very lower class should be excluded, but I think the number is not so great as to induce the risk of what would be a greater inconvenience, to effect their exclusion, for I should consider as such, the reducing the number of electors within too narrow bounds

In the mean time, however, an opportunity appears to me to present itself, by which, much may be done towards keeping the House itself within its proper bounds; by shewing it, that its proceedings are watched, and that it will not be suffered to outstep those limits by which its subordination to the Imperial Parliament is established, while it would tend to manifest that subordination, to the people, and perhaps lessen the confidence they now possess in their leaders, by shewing them that they are not all powerful, and that they may be in the wrong.

The House by rendering a certain class of His Majesty's subjects ineligible to a seat, by a vote of its own, has clearly violated the Act of the British Parliament, by which the House itself exists; and should this assumption of theirs be submitted to, they will successively vote every class of His Majesty's servants to be ineligible; I do not speak this hypothetically, my Lord, as what they may do, I mean it literally, as what I firmly believe they will do.

I have not a doubt that much good would result from a retaliatory act of the Imperial Parliament, forbidding the Governor to permit the House to proceed to any business of any sort whatever, and directing him to prorogue or dissolve them, as he may see occasion, whenever they attempt to proceed to any vote, or on any other motion, except that of rescinding their resolve, and expunging it from their Journals. It would be done without a moment's hesitation. It would teach them caution in future, and it would make them view their situation in a different light from what they do now.

This correction proceeding from Parliament would certainly be the most effectual. If, however, from reasons which are beyond my competency in judging, it should not be thought advisable to move such a measure in the Imperial Parliament, it might perhaps be nearly as effectual, if I were authorised to recommend it in His Majesty's name, should His Majesty, in His wisdom permit me so to do. In this case, I presume, the message to be delivered, would be prescribed to me; otherwise, I should express His Majesty's confident hope and expectation that they would see the expediency of proceeding immediately and in the first step, to a measure required of them upon every principle of justice to the people, and of deference to the Imperial Parliament; and in the event of their attempting to enter on any other business whatever, or even admit of a motion other than one which might be necessary for the purpose of carrying His Majesty's recommendation into effect, I would immediately prorogue them; and, should they shew the same spirit of resistance a second time, which is not to be expected, I would dissolve them again.

Should I adopt this course as of myself, under His Majesty's instruction, though without his name, I fear it would produce infinite confusion, and an endless controversy. They would certainly resist it in the first instance; how far they would carry their resistance it is impossible to say; but though they might comply at last, and probably would, they would accompany that compliance with resolutions and proceedings, that would only tend to keep us at variance, and to impede all public business; after all, the effect upon them and upon the people, would fall infinitely short of what might be expected in either of the other ways to which I have alluded.

In adverting to the little means of influence that the Governor possesses, I am at a total loss how to propose any means (except in the obvious instance to which I shall presently allude) by which it may be increased. The militia furnishes little or no means; the great body of the officers, that is, those of the country companies is composed of habitans, but a shade removed above the others in intelligence, though they are chosen from the most respectable among them. They are, generally speaking, the first to whom the agents of the party address themselves, and they are represented to me, as among the most disaffected in the Province. As credulous as their comrades, they listen to and believe what is told them, while they are under the same infatuation of mistrust of every body of an order higher than themselves: there are no means of disabusing them. I am certain that if I were to dismiss every officer against whom information has been given me, I should change one-third of the militia of the Province. Unfortunately, my Lord, the great source of not only the most extensive but also of the most powerful and useful influence, is in the hands of an individual, who is himself, as I am assured, (and that from no bad authority), at this moment a suffragan of an Archiepiscopal See in France. I have already adverted to the power exercised by the Bishop in the appointment and removal at pleasure of the Clergy of this Province.

Upon a careful enquiry into the subject, I find that, previous to the conquest, the Bishop did exercise the right of appointment. In the year 1667 a Royal Edict gave the right of patronage to the Seigneurs or founders of the Church; but a subsequent Edict of the year 1699 gave it to the Bishops; but, in order to render this matter more clear, I shall enclose a memorandum given me on the subject by the Chief Justice.

His Majesty's right to the nomination is clear and incontestable. So much so, that were a *habitant* to refuse to pay his tythes, the church might excommunicate him, but *for want of that nomination, it is held, that the Cure could not in any of His Majesty's Courts of Law compel him to pay.* The resumption of this right, appears to me, to be *indispensable*, to any hope that may be entertained of retaining the dominion of the Colony, and *this* I confess *seems to me to be the moment for effecting that resumption.* It may be accomplished now; twenty years hence it will be more difficult, if not impracticable, but the truth is, THE DANGER PRESSES. This influence is universally believed, and *I believe it myself to be now silently working against us.* I do not know that the proposed change would turn its current, but I am sure, it would lessen the force of it very much.

The person who at present exercises the Episcopal functions, is not, I think, of a turbulent disposition, but he is a man of *great ambition* and some art. I doubt whether the former is not such as to preclude any great hope of succeeding with him, by a negociation voluntarily to resign the powers he now holds. I am inclined to believe that he himself would prefer, that his submission should bear the appearance of an act of necessity, under the power of an Act of the Imperial Parliament, or of the just exercise of His Majesty's right. At the same time, however, if, whether it be accomplished by negociation or otherwise, he comes into it with a good grace, I imagine it will be thought reasonable that his allowance should be increased. He has now only £200 : it might not be amiss to hint to him, that his salary should be increased to the extent that His Majesty in the exersise of His liberality might think proper to permit. On this very important subject, permit me, my Lord, to refer to a letter from Sir Robt S: Milnes, together with a memorial from the Bishop, Denaut, predecessor to the present, copies of which, I enclose. From some circumstances that occurred at that moment, no Instructions were sent here in consequence, otherwise, there is no doubt that, the measure might have been effected.

As to the Curés themselves, it is understood that they are at present rather uneasy at the power exercised over them, and the obvious amelioration of their situation, would, I think, soon reconcile them to the change. It would be proper to give them a freehold in their livings, of which they could not be deprived, unless it were in consequence of the sentence of the Bishop, who on a complaint against a Curé, being referred to him by the Government, should be empowered to call in to his assistance his Grand Vicaires and to examine into it, from which sentence however, the party should have his appeal in His Majesty's courts. It is thought that it would be dangerous to give him the right of enquiring into complaints, *without their being referred to him by the Government*. The removal from a living to a better, to be of course at the pleasure of the Crown. It must be recollected that the appointment of the Grands Vicaires must also rest with the Crown: at present they are named by the Bishop, without even the ceremony of presenting them to the Governor.

The resumption of the lands held by the Seminary of Montreal, would, in like manner, tend to an exercise of the influence of Government, and would, to a certainty, lessen that of the *self created* community, in whose possession they now are. The right is incontestable, and they are so sensible of it, that they make a rule of dropping all claims by which the discussion might be brought into court.

The majority of the present members of the Institution are French Emigrant Priests, and are *not amongst the least dangerous persons in the colony*. The person at the head of it, particularly, is of that description; a very able, but a very artful, designing man, whose predilection for France is not doubted. The estate, under proper management, would probably produce ten thousand pounds a year, and four would be an ample allowance to them to carry on their establishment.

The Seminary of Quebec is also in the possession of large property, to which they have an undoubted claim, and the two together from an ample provision for the education of their youth.

I will not detain your Lordship any further, by a word more of apology, for the extreme length of this despatch. The occasion has seemed to me to require it, and I am yet sensible of the very deficient manner in which I have treated the subject which I have felt it to be my duty to undertake. To remedy this deficiency, I have confided my despatch to Mr. Ryland, my Civil Secretary. This gentleman has been in office here, seventeen years, during the greater part of which he has been in the station he now holds under my administration. He possesses my entire confidence, and I am persuaded, is most properly qualified to give every information that your Lordship may desire. My motive, indeed, for sending him, is that your Lordship may have a more purfect and detailed account than it is possible to convey in a letter, however long it may be.

I have the honor to be,
My Lord, &c.
J. H. CRAIG.

To the Right Honourable }
the Earl of Liverpool. }

LETTER OF INSTRUCTIONS from Sir J. H. Craig to Mr. Ryland, on despatching that gentleman to England with the above despatch.

Quebec, 10th June, 1810.

DEAR SIR,—As you are charged with despatches to His Majesty's Secretary of State, some of them of a very important nature, it may not be inexpedient, that I should address you something in the form of instructions, by which you may be enabled to proceed in the manner best calculated to answer the view I have in sending you.

The principal object of your mission is to be at hand, to afford every explanation, and every information in your power, and that His Majesty's Ministers may require on the several subjects on which I have written, particularly with regard to the actual state of the Province; I have announced you in my despatch, as well qualified to do so, and as possessing my entire confidence.

You will particularly recollect that in what I have said in my despatch, it has not been my intention to represent the leaders of the popular party here, as being in an actual intercourse with France, or, that an attempt at revolution is to be *immediately* apprehended. Of the former, I have no proof, and I have no reason to suppose that any organization of the people, or other preparation for the latter, has taken place, what I mean is, that such is the state of the people's minds, that sooner or later, revolution may be looked for, and that, perhaps, without any view to an immediate occurrence of such an event, the proceedings of the party all tend to facilitate and prepare the way for it; there is every reason to believe, however, that Tureau* is setting engines to work among us.

You are well acquainted with the state of the House of Assembly, and if called on by the Secretary of State, but particularly in your conversations with the under Secretary, with whom your communications will probably be more frequent, you will endeavour strongly to impress upon their minds, the utter impossibility of conducting the public business, unless some alteration takes place. Their jealousy and their ignorance is more prejudicial than even any bad design, with which we may suppose them to be endued. It may be proper to remark that all the English are impressed with the same opinion.

A good deal may be said in favor of fixing a qualification for Electors, as well as for Representatives; it is a subject upon which, from want of information, I have scarcely made up my mind; perhaps it might not be amiss to fix it at ten pound's annual value; that might not limit the right within too narrow bounds, at the same time that it certainly would exclude a part of that class, from which much of the inconvenience of elections now arises.

The resumption of the right of nomination to the *Cures* of the Roman Catholic Parishes, is an object of particular importance on which you will not fail to insist. You are well acquainted with all that

---

* French Ambassador to the United States.

has taken place already with this view, and you know the character of the person we should have to deal with. I have not attempted to renew a negotiation on the subject, because I do not think it would be prudent at this moment, nor indeed would it have been so at any time, since I came here, to give cause for suspecting that to be in view, which I am very clear should not be attempted, but under the determination to carry it into effect.

I think if an opportunity occurs, you should explain what passed before the Council, and with respect to the publication of the Proclamation.

The resumption of the Estate, now in the hands of the Seminary at Montreal, is likewise an object of some importance, not merely as an object of revenue, but as a circumstance that would materially increase the influence of Government.

It is of very great importance, that you should obtain for me a decision on the question I have put, as to the conduct to be persued towards the next Parliament. I consider it as indispensably necessary that their resolution for incapacitating the Judges should be noticed,—if it passes by disregarded, I know not the lengths to which they may not go. You will recollect that I must call them together by the 26th February, and I shall be exceedingly embarrassed indeed, if I do not receive instructions on the subject, prior to that day. If I do not, the only remedy appears to me at present, to be, to prorogue them at the same time, that I approve of the Speaker. The misfortune is that you will probably not arrive in England until after the end of the present Session; consequently, the mode of correction which I have pointed out as the most efficacious, which is to oblige them to rescind that vote, by an Act of the Imperial Parliament, can hardly take place so that I should receive the Act by the period on which I must assemble them. This, however, depends upon the time when the Imperial Parliament may meet next year. At any rate, should it be resolved on to pursue that method, I can, if I am made acquainted with it, act as I have pointed out by proroguing this Parliament when I approve of the Speaker. By the bye, if you should observe an unwillingness to come to any determination as to the adopting of any measures with respect to the Parliament of this country, it might not be amiss to advert to this, of calling them together once every twelve months, and then adjourning them. This might be followed until it were thought proper to take some decisive step.

Among the suggestions offered to Ministers, you will find one for supplying the three annual Bills that have been usually passed by Acts of the Imperial Parliament; this would certainly be adding very greatly to the power of Government here. I think it not improbable that this proposal may bring on much conversation; and that I may be thought inclined to overlook every right enjoyed by this people. On this subject you may say, that I confess I consider the rights of the people of Canada as standing upon a different footing from those of the inhabitants of His Majesty's other Colonies. These latter, or rather their ancestors, were English when they settled the Colonies which they now inhabit, and it may be argued, that they carried the rights and privileges of such with them, such at least is their claim; but the people of Canada were a conquered people, to whom the Government of Great Britain thought proper to give a Constitution, to which they could lay no claim as of right. I therefore, think that the same Government which gave, may modify, or take away that Constitution, if the ends for which it was given are not answered; and, still more, if it is found that that very Constitution is likely to be turned against the power that so generously conferred it.

" Point out the great difficulty of our communication

during the winter, by the despatches from the Secretary of State's Office coming round by Halifax; those from the Commander in Chief, from the Treasury, and from the War Office, all come through the States.— Any thing particular might be put under cover to Mr. Barclay, who will always find opportnnities, by which to send it to me.

You will observe what 1 have written on the subject of the renewal of the Gaol Act, which they will certainly attempt. It will create a very great clamour amongst the English people, and you will not scruple to say, that in the arduous situation in which I find myself, I shall be exceedingly unwilling to lose the only support I have in the Province. With regard to the payment of the Civil Expenditure, you know how it stands, and the views with which it is brought forward. I think it almost certain, that the House will clog their Bill with conditions that will render it inadmissable. However, as they did not make a sufficient progress in the business last year to enable us to judge of the detail of their intentions, (except as one of their followers, let it out, that £250 was a sufficient salary for the Judges,) I had it not in my power to enter so fully into it as I could have wished. I should be glad, however, if you could obtain for me some hint, at least, of what is wished on this head.

Press the subject of the Jesuits' property upon the attention of Ministers. I shall call on Mr. Caldwell for the balance in his hands, but he will require time to pay it. The great object is to get a grant of this property, at least, if we cannot get that of the Seminary at Montreal, as a Fund, for an efficient establishment for the education of the English part of the Colony. If any hopes are given of this, I should be glad to be enabled to place the Jesuits' money now amounting to upwards of £9,000, in the Stocks at home, so as to make it a productive fund.

The Attorney General must be removed, and immediately; it is not fair that Mr. Bowen should be doing the duty without the salary: remember I am earnest in my recommendation of Bowen. If any conversation should arise upon the subject of the insufficiency of Mr. Uniache, you will observe that I have never yet, I believe, received one draught, or report from him which I was not under necessity of altering. Mr. Somerville's commission was absolution nonsense, the Proclamation for the general pardon was the same, and when I referred to him, the question of what would be the effect of the Act for regulating the inland trade with America, being suffered to expire, his answer was that it would be to place it upon the footing on which it was, when the Act passed. You have his draught of the lease of the St. Maurice Forges, with the report of the Council upon it.

Among the letters given you, you will find one for Greenwood; call and deliver it yourself. If he should happen to be out of town, which is seldom the case, desire Mr. Cox, or Mr. Hammersley, to open it. It is to introduce you to them, because I shall put all letters that I may have occasion to write, under cover to them, so that you may settle how to get them.

With respect to your return, it must, of course, depend upon Ministers. I shall be very anxious until you come back, and should you not be able to come before the navigation closes, I shall expect you by way of New York; at any rate, always bear in mind the 26th of February, as the day on which I must assemble the Parliament at furthest. If you have occasion to write by way of New York, put your letters under cover, to Thos. Barclay, Esq., His Britannic Majesty's Consul.

I need scarcely add a request, that I may hear from you as frequently as possible, and that you will write opinions, as well as facts. What you desire shall be strictly confidential. Wishing you a good voyage,

I remain, dear Sir,
Yours, most faithfully,
J. H. CRAIG.

H. W. RYLAND, Esq.

(*Additional instruction of Mr. Ryland.*)

Should His Majesty's Ministers be disposed to accede to what I have recommended with respect to the resumption of the patronage of the Romish Church, and wish to know in what way I think it most advisable the measure should be brought forward, you will inform the Secretary of State that, in my opinion, the most eligible means of accomplishing this object would be, by His Lordship's instructing me to inform Mr. Plessis, the present Roman Catholic Bishop, that the petition of his predecessor, the Revd. Mr. Denaut, of the 18th July, 1805, to the King, has been taken into serious consideration, that His Majesty is graciously disposed to accede to the prayer of the said petition by granting to the Roman Catholic Bishop the powers and authorities requisite to enable him to be recognized in the King's Courts, and for this purpose to grant to him Letters Patent, appointing him to be Snperintendent of the Romish Church in the Province of Lower Canada; that a salary suited to the dignity and importance of this office will be granted by His Majesty to the person holding the same; that for the purpose of giving to the Roman Catholic Clergy a *legal* title to the privileges and emoluments of their respective Cures, His Majesty has been pleased to authorize the Governor to issue, in favor of each of them, Letters of Induction, in like manner as is practiced with regard to the Provincial Clergy of the established Church, which Letters of Induction or confirmation will, in the first instance, be issued free of expense, on the Governor's receiving from the Roman Catholic Bishop a Return of the present incumbents.

That as, in many instances since the cession of the Province to the Crown of Great Britain, Parishes have, without due authority, been laid out, and Curates appointed thereto, who, for want of such authority could not legally exercise their functions or enforce payment of tithes, His Majesty has been graciously pleased to empower the Governor to issue Letters Patent under the great Seal of the Province, confirming and establishing such Parishes.

That on a full consideration of the advantages thus proposed to be granted and confirmed to the Clergy of the Romish Church in Lower Canada, His Majesty trusts His subjects professing the Romish Religion in that Province will be sensible of his paternal regard for their interests; that the bonds of duty and attachment towards his person and Government will thereby become the stronger, and the general welfare and tranquility of the Province be essentially promoted.

J. H. CRAIG.

Castle of St. Lewis,
   Quebec, 14th June, 1810.

R. WORTHINGTON:
MONTREAL.
Publishes the Following Books:

GARNEAU'S HISTORY of CANADA:
New Edition—in 2 vols. $3.00.

HISTORY OF LOWER CANADA:
By the late Robt. Christie.
In 6 vols. Just Ready. Price $6.00.

ARTEMUS WARD—"His Travels,"
In 1 vol—with 17 Illustrations. Price 50c.

ARTEMUS WARD—"His Book:"
With 18 Illustrations—in 1 vol. Price 25 cts.

THE BIGLOW PAPERS:
In 1 Volume. Illustrated. Price 25 cents.

THE ADVOCATE:
A Novel—By Mr. C. Heavysege—in 1 Vol. $1.00.

HARP OF CANAAN:
By the Rev. J. Douglas Borthwick—in 1 Vol.

Other NEW WORKS are in course of preparation.

R. W. IMPORTS ENGLISH AND AMERICAN
BOOKS AT LOWEST CASH PRICES.

ORDERS SOLICITED.

www.ingramcontent.com/pod-product-compliance
Lightning Source LLC
Chambersburg PA
CBHW022136300426
44115CB00006B/207